OXFORD MODERN LANGUAGES AND LITERATURE MONOGRAPHS

Pop-Feminist Narratives

*The Female Subject under Neoliberalism
in North America, Britain, and Germany*

EMILY SPIERS

OXFORD
UNIVERSITY PRESS

OXFORD
UNIVERSITY PRESS

Great Clarendon Street, Oxford, OX2 6DP,
United Kingdom

Oxford University Press is a department of the University of Oxford.
It furthers the University's objective of excellence in research, scholarship,
and education by publishing worldwide. Oxford is a registered trade mark of
Oxford University Press in the UK and in certain other countries

First Edition published in 2018

Impression: 2

Published in the United States of America by Oxford University Press
198 Madison Avenue, New York, NY 10016, United States of America

British Library Cataloguing in Publication Data
Data available

Library of Congress Control Number: 2017953560

ISBN 978–0–19–882087–1

Printed and bound by
CPI Group (UK) Ltd, Croydon, CR0 4YY

Acknowledgements

Far too many people to include fully deserve thanks for supporting me while I was writing this book. Just some of them are my wife, Rachel; my family, Sue, Josh, Lucie, and James; the intellectual 'mothers of my heart', Georgina Paul, Karen Leeder, and Rebecca Braun. The Women in German Studies, but especially Sarah Colvin, Birgit Mikus, Allyson Fiddler, Helen Finch, Simone Schroth, Emily Jeremiah, Lyn Marven, Sara Jones, Clare Bielby, and Charlotte Ryland for the many chances to test out my ideas; Laura Marcus, Maggie McCarthy, Maria Stehle, Christina Scharff, and Carrie Smith-Prei for allowing me to publish some of them. Lastly, Mike Tennant, who introduced me to Rilke when I was fourteen years old and changed my life.

A section of Chapter 1 has appeared as part of the article ' "Alpha-Mädchen sind wir alle": Subjectivity, Agency and Solidarity in Anglo-American and German Popfeminist Writing', in *Angermion: Yearbook for Anglo-German Literary Criticism, Intellectual History and Cultural Transfers*, ed. by Rüdiger Görner, 5 (2012), 191–217. A section of Chapter 2 has appeared in ' "Killing Ourselves is not Subversive": Riot Grrrl from Zine to Screen and the Commodification of Female Transgression', *Woman: A Cultural Review*, 26.1–2 (2015), 1–21 (www.tandfonline.com). Sections of Chapter 5 have appeared in 'The Long March through the Institutions: From Alice Schwarzer to Pop Feminism and the New German Girls', in *Post-War Literature and Institutions*, special issue of *Oxford German Studies*, ed. by Sean Williams and Daniel Wilson, 43.1 (2014), 69–88 (www.tandfonline.com); and ' "Mädchen haben keine Lobby im Pop": Writing the Performative Popfeminist Subject', in *German Pop Literature: A Companion*, ed. by Margaret McCarthy (Berlin: De Gruyter, 2015), pp. 143–65.

Contents

List of Illustrations

List of Abbreviations

Kathy Acker
BG   *Blood and Guts in High School*
GE   *Great Expectations*
ES   *Empire of the Senseless*

Mary Gaitskill
S   'Secretary', in *bad behavior*
V   *Veronica*
TG   *Two Girls, Fat and Thin*
WT   'The Wrong Thing', in *Because They Wanted To*
AF   'The Agonized Face', in *Don't Cry*

Maggie Nelson
TA   *The Argonauts*

Sheila Heti
HPB   *How Should a Person Be? A Novel from Life*

Michelle Tea
Va   *Valencia*
HGU   *How to Grow Up: A Memoir*

Gwendoline Riley
CW   *Cold Water*

Helen Walsh
B   *Brass*

Scarlett Thomas
EY   *The End of Mr. Y*

Charlotte Roche
SG   *Schoßgebete*
F   *Feuchtgebiete*

Kerstin Grether
Z   *Zuckerbabys*

Alina Bronsky
S   *Scherbenpark*

Helene Hegemann
A   *Axolotl Roadkill*

Antonia Baum
V   *Vollkommen leblos bestenfalls tot*

Note about Translations

All translations of the German texts are my own except one. See Chapter 5, p. 224, note 157.

Introduction
Assembling the Narrative Threads

In the first decade of the twenty-first century, a striking number of popular guides to feminism were published in North America, Britain, and Germany. The authors were predominantly women, journalists, and freelance writers, often engaged in the development of online feminist blogs and networks, such as *Feministing* in the US or *Mädchenmannschaft* [the girls' team) in Germany, or the creation of zines.[1] Their texts, often combining elements of memoir with the essayistic mode, emerged against a backdrop of growing feminist activism and digital networking across North America and Europe, which, by the end of the decade, would contribute to the transnational presence of groups like Femen, events such as Ladyfest, movements like SlutWalk, and Twitter campaigns such as #everydaysexism, #Aufschrei [outcry] and #YesAllWomen.[2]

Those feminist handbooks, which constitute the departure point for this book, elicited widespread mainstream debate concerning the continued relevance of feminist thinking for young women in the new millennium. Their authors distanced themselves from postfeminist narratives that consigned the need for feminist engagement to the past, instead announcing a new departure in feminist thinking. While not all of the authors self-identified as 'pop-feminist', their texts share a mode of engagement and self-presentation, as well as thematic concerns, which allow them to be considered under the umbrella term 'pop'. 'Pop' signifies more than simply 'popular'. It activates a range of connotations connected with aesthetics and genre, target audience, the politics of production, and the processes of global versus local transmission. Pop-feminist texts engage playfully with celebrity culture, or even constitute the medium of choice for today's 'celebrity feminists', such a Caitlin Moran, who, as the 'public embodiment of feminism, [...] have come to mediate what this complex social movement means in the public imaginary'.[3] The texts also engage with contemporary media, including music, TV,

---

[1] The term 'zine' (derived from 'fan magazine', which became 'fanzine', then 'zine') refers to formally heterogeneous, hand-made graphic and textual productions circulated among small groups of people interested in a certain topic, issue, musical group, or literary genre. They often include political essays, creative writing, confessional passages, and graphic art.

[2] Femen, which first emerged in Ukraine in 2008, is the name of a group of feminist activists. Members typically demonstrate topless or naked. The term 'Ladyfest' refers to a women-only festival featuring female artists, feminist workshops, and creative activities. The first of these events took place in Olympia, Washington in 2000. SlutWalk is the name given to a series of demonstrations originally organized by a group of young Canadian women in 2011. They were responding to a Toronto police officer's comments that young women should avoid dressing like 'sluts' in order to prevent rape or sexual assault.

[3] See Anthea Taylor, *Celebrity and the Feminist Blockbuster* (London: Palgrave Macmillan, 2017), p. 2.

film, and social networking, perching on the axis of local situatedness and the transnational channels of pop-culture; they are often ironically self-conscious about their own complicity with neo-capitalism and consumer culture; and their readership is usually young and celebrity literate. The term 'pop-feminist' has recently gained intellectual purchase in media coverage of the current moment in both Anglophone and European contexts and as an analytical category not only in German studies but also in Anglophone feminist media studies.[4] However, this volume makes a key intervention in those fields by providing a comparative perspective. In particular, an analysis of German pop-feminism has played little to no part in English-language accounts of pop-feminism and postfeminism up till now (Christina Scharff's work is an exception).

The entanglement of modes of cultural and political critique with neoliberal economics has been systematically unpicked in studies of popular culture and pop-literature, in particular. One seemingly ubiquitous formal feature of pop is the tendency to draw on the paraphernalia of consumer culture and to name-check specific products or brands as a matter of course. This characteristic has often been cited in order to substantiate arguments that lament pop's unreflecting affirmation of the neoliberal status quo.[5] Other pop-theorists seek to salvage pop's critical potential. Thomas Ernst, for example, argues that the pop gesture enacts both an ironic critique and an indirect glorification of mass culture.[6] As Heinrich Kaulen notes, however:

> Das Problem dieser Kritik liegt darin, dass sie, ganz im Stil der überkommenen Ideologiekritik der 1970er Jahre, heteronome politische Wertmaßstäbe umstandslos auf ein Textkorpus appliziert, das sich solchen Kriterien bewusst zu entziehen sucht, weil es mit einer Ästhetik der Ambivalenz operiert und konzeptionell gerade am Indifferenzpunkt von Gesellschaftskritik und Affirmation angesiedelt ist.

> [This view is problematic because it blithely applies heteronomous political standards in the outdated style of 1970s ideology critique[7] to a body of works which consciously

---

[4] See, for example, Ann Friedman, 'Pop Feminism Doesn't Mean the End of the Movement', *nymag.com*, 1 June 2016, available at http://nymag.com/thecut/2016/05/andi-zeisler-pop-feminism-movement.html; Andi Zeisler, *We Were Feminists Once: From Riot Grrrl to CoverGirl®, the Buying and Selling of a Political Movement* (New York: Public Affairs, 2016); Maria Stehle and Carrie Smith-Prei, *Awkward Politics: Technologies of Popfeminist Activism* (Montreal: McGill-Queen's University Press, 2016); Maria Stehle, Carrie Smith-Prei, and Christina Scharff (eds.), 'Digital Feminisms: Transnational Activism in German Protest Cultures', special issue of *Feminist Media Studies*, 16.1 (2016); Hester Baer (ed.), 'Contemporary Women's Writing and the Return of Feminism in Germany', special issue of *Studies in Twentieth and Twenty-First Century Literature*, 35.1 (2011).

[5] For an overview of these arguments, see Sabine von Dirke, 'Pop Literature in the Berlin Republic', in *Contemporary German Fiction: Writing in the Berlin Republic,* ed. by Stuart Taberner (Cambridge: Cambridge University Press, 2007); Frank Finlay, 'Literary Debates and the Literary Market since Reunification', in *Contemporary German Fiction,* ed. by Taberner. See also Thomas Anz, 'Generationenkonstrukte: Zu ihrer Konjunktur nach 1989', in *Konkurrenzen, Konflikte, Kontinuitäten,* ed. by Andrea Geier and Jan Süselbeck; Heinz Drügh, 'Konsumknechte oder Pop-Artisten? Zur Warenästhetik der jüngeren deutschen Literatur', in *Konkurrenzen, Konflikte, Kontinuitäten*; Heinrich Kaulen, 'Popliteratur als Generationsphänomen: Jugendliche Lebenswelten im Spiegel der Popliteratur der 1990er Jahre', in *Konkurrenzen, Konflikte, Kontinuitäten*.

[6] See Thomas Ernst, *Popliteratur,* p. 25.

[7] Heinrich Kaulen cites the following as his source for this comment: Jost Hermand, *Pop international: Eine kritische Analyse* (Frankfurt am Main: Athenäum Verlag, 1971).

seek to evade those criteria. These texts operate with an aesthetics of ambivalence and are conceptually situated exactly at the juncture of indifference located between social criticism and affirmation.[8]]

Ernst and Kaulen's comments, which relate to a discussion of pop-literature, can be applied to other forms of pop-cultural media, including the essayistic pop-feminist texts discussed here. Nevertheless, if pop's attitude is indeed one of ambivalence as it straddles the line between glorifying the mass-media culture from which it springs and critiquing the same, then the term 'pop-feminism' must surely be an oxymoron. Historically, feminism has been understood as a discourse predicated on critique. Moreover, much contemporary feminist scholarship contends that mainstream popular culture neutralizes feminist politics, even bolstering the notion that feminism is redundant.[9] Yet the space beyond an absolutist stance on the political potential of pop remains a compelling one to explore. At its core, pop-feminism illuminates the tension inherent in the encounter between political activism and popular culture in a neoliberal economy. Pop-culture offers a significant platform for counter-cultural expression. Yet the platform, whether print or digital, is itself constituted by the economic apparatuses of the neoliberal status quo.

The texts under discussion transcend their domestic contexts by engaging with the global channels of popular culture and with transnational feminism while simultaneously retaining qualities specific to their linguistic and cultural origins. The website *Maedchenmannschaft*, for example, combines German-language texts with links to English-language blogs and engages with local and transnational feminist issues, creating 'localities that do not transcend political questions emerging in national arenas but instead infuse them with new meaning and context'.[10] The authors of the print volumes often employ local slang mixed with the idiom and symbols of feminist digital culture and social media.[11] In the German guides, colloquial German becomes interspersed with Anglicisms. This choice of informal register underpins the authors' insistence on the relevance of their arguments for young women between the ages of approximately fifteen and thirty-five and on their ability to offer a different kind of feminism from previous generations. As shown in Fig. 1, the book covers are brightly designed, often featuring stylized images of the female form; these images function as a visual clue to the texts' often

---

[8] Heinrich Kaulen, 'Popliteratur als Generationsphänomen', p. 141.

[9] Yvonne Tasker and Diane Negra, 'Feminist Politics and Postfeminist Culture', in *Interrogating Postfeminism,*ed. by Tasker and Negra, p. 1. See espcially Angela McRobbie, 'Postfeminism and Popular Culture', in *Interrogating Postfeminism: Gender and the Politics of Popular Culture*, ed. by Yvonne Tasker and Diane Negra (Durham; London: Duke University Press, 2007), originally published in *Feminist Media Studies*, 4.3 (2004), 255–64.

[10] Christina Scharff, Carrie Smith-Prei, and Maria Stehle, 'Digital Feminisms: Transnational Activism in German Protest Cultures', *Feminist Media Studies*, 16.1 (2016), 1–16 (p. 2).

[11] An important local specificity is the continued presence of German in German-language feminist digital activism. A recent study of language use on the internet revealed that German is the eighth most dominant language used in communications online, with 81.1 million users in 2013. Figures from the source Internet World Stats were published in a British Academy study by Holly Young, 'The Digital Language Divide: How Does the Language You Speak Shape Your Experience of the Internet?', *The Guardian*, available at http://labs.theguardian.com/digital-language-divide/ [accessed 16 February 2017].

Fig. 1. The pop-aesthetic and stylized cover of *Wir Alpha-Mädchen*. Copyright © 2008 by Hoffmann und Campe Verlag, Hamburg.

playful approach towards contemporary body politics, where the vicissitudes of fashion play a pivotal role in self-fashioning and identity performance.[12]

Pop-feminism is one of the 'varieties' of feminism that have become increasingly visible in the new millennium.[13] Aside from their focus on and employment of modes of pop-cultural expression, what defines the work of pop-feminists is their preoccupation with sexuality and transgression as potential generators of agency, their frequent thematization of the relationship between intergenerational feminist difference and the question of establishing female/feminist identity in the early twenty-first century. As I will show, however, paying attention to the precise qualities of pop-feminist narratives reveals striking differences between them. Pop-feminism is a heterogeneous mode of popular feminism. Yet a defining distinction between protagonists is the extent to which they 'buy in' to the promises and premises of neoliberalism, and how that affects their engagement with pop-culture itself.

The texts under discussion include the American blogger and journalist Jessica Valenti's *Full Frontal Feminism* (2007), which has the subtitle *A Young Woman's Guide to Why Feminism Matters* inscribed upon a cover image of a naked female torso; the English journalist Ellie Levenson's *The Noughtie Girl's Guide to Feminism* (2009), whose cover, with its slim female silhouette in high heels surrounded by cartoon stars, echoes the visual tropes of chick-lit novels; the British journalist Caitlin Moran's *How to Be a Woman* (2011); American journalist Hadley Freeman's *Be Awesome: Modern Life for Modern Ladies* (2013); and Polly Vernon's *Hot Feminist* (2015). In the German-language context, I include Barbara Streidl, Meredith Haaf, and Susanne Klingner's *Wir Alpha-Mädchen: Warum Feminismus das Leben schöner macht* [*We Alpha Girls: Why Feminism makes Life more Beautiful*] (2008), which employs a pop montage of infants, tape measures, and nostalgic, black-and-white photographs of women in 1950s underwear on its cover; and Jana Hensel and Elisabeth Raether's autobiographical account, *Neue deutsche Mädchen* [*New German Girls*] (2008), and I refer to Thea Dorn's selection of interviews, *Die neue F-Klasse: Wie die Zukunft von Frauen gemacht wird* [*The New F-Class: How Women are Making the Future*] (2006) and Mirja Stöcker's edited work *Das F-Wort: Feminismus ist sexy* [*The F Word: Feminism is Sexy*] (2007).

Other writers, who remain wary of pop-culture's entanglement with neoliberal consumer culture, have also declared themselves to be pop-feminist, or work critically within the pop mode without using the term pop-feminism themselves. They also

---

[12] My understanding of pop in relation to literature and feminism has been informed by the following sources: Moritz Baßler, *Der deutsche Pop-Roman: Die neuen Archivisten* (Munich: Beck, 2002); Thomas Ernst, *Popliteratur* (Hamburg: Europäische Verlagsanstalt/Rotbuch, 2001); Kerstin Gleba and Eckhard Schumacher, eds., *Pop seit 1964* (Cologne: Kiepenheuer & Witsch, 2007); Heinrich Kaulen, 'Popliteratur als Generationsphänomen: Jugendliche Lebenswelten im Spiegel der Popliteratur der 1990er Jahre'; Angela McRobbie, 'Postfeminism and Popular Culture'; Imelda Whelehan, *Overloaded: Popular Culture and the Future of Feminism* (London: Women's Press, 2000); see also Footnotes 3, 4, and 5.

[13] For a thorough account of why the 'varieties' of feminism in different countries matter, see Myra Marx Ferree, *Varieties of Feminism: German Gender Politics in Global Perspective* (Stanford: Stanford University Press, 2012).

instrumentalize popular culture in order to reach a new target audience.[14] Yet they insist that feminism must not be compromised in order to make it palatable to pop.[15] Instead, feminism should permeate pop-culture in order to transform it.[16] Writers in this category include the American writer Roxane Gay, and journalist Ariel Levy, whose *Female Chauvinist Pigs: Women and the Rise of Raunch Culture* (2005) examines the ways in which the media encourages young women to collude in their own sexual objectification. I also include the latest volume by Jessica Valenti, *Sex Object* (2016), which marks a notable shift in its author's thinking since the 2007 publication of *Full Frontal Feminism*, and the co-founder of the American pop-feminist website *Bust*, Andi Zeisler's, latest publication *We Were Feminists Once: From Riot Grrrl to CoverGirl®, the Buying and Selling of a Political Movement* (2016). The British authors I refer to include the founder of *The F Word* blog and the London Third-Wave network, Catherine Redfern, and the sociologist Kristin Aune, whose *Reclaiming the F Word: The New Feminist Movement* combines scholarly accuracy and sustained attention to the history of feminism with the textual strategies of the popular magazine medium. I also include the German journalist Sonja Eismann, whose *Hot Topic: Popfeminismus heute* [*Hot Topic: Pop-Feminism Today*] (2008) counts as the foundational pop-feminist text in twenty-first-century Germany.

This second group of pop-feminist authors seeks to challenge the discriminatory elements of popular culture directly without necessarily decrying popular culture per se; they view pop as a medium that retains emancipatory potential for a young generation of pop-literate women and girls despite its entanglement with commercial forces. They consciously practise, in Carrie Smith-Prei and Maria Stehle's terms, 'awkward politics'. According to Smith-Prei and Stehle, awkwardness emerges through the 'new forms of dissemination and reception' of political moments or events and, in particular, their 'multi-media circulation'.[17] These moments are awkward:

> not only because a neoliberal digital economy enables them but also because these activisms, which doggedly persist in their political actions in spite of this enabling, simultaneously reveal the false promises of neoliberal capitalism. They do not or cannot detach from the economy that enables them; rather they stick to that economy in an uncomfortable, awkward manner.[18]

I draw on the work of these 'awkward' pop-feminists to support my critique of the more unreflecting strand of pop-feminism represented by the first group of texts listed above, in which the entanglement with neoliberalism appears as a comfortable, rather than awkward, arrangement.

While both groups of pop-feminist writers assert that feminist thinking is still viable and necessary, the more unreflecting among them rely upon the contention that second-wave feminism is now a redundant paradigm and that women must

---

[14] Sonja Eismann, 'Einleitung' [Introduction], in *Hot Topic: Popfeminismus heute*, ed. by Sonja Eismann (Mainz: Ventil, 2007), p. 10.
[15] Ibid.   [16] Ibid.
[17] Carrie Smith-Prei and Maria Stehle, *Awkward Politics*, p. 11.   [18] Ibid.

both create and safeguard their own opportunities when it comes to their careers, appearance, sexuality, and reproductive capacities. The more critically attuned pop-feminists, however, examine the socio-political and economic structures that sustain gender inequality. The first group appeal to younger women by celebrating their autonomy, proclaiming the right to individual choice in the realm of body politics and, in particular, (hetero)sexual self-expression. This is due in part to their foregrounding, consciously or not, mass-media culture's preoccupation with the sexualized female form. These issues often dominate the texts' content, while questions relating to careers, reproduction and child care are frequently afforded less space.[19] Non-heterosexual perspectives, as well as discussions of class and ethnicity, are seldom included.

From the vantage point of 2017, distinguishing between these types of pop-feminism, as I have begun to do here, seems more important than ever. The call for a reinvigoration of feminist thinking and activism unites them, and over the last ten years what has been called the heightened 'visibility' or 'luminosity' of feminist debates in mainstream journalism and on social media across cultural and linguistic contexts cannot be repudiated.[20] This has led to talk of a putative 'fourth wave' of feminism and to debates about 'new' or 'neo'-feminisms in Anglophone and European contexts, to the extent that there have been recent calls to scrutinize the continued value of the term 'postfeminism'.[21] Commentators argue that, if understood as cognate to 'after', then 'postfeminism' must by now be understood as a misnomer, a misplaced analytical category unsuited to the current moment. They ask whether the prevalence of feminist politics in both activist and mainstream media over the last few years does not in fact 'complicat[e] the logic that feminism is in retreat'.[22]

Others, like Diane Negra and Yvonne Tasker, have in fact recently linked the fundamental gesture of postrecessionary popular culture to postfeminism, making the case for the continued usefulness of postfeminism as an analytical category that is relevant to a discussion of pop-feminism in the pre- and post-financial crash period.[23] Negra has recently argued that:

> Just as postfeminist culture suggests that it is individual women (rather than systems of gender hierarchy) who require modification, recessionary popular culture consistently implies that it is management of the self that is necessary to survive adverse economic conditions. Though governments seem increasingly unable to act in the interests of citizens, media and print texts offer reassuring vignettes of individual agency as compensation to the ill-defined yet intensely valorised power of 'the market'.[24]

---

[19] Thea Dorn's volume is an exception here, as it sets out to examine a variety of women's professional lives.

[20] See Rosalind Gill, 'Post-postfeminism? New Feminist Visibilities in Postfeminist Times', *Feminist Media Studies*, 16.4 (2016), 610–30.

[21] See Jessalynn Keller and Maureen Ryan, 'Call for Papers: Emergent Feminisms and the Challenge to Postfeminist Media Culture', 2015 http://arcyp.ca/archives/4244 [accessed 16.2.2017].

[22] Ibid.

[23] See Diane Negra and Yvonne Tasker (eds.), *Gendering the Recession: Media and Culture in an Age of Austerity* (Durham, NC: Duke University Press, 2014).

[24] Diane Negra, 'Claiming Feminism: Commentary, Autobiography and Advice Literature for Women in the Recession', special issue of *Journal of Gender Studies* 'Feminism, Academia, Austerity', ed.

A closer look at what differentiates pop-feminists from each other reveals the need, identified by Clare Hemmings, for continued close scrutiny of the types of feminist 'stories' that get told,[25] and suggests the continuing usefulness of the category of 'postfeminism' in order to parse them. As Rosalind Gill comments, it is important to understand the 'meaning of the apparent new visibility of feminism' and to understand the 'multiplicity of different feminisms currently circulating in main-stream media culture—which exist in tension with each other'.[26] Like Gill, I use postfeminism as an analytical category to investigate the 'sensibilities' emerging from different strands of pop-feminism, which are often contradictory, but ultim-ately 'intimately connected' to neoliberalism.[27]

This book has two principal focuses. The first is the model of subjectivity that emerges from pop-feminist handbooks. What interests me particularly is how this model relates to pop-feminist conceptualizations of identity and agency and what they imply for feminist politics. The second focus is a corpus of American, British, and German pop-literary fiction, specifically first-person novels and 'autofictions' written by women that address the same issues concerning subjectivity, identity, and agency as the pop-feminist handbooks, but in a manner which I contend is more useful for feminist politics.[28]

My understanding of subjectivity holds it to be a capacity of consciousness. This capacity processes thought, hosts reflection upon events and actions, and constitutes the site where the 'I' may be articulated. Yet it does not constitute an omniscient, permanent or coherent entity. Identity, on the other hand, constitutes a 'signifying practice', which contains within it the possibility of agency.[29] Agency, as I understand it, does not signify a capacity for action predicated on unfettered subjective access to a prediscursive 'I'. Instead, agency emerges at a variable, and often indeterminable, point between subjective capacities, identity's socially constituted articulation, and ethical intersubjective relations.

Pop-feminism operates in a theoretical environment in which understandings of subjectivity, identity, and agency have been transformed by, among others, femin-ist predecessors: this climate can be characterized by a shift from invoking a unified

by Helen Davies and Claire O'Callaghan, 23.3 (2014), 275–86 (p. 275). For further reading on post-recessionary feminism, see Mary Evans, 'Feminism and the Implications of Austerity', *Feminist Review*, 109 (2015), 146–55; Gary Minda, 'Lessons from the Financial Meltdown: Global Feminism, Critical Race Theory, and the Struggle for Substantive Justice', *American University Journal of Gender Social Policy and Law*, 18.3 (2010), 649–83.

[25] Clare Hemmings, *Why Stories Matter: The Political Grammar of Feminist Theory.* (Durham, NC, Duke University Press, 2011).

[26] Rosalind Gill, 'Post-postfeminism?', p. 1.   [27] Ibid.

[28] The term 'autofiction' refers to a 'fictionalization of the self' in narrative. (This is Genette's for-mulation. See Gerard Genette, *Palimpsestes* (Paris: Seuil, 1982)). French academic, Jacques Lecarme, defines it in the following way: 'l'autofiction est d'abord un dispositif très simple: soit un récit dont auteur, narrateur et protagoniste partagent la même identité nominale et dont l'intitulé générique indique qu'il s'agit d'un roman' ['Autofiction is first of all a very simple device: it is a narrative whose author, narrator and protagonist share the same nominal identity and whose generic title indicates that it is a novel']. See Jacques Lecarme, 'Autofiction: un mauvais genre?', *Autofictions & Cie.*, RITM, 6.1 (1993), 227–49 (p. 227).

[29] Judith Butler, *Gender Trouble: Feminism and the Subversion of Identity*, 3rd edition (New York; London: Routledge, 2006), p. 198.

category of 'woman' to broader, intersectional considerations of 'women' and to the examination of the social, cultural and discursive factors that influence the subject's ability to act autonomously. Pop-feminist accounts of subjectivity thus draw heavily—if implicitly—upon poststructuralist notions of pluralistic, unstable identity and Judith Butler's concept of performativity, in particular. This understanding of subjectivity aligns neatly with a pop-cultural aesthetic strategy of sampling, or mash-up.[30]

The less reflective pop-feminist texts often retain the assumption that, underlying these playful or at times ironically executed identity performances, there remains a sovereign subject capable of mediating reflexively and maintaining full autonomy over such performances. As body politics, sexuality, and generational discord connote the primary areas of discussion in the pop-feminist guides, 'transgressive' sexualities frequently become linked with the expression of autonomy and an up-to-date feminist identity.[31] Some strands of pop-feminism thus underestimate, in alignment with neoliberal narratives of self-entrepreneurialism and individual choice, external forces of social constraint upon behaviours. In a twenty-first-century consumer-driven climate, pop-feminist agency resides all too often in the act of choosing from an array of lifestyle options and products and not in seeking to understand or challenge the forces that constitute the subject and impinge upon the 'choices' available. In exploring the theoretical blind-spots of pop-feminist claims to autonomy and agency, this book sets out to demonstrate that many pop-feminist handbooks lack a coherent feminist politics.

Instead, such volumes draw on the rhetoric of collective feminist intervention while, in fact, rejecting the possibility of intersubjective relations in the form of coalitional feminist engagement. The collective 'we' or the autobiographical 'I' employed in the essayistic mode restrict the exploration of selfhood and agency either by conjuring a unified—if ultimately chimerical—generalized collective (as in *Wir Alpha-Mädchen* [*We Alpha Girls*]), or by presenting an overly specific and thus exclusionary model of being (the autobiographical 'I' unmediated by self-reflexive fictional play). On the other hand, the fictitious 'I' employed in the first-person novels or the mediated authorial persona deployed performatively in the autofictions to muddy the categories of fact and fiction do not rely on making claims to authority, prompting instead an imaginative and extrapolative process of identification and dis-identification in the reader. Choice of genre and mode therefore play a role in the conceptualization of self and agency in the volumes.

The literary authors I discuss include the American writers Kathy Acker and Mary Gaitskill, who I consider to be important literary precursors for the North American writers Sheila Heti, Maggie Nelson, and Michelle Tea, as well as for the

---

[30] According to the *Oxford English Dictionary*, the term 'mash-up' refers to a fusion of disparate elements. Since the early 2000s, it is used predominantly in relation to a 'piece of popular music created by merging the elements of two or more existing songs using computer technology and production techniques'.

[31] My understanding of 'transgression' aligns with the *OED*'s definition: 'The action of transgressing or passing beyond the bounds of legality or right; a violation of law, duty, or command; disobedience, trespass, sin.'

British and German authors I discuss. I then go on to explore the work of British authors Gwendoline Riley, Helen Walsh, and Scarlett Thomas and the German writers Charlotte Roche, Kerstin Grether, Alina Bronsky, Helene Hegemann, and Antonia Baum. My selection of literary texts is determined by three criteria. First, they engage with the same questions concerning contemporary female identities, agency, sexuality, and socio-psychological constraint as the pop-feminist guides. The authors all employ and depict transgressive tropes and behaviours, particularly in the realm of sexuality. They pursue these issues in an aesthetically innovative pop-literary mode that targets their work at a similar social and age demographic to the feminist handbooks. Second, despite their contrasting language and cultural contexts, the texts' central protagonists bear striking resemblances to each other in terms of their depicted behaviours, view of themselves and the world around them. Third, the authors employ a first-person narrative voice in the mode of fiction or autofiction. Their texts can be defined as novels or as novelistic autofictions; the autofictions combine an often uncertain and ambiguous relationship with the biography of the author, often constructing a nominal correlation between the author and the mediating narrative voice. The first-person voice in all cases functions to sharpen the interplay between narrator and the representation of consciousness in narrative form. In their depictions of a single consciousness these works explore how subjects are constituted by discourse and matter but also how the subject may shape her choices and actions. Narrative fiction, in short, can hold the ambiguity inherent in this dynamic in a productive and irresolvable tension without resorting to a rhetoric of personal choice.

This volume is thus ultimately concerned with shifting conceptions of subjectivity, identity, and agency in feminist discourse since the impact of poststructuralism and to discover whether literary fiction offers a more probing engagement than the handbooks with the neoliberal socio-cultural constellations that inform any productive discussion of agency.

I have selected texts from North America, the UK, and Germany for several reasons. First, the historical, cultural, and linguistic links that bind the US, Canada, and the UK have generated a long-standing dialogue between feminist thinkers in those contexts, to the extent that 'Anglo-American' remains a term that carries significance in international feminist discourse. The influence of Anglo-American feminism on German feminist movements has been well documented.[32] Yet commentators note the cultural specificities that mark the second wave in Germany, known as *Neufeminismus* [the New Feminism], as distinct from, if influenced by, Anglo-American feminist discourse.[33] As other recent works have shown, comparing the German context with Britain and North America will therefore provide insight into the transnational flow of feminist discourse and its

---

[32] See Edith Hoshino Altbach et al., eds., *German Feminism: Readings in Politics and Literature* (Albany, New York: State University of New York Press, 1984); Myra Marx Ferree, *Varieties of Feminism*; Emily Spiers, 'The Long March through the Institutions: From Alice Schwarzer to Pop Feminism and the New German Girls,' *Post-War Literature and Institutions*, special issue of *Oxford German Studies*, ed. by Sean Williams and Daniel Wilson, 43.1 (2014), 69–88.

[33] See Myra Marx Ferree, *Varieties of Feminism*.

impact on the local.[34] Second, these three countries represent a fruitful comparative constellation due to the political and economic resonances they have shared since the ascendance of so-called 'Third Way' politics in the Clinton-Blair-Schröder era. Given the emphasis I place on the role of neoliberal ideologies in the development of pop-feminism, comparing three culturally and linguistically variant contexts that have nevertheless adopted similar ideological trajectories yields compelling insights into the interplay between the global and the local in political and economic paradigms. Third, Britain's geographical and cultural role as a conduit or Janus figure positioned between North America and Europe further warrants the comparison of these contexts, although it remains to be seen how the decision to leave the EU made in the 2016 referendum will affect this role. Fourth, and finally, the findings yielded by this comparison contribute to debates concerning the 'Americanization' of German literature, where 'Americanization' signifies a perceived turn to mass-market-driven publishing practices and, textually, the foregrounding of narrative and entertainment value over social critique.[35] While I trace a line of influence from American postmodern feminist writers Kathy Acker and Mary Gaitskill to early twenty-first-century British and German writers, my close reading of the German pop-literary fiction provides insight into the contention that the alleged Americanization of German literature equates with a withdrawal from social critique.[36] Furthermore, other important lines of influence on the German pop-feminists and pop-literary authors from preceding German-language writers like Sibylle Berg, Austrian Nobel Prize winning author and playwright Elfriede Jelinek, or the film-maker Monika Treut, have also begun to be explored.[37] Significantly, comparable concerns in the British context relating to publishing models and the role of literature become articulated in a language devoid of the idiom of national integrity, providing insight into the role that literature plays in perceptions of Germany's place on a global stage.

The pop-feminist guides become a fixed point of reference throughout this book. Chapter 1 establishes the theoretical framework guiding my analysis of subjectivity and agency in relation to the pop-feminist handbooks and the first-person narrative fictions. This chapter teases out the continuities and discontinuities between their respective models of subjectivity and agency. Close reading of the literary

---

[34] For example, Myra Marx Ferree, *Varieties of Feminism*; Christina Scharff, Carrie Smith-Prei, and Maria Stehle, 'Digital Feminisms: Transnational Activism in German Protest Cultures', p. 8.

[35] See Agnes C. Mueller, 'Introduction', in *German Pop Culture: How 'American' is it?*, ed. by Agnes C. Mueller (Ann Arbor: University of Michigan Press, 2004); Stuart Taberner, 'Literary Debates since Unification: "European" Modernism or "American" Pop?', in *German Literature of the 1990s and Beyond: Normalization and the Berlin Republic* (Rochester, NY: Camden House, 2005).

[36] See Thomas Anz, 'Konkurrenzen, Konflikte, Kontinuitäten'; Matthias Politycki, 'The American Dead End of German Literature', in *German Pop Culture: How 'American' is it?*

[37] See for example, Maria Stehle, 'Pop, Porn, and Rebellious Speech: Feminist Politics and the Multi-Media Performances of Elfriede Jelinek, Charlotte Roche, and Lady Bitch Ray', *Feminist Media Studies*, 12.2 (2012), 229–47; See also the articles gathered in Birgit Mikus and Emily Spiers (eds.), *Fractured Legacies: Historical, Cultural and Political Perspectives on German Feminism*, special issue of *Oxford German Studies*, 45.1 (2016); Hester Baer and Alexandra Merley Hill (eds.), *German Women's Writing in the Twenty-First Century* (Rochester, NY: Camden House, 2015); Margaret McCarthy (ed.), *German Pop Literature: A Companion* (Berlin: De Gruyter, 2015).

texts occurs within each subsequent chapter due to their specific literary contexts, although commonalities and specificities emerge as the book progresses. Together, the volumes signify a feminist pop-literary interest, spanning approximately three decades and shifting across cultural contexts, in subjectivity, female identity and agency in the face of neo-capitalist structures of social constraint.

I begin my investigations in Chapter 2 with Kathy Acker and Mary Gaitskill. I trace what I consider to be a depoliticizing trend apparent in much mainstream feminist discourse over the subsequent thirty years by observing the mobilizations of the transgressive feminist gesture in the North American riot-grrrl movement followed by its circulation in commercial popular culture. Chapter 3 begins with a discussion of the growth and axiomatization of digital feminist activism, which at times becomes just as prone to political blind-spots and commercialization as printed feminist discourse. My discussion of the recent work of Roxane Gay, Jessica Valenti, Maggie Nelson, Sheila Heti, and Michelle Tea draws on my analysis of the narrative qualities of selfhood developed in Chapter 1 and goes on to link the appropriation of the transgressive gesture identified in Chapter 2 to the process of queer normalization in a neoliberal climate, as explored in the works of Nelson and Tea, in particular.

Chapter 4 pursues the mainstreaming of female transgression and simultaneous disarming of politicized feminism from the 1990s onwards through the lens of the British publishing landscape. Instead of focusing on the already well-documented threshold moment in British publishing known as chick-lit, I dwell on statistical analysis of the publishing industry combined with data gathered from interviews with contemporary female authors. I then arrive at a close reading of British pop-literary fiction and the British pop-feminist guides. Chapter 5 examines the German pop-literary and pop-feminist landscape, whose comparative lateness offers fresh insights into the effect on feminism of pop-culture and the consequences for feminist politics.

THIRD-WAVE AND POSTFEMINIST LEGACIES

Before embarking upon these discussions, it is important to understand how pop-feminism relates to developments in feminist discourse since the early 1990s and the consolidation of neoliberalism in the West. Among the varieties of pop-feminist writing, I have identified a cluster of texts that demand reinvigorated feminist debate while simultaneously perpetuating some of the more problematic issues inherent in postfeminism. By this I mean that, despite their employment of feminist rhetoric, the authors' repudiation of their feminist forbears in the form of theoretical and/or second-wave feminism 'intersect[s] with wider institutionaliza-tions of gendered meanings' that consign feminism to the past wholesale.[38] Further, they ultimately reinforce the neoliberal status quo by deferring to an individualist logic whereby individual choice, likened to consumer choice, takes precedence over

---

[38] Clare Hemmings, *Why Stories Matter*, p. 1.

a coherent political framework. Their titles often draw on the language of the self-help guide, which relocates transformation to the private realm of self-improvement, self-discipline, and self-calibration in relation to the demands of neoliberal consumer culture. While these strategies appear to be intended to ameliorate the beleaguered image of feminism in the early twenty-first century and increase its popularity among a younger target audience, one consequence of this manoeuvre is the forfeiture of a concrete political dimension, including strategies for change. Conversely, other pop-feminists seek to engender continuity between feminisms past and present; they also remain alert to their 'awkward' attachment to the neoliberal paradigm, seeking actively to expose neoliberalism's systemic fault lines and the 'false promises' that impinge upon the individual.[39]

Such variance can be usefully compared to an earlier critical divergence in feminist concepts and approaches. By this I mean the perceived distinction between third-wave feminism and postfeminism in the mid-1990s. Deborah Siegel observes that in the 'mid-1990s, as the postfeminists were busy pronouncing the personal no longer political, the newly self-identifying third-wavers proclaimed the opposite'.[40] Stéphanie Genz and Benjamin Brabon refer to the perceived 'division between postfeminism and third-wave feminism, whereby the former is interpreted as middle-of-the-road and depoliticized while the latter is more subcultural and activist'.[41] Mapping pop-feminism onto this model aligns the more market-oriented, individualistic pop-feminism with conceptualizations of 'middle-of-the-road' postfeminism and suggests an even earlier continuity with liberal feminism per se.[42] In contrast, other pop-feminists express a particularly strong sense of aesthetic and ideological indebtedness to the North American riot-grrrl movement, which I discuss in Chapter 2, as well as the third wave. Riot grrrl often becomes linked with third-wave feminism in Anglophone theoretical volumes such as Siegel's and Genz and Brabon's, and they become potent touchstones for the German pop-feminist volumes, in particular.[43]

Diane Negra and Yvonne Tasker initiate their interrogation of the term postfeminism with a definition that gestures towards its complexity: postfeminism 'encompasses a set of assumptions, widely disseminated within popular media forms, having to do with the "pastness" of feminism, whether that supposed pastness is merely noted, mourned, or celebrated'.[44] For Diane Negra, Yvonne Tasker, and other scholars like Angela McRobbie and Rosalind Gill, postfeminism connotes a critical object of study, rather than a feminist methodology. In her influential essay

---

[39] Carrie Smith-Prei and Maria Stehle, *Awkward Politics*, p. 11.

[40] Deborah Siegel, *Sisterhood, Interrupted: From Radical Women to Grrls [sic] Gone Wild* (New York; Basingstoke: Palgrave Macmillan, 2007), p. 132.

[41] Stéphanie Genz and Benjamin A. Brabon, *Postfeminism: Cultural Texts and Theories* (Edinburgh: Edinburgh University Press, 2009), p. 81.

[42] Making a strong case for understanding 'feminism-lite' or 'fun feminism' as a contemporary manifestation of liberal feminism are Miranda Kiraly and Meagan Tyler (eds.), *Freedom Fallacy: The Limits of Liberal Feminism* (Brisbane: Connor Court, 2015).

[43] See Stéphanie Genz and Benjamin Brabon, *Postfeminism*, pp. 80–1; Deborah Siegel, *Sisterhood, Interrupted*, pp. 148–9.

[44] Yvonne Tasker and Diane Negra, 'Feminist Politics and Postfeminist Culture', p. 1.

'Postfeminism and Popular Culture' (2004), McRobbie defines postfeminism as 'an active process by which feminist gains of the 1970s and 1980s come to be undermined'.[45] Both in this essay and the ensuing monograph, *The Aftermath of Feminism* (2009), McRobbie builds upon the American scholar Susan Faludi's notion of 'backlash', which the latter employs to describe the negative conservative response, occurring from the early 1990s onwards, to the achievements of feminism.[46] For Negra and Tasker, as for McRobbie, postfeminism implies a more 'complex relationship between culture, politics, and feminism than the more familiar framing concept of "backlash" allows'.[47] Defining her concept of 'double entanglement', McRobbie argues that 'elements of contemporary popular culture are perniciously effective' in undermining feminist achievements while 'simultaneously appearing to be engaging in a well-informed and even well-intended response to "feminism"'.[48] She refers to the assimilation of feminist values across a variety of institutions, including the law, education, employment, and the media, which lead to certain newsworthy achievements by women and girls being profiled in the media. Items of this kind 'show the institutions to be modern and abreast with social change'.[49] On the other hand, McRobbie identifies 'various sites within popular culture where [the] work of undoing feminism with some subtlety becomes visible'.[50]

Advertisements that feature women adopting sexually objectifying roles seemingly out of choice take 'feminism into account by showing it to be a thing of the past, by provocatively "enacting sexism" while at the same time playing with those debates in film theory about women as the object of the gaze and even with female desire'.[51] The young female viewer, who is 'educated in irony and visually literate', is not angered by such mobilizations of sexism. In fact, she 'appreciates its layers of meaning; she "gets the joke"'.[52]

McRobbie stresses the importance of viewing this process within the context of the 'full enfranchisement of women in the West, of all ages, as audiences, as active consumers of media and the many products they promote'. In this context, female achievement becomes aligned with '"female individualism"' rather than feminism.[53] In the advertisements McRobbie describes, 'tradition is restored' for male viewers. For women, on the other hand, 'what is proposed is a movement beyond feminism to a more comfortable zone where women are now free to choose for themselves'.[54] While the narrative of 'choice' indeed signals a 'movement beyond feminism', the word itself also echoes the language of second-wave feminism, in particular idea of a 'woman's right to choose' in relation to reproductive capacities. At the same time, it evokes the language of consumerism in relation to 'consumer choice'. Thus, the

---

[45] Angela McRobbie, 'Postfeminism and Popular Culture', p. 27.
[46] Susan Faludi, *Backlash: The Undeclared War against Women* (London: Vintage, 1992).
[47] Yvonne Tasker and Diane Negra, 'Feminist Politics and Postfeminist Culture', p. 1.
[48] Angela McRobbie, 'Postfeminism and Popular Culture', p. 27.   [49] Ibid., p. 30.
[50] Angela McRobbie, 'Postfeminism and Popular Culture', p. 32.
[51] Ibid. Here, McRobbie is referring to the pivotal work of Laura Mulvey and her concept of the 'male gaze', developed in Laura Mulvey, *Visual and Other Pleasures* (Basingstoke: Palgrave Macmillan, 1989).
[52] Angela McRobbie, 'Postfeminism and Popular Culture', p. 33.
[53] Ibid.   [54] Ibid.

potency of this motif lies in its straddling multiple narratives: it implies that feminism has been taken into account, but it also gestures towards a movement beyond those elements of feminist ideology perceived as restrictive of individual choice, relocating the locus of feminist empowerment in purchasing power. Ultimately, the assimilation of feminist values within cultural, political, and social institutions, and public media profiling of the same, combines with pre-feminist, conservative tendencies in the media, in which female consumers are also implicated. In the sphere of popular culture, feminism is thus invoked 'as that which can be taken into account' because equality has purportedly been achieved. As a result, feminism becomes associated with a 'whole repertoire of new meanings' that imply that it constitutes a 'spent force'.[55]

Nevertheless, when the term initially appeared, it was understood by some advocates to signify a new positive departure in feminist discourse. Sophie Phoca, who co-authored *Introducing Postfeminism* in 1999, claimed that postfeminism constituted a different form of feminism rather than being anti-feminist.[56] In fact, she thought it spoke to a younger generation of women. In 1997 Ann Brooks, also drawing on the generational analogy, argued that postfeminism had arisen out of a conceptual shift in feminist theory from a preoccupation with equality issues to a welcome confrontation with matters of difference.[57]

Today, most scholars agree at least with this part of Brooks's assessment: that the rise of postfeminism coincided with what McRobbie calls 'the moment of definitive self-critique in feminist theory'.[58] By the early 1990s, the influence of poststructuralism on feminist discourse had already been instrumental in shifting the focus of feminist critique from monolithic notions of patriarchy and the law to decentralized nexuses of power instantiated in the convergence of discursive flows and institutional contexts; this shift in theoretical approach occurred concomitantly with the ascendance of postcolonial studies and resonated with the already long-established work of theorists of colour, whose work challenged the universalist representational claims of second-wave feminism and its 'dominant and colonizing voice'.[59]

However, internal fragmentation did not cauterize feminist debate completely. In 2000 Imelda Whelehan argued convincingly that there had been, in the Anglo-American context, two responses to the then established 'cultural climate', by which she means one in which 'feminism is at one and the same time credited with furthering women's independence and dismissed as irrelevant to a new generation of women who no longer need to be liberated from the shackles of patriarchy because they have already "arrived" '.[60] Whelehan contends that while some

[55] Yvonne Tasker and Diane Negra, 'Feminist Politics and Postfeminist Culture', p. 1.

[56] Sophie Phoca, interviewed by Melaine Ashby, 'Beyond the New Feminism?', *Sibyl*, May–June: 8 (1999), 34 (p. 34).

[57] Ann Brooks, *Postfeminisms: Feminism, Cultural Theory, and Cultural Forms* (New York: Routledge, 1997).

[58] Angela McRobbie, 'Postfeminism and Popular Culture', p. 29.

[59] Lynne Alice, *What is Postfeminism? Or, Having it Both Ways: Feminism, Postmodernism, Postfeminism* (New Zealand: Massey University, 1995), p. 11.

[60] Imelda Whelehan, *Overloaded*, p. 3.

thinkers described this 'staging point' as postfeminism, others 'incorporated aspects of this with an "old" feminist perspective and christened it "new feminism"'.[61] Referring to the work of Naomi Wolf, Natasha Walter, and Rene Denfeld in Britain and the North America, Whelehan sketches the emergence of these so-called 'new feminisms':

> [A]t the beginning of the new millennium, feminists have been positioned as the cultural oppressors of 'normal' women against which a younger generation of 'new' feminists offers as antidote a marked individualistic kind of 'radicalism'. This radicalism pretends the power of self-definition is all about being 'in control' and 'making choices', regardless, it seems, of who controls the 'choices' available. Being 'in control' became one of the catchwords of the nineties in the parlance of women's magazines, but control always seemed to be about the right to consume and display oneself to best effect. [. . .] It was an expression of withdrawal from a wider political arena.[62]

Some strands of pop-feminism in both the Anglo-American and German contexts take up where 1990s 'new feminism' left off; their authors, while younger than Walter and Wolf, are nevertheless influenced by their work, in particular their emphasis on individual self-definition and a sense of antagonism towards second-wave feminism.

By the late 1990s, the subversive third-wave figure of the riot grrrl had arrived in Germany. This was due in part to the publication in Germany of an anthology of riot-grrrl work, *Lips Tits Hits Power?*, edited and published by Anette Baldauf and Katharine Weingartner in 1998. Baldauf and Weingartner, two German critics living in New York, assembled a selection of song lyrics, articles, art work, and accounts of feminist activism in a scholarly publication that sought to depict both the variety of the riot-grrrl movement and celebrate its subversive potential.[63] The music journalism of writers like Kerstin Grether, whose literary work features in Chapter 5, was also influential in promoting awareness of Anglo-American riot-grrrl culture in Germany. Before that time, riot grrrl's mainstream cognate, the 'Girlie', was a more familiar protagonist in German popular culture.[64] The mis-spelled Anglicism, 'Girlie', a term that reached prominence in the mid-1990s, alludes to the 'Girl Power' motto of the British Spice Girls, and denoted at that time a cheeky fashion sensibility for twenty-somethings and a fun-seeking attitude to life, love, and partying. German-language theoretical texts that pronounced either postfeminist, new feminist or third-wave feminist departures were much thinner on the ground in the 1990s; translations of English-language works filtered through after some lapse of time into a field still dominated by domestically produced texts by renowned feminist figureheads such as Alice Schwarzer and

[61] Ibid.   [62] Ibid., pp. 3–4.

[63] Anette Baldauf and Katharina Weingartner, eds., *Lips Tits Hits Power? Popkultur und Feminismus* (Vienna: Folio, 1998).

[64] See Katja Kauer, *Popfeminismus! Fragezeichen! Eine Einführung* (Berlin: Frank & Timme, 2009), pp. 77–90. Katja Kauer argues that the Girlie and riot-grrrl phenomena were important precursors of pop-feminism in Germany. See Katja Kauer, pp. 9–28.

other representatives of *Neufeminismus* [literally 'New Feminism' but what, in the Anglo-American context, is known as second-wave feminism].[65]

The reinvigoration of published popular feminist discourse arising in the mid-2000s in Germany was all the more striking as a result of this prolonged dominance in the public sphere. The absence of the wave metaphor in the German context, which symbolically links stages in Anglo-American feminist discourse while simultaneously distinguishing between them, also contributed to the sense of abrupt caesura upon the publication of the pop-feminist volumes in the first decade of the twenty-first century. Sonja Eismann, for example, evokes this cultural difference when she contends that German pop-feminism connotes an act of 'catching-up' with Anglo-American third-wave feminism.[66] As I demonstrate in Chapter 5, however, pop-feminism in Germany was also influenced by the boom in domestically produced pop-literature in the mid-1990s.

POP-FEMINISM AND NEOLIBERALISM

Understanding pop-feminism requires contextualization not only in relation to postfeminism but also neoliberalism. David Harvey provides a useful definition that describes neoliberalism as a 'theory of political economic practice that proposes that human well-being can best be advanced by liberating individual entrepreneurial freedoms and skills within an institutional framework characterized by strong private property rights, free markets and free trade'.[67] Scholars generally trace its recent historical prominence to the processes of deregulation and privatization that gained currency in the 1980s during the Reagan/Thatcher era. Neoliberal policies and ideologies proceeded to spread through the West, gaining sure footing over greater geographical distances due to the global interventions of international institutions like the World Bank, the International Monetary Fund, and the World Trade Organization.[68] As Hester Baer notes, German reunification paved the way for the increased adoption of neoliberal policies and ideologies, such as the Hartz concept, in re-unified Germany.[69] Such policies were successfully implemented despite a strong trade-union presence and traditionally amenable attitude towards

---

[65] Naomi Wolf's *The Beauty Myth* (1990) was published by Rowohlt in German in 1992. Natasha Walter's *The New Feminism* (1998) was not picked up by German publishers at all, yet her 2010 volume *Living Dolls* was, and almost immediately after publication in Britain. Translated by Gabriele Herbst, it was published by Krüger Verlag in 2011.

[66] Sonja Eismann, 'Einleitung', pp. 10–11. Eismann mentions the US third-wave feminist publications *Bitch* and *Bust*, in particular.

[67] David Harvey, *A Brief History of Neoliberalism* (Oxford: Oxford University Press, 2005), p. 2.

[68] For the purposes of my study, I focus on the spread of neoliberalism in Anglo-American and European contexts. For a more detailed discussion, see Stéphanie Genz, 'Third Way/ve: The Politics of Postfeminism', *Feminist Theory*, 7.3 (2006), 333–53.

[69] The Hartz concept of 2002 initiated a set of reforms in the German labour market, which, among other things, rewarded entrepreneurialism on the one hand, while implementing harsher measures for the unemployed on the other. For example, unemployment benefit and social welfare payments were combined (Hartz IV) in 2005 and the system of emergency payments for those in extreme need was abolished.

the provision of social welfare.[70] Some scholars argue that Eastern Germans have adapted more quickly and completely to neoliberalism than their West German counterparts. While the former East Germany was exposed in an unprotected manner to the prospecting incursions of global capitalist opportunists in the first years after reunification, the strong neoliberal narrative of freedom of choice and equal opportunity appears to have been positively and enthusiastically received in the east of Germany.[71]

Neoliberalism marks the intrusion of the market into every aspect of everyday life. Citing Peck and Tickell, Rosalind Gill focuses on the phase of neoliberalism from the early twenty-first century onwards, which is marked by a 'rolling-out' and 'intensification' of 'quasi-market mechanisms', which 'expand over an ever-widening range of activities'.[72] Elisabeth Prügl has recently argued in favour of differentiating between forms of neoliberalism, reminding us of the 'indeterminate way in which doctrines circulate and are resisted, and the process aspect of any class and governance project'.[73] Prügl refers not only to neoliberalism's multiple forms but also to its 'tremendous capacity to transform and adapt'.[74] Precisely this adaptability ensured that neoliberalism not only survived the financial crisis of 2008–9 and the years of austerity following it, but in some cases became more entrenched. According to Gill, this is because neoliberalism has become a 'force for creating actors who are rational, calculating and self-motivating, and who are increasingly exhorted to make sense of their individual biographies in terms of discourses of freedom, autonomy and choice—no matter how constrained their lives might be'.[75]

Pop-feminism constitutes both the creation of *and* response to postfeminism and neoliberalism. By this I mean that some pop-feminist attempts to articulate a feminist response to contemporary manifestations of discrimination and gender inequality involve them drawing on the principles of the very discourses upholding those oppressive practices. Pop-feminism's frequent foregrounding of playful self-fashioning, freedom of choice, and rhetorical claims to autonomy resonates with neoliberalism's discursive and structural prioritization of the individual and her freedom, its emphasis on the importance of deregulation in relation to regulatory structures like welfare systems. In the same way, many pop-feminists perceive

---

[70] Hester Baer, 'German Feminism in the Age of Neoliberalism: Jana Hensel and Elizabeth Raether's *Neue deutsche Mädchen*', *German Studies Review*, 35. 2 (2012), 355–74 (p. 359). For a detailed overview of neoliberalism in Germany, see Herbert Schui and Stephanie Blankenburg, *Neoliberalismus: Theorie, Gegner, Praxis* (Hamburg: VSA, 2002).

[71] See Stuart Taberner (ed.), *German Literature in the Age of Globalisation* (Birmingham: University of Birmingham Press, 2004), p. 13; and Laurence McFalls, 'Eastern Germany Transformed: From Postcommunist to Late Capitalist Political Culture', *German Politics and Society* 17.2 (1999), p. 3.

[72] Jamie Peck and Adam Tickell, 'Neoliberalizing Space', in *Spaces of Neoliberalism*, ed. by Neil Brenner and Nik Theodore (Oxford: Blackwell, 2002), cited in Rosalind Gill and Christina Scharff, 'Introduction', in *New Femininities: Postfeminism, Neoliberalism and Subjectivity*, ed. by Rosalind Gill and Christina Scharff (Basingstoke: Palgrave Macmillan, 2011), p. 6.

[73] Elisabeth Prügl, 'Neoliberalising Feminism', *New Political Economy*, 20.4 (2015), 614–31 (p. 616).

[74] Ibid.   [75] Rosalind Gill and ChristinaScharff, 'Introduction', in *New Femininities*, p. 6.

self-empowerment to be located in highly personalized, stylized performances of identity, a notion which facilitates the disarticulation of collective politics and bolsters consumer culture.

This understanding of agency aligns with the type of feminism that is 'thriving as feminism is walking the halls of corporate and state power', namely 'liberal feminism and individualist solutions to gender oppression'.[76] The wider impact of this institutional feminism is exemplified by the high sales achieved by business woman Sheryl Sandberg's 2013 publication *Lean In: Women, Work and the Will to Lead* in the two years after publication.[77] Rather than combatting capitalism, however, Prügl notes that liberal feminism has:

> gone to bed with capitalism, mixing at the meetings of the World Economic Forum in Davos as much as in the annual meetings of the World Bank and the International Monetary Fund. It engages women and men in business, academia, and government and speaks a new language of gender balance and equality as an asset for business and economic development.[78]

This kind of 'market' or 'free market' feminism[79] appears to be 'far from generating structural change'.[80] At the same time, scholars have noted the gendered characteristics of both pre- and post-crash neoliberal mobilizations in both economic and discursive terms. Raewyn Connell, for example, argues that the neoliberal 'entrepreneur' is coded masculine. This is because one effect of dismantling welfare structures has been the redistribution of wealth from women to men, as many women, often employed in lower-paid jobs (or sectors) than men in the first place, leave work to care for those who previously would have been cared for by the state. Connell furthermore views neoliberalism's distaste for political correctness and affirmative action as directly undermining the feminist gains predating the 1980s, offering some kind of redress for the threat to patriarchy posed by the women's movement.[81] It is no accident that, in Germany, 'public discourse blames women' for the drop in child-birth rate, which garnered significant public attention in the so-called 'demography debate' of the mid-2000s, while Hester Baer attributes the drop to the implementation of neoliberal policies, such as cut-backs in social welfare.[82] Myra Marx-Ferree, too, makes the point that the repeal of comprehensive welfare policies in neoliberal Germany, underpinned by Hartz IV, 'represents a step

---

[76] Elisabeth Prügl, 'Neoliberalising Feminism', p. 614.

[77] A 2015 BBC article claims that the volume had by that time sold 2.5 million copies worldwide. See Gianna Palmer, 'What impact has Lean In had on women?', 5 March 2015, available at http://www.bbc.co.uk/news/business-31727796.

[78] Elisabeth Prügl, 'Neoliberalising Feminism', pp. 614–15.

[79] See Johanna. Kantola and Judith Squires, 'From State Feminism to Market Feminism', *International Political Science Review*, 33.4 (2012), 382–400; Hester Eisenstein, *Feminism Seduced: How Global Elites Use Women's Labor and Ideas to Exploit the World* (Boulder, CO: Paradigm Publishers, 2009). See also Nancy Fraser, 'Feminism, Capitalism and the Cunning of History', *New Left Review*, 56 (2009), 97–117.

[80] Elisabeth Prügl, 'Neoliberalising Feminism', p. 615.

[81] Raewyn Connell, 'Understanding Neoliberalism', in *Neoliberalism and Everyday Life*, ed. by Susan Braedley and Meg Luxton (Montreal: McGill-Queen's University Press, 2010), pp. 33–4.

[82] Hester Baer, 'German Feminism in the Age of Neoliberalism', p. 360.

backwards in a country already perceived to be lagging the rest of the EU' in terms of women's access to full-time work, leadership roles, and pay equality.[83]

Gill and Scharff scrutinize the connection between postfeminism and neoliberalism.[84] They pay attention to the gendering of neoliberal narratives, observing that in popular culture it is '*women* who are called on to self-manage, to self-discipline. To a much greater extent than men, women are required to work on and transform the self, to regulate every aspect of their conduct, and to present all their actions as freely chosen'.[85] In contrast to Connell, Gill and Scharff reflect on the possibility that women become constructed as neoliberalism's 'ideal subjects'.[86] All too often, however, postfeminist neoliberal narratives in pop-culture encourage women to understand sexuality as the acceptable realm of entrepreneurial expression and achievement.[87]

SEXUALITY, TRANSGRESSION, AND AGENCY

One of the most striking features of all of the texts under discussion, from the pop-feminist guides to the pop-literary fiction, is their foregrounding of sex and sexuality as categories of analysis. In order to understand how these themes function within pop-feminist and wider cultural discourse, I turn to a body of scholarship that, since the first decade of the twenty-first century, has engaged with the alleged sexualization of Western culture. As Harvey and Gill contend, the term 'sexualization' is employed to 'capture the growing sense of Western societies as saturated by sexual representations and discourses, and in which pornography has become increasingly influential and porous, transforming contemporary culture'.[88] Feona Attwood itemizes the elements characterizing the transformed sexual landscape of the early twenty-first century:

> [A] contemporary preoccupation with sexual values, practices and identities; the public shift to more permissive attitudes; the proliferation of sexual texts; the emergence of new forms of sexual experience; the apparent breakdown of rules, categories and regulations designed to keep the obscene at bay; our fondness for scandals, controversies and panics around sex.[89]

---

[83] Myra Marx Ferree, 'Gender Politics in the Berlin Republic: Four Issues of Identity and Institutional Change', *German Politics and Society*, 28.1 (2010), p. 198.

[84] Rosalind Gill and Christina Scharff, 'Introduction', in *New Femininities*, p. 7; see also, Rosalind Gill, 'Postfeminist Media Culture: Elements of a Sensibility', *European Journal of Cultural Studies*, 10.2 (2007), 147–66.

[85] Rosalind Gill and Christina Scharff, 'Introduction', in *New Femininities*, p. 7. Original italics.

[86] Ibid.

[87] See Laura Harvey and Rosalind Gill, 'Spicing it Up: Sexual Entrepreneurs and *The Sex Inspectors*', in *New Femininities*; Joel Gwynne, *Erotic Memoirs and Postfeminism: The Politics of Pleasure* (Basingstoke: Palgrave Macmillan, 2013).

[88] Ibid. p. 53.

[89] Feona Attwood, 'Sexed-Up: Theorising the Sexualisation of Culture', *Sexualities*, 9.1 (2006), 77–94 (pp. 78–9).

Attwood contends that such controversies persist despite the fact that, in the twenty-first century, the 'explicit has become so familiar and sexual transgression so mainstream'.[90]

Scholarship on cultural sexualization remains ideologically and methodologically diverse in ways that resist categorization along the lines of the 'sex-positive' and 'sex-negative' binary of the so-called feminist sex wars of the 1980s. Some contemporary writers align themselves with a type of 'anti-sexualization' stance that recalls the critical position taken by second-wave feminist Andrea Dworkin in relation to heterosexual sex and by Dworkin and Catherine McKinnon in relation to pornography.[91] Ariel Levy's *Female Chauvinist Pigs* and Pamela Paul's *Pornified* are two examples of such popular critical works. Paul's volume contends that increasing exposure to pornography inflicts psychological damage on individuals and their families, while Levy examines the manner in which pornographic aesthetics and content are increasingly disseminated through popular media, delivering the message to young women that participation in 'raunch culture' represents a means to self-empowerment and agency.[92] By examining the brands and media conglomerates profiting from sexualized cultural practices and representations, Levy also makes the link between 'raunch culture' and commercialism, arguing that the 'new conception of raunch culture as a path to liberation rather than oppression is a convenient (and lucrative) fantasy'.[93] This is a connection made by Maggie Nelson in her hybrid theoretical-literary mash-up, *The Argonauts* (2015), which I explore in Chapter 3. The narrator views the ascendance of commercial raunch culture through the lens of queer critique:

> What sense does it make to align 'queer' with 'sexual deviance' when the ostensibly straight world is having no trouble keeping pace? [...] Has anyone looked at the endless list of fetishes on a 'straight' porn website recently? [...] If queerness is about disturbing normative sexual assumptions and practices, isn't one of these that sex is the be-all and end-all? What if Beatriz Preciado is right—what if we've entered a new, post-Fordist era of capitalism that Preciado calls the 'pharmacopornographic era', whose principal economic resource is nothing other than 'the insatiable bodies of the multitudes'?[94]

Echoing Nelson's comments on the relationship between sexuality and the queering of normative behaviours, Levy views sexualization as a type of rebellion by young women against the proscriptive theorizing of some protagonists in the so-called feminist sex wars of the 1980s. Since that period, queer theory and disability

---

[90] Ibid., p. 80.

[91] Andrea Dworkin, *Intercourse* (London: Secker & Warburg, 1987); Andrea Dworkin, *Pornography: Men Possessing Women* (London: Women's Press, 1981); Catharine A. MacKinnon and Andrea Dworkin, *In Harm's Way: The Pornography Civil Rights Hearings* (Cambridge, MA; London: Harvard University Press, 1997).

[92] See Pamela Paul, *Pornified: How Pornography is Transforming our Lives, our Relationships, and our Families* (New York: Times Books/Henry Holt & Company, 2005).

[93] Ariel Levy, *Female Chauvinist Pigs: Women and the Rise of Raunch Culture* (New York; London: Free Press, 2005), p. 82.

[94] Maggie Nelson, *The Argonauts* (London: Melville House, 2015), pp. 137–8.

studies have intervened in these debates in ways that have disrupted the logic of anti-sex reasoning, arguing for the rights of marginal groups to access a discourse of sexuality from which they had been previously excluded. As women have increasingly gained access to the modes of production, queer, feminist, and women-friendly porn is produced, disseminated, and consumed by women and men alike, and the field of feminist porn studies is growing rapidly.[95] Indeed, many contemporary feminist writers view their work on sex and sexuality as a continuation of the second-wave feminist project of 'deconstructing essentialist histories of sexuality' and reappraising the 'sources of women's sexual pleasure by specifically underscoring the relationship between suppressed sexuality and social powerlessness'.[96] For many second-wave feminists, this process was 'imperative to the endeavour of deconstructing patriarchal capitalist ideologies'.[97]

Theories of contemporary sexuality and sexualization thus exist on what Gill and Harvey call 'multiple axes of difference'.[98] My analysis draws predominantly on the work of scholars like Gill, Harvey, McRobbie, Gwynne, and Attwood, who examine sexualization as a cultural phenomenon linked with the processes of postfeminism and neoliberalism. Importantly, their work avoids adopting positions of moral authority, on the one hand, or reliance upon Marxist notions of false consciousness, on the other. Instead, it investigates the links between representations of female sexuality and agency, emphasizing how young women engaged in sexualized behaviours understand themselves to be acting autonomously. These protagonists cannot be viewed simply as victims of a wrong-footed patriarchy seeking to establish innovative methods of incorporating and then containing female agency. This is because these protagonists actively conceive of their behaviours as claiming a scene of agency even as 'postfeminist sensibilities of choice and empowerment [become] complicit in masking a social reality in which little has changed in terms of real world social practices'.[99]

My analysis of pop-feminism will demonstrate how postfeminism and neoliberalism combine to create a climate in which, all too often, feminist achievement becomes re-situated in the realm of self-empowerment, facilitated by the exercise of individual choice and the processes of self-improvement. The rhetoric of choice conceals the restrictions placed upon arenas of agency by the disciplinary forces of a decentralized patriarchy, underpinned by commerce and consumerism. Sex and female sexuality constitute one of the 'licensed' arenas of female agency. This is due to the manner in which these themes dovetail with the demands of the free market and consumer culture, but also with the compelling narrative that sexuality constitutes a private arena exempt from feminist scrutiny.[100] As Attwood observes, 'sex is increasingly linked to youth and consumer cultures; sexual discourse is increasingly

---

[95] See, for example, Tristan Taormino et al., eds., *The Feminist Porn Book: The Politics of Producing Pleasure* (New York: Feminist Press at the City University of New York, 2013).

[96] Joel Gwynne, *Erotic Memoirs and Postfeminism*, p. 4.   [97] Ibid.

[98] Laura Harvey and Rosalind Gill, 'Spicing it Up', in *New Femininities*, p. 54.

[99] Joel Gwynne, *Erotic Memoirs and Postfeminism*, p. 15.

[100] I borrow the term 'licensed' from McRobbie via her discussion of Butler's model of the 'phallicised dyke'. See Judith Butler, *Gender Trouble*, pp. 59–77.

organized by new cultural intermediaries and, in particular, is articulated in terms of a "therapeutic" culture that promotes a focus on sexuality and the self as a means to personal development and fulfilment'.[101]

In general, the pop-feminist guides I discuss remain entangled in a position on sex that draws on the legacy of revisionist feminist work on female sexuality while simultaneously resonating with postfeminist commercial ideations of the sexually active female. Drawing on Foucault's later ideas concerning 'technologies of selfhood', which opened up a less passive model of theorizing the subject's capacity for action than his earlier work, McRobbie views the entanglement outlined above as one of a range of postfeminist 'technologies of individualization'.[102] Such technologies 'regularly draw on elements from well-known feminist discourses in terms of independence and the desire for agency, but subject these qualities to further transformation so that they more fully conform with the dictates of a postfeminist sexual contract that seeks resolution to sexual inequality without challenge to or contestation of masculine hegemony and the heterosexual matrix'.[103] While the authors of pop-feminist handbooks generally remain alive to the more negative aspects of commercial sexualization, their frequent reliance on the rhetoric of choice prevents them from probing the fundamental question of how choices become made. The literary fiction I discuss, however, tends to complicate precisely those processes of self-reflection, choice, and agency, producing a more ambivalent exploration of the relationship between sexuality and agency.

Moreover, the fictions focus on the intersection of sex and sexuality with a group of other, transgressive behaviours that McRobbie argues belongs to the wider 'habits of masculinity'.[104] Drawing on Butler, McRobbie identifies the 'phallic girl' as a central respondent to the new postfeminist sexual contract, which construes sexuality as an 'urging to agency'.[105] These behaviours include 'heavy drinking, swearing, smoking, getting into fights, having casual sex, the consumption of pornography' as well as access to a type of 'licensed' homosexuality.[106] The literary narratives I discuss represent many of the kinds of behaviours listed above, often extending to the inclusion of a range of self-destructive practices like self-harm and disordered eating, which become linked with psychological pathologies like depression and anxiety. Many of the works also foreground characters who initially opt out of, or subversively 'queer', social trajectories of self-improvement, shunning careers, families, and aspirational behaviour in general. The literary narratives thus respond to a postfeminist neoliberal climate that ensures high visibility for the female subject as a well-educated, high achieving contributor to the processes of economic prosperity while simultaneously circulating a model of female agency that is

---

[101] Feona Attwood, 'Sexed- Up', p. 80. See also Kenneth Plummer, *Telling Sexual Stories: Power, Change, and Social Worlds* (London: Routledge, 1995), pp. 124–5.

[102] Angela McRobbie, *The Aftermath of Feminism: Gender, Culture and Social Change* (Los Angeles; London: Sage, 2009), p. 111. See also, Michel Foucault, 'Technologies of the Self', in *Technologies of the Self: A Seminar with Michel Foucault*, ed. by Luther H. Martin et al. (London; Amherst: University of Massachusetts Press, 1988).

[103] Angela McRobbie, *The Aftermath of Feminism*, p. 111.

[104] Ibid.   [105] Ibid.   [106] Ibid.

contained within the arena of female corporeality and sexuality. The majority of protagonists in the literary pieces I explore experience what McRobbie dubs 'illegible rage', engendered by the conflicting forces at work on their subjective development.

Drawing on Butler's notion of heterosexual melancholia in order to develop her own understanding of the contemporary pathologies afflicting young women, McRobbie contends that:

> [c]oncessions are made on the part of patriarchal authority in the direction of responding to desire for autonomy, or desire for distance from heterosexuality, but all the more so that unruly or disorderly desires can be safely contained, even if this requires the endorsement of normative pathologisation, such that symptoms of gender distress (self-harming, drug addiction, eating disorders) come to be established as predictable, treatable, things to be managed medically rather than subjected to sustained social scrutiny.[107]

For McRobbie, the root cause of these pathologies lies in the loss of the feminist alternative to postfeminist selfhood experienced by the young female subject in contemporary culture. McRobbie thus views their internalized rage as today's 'female complaint, where the values of feminist sociality are disavowed and replaced by a bolstered post-feminist self which is unviable, this unviability ensuring its status as subject for attention and treatment in accordance with the values and norms set by various experts, self-help gurus, and professionals. [...] [T]hese endless stagings of femininity conjure psychic landscapes and scenarios of loss, melancholia and illegible rage'.[108] Chapter 1 investigates in more detail the characteristics of these psychic landscapes and their consequences for questions of subjectivity and agency, as well as how they affect the relationship between the subject and the social. The remaining chapters make visible the link between sexualization, postfeminism, and neoliberalism as I trace the deployment of the sexually transgressive gesture in female-authored fiction from the early work of Kathy Acker and Mary Gaitskill to the twenty-first-century fiction of authors in North America, Britain, and Germany. My aim is to trace the processes of sexual mainstreaming referred to by Feona Attwood above not only in pop-literary fiction but also in wider pop-feminist discourse.

---

[107] Ibid., p. 112.   [108] Ibid., p. 111.

1

The Pop-Feminist Subject

Postfeminist enquiries into identity politics have been dominated by the work of Judith Butler for nearly two decades,[1] and pop-feminist debates are not exempt from this influence. In the pop-feminist guides, accounts of subjectivity and agency draw on the notion of social constructivism and on Butler's *Gender Trouble* (1990), in particular. Their authors demonstrate an awareness that identities arise out of a complex nexus of social conditions, are performed in a pluralistic, incoherent process of making the self identifiable within a regulatory social system, and that the concept of prediscursive coherent selfhood sustains essentialist notions of a 'natural' or 'universal', biologically determined gender identity. Pop-feminist guides often take up the debate from the point at which *Gender Trouble* left off, rarely referring to Butler's later work in which she addresses that formative work's shortcomings.[2]

As pop-feminists do not seek to be scholarly, their outlines of Butler's work become radically transformed from the densely written academic register of its initial form. It is difficult to ascertain whether Butler's work was already thus condensed in the women's/gender studies, literature, or political philosophy departments in which many of the North American and German pop-feminist authors studied (the British authors are predominantly trained journalists), or whether the pop medium their texts inhabit and their intended audience induce an over-simplified translation, whether inter- or intralingual. In general, pop-feminist volumes constitute a generative re-interpretation of Butler's thinking that aligns social constructivism and performativity with playful pop aesthetics and neoliberal consumer lifestyle. Katja Kauer identifies this connection when she discusses pop-feminist identity, expressed '[d]urch das Sampling, also das Spiel mit verschiedenen klassischen Weiblichkeitsentwürfen, die durch Musik, Fernsehen und Konsumprodukte am Leben erhalten werden' [through sampling, or playing, with various classic conceptions of femininity that have been sustained through music, television and consumer products.][3] This assessment is echoed in British author Ellie Levenson's description of her style of 'pick "n" mix feminism':

[1] Stephanie Clare, 'New Material Feminisms', *Gender Studies Lecture* (Oxford University, 16 February 2012).

[2] For example, Judith Butler, *Bodies that Matter: On the Discursive Limits of 'Sex'* (New York; London: Routledge, 1993).

[3] Katja Kauer, *Popfeminismus!*, p. 94.

Sometimes when I have wanted something, a refund in a shop perhaps, or a favour from my boss, I have shamelessly and knowingly flirted my way to getting what I wanted. At other times, I have deliberately played on the fact that I look young and have a girly voice to get what I want, to seem unthreatening, letting my eyes fill with tears so that people will let me get my own way. [...]. It is unrealistic to expect all of us to put being a feminist first all of the time, and even if we did my brand of feminism lets me play on being girly sometimes.[4]

This extract is noteworthy for several reasons. Levenson describes 'playing' or performing some of the 'classic female roles' mentioned by Kauer above. Also striking is her employment of the term 'brand', as if feminism were a mass-produced consumer product one could purchase in kit form and assemble in the desired format at home. Writing in a cultural context dominated by a bifurcated perspective on sexuality characterized by the extremes of abstinence-only sex education and normalized pornographic pop-cultural aesthetics, American author Jessica Valenti not only links popular culture with performance but also performance with sexuality. She argues that what 'all this porn/pop-culture has in common is performance. Sometimes performance can be a cool thing when it comes to sexuality'.[5] For Kauer, and as Levenson and Valenti's words illustrate, one of the strengths of performativity for pop-feminist writers is its potential appeal to a younger female audience based on precisely this kind of malleability, particularly when performativity becomes linked to sexuality.[6]

By enquiring into the nature of the pop-feminist 'subject', I acknowledge my own entanglement in a Hegelian epistemological tradition that, as Butler has it, 'conditions the very problematic of identity that it seeks to solve'.[7] Indeed, part of *Gender Trouble*'s project is to propose an alternative model of conceptualizing selfhood. Nevertheless, the term 'subject' remains useful for discussing both cognition and agency as aspects of consciousness informing how identities arise, overlap, and intersect. Butler is astute when she suggests that the 'foundationalist reasoning of identity politics tends to assume that an identity must first be in place in order for political interests to be elaborated and, subsequently, political action to be taken'.[8] In this model, the possibility of agency exists either through a subject who pre-exists cultural negotiations; or, if the subject is conceived as partially culturally embedded, agency emerges through a subject's ability to practice 'reflexive mediation', i.e. self-conscious reasoning in relation to its culturally embedded state.[9] These alternatives safeguard the pre-discursive subject, as cultural factors are deemed to foreclose on subjective agency by determining the subject. In the Hegelian model of self-recognition, cultural determination is avoided through the configuration of a subject/agent who is already intact before encountering its world, its language and itself as an object. The concept of self-recognition, along with Lacan's later

---

[4] Ellie Levenson, *The Noughtie Girl's Guide to Feminism* (Oxford: One World Publications, 2009), pp. 212–13.

[5] Jessica Valenti, *Full Frontal Feminism: A Young Woman's Guide to Why Feminism Matters* (Berkeley, CA: Seal Press, 2007), p. 54.

[6] Katja Kauer, *Popfeminismus!*, p. 94.   [7] Judith Butler, *Gender Trouble*, p. 196.

[8] Ibid., pp. 194–5.   [9] Ibid., p. 195.

interrogation of Hegel's model, will play a vital role in my discussion of the mirror-gazing scenes in the literary texts, in which the protagonists struggle to reconcile their discrete reflected images with their multiple subjective states. Of particular use is Lacan's 'mirror stage', during which the mirror becomes a tool for identification, whereby the developing subject recognizes that the *imago* of the self is not identical with the I, or as Julia Kristeva has it, when the subject transitions from the world of the semiotic to that of symbols.[10] The *Gestalt* in the mirror offers only a symbol of total form and stable interiority, an illusion constituting the reverse of the 'turbulent movements'[11] that the subject feels constitutes it.

My understanding of subjectivity, like Butler's, is predicated upon a contestation of the antagonistic and dichotomous Hegelian model of subject/object, in which the 'I' is established as a consequence of its opposition to the 'Other'. As Butler herself points out, the 'language of appropriation, instrumentality, and distanciation germane to the epistemological mode also belong to a strategy of domination that pits the "I" against the "Other" and, once that separation is effected, creates an artificial set of questions about the knowability and recoverability of that Other'.[12] Furthermore, this process 'reifies that opposition as a necessity, concealing the discursive apparatus by which the binary itself is constituted'.[13]

In *Gender Trouble*, Butler provides a genealogy of how the Hegelian epistemological model has led to the normalization of rigid hierarchies based on sex and gender, the naturalization of compulsory heterosexuality, and the entrenched notion of a 'global and globalizing subject'.[14] An important moment for pop-feminists is when Butler critiques second-wave feminist thinkers who employ the universalizing feminist 'we' in order to make representational claims in women's interest. This strategy, she argues, 'denies the internal complexity and indeterminacy of the term [woman] and constitutes itself only through the exclusion of some part of the constituency that it simultaneously seeks to represent'.[15] But she also takes issue with later theories of 'feminist identity' that 'elaborate predicates of color [sic], sexuality, ethnicity, class, and able-bodiedness'. This is because they 'invariably close with an embarrassed "etc." at the end of the list', as they seek, but fail, to encompass a comprehensively situated subject.[16] Instead, Butler posits the fundamental irrecoverability of subjective constitution. The subject is always already constituted, emerging as 'a consequence of certain rule-governed discourses that govern the intelligible invocation of identity'.[17] Nevertheless, she avoids alignment with deterministic models of subject formation by averring that identity is 'neither fatally determined nor fully artificial and arbitrary'. In fact, construction is 'not opposed to agency; it is the necessary scene of agency'.[18] What Butler means by this can be gleaned from her model of performativity, which I will go on to discuss in conversation with the starkly modified versions deployed in many pop-feminist guides.

[10] Jacques Lacan, *Écrits: The First Complete Edition in English*, trans. by Bruce Fink (New York; London: W.W. Norton, 2006); see also, Julia Kristeva, *La révolution du langage poétique* (Paris: Éditions du Seuil, 1974).

[11] Jacques Lacan, 'The Mirror Stage', in *Écrits*, p. 76.

[12] Judith Butler, *Gender Trouble*, p. 197.   [13] Ibid.   [14] Ibid., p. 202.

[15] Ibid., p. 194.   [16] Ibid., p. 196.   [17] Ibid., p. 198.   [18] Ibid., p. 201.

In their portrayal of Butler's thinking in *Gender Trouble*, pop-feminist texts often refer to Butler's alleged dismantling of the category woman, indeed of the subject itself. In her contribution to *Das F-Wort: Feminismus ist sexy*, Jenny Warnecke locates the origins of twenty-first-century feminist thinking in Butler's account of the incoherent subject and glosses the latter's impact:

> Mitten hinein in dieses Wir-Gefühl hat Judith Butler die Frau als Handlungssubjekt in Frage gestellt und philosophisch kurzerhand aufgelöst, stattdessen hat sie Bündnispolitik und Netzwerke empfohlen. Aktionen nehmen ihren Ausgangspunkt in einem gemeinsamen Problem und nicht in einer vermeintlichen Geschlechtsidentität.

> [Judith Butler interrupted this sense of a feminist 'we' by scrutinizing the acting subject category 'woman' and, without further ado, philosophically dismantling it. In its place, she proposed a politics predicated on alliances and networks. Actions originate in mutual problems and not in an alleged gender identity.][19]

Here, Warnecke oversimplifies Butler's thinking. Rather than dismantling the subject category 'woman', Butler argues that the subject is always already constituted, and that one of the discursively produced convergences of identity is sex and gender. Reluctant even to mention the word 'subject', Warnecke replaces it with the impersonal plural, 'Aktionen', removing any human 'subject' from the sentence's grammatical structure.

While Butler is often considered to have sounded the death knell for coalitional feminist politics, she in fact repeatedly acknowledges the strategic value of the feminist 'we', even while stressing its 'phantasmatic' nature.[20] Too often, pop-feminist texts jettison any sense of value in the feminist 'we', proceeding nonetheless to make the very representational claims they seek to critique. As Kauer notes, they acknowledge, on the one hand, identity's plurality and declare the concept of a fixed female identity obsolete,[21] and on the other their written interventions draw on the language of coalitional feminist politics, highlighting a latent conviction that within a limited context feminist identity and solidarity can indeed be claimed.[22]

Linguistically, pop-feminist writers distance themselves still further from the perceived representational claims of second-wave feminism by reconfiguring the term feminism and employing alternative descriptors. Feminism becomes 'das F-Wort' [the F Word] or merely a letter applicable to a certain class of women, the 'F-Klasse' [f-class], or the 'Alpha' [alpha] or 'neue' [new] 'Mädchen' [girls]. The word is also avoided completely at times, particularly in the British context, where pop-feminist authors proffer instead a guide to 'being a woman', or to 'modern life for modern ladies'.[23] The German pop-feminist texts, in particular, draw on the rhetoric of girlhood in order to enact an intergenerational caesura that relegates the work of previous feminist German generations to the realm of

---

[19] Jenny Warnecke, '"Das ist mir zu extrem!" Eine Generationen-Studie', in *Das F-Wort: Feminismus ist sexy*, ed. by Mirja Stöcker (Königstein/Taunus: Ulrike Helmer Verlag, 2007), p. 36.
[20] Judith Butler, *Gender Trouble*, p. 194.
[21] Katja Kauer, *Popfeminismus!*, p. 94.   [22] Ibid.
[23] Hadley Freeman, *Be Awesome: Modern Life for Modern Ladies* (London: Fourth Estate, 2013); Caitlin Moran, *How to be a Woman* (London: Ebury, 2011).

obsolescence. Very often the attributives employed in the titles of these texts link feminism explicitly with sex, and it becomes 'full frontal' or the obligatory lifestyle accessory for the 'noughtie girl'. (The latter, as it appears in the title of Ellie Levenson's volume, plays with the slippage between the shorthand for the first decade of the twenty-first century and its homophone 'naughty').[24] The sexualization of the linguistic and visual elements of these publications evinces pop-feminism's entanglement with the mores of postfeminist culture; all too often feminist thinking becomes licensed only to the extent that it conforms to a model of self-expression and agency linked to sexualized heterosexual femininity.

Many pop-feminists distance themselves from postfeminist media-based conceptions of feminism that configure feminists as 'hässlich, spaß- und männerfeindlich, ironiefrei und unsexy' [ugly, anti-fun, anti-men, irony-free, and unsexy].[25] However, few writers acknowledge that popular culture's prohibitively negative attitude towards feminism belongs to the same paradigm that exerts insidious pressure upon women to behave according to prescribed conceptions of contemporary sexualized femininity; and their frequently unreflecting insistence on the sex-positive nature of current feminism merely reiterates the very cultural pressures they seek to combat. For example, Valenti, Stöcker, Haaf, Klingner, and Streidl make the claim that being a feminist means a better sex life.[26] The authors of *Wir Alpha-Mädchen* describe the advantages for men in adopting feminist behaviours and in supporting women who do: men who try out progressive roles and behaviours are, the volume assures an implied male reader, seen as 'super sexy' by women and they will also have better sex with a girlfriend who is a feminist.[27]

Sex and sexuality occupy the foreground of pop-feminist discussions of identity, to the extent that they often become almost interchangeable. Valenti, for example, writes:

> It shouldn't be that hard to develop an authentic sexuality—or even personhood, for that matter. But the prevalence of porn/pop makes it pretty frigging difficult to negotiate how we separate good kinds of performance from bad and how we develop an identity that isn't mired in all this ridiculous crap.[28]

The 'crap' Valenti refers to is the 'porn/pop' culture that, she argues, interferes with the processes of identity formation. Valenti's mode of expression is steeped in the language of poststructuralism: personhood is 'negotiated' and 'performed', identity is 'developed'. Yet her use of the term 'authentic' reveals a yearning for self-identity and subjective cohesion and a desire to believe in an intact subject who pre-exists—and is thus not determined by—the 'crap'. But Butler suggests that this is not possible. Furthermore, she contends that the belief—or even the

[24] Ellie Levenson, *The Noughtie Girl's Guide to Feminism*.

[25] Meredith Haaf, Susanne Klingner, and Barbara Streidl, *Wir Alpha-Mädchen: Warum Feminismus das Leben schöner macht* (Hamburg: Hoffmann und Campe, 2008), p. 13.

[26] Meredith Haaf, Susanne Klingner, and Barbara Streidl, *Wir Alpha-Mädchen*, p. 63; Jessica Valenti, *Full Frontal Feminism*, p. 19. See also the title of Mirja Stöcker's edited volume, *Das F-Wort: Feminismus ist sexy*.

[27] Ibid., pp. 23–7.   [28] Jessica Valenti, *Full Frontal Feminism*, p. 55.

desire for the belief—in an intact prediscursive subject perpetuates the hierarchies of exclusion inherent in the foundationalist model of subjectivity as well as concealing the discursive forces that regulate behaviour. What Butler suggests does exist is the *possibility* of disrupting the regulated processes of repetition that signify identity through slight variations and parodic renditions of 'natural' identity or denaturalizing 'performances' of the same, in order to generate potentially subversive moments. In the above quotation, Valenti remains conceptually 'trapped within the unnecessary binarism of free-will and determinism'.[29] On the one hand, there exist social influences and 'baffling expectations' and, on the other, the 'authentic expression of yourself', which those social constraints render 'impossible'.[30]

In her discussion of performativity, Butler argues that 'acts, gestures, and desire produce the effect of an internal core or substance, but produce this on the surface of the body [...]. [S]uch acts, gestures, enactments [...] are *performative* in the sense that the essence or identity that they otherwise purport to express are *fabrications* manufactured and sustained through corporeal signs and other discursive means'.[31] She suggests that identity performances are manufactured externally, not from an inner subjective core. But, as Valenti's comment shows, performativity is construed by many pop-feminists as an autonomous act (i.e. it *is* possible to distinguish 'good' from 'bad' performances), whereas, for Butler, it is fundamentally *not* autonomous. Valenti's comment that 'some performances are thought out and some are not' implies a residual belief in the mediating potential of a prediscursive subject.[32]

Butler views this understanding of performance as an act of free will as a pernicious and normative tool: '[i]f the "cause" of desire, gesture, and act can be localized within the "self" of the actor, then the political regulations and disciplinary practices which produce that ostensibly coherent [identity] are effectively displaced from view'.[33] Here, the subject's *belief* in the autonomy of its identity performances is vital for both the perpetuation *and* the invisibility of the public and social discourses that regulate identity.

While Butler's observations concern the normative 'regulation of sexuality within the obligatory frame of reproductive heterosexuality',[34] it is possible to extend this model to include the full spectrum of identity performances. In this way, the pop-feminist mandate for autonomous action can be viewed as an illusory belief that merges with the neoliberal discourse that regulates identity within the 'obligatory frame' of individualism, self-entrepreneurship, and consumer choice, the same illusions underpinning free-market capitalism. This manifestation of the pop-feminist subject believes that she still retains agency in the form of reflexive mediation, holding the types of cultural influence she confronts daily at arm's length.[35]

Valenti engages with the question of social construction when she acknowledges that '[o]bviously everything we do is affected to a certain degree by social norms

---

[29] Judith Butler, *Gender Trouble*, p. 201.   [30] Jessica Valenti, *Full Frontal Feminism*, p. 54.
[31] Judith Butler, *Gender Trouble*, p. 185. Original emphasis.
[32] Jessica Valenti, *Full Frontal Feminism*, p. 55.   [33] Judith Butler, *Gender Trouble*, p. 186.
[34] Ibid.   [35] Ibid., p. 195.

and what pop culture demands of us'.[36] However, she retains space for a subject who can knowingly 'go along with these to a certain extent', with the proviso that 'you're always cognisant of why you're doing it'.[37] This casual demand for comprehensive, continual self-awareness presents the reader with a troubling problem: Valenti, toeing the social constructivist line, implies that the extent of pop-culture's influence on the subject is, on the one hand, irrecoverable, i.e. epistemologically opaque. On the other hand, subjects are expected to be able to differentiate between autonomous action and action induced without consent by external social forces. Ellie Levenson goes further, demanding none of the self-reflection encouraged by Valenti. For Levenson, the only criterion for feminist action is personal desire. She refers, for example, to a female friend who goes to pole dancing lessons. Levenson asks whether this means her friend cannot be a feminist and answers:

> No, because noughtie girl feminism says what is most important is that we are free to make our own choices, which is exactly what she has done. If she felt pressured into pole dancing by men, or because society told her that women have to learn sexy moves, then it might be anti-feminist, but that is not the case.[38]

This slippage between contingency and desire is symptomatic of many pop-feminist interpretations of Butlerian models of plural, performative subjectivity more generally. All too frequently, performance is divorced from its contingencies and becomes the illusion of an autonomous act, implying a singular, irreducible subject behind the multiple fragments of external identity markers; this subject is perceived as being intrinsically intact and capable of sovereign action, namely, the discerning and playful selection of identity from an endless array of choices. However, the types of performance on offer, whose 'subversive' potential is celebrated, are often limited to a predictable selection of what Kauer has called 'classic conceptions of femininity', those which, as Valenti notes, are in any case 'demanded' of women by pop-culture.

Valenti takes up the question of performativity's subversive potential in relation to sexuality, asking whether a performance can 'really be a subversive way of playing with your sexuality'.[39] She responds affirmatively, but then qualifies her response by referring again to the notion of a mediating consciousness capable of distinguishing free-will from contingent action. The trump card, however, as in Levenson's discussion, remains the degree of individual choice and enjoyment. Valenti argues that the degree of subversion remains an 'individual thing and depends on how much you're buying in to the bullshit notions of what sexy is. [. . .] And again, if you want to show your tits just for the pure fun of it—go for it'.[40] Here, fun becomes prioritized over the degree of potential political subversion generated by the act of baring breasts or not.

To some extent this reinterpretation of Butler's work is understandable, as her identification in *Gender Trouble* of the possibility of subverting normative identity

---

[36] Jessica Valenti, *Full Frontal Feminism*, p. 57.   [37] Ibid.
[38] Ellie Levenson, *The Noughtie Girl's Guide to Feminism*, pp. 210–11.
[39] Jessica Valenti, *Full Frontal Feminism*, p. 55.   [40] Ibid. Original italics.

performances at some point in the process of repetition also does not fully address how the socially constructed subject may identify the pivotal moment to enact her subversion.[41] *Gender Trouble* posits the notion of parodic performance as a subversive tool in the process of denaturalizing normative identity categories.[42] In particular, Butler refers to the ways in which transvestism, or drag, parodies the concept of an 'original', that is, 'natural', sex and gender, claiming that in 'imitating gender, drag implicitly reveals the imitative structure of gender itself–as well as its contingency.'[43] The concept of displacing any idea of an authentic original behind the performance resonates with pop-literary understandings of 'reality', according to which no 'authentic' repository of the 'real' exists beyond the process of *Inszenierung* [staging or production].[44] Just as this observation has led to a critique of pop-literature's free-floating apoliticism, the recourse to parody remains potentially problematic for emancipatory politics. As I pointed out earlier, a postfeminist climate absorbs, disarms, and redeploys parodic critique or ironic subversion. This co-option gestures towards the slippery ambiguity of the ironic gesture within popular culture.

To take one example, a woman presenting herself in a hyper-feminine and/or sexualized manner may understand herself to be 'performing' a subversive parody of outdated notions of female identity and sexuality, while simultaneously affirming and reifying those notions, as they have been historically and discursively deployed, in the act of performance. This subject, who, importantly, understands herself to be behaving autonomously and with ironic self-awareness, becomes enabled in that understanding by commercial forces that profit from the association of female empowerment with hyper-femininity and the accoutrements of that *imago*. The sense that, in postfeminist culture, feminism may now be 'taken for granted' facilitates the deployment of supposedly parodic, naturalized, and gender-normative identity performances that deny their normative function even as they enact it throughout commercial pop-cultural channels. The subject's own belief and/or desire that feminism has become irrelevant entails too that on a psychological level, she understands herself to be an agentic participant in the construction of her identity, rather than a co-conspirator with the normative discourses regulating identity.

KNOWING WHAT I (DO NOT) KNOW

Up to this point, I have argued that many pop-feminist models of subjectivity benefit from a radically modified understanding of Butler's model of performativity in which, superficially at least, the subject replaces coherent self-identity with a multiplicity of performances selected at will. Furthermore, I have suggested that this conceptualization still leaves room for the idea of an intact, pre-discursive subject capable of self-reflexive mediation and autonomous action. Moreover, the

---

[41] This is a shortcoming she admittedly seeks to address in her later works *Excitable Speech* (1997), *The Psychic Life of Power* (1997) and *Giving an Account of Oneself* (2005).
[42] See Judith Butler, *Gender Trouble*, pp. 183–93.   [43] Ibid., p. 187.
[44] See Kerstin Gleba and Eckhard Schumacher, *Pop seit 1964*, pp. 11–12.

merging of pop-feminist re-appropriations of performativity with neoliberal narratives of individual choice and female self-empowerment strengthens the illusion of agency for the pop-feminist subject. Angela McRobbie notes that as young Western women have been encouraged to 'come forward and make good use of the opportunity to work, to gain qualifications, to control fertility and to earn enough money to participate in [...] consumer culture', the range of identity performances available to women in the twenty-first century appears to have expanded. In fact, as both McRobbie and Nina Power note, this coming forward onto the global labour market coincides with the rolling back of feminism and the dominance of consumerism, which all too often redirects the range of identity options to a menu of preconceived options marking one's lifestyle affiliation or shopping preferences.[45]

As already indicated, narratives of self-empowerment and consumerism collide and become amplified in the realm of female sexuality. Consider, for example, the language and imagery in the following excerpt taken from *Wir Alpha-Mädchen*:

> Pornographie kann neue Dimensionen der eigenen Persönlichkeit eröffnen, wenn es einem bei den Bildern einer erotisch gefesselten Frau plötzlich zwischen den Beinen kribbelt. Oder man feststellt, dass die Fesseln eher langweilig, aber das, was eine andere mit dem Vibrator an ihrem Hintern tut, ziemlich interessant aussieht.

> [Pornography can reveal new aspects of your personality. Say, for example, you suddenly feel a tingle between your legs when you see pictures of a woman being erotically tied up. Or if you decide that the bondage ropes are in fact boring, but what another woman is doing to her arse with that vibrator looks pretty interesting.][46]

Their approach to pornography foregrounds the manner in which sexual self-expression empowers the acting subject. Yet the type of empowerment that their language evokes is that of an empowered consumer, whose sexual explorations are enabled through the purchase of the appropriate accessories, selected with the discerning eye of the inveterate bargain hunter or with the studied disinterest of the chronic consumer accustomed to ever-increasing choice. But the language of consumerism pervades many areas of pop-feminist discourse, often in relation to descriptions of pop-feminism itself. In her introduction to *Das F-Wort*, Mirja Stöcker, like Levenson, gestures towards the variety and conviviality characterizing pop-feminism by inviting the reader, not without irony, to reimagine gender identities in the form of a large shopping mall: 'eine Art Outlet-Store der unbegrenzten Geschlechtermöglichkeiten' [a kind of outlet store for unlimited varieties of gender.][47] She continues:

> Ich meine, die meisten von uns sind doch bestens kapitalistisch-konsumistisch getunt [sic], nur beim Geschlecht soll die freiwillige Selbstbeschränkung hochleben? Schnuppern Sie doch mal in die Auslage hinein! Kaufen Sie nur das, was Ihnen *wirklich* gefällt! Das Angebot ist nämlich gigantisch.

---

[45] Angela McRobbie, *The Aftermath of Feminism*, 55–83; Nina Power, *One-Dimensional Woman* (Winchester: O Books, 2009), 27–37.

[46] Meredith Haaf, Susanne Klingner, and Barbara Streidl, *Wir Alpha-Mädchen*, p. 105.

[47] Mirja Stöcker, 'Die Sache mit dem F-Wort', in *Das F-Wort: Feminismus ist sexy*, p. 14.

[I mean most of us are savvy little capitalist consumers after all. And we're supposed to limit ourselves voluntarily when it comes to gender? Have a browse around the display! Only buy what you *really* like! There are some humungous deals to be had.][48]

While Stöcker's volume strives for critical breadth and differentiation, the fore-grounding of sexiness and reliance on the mores of consumer culture implicates the text in a collusive relationship with postfeminist neoliberalism. In the above, pop-feminism's performative subject is a highly practised consumer, convinced that she is only marginally affected by regulatory social discourse, which she may overcome through mediating reflection carried out by an authentic self. The upbeat rhetorical gestures necessitated by the genre of the self-help guide, as well as the anticipated negative reception of feminist writing in postfeminist culture, entail that many pop-feminists avoid probing too deeply the question of what remains irrecoverable in the processes of identity formation and action. Critique, however, 'finds that it cannot go forward without a consideration of how the deliberating subject comes into being and how a deliberating subject might actually live or appropriate a set of norms'.[49] Too frequently, the pop-feminist actor in these guides perceives herself to be a subject playing with versions of her 'self' in an expression of self-reflexive cognition and agency. 'This is who I am' becomes 'this is one possible version of me *and* I know it'. The 'I' in the latter statement denotes the moment of persisting attachment to the sovereign self behind the iterations. While this subject labours under the illusion that she constitutes her 'self' by means of an array of temporary, even processual, yet still autonomous performances, she remains, in Wendy Brown's terms, 'buffeted and controlled by global configurations of discip-linary and capitalist power of extraordinary proportions'.[50] Far from existing as a self-empowered individual agent, subjects in neoliberal societies become 'nakedly individuated, stripped of reprieve from relentless exposure and accountability for themselves'.[51]

Many pop-feminist texts embody this relentless individuation and stress the subject's accountability for herself. This characteristic becomes revealed in the generic moulding of the volumes themselves, which positions the pop-feminist volumes predominantly as self-help guides to a better quality of life, or, as Valenti has it, 'self-help times one hundred'.[52] Yet the authors' claim to feminist engage-ment suggests a contesting drive. To engage in emancipatory politics of any sort, the pop-feminist subject must make herself, in Butler's terms, 'reducible' (i.e. non-unique and capable of being recognized by others) in order to narrate her 'self' and for recognition, considered by Hegel to be the motivation behind being, to take place. By this I mean that intersubjective relations that rise above the cult of the individual must occur in order for ethical deliberation and progressive politics to take place.

---

[48] Ibid. Original italics.
[49] Judith Butler, *Giving an Account of Oneself* (New York: Fordham University Press, 2005), p. 8.
[50] Wendy Brown, 'Wounded Attachments', *Political Theory,* 21. 3 (1993), 390–410, p. 402.
[51] Ibid.   [52] Jessica Valenti, *Full Frontal Feminism*, p. 7.

Butler proposes that the foundation of ethical conduct is located in the very impossibility of what I have called 'knowing what I (do not) know'. She argues that a 'theory of subject formation that acknowledges the limits of self-knowledge can serve a conception of ethics, and, indeed, responsibility'.[53] She goes on:

> [T]he opacity of the subject may be a consequence of its being conceived as a relational being, one whose early and primary relations are not always available to conscious knowledge. [...] If we are formed in the context of relations that become partially irrecoverable to us, then that opacity seems built in to our formation and follows from our status as beings who are formed in relations of dependency.[54]

Ethical responsibility becomes predicated not only on the 'subject's opacity to itself', but also its dependency on others. The emphasis on individual choice in some pop-feminist texts not only upholds the sovereign subject, it also prevents them from understanding the dynamics of intersubjective dependency as an ethical responsibility. While understanding subjectivity as an always already situated agglomeration of incoherent fragments constituted by social forces evinces its own potentially challenging set of ethical questions, including the question of where agency might reside in such a model, renouncing the 'we' is, as I will demonstrate equally problematic, as it abolishes the need for an ethics of intersubjective accountability.

THERE IS NO 'I' IN 'WE'

> The uniqueness of the other is exposed to me, but mine is also exposed to her. This does not mean we are the same, but only that we are bound to one another by what differentiates us, namely, our singularity.[55]

The rhetoric of choice based on individual preference, experience, and lifestyle employed in many pop-feminist texts can also be seen as a misguided interpretation of feminist theories of difference that sought to dismantle the universalizing voice of Anglo-American second-wave feminism, in particular, and to develop an intersectional framework for reflecting on questions of identity and women's heterogeneous experiences of oppression. Narratives of difference and choice combine in much pop-feminist writing to legitimize the exclusion of other women's experiences within the texts. Levenson, for example, includes a set of disclaimers concerning her decision to exclude discussions of, as she puts it, 'foreign women', or 'women who are lesbians'.[56] Haaf, Klingner, and Streidl add a disclaimer about the lack of 'Perspektiven lesbischer Frauen oder etwa Migrantinnen' [lesbian or, say, migrant perspectives] in their book, justifying this omission with the argument that they are reluctant to perpetuate the mistakes of second-wave feminism by generalizing

---

[53] Judith Butler, *Giving an Account of Oneself*, p. 19.   [54] Ibid. p. 20.
[55] Ibid., p. 34.   [56] Ellie Levenson, *The Noughtie Girl's Guide to Feminism*, p. 6 and p. xviii.

about 'the' female experience.[57] Yet their disclaimers are succeeded by the construction of just such a homogenous and exclusionary group of readers when they claim that their volume deals with the issues affecting the majority of women in Germany.[58] Levenson, too, enacts a similar manoeuvre by hoping her book remains 'interesting to all women' despite its restricted perspective.[59] This reluctance to perceive the double exclusion their language enacts (one explicit and one implicit) replicates the exclusionary violence at work in many pop-feminist models of subjectification, which, despite Butler, remain indebted to a Hegelian model of self that posits the subject in relation to the Other, whose alterity is either assimilated by the subject or antagonistically rejected.

The overriding tension inherent in most pop-feminist texts arises from the attempt to accommodate both the individual's right to choose how to live (the individualist gesture undergirded by free-market capitalism) and the recognition that establishing some common ground may be productive (the collective gesture). This tension often creates an awkward slippage in pop-feminist logic. Commentators insist that '[b]eing a feminist is what you want it to be',[60] because '[d]ie Frau im Plural gibt es nicht mehr. Das ist seit Judith Butlers Buch *Gender Trouble* klar' ['woman' in the plural doesn't exist anymore. That's been clear ever since Judith Butler's *Gender Trouble*].[61] Some thinkers, like Levenson, portray feminism as a lifestyle choice that, once a few basics are established, can be tailored to every imaginable individual need. Levenson appears at first almost antagonistic towards other women, stating that 'once we have these choices and equality, frankly I don't care what other women do with it'.[62] Yet she slips seamlessly into precisely the kind of universalist language that the explicit content of her text ostensibly rejects. She argues that '*[w]e all* make different choices'[63] and '*we all* live contradictory lives to some extent'.[64]

Equally, Valenti is at pains to emphasize the individual's right to make mistakes in the process of identity formation without fear of censure from other feminists. She attempts to speak only from her own idiosyncratic subject position, employing such disclaimers as 'I guess what I've come to—and this is what works for me—is that you have to find your own middle ground' and champions the right of young women to carve out identity alone, stating that '[t]here has to be space for young women to figure shit out on their own'.[65] Yet when she comes to imagining what that space might look like, it involves the collective she has distanced herself from: 'we just have to talk it out, hopefully with each other and with women who have been there and done that'.[66]

---

[57] Meredith Haaf, Susanne Klingner, and Barbara Streidl, *Wir Alpha-Mädchen*, p. 8.
[58] Meredith Haaf, Susanne Klingner, and Barbara Streidl, *Wir Alpha-Mädchen*, p. 8.
[59] Ellie Levenson, *The Noughtie Girl's Guide to Feminism*, p. xviii.   [60] Ibid., p. xviii.
[61] Jenny Warnecke, ' "Das ist mir zu extrem!" ', p. 25. It is striking that pop-feminists in general focus on Butler and not feminists of colour like Kimberlé Crenshaw or bell hooks who intervened in debates concerning the universal female subject before Butler.
[62] Ellie Levenson, *The Noughtie Girl's Guide to Feminism*, p. xix.   [63] Ibid., p. xviii.
[64] Ibid., p. 1. My emphasis.   [65] Jessica Valenti, *Full Frontal Feminism*, pp. 48–9.
[66] Ibid.

Haaf, Klingner, and Streidl provide perhaps the most extreme example of this tension between individualist and collective rhetoric. Their text begins with a surprisingly forthright expression of putative group identity:

> Eines muss gleich zu Anfang geklärt werden: Alpha-Mädchen sind wir alle. Nicht nur die Autorinnen dieses Buches, sondern alle jungen Frauen, die mitdenken und Ziele haben; die sich für die Welt interessieren und frei und selbstbestimmt leben möchten, jede nach ihrer Art—das sind wir Alpha-Mädchen.
>
> [Let's make something clear right from the start: we're all alpha girls. Not only the authors of this book but all young women who think for themselves and have goals, who are interested in the world and would like to live freely and autonomously, each in her own way—that's us: alpha girls.][67]

Yet, they are careful to remain vague about the actual shape of a life lived in a 'free and autonomous' manner, for this is achieved by women 'each in her own way'. Their volume, they suggest, does not aspire to unite all points of view because they know 'dass nicht alle jungen Frauen in Deutschland gleich leben. Schließlich trifft jede ihre Entscheidungen doch am Ende selbst' [that not all young women in Germany live the same way. After all, everyone makes their own decisions at the end of the day].[68] Yet, the effect of this oscillation between rhetorical gestures of collectivism and the insistence on multiple, irreducible narratives of identity is to raise the perspective of the authors to a universalist position in their own right. This text is written, after all, from the perspective of three white, middle-class heterosexual women and it therefore implicitly excludes women who do not identify with those categories from its 'wir' [we], as well as, in a more explicit fashion, the LGBTQ+ community and those with a migrant background.

The most common strategy employed to overcome the problems concerning group/individual identity is to emphasize the importance of issues over identity-based politics. Warnecke, for example, clarifies her use of the first-person plural thus: 'Wer ist nun mal dieses Wir? Es ist die Summe der Subjekte, die in wechselnden Bündnissen für ihre Ziele kämpfen.' [Now, who is this 'we' then? It is the sum of subjects fighting for their goals in shifting alliances.][69] Haaf, Klingner, and Streidl, too, claim to concentrate first and foremost on the issues affecting the bulk of young women living in Germany today.[70] For Levenson, the concept of 'sisterhood' means that 'we are a movement that is greater than the sum of its parts, made up of women who might not agree with each other on every subject, but who have the same basic demands'.[71]

But the collective 'we' appears only to be deployed for rhetorical impact; ultimately readers are encouraged to adopt a stringent policy of self-accountability. The avoidance of identity politics also forecloses upon a genuine discussion of the issues at hand and diminishes the impact of the volumes' political dimension. This is

---

[67] Meredith Haaf, Susanne Klingner, and Barbara Streidl, *Wir Alpha-Mädchen*, p. 7.
[68] Ibid., p. 45.   [69] Jenny Warnecke, '"Das ist mir zu extrem!"', p. 25.
[70] Meredith Haaf, Susanne Klingner, and Barbara Streidl, *Wir Alpha-Mädchen*, p. 8.
[71] Ellie Levenson, *The Noughtie Girl's Guide to Feminism*, p. 2.

because the issues they foreground arise through and become perpetuated by a normative and regulatory discursive framework that recognizes subjects and constitutes agency *unequally*.

NARRATIVE SELVES AND COHERENCE

This section moves away from performativity as a model for considering subjectivity, identity, and agency in anticipation of my study of the first-person narratives commencing in Chapter 2. Drawing on Butler's post-*Gender Trouble* work functions as a springboard for reflecting on the role that narrative plays within theories of selfhood that seek to carve out a space for agency away from the binary of social determinism and prediscursive subjective sovereignty, a binary some strands of pop-feminism ultimately revert to. I do this in order to prepare the ground for my argument that literary fiction generates a more probing exploration of selfhood and a more powerful political critique than the pop-feminist handbooks when it comes to questions of identity, agency, and constraint.

The question of subjective coherence and its relation to agency and ethical intersubjectivity constitutes a particularly important aspect of both the pop-literary novels and the theories of narrative selfhood explored here. The foregrounding of subjective incoherence in the literary narratives constitutes a significant element of the social critique they enact and contrasts with the model of sovereign subjectivity and individual self-empowerment proposed by many pop-feminist guides. On the other hand, the narrative representations of incoherent selfhood co-exist in productive tension with a desire for coherence and unity that fundamentally relates to an ethics of intersubjective relations in Butler's sense. Aside from Butler, I draw on the work of Adriana Cavarero and Lois McNay in order to illuminate the first-person narratives as model representations of selves attempting to generate a sense of self. What interests me is how these works represent the narration of 'self' and foreground the role played by the desire for unity, in the form of a generative intersubjective encounter preceding narrative closure, in that self-narration.

The mode of address employed by the pop-feminist guides discussed above, by which I mean the plural 'we', conceptualizes a plurality of readers that incorporates the authors. This imagined plurality, based as it is on implicit hierarchies and exclusions, remains both misleading and ultimately phantasmagorical due to the authors' frequent capitulation to the neoliberal narrative of individual choice. The first-person narrative fictions create a contrasting rhetorical arena due, in part, to their mode of address. From the novels to the autofictions, the reader encounters a single, fictional, or performative I, whose author hovers behind the scenes of textual engagement. This imaginative meeting between narrator and reader thus empowers the reader in the creative construction of meaning, opening up, rather than closing down, interpretive opportunities. This sense of 'opening up' stems from literature's capacity for ambiguity and plurality of meaning. Significations and interpretations proliferate, existing side by side simultaneously, often destabilizing as much as reinforcing each other. As Sarah Colvin, drawing on Martha

Nussbaum, notes, literature 'allows more than one thing to be true at once'.[72] Many of the pop-feminist handbooks demonstrate a contrasting drive, characterized by the tendency to close down the viability of alternative interpretations in favour of a central rhetorical premise, seeking to fix meaning permanently in order to convince.

My assessment of the enhanced critical dimension in the first-person narratives therefore rests not only on the textual encounter between the narrating self, her diegetic other(s) and their (auto)fictional world, but also on the relationship between the narrating protagonist, the implied and actual reader. This relationship can be characterized as fluid and intersubjectively expansive. I use the term 'intersubjective' deliberately: despite the narrator's status as an (auto)fictional entity, she functions as a 'model' representation of the actual reader's 'other', therefore replicating an intersubjective encounter. The reader, both implied and actual, is a necessary component in the 'telling' of the narrator's story. By reading the narrative, the reader complements the narration of self undertaken by the narrator. She actively facilitates the scene of address and permits the achievement of coherence, at least in narrative terms, by appearing as the narrative's other (implied reader) and remaining engaged until closure becomes achieved (actual reader).

An encounter with the other's consciousness in the realm of narrative (auto) fiction has the capacity to generate a continual process of self-reflexive assessment, reconsideration, and self-adjustment on the part of the actual reader. Confronted with another entity reflecting upon the familiar tangled complexity of lived experience, the reader undertakes a chain of creative extrapolations grounded in cognitive and affective comparisons with her self, which are characterized by moments of identification, but also difference. This encounter can be understood as augmenting the self, as the reader steps into the shoes of the fictional character even for a moment (identification), or as dissolving the contours of the self. Dissolution occurs when the reader confronts alterity, in the sense that the other may present an aspect of experience, reflection, or affect that exists outside the understanding of the reader.

Reflection upon the internal responses produced by this point of tension constitutes an arena of potential self-critique, in which the reader is provided imaginative space to consider her own motivations for judgement, disagreement, revulsion etc. The extrapolative function of reading literature continues, however, and the reader is compelled to step outside the boundaries of the 'self-up-to-this-point'. Even this quality of dissolution can be considered an augmentation of self as the boundaries re-knit around the newly imagined experience or reflection, which might be called a process of empathic identification.[73] Alternatively, some encounters might prove

---

[72] Sarah Colvin, 'You have to Change Your Life?', *Schröder Lecture* (Cambridge, 25 October 2013), pp. 2–3.

[73] While the term 'empathic identification' is my own, I have found the following sources useful for reflecting on reading in relation to the textual other, ethics, and critique: Derek Attridge, 'Innovation, Literature, Ethics: Relating to the Other', *PMLA*, 114. 1 (1999), 20–31; Sarah Colvin, 'You have to Change Your Life?'; Garry L. Hagberg, 'Self-Defining Reading: Literature and the Constitution of Personhood', in *A Companion to the Philosophy of Literature*, ed. by Garry L. Hagberg and Walter Jost (Oxford: Wiley-Blackwell, 2010).

so unparseable that the reader confronts a boundary of self that appears intractable. This experience means that the 'uniqueness of the other' becomes exposed to the reader/self. The ethics of the intersubjective moment rest upon 'permitting other kinds of knowledge, and other experience, to exist alongside mine, and exposing myself to the risk that it will challenge me, or perhaps even demand that I change my life'.[74] Narrative fiction, in short, provides the reader with the opportunity to consider her own subjectivity, testing the boundaries of self alongside those of another, permitting those boundaries to be modified through exposure to critique, and remaining empathically engaged when she encounters intractable alterity. This imaginative role-play activates a critical sensibility within the reader that is applicable to the ex-diegetic world. Of course, genre recognition also plays a significant role in the reader's interpretive actions. For this reason, I conclude this chapter and prepare the ground for the close readings with a discussion of genre, which not only considers novelistic and autofictional explorations of selfhood and agency but also examines how those investigations become transformed, sustained, or undermined by the specifically gendered ways in which texts circulate on complex literary markets.

Contemporary scholars investigating subject formation from disparate disciplinary fields have profited from employing narrative theory as a tool for conceptualizing not only subjectivity but also agency. Cavarero and Butler's philosophical enquiries lead them to understand subject formation in terms of articulating a narrative of self.[75] Lois McNay draws on Paul Ricoeur's work on narrative in her response to poststructuralist theories of subject formation, like Butler's, which McNay claims conceptually diminish the subject's capacity for action.[76] For Anthony Giddens, too, the 'reflexive project of the self' consists in the 'sustaining of coherent, yet continuously revised, biographical narratives'.[77]

To some extent, Cavarero and McNay develop their models of subjectification and agency in response to theories, like Butler's, which view the subject as a pluralistic and incoherent entity constructed discursively prior to any capacity for self-reflexive mediation. Their point of contention focuses on poststructuralism's model of fragmented subjectivity, as well as the, to their mind, deterministic implications of social construction, which they claim diminishes the subject's capacity for action. Butler's *Giving an Account of Oneself* constitutes a thoughtful response to Cavarero's work, *Relating Narratives: Storytelling and Selfhood*, first published in Italian in 1997. Butler draws on Cavarero's narrative model, but remains insistent on her notion of incoherent selfhood, an idea Cavarero seeks to modify. In *Giving an Account of Oneself*, Butler continues the work she began in *Gender Trouble* to carve out a space for agency in her model of the socially-constructed subject, and

---

[74] Sarah Colvin, 'You have to Change Your Life?', p. 14.

[75] Judith Butler, *Giving an Account of Oneself*; Adriana Cavarero, *Relating Narratives: Storytelling and Selfhood*, trans. by Paul A. Kottman (London: Routledge, 2000).

[76] Lois McNay, *Gender and Agency: Reconfiguring the Subject in Feminist and Social Theory* (Cambridge; Malden, MA: Polity Press, 2000).

[77] Anthony Giddens, *Modernity and Self-identity: Self and Society in the Late Modern Age* (Cambridge: Polity Press, 1991), p. 5.

to defend her theory against the critique that this model precludes the capacity for ethical deliberation as well as human agency. This critique is not unfounded. If the 'I', as both Foucault and Butler have argued, exists prior to its knowledge—that is, if it is constituted by social factors opaque to consciousness—and the act of address and the channels of address (language) also influence the narrative the 'I' tells about itself, how can 'I' know what 'I' am and how can 'I' comprehend what agency might be, let alone experience it?[78] In Valenti's terms, how can one separate 'good' performances from 'bad'?

Cavarero rethinks the 'metaphysical profile of the subject' using a constitutive and relational ontological model of unique, desiring selfhood, which views 'narrated identity as the tangible expression of existence'.[79] Cavarero's work challenges the universal and abstract subject of classical metaphysics as well as the fragmentary, discontinuous non-identity posited by postmodernism and poststructuralism.[80] She does this by redefining the subject as a 'narratable self', who is narratable because she is exposable to others from birth. The earliest stages of this exposure remain necessarily opaque to the self and cannot therefore be narrated by it. Butler calls this experience 'non-narrativizable exposure' because, she observes, there is a 'history to my body of which I can have no recollection'.[81] In Butler's account, this early exposure is compounded by a subsequent 'dispossession in language', where the 'narrative structure' of a subject's account of themselves becomes 'superseded by [...] the *structure of address* in which it takes place'.[82] Cavarero, however, avoids entrenchment in the linguistic paradigm by focusing on the role played by ontological memory: for her, the existent is precluded from narrating herself because she immediately experiences the impossibility of 'personally objectifying the material of her own desire without falling into the perspectival mistake of memory'.[83] Nevertheless, Cavarero's self, as Butler's, is 'constitutively precluded' from self-knowledge and is thus dependent on an*other* (who, importantly, is not an abstract Other) to narrate who she is for her.[84] This notion resonates with Butler's concept of ethical intersubjective dependency discussed above. In Cavarero's view, the existent:

[a]t once exposable and narratable, [...] always constitutes herself in relation to an other. With all the inimitable wisdom of a familiar feeling [*sapore*] she knows that she is an unrepeatable uniqueness, but does not know *who* she is, or *who* is exposed. She knows she is a narratable identity, but also knows only another can correct the fallacy of the autobiographical impulse. The unity of the desire—namely, the unity entrusted to the tale that everyone desires—is not, in fact, an aspect of unconsciousness or a problem of introspection. It is rather the irreflexive object of the desire *for* the unity of the self in the form of a story.[85]

[78] See Volume II of Michel Foucault, *The History of Sexuality*, trans. by Robert Hurley (Harmondsworth: Penguin, 1990).
[79] Adriana Cavarero, *Relating Narratives*, p. 69 and p. 67.　　[80] Ibid., p. 43.
[81] Judith Butler, *Giving an Account of Oneself*, p. 39 and p. 38.　　[82] Ibid., p. 39.
[83] Adriana Cavarero, *Relating Narratives*, p. 56.　　[84] Ibid., p. 45.
[85] Ibid., p. 40.

The self is thus a 'unique existent' who is mobilized by the desire for unity in the form of the story of herself narrated to her by an equally unique other.[86]

In contrast to Cavarero, and in keeping with her earlier work, Butler continues to insist upon incoherence and contingency as fundamental elements of subject formation. This assertion is made in order to pursue an ethical argument: 'Suspending the demand for self-identity or, more particularly, for complete coherence seems to me to counter a certain ethical violence.'[87] The violence she imagines connotes the demand for sustained self-identity, which the subject consequently expects from others. Instead, Butler contends, an 'ability to affirm what is contingent and inco-herent in oneself may allow one to affirm others who may or may not "mirror" one's own constitution. [...]. It would be, perhaps, an ethics based on our shared, invariable, and partial blindness about ourselves.'[88] Cavarero, however, is careful to highlight that coherence, as she imagines it, comes not from the 'contents' of the narrative (the 'what', rather than the 'who' someone is), which Butler might envis-age constituting self-identity. This is because, for Cavarero, the 'contents of this text are necessarily discontinuous—fragmentary, fleeting, and even casual—because the weaving-work of memory is itself discontinuous, fragmentary, fleeting and casual'.[89] Coherence stems instead from the *desire* for unity.

The work of political theorist Lois McNay dovetails with Cavarero's in the for-mer's project to conceptualize a generative and relational model of agency that escapes poststructuralism's emphasis on the negative paradigm of subjectification (i.e. the elements of constraint and contingency—rather than liberty—involved in the process of subjectification). In McNay's view, much poststructuralist writing, such as Butler's, places an emphasis upon 'discursive construction', i.e. the contingency of the subject, which in turn then becomes a 'form of determinism because of the frequent assumption, albeit implicit, of the essential passivity of the subject'.[90] Many poststructuralists, she contends, 'highlight the retentive dimension of the sedimented effects of power on the body'.[91] Instead, McNay develops a generative logic to subject formation, imagining in the process a more creative stratum to action. She claims that it is 'crucial to conceptualize these creative or productive aspects immanent to agency in order to explain how, when faced with complexity and difference, individuals may respond in unanticipated and innovative ways which may hinder, reinforce, or catalyse social change'.[92]

McNay, like Cavarero, draws on Ricoeur's work on narrative, which confers greater agency to the subject in the process of configuring the self:

> The coherence of the self is not conceived as an exogenously imposed effect, but as the result of an active process of configuration whereby individuals attempt to make sense of the temporality of existence. Narrative is the privileged medium of this process of self-formation. The process of active appropriation immanent in the construction of narrative identity suggests a more autonomous model of agency than is offered in the negative paradigm.[93]

---

[86] Ibid., p. 20. [87] Judith Butler, *Giving an Account of Oneself*, p. 42.
[88] Ibid., p. 41. [89] Adriana Cavarero, *Relating Narratives*, p. 35.
[90] Ibid., p. 3. [91] Ibid., pp. 4–5. [92] Ibid., p. 5. [93] Ibid., p. 27.

Cavarero, too, argues for the active role played by the self in the process of subject formation. Establishing the ontological status of the narratable self, Cavarero insists that the subject is not the '*product* of the life-story which the memory recounts. She is not, as the experts of narratology would say, a construction of the text, or the effect of the performative power of narration'. Instead, she 'coincides [...] with the uncontrollable narrative impulse of memory that produces the text, and is captured in the very text itself'.[94] Memory's relentless narrative impulse dovetails with what Cavarero calls the subject's desire for unity of the self in the form of a story.

Importantly, Cavarero distinguishes between 'text' and 'story'. She associates the term 'text' with a post-Barthian 'tradition of critical reflection that privileges the text'. This tradition, of which Butler's early work is arguably a part, combines with poststructuralist thinking that posits the self as 'only an effect of language'.[95] The consequence of this tradition, she argues, is that 'by swallowing life, the text also risks swallowing the unrepeatable uniqueness of the existent'. In contrast, the 'story' conceptually incorporates the corporeal and ontological aspects of existence that contribute to the 'unrepeatable uniqueness of the existent'.[96]

Lynne Layton also challenges the confinement of the subject to the realm of language and seeks in her work to consider the socially and psychically embedded subject. Of particular importance to the trajectory of the present discussion is her criticism of the model of fragmented subjectivity employed by thinkers like Butler. Layton's work on fragmentation engages directly with Butler and others to counter abstract theorizations of so-called 'ludic' fragmentation by drawing on genuine clinical observations of individuals suffering from what she calls 'traumatic fragmentation'.[97] In 1995, five years after the publication of *Gender Trouble*, Layton argued that, over the previous two decades, strains of poststructuralist thought combined with Lacanian theory and Cultural Studies had come to celebrate notions of 'diversity, ambiguity and fragmentation' as a productive theoretical tool. Layton refers to theorists and literary scholars as diverse as Butler and Ellen G. Friedman, contending that their theories 'posit the fragmentation of the subject as a strategy of resistance and/or guarantee of indeterminacy, especially gender indeterminacy'.[98] The fragmented subject is thus viewed as occupying an alternative space to hierarchically structured, gendered identity, a position of marginality re-valorized that allows the free-play of subjectivity and increasing the potential for subject-agency. Layton suggests that trauma, and the consequent subject-splitting it may induce, had become postmodernism's dominant mode. This is due to the association of fragmentation with the potential for reinventing the self, and in the literary field, as I will demonstrate, it has become the arena in which many authors explore the tension between agency and the exigencies of social circumstance.

---

[94] Adriana Cavarero, *Relating Narratives*, p. 35.   [95] Ibid., p. 69.   [96] Ibid., p. 42.
[97] Lynne Layton, 'Trauma, Gender Identity and Sexuality: Discourses of Fragmentation', *American Imago*, 52. 1 (1995), 107–25.
[98] Ibid., pp. 107–8.

In the field of clinical psychology, however, fragmentation is viewed as a debilitating defence mechanism: 'splitting', as Layton notes, connotes a 'defense [sic] that operates to keep separate good and bad affects, good and bad self-representations, and good and bad object representations'. In the context of psychology, clinicians note that the resulting black-and-white view of the world entails that the fragmented subject 'oscillates between self-depreciation and grandiosity'.[99] Layton suggests that the strategic deployment of traumatic fragmentation poses problems in both theory and literature inasmuch as it runs the risk of obscuring the pain of the fragmented subject. Layton refers to Kathy Acker's fiction, as well as Acker scholarship (discussed in the following chapter), as examples of an aestheticization of female suffering. This process, Layton contends, universalizes suffering, and fragmentation is no longer viewed as a result of specific social or historical circumstances but as a condition of selfhood itself. Layton's work on fragmentation provides a useful framework for my close reading of the works of literary fiction. This is because the first-person narratives grapple with the tension identified by Layton between the usefulness of models of fragmentation for conceptualizing subjectivity in the literary mode and the consideration of the socially embedded aspects of fragmentation, which become linked in the fictions with specific occasions of trauma.

This brief overview of thinkers who have challenged the models of pluralistic fragmented subjectivity generated by poststructuralist theorists like Butler, but also Deleuze and Guattari, whose work forms the theoretical framework for Chapter 2, suggests a post-poststructuralist turn towards exploring coherence and intersubjective dependency in the processes of subjectification and agency. McNay and Cavarero do not return to coherence as a strategy for rehabilitating the totalizing humanist subject; they seek instead to find alternative models that move beyond the binaries of stasis (essentialism) or change (construction) and the linguistic paradigm. They incorporate in part the legacy of poststructuralist thinking about the role flux plays in selfhood, acknowledging that the 'self may always be in a state of reconfiguration in order to incorporate the flux of experience'.[100] McNay, who attempts to overcome the linguistic emphasis and abstraction inherent in some poststructuralist thought by thinking through the temporal and embodied aspects of subject formation, contends that this reconfiguration is nevertheless not 'completely arbitrary or open-ended'.[101] Cavarero, in turn, seeks to overcome the politics of non-identity posited by performative conceptualizations of selfhood by insisting on the uniqueness of the embodied existent and the role that desire plays in identity formation. As a result, their challenge interrogates the continuing advantages of incoherence and performativity, suggesting that what was once a useful disruption may now represent a hindrance to conceptualizing agency.

The specific usefulness of narrative as a model to think through these matters arises from its temporal qualities, its open, interactive function, its foregrounding of the processes of cognition and reflection against a backdrop of external events, and the drive to coherence in the form of narrative closure. The resonance between narrative form and the processes of subjectification and agency provides me with a

---

[99] Ibid., p. 108.   [100] Lois McNay, *Gender and Agency*, p. 93.   [101] Ibid.

framework for considering the first-person narratives I go on to discuss. This model proves useful for exploring the textual encounter between the narrating self and her diegetic other(s), where the 'assertion of self' undertaken by the first-person narrator, generated by the 'tension between the moments of distanciation and identification' in relation to the other protagonists in the narrative, becomes profoundly connected with agency in the form of the narrator's 'capacity for critique', directed both externally and internally.[102]

The literary texts I have selected explore the tensions at work between the pluralistic discordance of the self's interiority and the drive to coherence engendered by the narrative form. Experimental writers such as Acker radically subvert this drive by providing multiple endings and interrupted closures. They work with multiple voices, modes, and registers to disrupt any notion of a single consciousness in the first place. The postmillennial writers I discuss work with similar models of incoherence, but their texts resound with an intangible desire for coherence on the part of the first-person narrators that resonates with modes of critical thinking about selfhood, agency, and narrative. The protagonists' sense of fragmented interiority and their ensuing transgressive behaviours become suspended within a narrative form that implies their desire to escape those paradigms. These works of (auto) fiction thus employ literary, rather than philosophical, strategies to interrogate the usefulness of poststructuralist models of incoherent selfhood like Butler's.

The narrative model also provides a way of conceptualizing the relationship between the narrating protagonist and the reader over the course of the reading process. First-person narrative fiction challenges the reader to asses, or re-assess, their own interior processes, generating room for the accommodation and also exercise of critique. The fundamentally linear mode of reading automatically produces readerly interaction with a subject through time and in flux, yet the convention of narrative resolution—the physical end of the book—entails that this process, like McNay's concept of subjective reconfiguration, cannot remain 'open-ended'. In both diegetic and metafictional paradigms, the narrative model provides a way of thinking through the relationship between the intersubjective encounter and the desire for coherence, as well as considering the importance of those phenomena to agency and the process of subjectification .

GENDER MELANCHOLIA AND RAGE

In *The Aftermath of Feminism* McRobbie draws on Butler's work from *The Psychic Life of Power* (1997), in which Butler indirectly addresses the concerns voiced by Layton about traumatic fragmentation by seeking to theorize the impact of the social on the psyche. McRobbie finds Butler's work useful for developing her position on the transgressive self-harming practices prevalent among young women and girls, such as self-mutilation, disordered eating, excessive consumption of drugs and alcohol, and violence. McRobbie's arguments help me frame the socio-political

---

[102] Lois McNay, *Gender and Agency*, p. 109.

critique levied by the later North American, British, and German first-person fictions I discuss in Chapters 3, 4, and 5. Their protagonists have, in the past or the present, drunk heavily, taken drugs, enacted violence upon others and/or themselves, and withdrawn from the demands of familial or wider social paradigms from which they feel fundamentally alienated. In the case of Michelle Tea, Maggie Nelson and, to an extent, Helene Hegemann's work, queer communities provide an alternative sociality to the (hetero)normative paradigms from which they distance themselves. The older American narratives I discuss in the following chapter anticipate this literary concern, but, as I show in Chapter 2, the qualitative shift in context between the 1980s and the twenty-first century entail that the transgressive literary gesture signifies differently. The twenty-first-century works are positioned on the cusp between a Butlerian mode of thinking about fragmented and performative identity within the linguistic paradigm and the narrative models of embedded selfhood and agency outlined above.

McRobbie views such transgressive behaviours as cultural phenomena, rather than private pathologies, which constitute a direct response to the violent regulations enacted upon the female subject in postfeminism. Whereas Butler conceptualizes this 'female complaint', as McRobbie calls it, within a framework of 'heterosexual melancholia', McRobbie applies it to all aspects of female identity in neoliberal postfeminist culture. She argues:

> The insistent bolstering of the female ego, the requirement of feminine coherence and mastery, are as Butler says forms of violent constraint and female confinement. It is by these dictates that forms of gender re-stabilisation are secured at a cost. Young women find themselves, if no longer trapped within the home, then confined to the topographies of an unsustainable self-hood, deprived of the possibilities of feminist sociality, and deeply invested in achieving an illusory identity defined according to a rigidly enforced set of feminine attributes.[103]

The illusory feminine identity required of this bolstered female self in neoliberalism is, in McRobbie's view, 'unviable', leading to what she calls the 'illegible rage' expressed by the figure of the sick girl in postfeminist culture. This young woman or girl has been compelled to relinquish the 'values of feminist sociality', encouraged to aspire to the heights of socio-economic productivity—which she may also desire herself—and to sustain simultaneously a rigidly enforced set of idealized feminine attributes and behaviours.[104] Repeatedly urged to agency yet constrained by impossible demands, the young woman at the turn of the twenty-first century is required to forego feminism, precisely the 'form of power which might challenge these punitive norms of social approval'.[105] The loss of the feminist alternative is non-negotiable yet mourned by the young woman, whose grief becomes prohibited (and thus illegible) in a postfeminist culture where feminism has been thoroughly repudiated in popular culture, and a structurally ineffective 'market feminism' walks the 'halls of corporate and state power'.[106] As a result, the 'young woman's

---

[103] Angela McRobbie, *The Aftermath of Feminism*, p. 120.   [104] Ibid., p. 111.
[105] Ibid., p. 119.   [106] Elisabeth Prügl, 'Neoliberalising Feminism', p. 614.

illegible rage expresses the powerlessness in the forced abandonment of this public feminist ideal'.[107]

On the one hand, the lapse into melancholia, self-harm, excessive intoxication, or violent rage connotes a socio-cultural transgression, a refusal to participate, on the part of the sick girl; McRobbie calls this a 'crushed rebellion'.[108] The melancholic female subject turns away from the demands of the social realm and abdicates responsibility for the levels of productivity and perfection required of her. The self-destructive nature of her transgressive gesture constitutes, in Butler's view, the 'violence of social regulation' itself. This is because this violence is 'not to be found in unilateral action, but in the circuitous route by which the psyche accuses itself of its own worthlessness'.[109]

The unviability of this 'masquerade' of feminine identity, resulting in abjection, ensures her status as a 'subject for attention and treatment in accordance with the values and norms set by various experts, self-help gurus, and professionals'.[110] Furthermore, the 'State, media and popular culture converge in the production of female melancholia and illegible rage to pre-empt the re-invention of feminist politics through a wide range of individualizing strategies and technologies of the self, many of which draw on and even cite with a degree of approval early feminist books and interventions'.[111] Thus, the ruthless individualization of self-destructive pathologies prevents them from being viewed as a wider phenomenon and a cause for general concern; they remain culturally 'illegible'. Yet the media and popular culture remain fascinated and not a little thrilled by the figure of the transgressive, sick girl. As McRobbie argues, the production of a narrative and industry around such behaviours, in the form of expert professionals and self-help guides, has normalized these female pathologies. She goes on:

> Cutting themselves, endlessly on diets, fearful of their weight, prone to low self-esteem, frequently anorexic? These are all now healthy signs of an unhealthy femininity, normalised in the Foucault sense, but also dynamic features of the heterosexual matrix in the Butler sense. Better to be an ill girl than a girl who gets up out of her sickbed and challenges the power of the heterosexual matrix.[112]

The abject state of the sick young woman thus 'speaks of a normative pathology on the basis of the impossibility of femininity in its struggle for autonomy' for which there appears to be no radical alternative.[113] Relentlessly called to action as the high-achieving new figurehead of so-called postfeminist equality, the overstretched young woman withdraws from the social in an act of rebellion that paradoxically requires the destruction of the object—her body—placed under so much scrutiny. Yet the call to agency continues even during the period of sickness and rebellion; as McRobbie notes, she 'who suffers (along with her fellow-sufferers) is no longer passive, indeed she is expected to be highly active in her struggle to overcome her

---

[107] Angela McRobbie, *The Aftermath of Feminism*, p. 119.   [108] Ibid., p. 116.
[109] Judith Butler, *The Psychic Life of Power: Theories in Subjection* (Stanford, CA: Stanford University Press, 1997), p. 116.
[110] Angela McRobbie, *The Aftermath of Feminism*, p. 111.   [111] Ibid., p. 119.
[112] Ibid., p. 96.   [113] Ibid., p. 108.

afflictions'.[114] This message is provided by the wealth of material circulating to bolster the female ego, to provide guides to improving self-esteem and overcoming disordered eating or other self-destructive patterns. Yet, as McRobbie points out, the sources of this material, often fashion or women's magazines, remain contradictory in their treatment of such subjects due to their practice of juxtaposing images of feminine perfection and weight-loss guides in between the narratives dedicated to health and recovery. This confusing cultural material fosters the awareness among young women that 'female bodily anxieties are intricately tied up with the need for social approval and more generally with the high value that society places on spectacularly coded styles of feminine beauty and sexuality at the expense of other capacities'.[115] The coexistence of contradictory narratives therefore produces in the female subject a sense of entrapment within a pernicious paradigm that appears somehow inevitably part of being female.

Pop-feminist handbooks focus as a matter of course on the matter of female bodily anxieties and their relationship to cultural forces, the media, and beauty industries. The volumes respond to these issues with varying degrees of subtlety, often depending on whether the authors have had some experience of mental health issues relating to body image or eating disorders. At one end of the spectrum, Haaf, Klingner, and Streidl, who spend only ten pages on this area, call on women to take responsibility for the degree to which they are affected by what they call the 'Schönheitslüge' [beauty lie].[116] They claim simply that '[d]em Schönheitsterror kann jeder [sic] aus dem Weg gehen, der will' [everyone who wants to avoid being terrorized by the beauty myth can], while reminding readers of the seemingly all-important common denominators in their text: sex and fun. They remind readers that those affected by body image issues statistically enjoy worse sex.[117]

Valenti, who at first expresses her 'faith that younger women can look at pop culture and analyse it in a way that's positive', later observes that there is 'something seriously amiss when women are spending so much of their time and energy, you know, killing themselves than they are actually living their lives'.[118] Similarly, her solution is to place the responsibility for recovery on the young women themselves: 'So please, gals. Eat something.' She continues: '[w]e're not going to be changing the world of beauty expectations any time soon. But we can do one thing that, while totally simple, is completely revolutionary: We can stop hating ourselves so much. [. . .]. I'm so self-help, I know.'[119]

Hadley Freeman offers perhaps a more nuanced discussion of eating disorders, focusing predominantly on the prurient fascination within certain strands of the media with anorexia and on their short-sighted tendency to blame very thin models for perpetuating such illnesses. Freeman argues instead that eating disorders, 'like any mental illness, do not come from an outside agency [. . .]. They are a means of

---

[114] Ibid., p. 98.   [115] Ibid., p. 118.

[116] Meredith Haaf, Susanne Klingner, and Barbara Streidl, *Wir Alpha-Mädchen*, p. 47.

[117] Ibid., p. 55 and p. 58. Note here the unconscious (and unintentionally ironic) use of the generic masculine in their discussion of the pressures exacted on women.

[118] Jessica Valenti, *Full Frontal Feminism*, p. 43 and p. 211.   [119] Ibid., pp. 211–12.

expressing extreme unhappiness, and it happens that the medium used to express it is food and the body, just as other people use drugs, alcohol or cutting'.[120] Unfortunately, Freeman fails to make the link between personal pathology and wider socio-cultural paradigms even while criticizing the tabloid media's role in scapegoating the fashion industry. This results in her downplaying the cultural factors that her volume had been critiquing up to that point. She contends that these factors 'obviously play a part' and 'might create an environment in which eating disorders can fester, [...], but they do not cause them'.[121] Instead, Freeman argues that a complex 'unhappiness from within' leads to eating disorders, language which locates the cause of and the solution to such pathologies within the sufferer herself.

Butler is more generally interested in how the violence of regulatory norms facilitates the process of subjectification, or, in Claire Colebrook's terms, how the 'fiction of identity is constituted through an originary violence that turns the will against itself in a mode of subjection'.[122] To apply that model to the figure of the sick young girl, as McRobbie does, entails perceiving the extent to which the girl's emergence as a subject is predicated on the enforced loss of feminist sociality. Critical agency pits the young woman's ego against her self as she tries and fails to comply with normative and unviable narratives of femininity. The melancholia induced by the loss of the feminist ideal—which in Butler's account becomes the loss of the same-sex object of desire—generates self-violence as a type of failed rebellion against the wider constraints from which she seeks to escape, but also as self-punishment for the act of relinquishing the ideal.

The sick young woman is furthermore compelled to exercise her will in an autonomous act of overcoming her own self-destructive behaviour. Butler argues, however, that the abandonment of autonomy provides the key to actual recovery through the re-acceptance of the social realm from which she has withdrawn. Butler's thinking here anticipates her ethical account of intersubjective dependency developed in *Giving and Account of Oneself* and, as a counter-model to the relentless bolstering of the female ego in postfeminist neoliberalism, Butler suggests that to 'claim life in such circumstances is to contest the righteous psyche by submission to a sociality that exceeds the bounds of the ego and its autonomy'.[123] Survival, she contends, does not occur because an 'autonomous ego exercises autonomy in the face of a countervailing world (i.e. autonomy is not the solution), on the contrary no ego can emerge except through animating reference to such a world'.[124] What remains unclear in Butler's account, however, is how the sociality to which the recovering young girl submits can foster an alternative mode of being from the options on offer within the social realm that precipitated her sickness in the first place.

This is precisely the question posed by the first-person fictions I discuss in Chapters 3, 4, and 5, with the exception perhaps of Maggie Nelson's autofiction,

---

[120] Hadley Freeman, *Be Awesome*, p. 102.   [121] Ibid., p. 103.
[122] Claire Colebrook, 'From Radical Representations to Corporeal Becomings: The Feminist Philosophy of Lloyd, Grosz and Gatens', *Hypatia*, 15. 2 (2002), 76–93 (p. 88).
[123] Judith Butler, *The Psychic Life of Power*, p. 197.   [124] Ibid., p. 195.

discussed in Chapter 3, which begins at the moment when the narrator re-enters animating sociality in the form of her relationship with Harry Dodge. Suffering from gender melancholia and illegible rage, the protagonists' fragmented selves represent a disruptive force in respect of gender normativity and identity politics, as well as subverting the narratives of self-improvement promulgated by some pop-feminists. Yet these radically transgressive and politically-charged characters become suspended in a narrative form that foregrounds the intangible but relentless desire for subjective coherence, whose telos is recovery, recognition, and resolution. Recovery often becomes facilitated by re-entering the social and familial arenas from which they had exiled themselves. Coherence is attained even if it is merely in the form of narrative resolution, constituted by a moment of recognition between central protagonist and a previously excluded other, often represented by the figure of the mother, the female friend, or partner.

In contrast to the pop-feminist handbooks, in which the illusion of autonomy functions frequently as a cornerstone of what political dimension they retain, the first-person narrators in the narrative fictions relinquish their claims to autonomy by acknowledging their dependency upon others. The by-product of this move, however, is the collapse of the radical self introduced at the beginning of the stories. While their illegible rage functions as a stringent indictment of society and its norms, recovery and/or reconcilement might entail recanting this critique and capitulating to the social realm and, inevitably, to its demands.

GENRE AND WRITING THE SELF

In order to avoid making the mistake outlined above of reading young women and girls' rage or melancholia as the illegible outpourings of a unique psyche, it is important to account for the genre dynamics that inform the meanings these texts accrue and disseminate as they circulate on literary marketplaces. I suggest that the first-person narratives extend beyond accounts of unsettled individual pathologies and intervene in wider debates about female selfhood and agency in neoliberal postfeminism. Before they circulate on the literary market and enact their interventions, however, constitutive and interpretive acts based on genre precede and inform the encounter between reader, text, and narrator. This is of course the case for the pop-feminist guides, too. Although my interest lies predominantly in the portrayals of selfhood and agency in both groups of texts, it remains nonetheless important to consider how those portrayals become informed, sustained, or undermined by the ways in which texts are constructed, marketed, and interpreted in relation to genre.

Pop-feminism navigates multiple media channels, such as web-based and hard-copy zines, internet forums, blogs, music, poetry, and theatre, but I focus on pop-feminist handbooks and first-person (auto)fictions. This is because feminist enquiry has historically highlighted the dialogical relationship between feminist theoretical writing and fiction written by women—first-person narratives, in particular. As Leigh Gilmore observes, '[e]ven as feminist theory has unsettled and inspired self-representation, self-representation has challenged theory in a reciprocal reworking of subjectivity, identity and politics'.[125] This well-documented exchange permits an examination of the first-person narratives outlined above through the lens of pop-feminist writing and vice versa.

Nevertheless, as my introductory comments about the pop medium indicated, problems of generic categorization immediately arise when approaching pop artefacts. Pop resists definition, revels in generic ambiguity and multiplicity, performing mimetic representation without necessarily subscribing to any belief in an authentic and original essence behind the medialized object. I have also highlighted the central ambiguity inherent in the pop-feminist guides, namely, that pop has traditionally been understood as withdrawing from ideological critique. Furthermore, the volumes I have gathered under the title 'pop-feminist' are not always categorized as such by the publishing industry, or by critics, and do not always display either generic signifier themselves.

Genres themselves, however, are not fixed and stable categories that alone construct meaning. John Frow argues that 'genre is not a property of a text but is a function of reading'.[126] By this he means that genre is 'pragmatic, a use, not a class, but a classifying act'.[127] Frow's understanding of genre as an active process of interpretation allows me to gather the essayistic volumes discussed under the umbrella term 'pop-feminist'. But it also supports my model of the reading process developed above in relation to the literary fiction, by which I mean the generative role played by the reader as the other encountering the narrating self.

Nonetheless, Amy Devitt suggests that both the individual situation, i.e. the encounter between reader and text/narrator, *and* the wider social context influence both the act of classification (including the person classifying) and the preceding selection of genre by the writer.[128] Devitt's point highlights the importance of long-standing practices of genre interpretation. As Fredric Jameson observes, 'texts come before us as the always-already-read; we apprehend them through layers of previous interpretations, or—if the text is brand new—through the sedimented reading habits and categories developed by [...] inherited interpretive traditions'.[129] Devitt contends that people in fact construct a 'recurring situation' by means of their awareness and use of genres. Hence, '[p]re-existing genres are part of what enable individuals to move from their unique experiences and perceptions to a shared construction of recurring situation and genre'.[130] Of course, the act of genre interpretation and classification constitutes not only a vital part of reading but also plays a fundamental role in the marketing of books, a theme I will return to when I explore individual fictional texts in Chapters 2–5.

---

[125] Leigh Gilmore, 'Autobiographics', in *Women, Autobiography, Theory: A Reader*, ed. by Sidonie Smith and Julia Watson (Madison, WI: University of Wisconsin Press, 1998), p. 184.

[126] John Frow, *Genre* (London: Routledge, 2006), p. 102.   [127] Ibid.

[128] Amy J. Devitt, *Writing Genres* (Carbondale: Southern Illinois University Press, 2008), p. 31.

[129] Fredric Jameson, *The Political Unconscious: Narrative as a Socially Symbolic Act* (London: Routledge, 2002), pp. ix–x.

[130] Amy J. Devitt, *Writing Genres*, pp. 20–1.

Pop-feminist handbooks therefore become interpreted in terms of the theoretical feminist texts that preceded them, interpretations which include an assessment of the ways in which they conform to generic expectations or deviate from generic standards set by those forerunners. Equally, the fact of these texts' appearance constructs the context: the mid-2000s becomes perceived as a period of feminist reinvigoration *because* the meaning has been constructed through a genre. By producing feminist texts within the medium of the popular journalistic essay, writers of pop-feminist guides engage in what Stephen Heath calls the 'politics of representation', where 'change and innovation' are 'implicated in crises as to who and what is represented and how and to whom'.[131] This is because:

> [t]ypically such crises involve disturbance of and resistance to existing genres from the perception of and appeal to a reality that the resulting new or transformed genres will help precisely to *know*, to bring into meaning. Genres, that is, are attempts to make representational and representative sense.[132]

Many pop-feminist volumes in North America, Britain, and Germany portray dissatisfaction with the politics of much second-wave feminist writing and its perceived academic or theoretical tone, in particular. The pop-feminist writers introduced above emphasize instead how their texts offer a relevant, common-sense approach to feminism based on day-to-day experiences. Levenson, for example, cites a complex statement from Germaine Greer's *The Female Eunuch*, concluding that '[t]his kind of language is immediately off-putting, not just because I don't have a clue what she is talking about but because the academic framework of this kind of book immediately seems removed from our everyday lives'.[133] Caitlin Moran, too, argues that '[f]eminism is too important to only be discussed by academics. [...] Now is really the time for it to be championed by a light-hearted broadsheet columnist and part-time TV critic who has appalling spelling'.[134] While Moran's distaste for academic feminism forms an important function in terms of her performance of working-class authenticity, pop-feminist guides generally avoid abstract theoretical writing by employing instead a ludic journalistic style combined with pop-cultural references and autobiographical detail. This tactic arguably betrays a feminist 'crisis'—to employ Heath's term—in representation: the rejection of one genre of conceptual second-wave writing by pop-feminists as inadequately representative of their concerns.

But this kind of explicit distancing belies the manner in which contemporary pop-feminist writing—even Levenson's—nevertheless draws on many of the generic strategies developed by precisely those second-wave thinkers from whom they seek to distance themselves. Greer's text, for example, is hardly a dry academic volume. In *The Female Eunuch*, she references the pop-cultural artefacts of

---

[131] Stephen Heath, 'The Politics of Genre', in *Debating World Literature*, ed. by Christopher Prendergast and Benedict R. Anderson (London: Verso, 2004), p. 170.

[132] Ibid., p. 171. Original italics.

[133] Ellie Levenson, *The Noughtie Girl's Guide to Feminism*, p. 210. See also Jana Hensel and Elisabeth Raether, *Neue deutsche Mädchen* (Reinbek bei Hamburg: Rowohlt, 2008), p. 14.

[134] Caitlin Moran, *How to be a Woman*, p. 12.

the time: women's magazines, newspapers, pornography, music magazines, and songs, as well as drawing on a wealth of theoretical and literary theory. Her language is often humorously demotic and she also mixes autobiographical aspects with theory.[135]

In other words, pop-feminist theorists employ genre strategies that resemble those of many second-wave writers, but which often deviate from the expectation of abstract theoretical discussion associated with those strategies. Whatever action the genre of second-wave feminist writing performed upon original publication, it is now implicated in a homogenizing postfeminist narrative that characterizes second-wave writing as intellectually elitist, proscriptive, humourless and obsolete. Pop-feminist texts benefit from readers' recognition of previous feminist genres—recognition which imbues the later text with the authority and attraction of an established genre—but claim greater relevance by dissociating themselves explicitly from certain perceived features of that genre, including abstract or theoretical thought.

This strategy is arguably designed to enhance the pop-feminist texts' authority, plausibility, and relevance for their target readership. In his influential work, *Anatomy of Criticism*, Northrop Frye contends that non-literary prose depends upon rhetoric to attain authority and plausibility, and to enact persuasion, in short that the 'nature and conditions of ratio [...] are contained by oratio'.[136] Kenneth Burke, taking issue with the 'classical notion of clear persuasive intent' as the basis of rhetoric, claims that persuasion is 'not an accurate fit for describing the ways in which the members of a group promote social cohesion by acting rhetorically on themselves and one another'.[137] Instead, Burke locates the source of rhetorically induced co-operation in identification. This is because, in Burke's terms, '[o]nly those voices from without are effective which can speak the language of a voice within'.[138]

While Frye and Burke refer explicitly to non-fiction, the production of a sense of identification between reader and narrator has played a major role in Western feminist writing historically, whether in theoretical essays, first-person narratives, autofiction or complex hybrids of theoretical writing mingled with autobiographical or confessional modes. The historical emphasis on identification gestures towards the conviction that a political dimension always inheres in private experience. Identification creates recognition, drawing reader, narrator, and implied author out of uniqueness of experience to establish connections and commonalities—especially in the potentially isolated realm of private experience. As the literary scholar Jeanne Perreault notes:

She who is feeling crazy is certainly (whatever else) feeling dislocated from her world. The discourse communities of which she is a part are inadequate to her 'feeling' or

---

[135] For example, 'No woman wants to find out that she has a twat like a horse-collar'. See Germaine Greer, *The Female Eunuch* (London: Harper Perennial, 2006), p. 45.

[136] Northrop Frye, *Anatomy of Criticism: Four Essays*, ed. by Robert D. Denham (Toronto, ON; London: University of Toronto Press, 2006), p. 316.

[137] Kenneth Burke, *A Rhetoric of Motives* (Berkeley: University of California Press, 1969), p. xiv.

[138] Ibid., p. 39.

'experience'. It is this gap between the conceptual and the experiential that feminist self-writers (and theorists) explore as the zone most available for modification.[139]

The pop-feminist guides I discuss ground themselves in personal accounts of lived experience in order to engender readerly identification, and—to use the term employed by Lisa Maria Hogeland in relation to a grouping of second-wave feminist novels—to practise 'consciousness raising'.[140] Hensel and Raether reveal their intention 'ein Buch darüber zu schreiben, wie es ist, heute eine Frau zu sein. Ein ehrliches Buch, ein persönliches, mit allem, was wichtig ist. Woher kommt man, was hat einen geprägt, worüber denkt man nach, was erzählt man seinen Freunden?' [to write a book about what it's like being a woman today. An honest and personal book, with everything that's important. Where do you come from? What's influenced you? What do you think about? What do you tell your friends?].[141]

Levenson's book is a 'window',[142] providing access to a 'journey through various aspects of a noughtie girl's life to persuade you that feminism is a real issue for today's women and not just an embarrassing word'.[143] *Wir Alpha-Mädchen*, *Full Frontal Feminism*, *Reclaiming the F Word* and *Female Chauvinist Pigs* all begin with the assertion of an 'I' or a 'we' in the guise of the authorial voice, which goes on to act as narrative guide. Their introductions all narrate the material conditions that led to the author's feminist enquiries and subsequent textual endeavours, which strategy grounds the texts' discussions in the experiential and not just the conceptual. In her introduction to *Hot Topic*, Sonja Eismann explains:

> Bewusst habe ich den Autorinnen nahe gelegt, Themen, die ihr Leben oder ihr Denken bestimmen, mit einem persönlichen Zugang—das Private ist schließlich nach wie vor politisch—zu einem theoretischeren Diskurs-Level zu führen, um zu demonstrieren, dass Feminismus kein abstraktes Konzept ist, sondern als gelebte Alltagskultur alle Lebensbereiche durchdringt.
>
> [I deliberately advised the authors to approach the themes which condition their lives or thinking from a personal as well as discursive theoretical angle—the private is after all still political. This demonstrates that feminism isn't an abstract concept but rather it permeates everything through the practices of daily life.][144]

Although Eismann states that readers will discern productive differences between their own lives and those of other women, she distances herself from the identity politics she considers a feature of the American third wave.[145] In her view, identity politics tends to undermine the legitimacy of a shared basis for action by emphasizing difference. Her willingness to draw on, but still modify, North American third-wave discourse demonstrates how global discourses generate locally specific differences. For example, her readiness to prioritize commonality over difference is one example

---

[139] Jeanne Perreault, 'Autograph/Transformation/Asymmetry', in *Women, Autobiography, Theory,* ed. by Smith and Watson, p. 193.

[140] Lisa Maria Hogeland, *Feminism and its Fictions: The Consciousness-Raising Novel and the Women's Liberation Movement* (Philadelphia: University of Pennsylvania Press, 1998).

[141] Jana Hensel and Elisabeth Raether, *Neue deutsche Mädchen*, p. 16.

[142] Ellie Levenson, *The Noughtie Girl's Guide to Feminism*, p. xviii.   [143] Ibid., p. xvii.

[144] Sonja Eismann, 'Einleitung', p. 12.   [145] Ibid.

of how Eismann's text works to build bridges between the specifically German second-wave and pop-feminism. Yet, the pop-orientation of her work can be discerned in the emphasis she places on affect in relation to the reading experience: the process of ascertaining the points of identification and difference between reader and narrator is designed as much to entertain as to inform. Accounts of lived experience not only aid the formulation of shared issues and demands they are also interesting to read.[146]

The genre employed by Eismann—the multiply-authored essay collection—pre-empts potential claims that the text unilaterally usurps representational authority by universalizing individual experience and overlooking differences between women. Featuring multiple contributors provides a variety of voices, experiences, and outlooks. Stöcker also employs this strategy and, unlike Eismann, she also includes three essays written by men. Catherine Redfern and Kristin Aune ground their observations and experiences in solid statistical evidence and they also scatter text boxes throughout chapters that cite verbatim the women who took part in their research. Ariel Levy is the sole author of *Female Chauvinist Pigs*, and her particular style of intimate, first-person journalism might risk creating an exclusively experiential account of the postfeminist raunch culture she investigates. However, she provides a solid conceptual framework and grounds her observations in accurately-sourced and well-documented evidence.

The multiply-authored *Wir Alpha-Mädchen* is divided into thematic sections but each is co-written by the three writers. This text demonstrates perhaps the greatest anxiety concerning the claim to representational authority. On a linguistic level, the collective authorship entails the consistent use of the first-person plural, which tends to reach beyond immediate reference to Meredith Haaf, Susanne Klingner, and Barbara Streidl to include all women/readers. While this is a rhetorically powerful technique (readerly identification is rather persuasively taken for granted), it also imbues the particular experiences of the authors with a universal authority. Despite their initial disclaimer that they do not seek to speak for all women in Germany, this remains a problem on a structural and linguistic level. A thread of anxiety concerning any claims to representation runs through Jessica Valenti's singly authored *Full Frontal Feminism*, whereas the authors of *Neue deutsche Mädchen* have few qualms about conflating themselves and 'andere Frauen in unserem Alter' [other women of our age], which entails they often overlook important differences between them and many other women for whom they claim to speak.[147]

Pop-feminist guides range between those that operate on a highly autobiographical level while eschewing a firm conceptual framework and those that draw on the experiential in autobiographical form while still linking these explicitly to an objective analysis and overarching conceptual framework. Aune and Redfern's aim, for example, is to 'represent feminism fairly'.[148] For these two academic authors, this entails respectfully accounting for the rich history of feminism. In their introduction,

---

[146] Ibid. [147] Jana Hensel and Elisabeth Raether, *Neue deutsche Mädchen*, p. 15.
[148] Catherine Redfern and Kristin Aune, *Reclaiming the F Word: The New Feminist Movement* (London: Zed Books, 2010), p. x.

they insist that '[t]his isn't going to be one of those "new feminist" books that reiterate negative stereotypes about 1970s feminism and position younger feminists in opposition to it. We're not interested in pushing forward a hip, "fashionable" kind of feminism'.[149] Levenson argues conversely that she does not 'need to know' her place in 'feminist history' before going on to rehearse precisely the negative stereotypes of second-wave feminism that Redfern and Aune warn against.[150]

Among the pop-feminist handbooks generally, there is a correlation between the degree of antipathy to conceptual (read second-wave) writing, the degree of ignorance about the history and writings of the second wave, and the weighting placed on the autobiographical. The less reflective volumes, like *Wir Alpha-Mädchen*, *Neue deutsche Mädchen*, *Full Frontal Feminism*, and *How to be a Woman*, often explicitly foreground the superior relevance and entertainment value of experiential over conceptual matters. Their dissociation from elements of past feminist discourse, even as they draw on the writerly strategies of the second wave, entails that their arguments sometimes lapse into incoherence, or that they unwittingly adopt an essentialist stance. Their preoccupation, for example, with 'those littler, stupider, more obvious day-to-day problems with being a woman' implies that there is an essence of womanhood beyond the problems women often encounter due to gendered inequalities built in to the socio-cultural and political structures.[151] Ultimately, the lack of an over-arching conceptual framework, combined with self-conscious and frequent disassociations from second-wave thought, entails that these volumes tend to withdraw from political critique. This is because their emphasis on the experiential frequently combines with a lapse into subjective relativism, which results in the authors' admission that their view can only ever be 'just' their 'take' on matters.[152] The insistence on subjective relativism, which connotes one strategy for avoiding accusations of authoritarianism, conflicts in a perplexing manner with their otherwise universalizing rhetoric, and resonates further with an individualist ethos.

Celia Lury's thoughts on the subject of first-person narrative fiction when the protagonist and author are both female guide my consideration of the pop-literary fiction I juxtapose with the pop-feminist guides. Lury highlights how the attribution of genre and understandings of genres' qualities can reflect groups' contrasting values and are concomitantly implicated in the discursive exercise of power. All too often, the author's gender combines with the generic choice of the first-person voice to activate a range of gendered expectations about the text's function, theme, aesthetics, and representational claims.

Thus, genres enable the construction of meaning, yet they can simultaneously restrict meaning to the limits of one dominant genre frame. Thomas Ernst, for example, argues that the furore surrounding the German author Helene Hegemann's alleged plagiarism, discussed in Chapter 5, arose as a result of literary critics initially miscategorizing her debut as an original coming-of-age novel with autobiographical

---

[149] Ibid., p. xi.   [150] Ellie Levenson, *The Noughtie Girl's Guide to Feminism*, p. xv.
[151] Caitlin Moran, *How to be a Woman*, p. 13.
[152] JessicaValenti, *Full Frontal Feminism*, p. 3.

elements. Ernst argues that critical oversight of her intertextual pop sampling, brought about by assumptions based on her gender and age, generated outraged accusations of plagiarism when the initial categorization was corrected.[153]

In her work on first-person narrative fictions, Lury cites criticism from within and without feminist quarters concerning women writers' use of first-person narrative strategies when the protagonist is female. Lury observes that poststructuralist and postmodern feminist critics argue that in the first-person 'journey of self-discovery [...] there is an essentialist identification of the author with the protagonist, and of both with all women, a conflation which is made explicit when women's writing is marketed as the autobiography of a gender'.[154] These critical voices also condemn the alleged aesthetic normativity of the first-person mode, which leaves first-person novels 'closely tied to conventional forms and values, such as the use of a linear narrative, and the emphasis on female sexuality as the key to women's identity'.[155]

Lury is critical of such arguments and of those voices that disparage the 'naive appropriation of the autobiographical mode' by women writers. This appropriation supposedly 'denies the aesthetic nature of writing, since the effect of the (assumed) identification between author, text, and reader is to obscure the displacement present in all forms of writing in the distance between the subject and representation'.[156] This critique dovetails with androcentric notions of post-romantic literature, which emphasize its required 'fictional character, and its ability to transcend the purely personal'.[157] Lury, on the other hand, views the employment of the first-person narrative 'positively as a space from which to construct a feminine position in opposition to that of the universal male position'. She posits that this aesthetic will remain important so long as certain issues 'still retain their urgency for the women's movement as a whole: sexuality, subjectivity, self-and group-representation and political practice'.[158] The critics who Lury refers to above are arguably responding in a somewhat pragmatic—if defeatist—manner to the gendered interpretive practices of wider mainstream culture outside the realm of feminist scholarship. The solution they offer is to step outside those genre boundaries that have both facilitated and contained women's writing and its significations historically.

Yet, as Devitt contends, 'it is not genre that has agency, not genre that creates a social agenda'. The social agenda pre-exists the question of genre and, like other 'standards, genre is used by society to accomplish its ends'.[159] Merely avoiding the use of a mode or genre associated with and thus allegedly limited by a specifically female perspective does not address the gender inequalities characterizing the field of literary criticism and publishing. As this discussion demonstrates, it is important

---

[153] Thomas Ernst, ' "The Author is a DJ!" Plagiarism vs. Intertextuality in the Discourse of Pop Literature. A Look at Helene Hegemann's *Axolotl Roadkill* ', in *German Pop Literature: A Companion*, ed. by Margaret McCarthy.

[154] Celia Lury, 'Reading the Self: Autobiography, Gender and the Institution of the Literary', in *Off-Centre: Feminism and Cultural Studies*, ed. by Sarah Franklin, Celia Lury, and Jackie Stacey (London: HarperCollins Academic, 1991), p. 99.

[155] Ibid.   [156] Ibid., p. 100.   [157] Ibid., p. 97.

[158] Ibid., p. 106.   [159] Amy J. Devitt, *Writing Genres*, pp. 86–7.

to reflect upon the politically charged dialogue women writers of fiction enter into when they write 'I', as well as the power dynamics that are rehearsed when publishers, marketers, and literary critics imply an autobiographical element in first-person narrative fictions written by women. As Lury noted in 1991, 'although women's fiction has a range, a power, and a public political presence today that is has rarely had before, it is nevertheless true to say that "she" still continues to be read as an indexical symbol rather than a pure sign by the literary establishment'.[160] As my work on the three literary contexts will demonstrate, such power dynamics continue to be rehearsed in the twenty-first century.

The current popularity of autofiction in North America exemplified in works by Maggie Nelson, Michelle Tea, and Sheila Heti, but also Nell Zink and Ben Lerner, has its roots in the dogged pursuit of the 'I''s potential by second-wave writers, as well as queer and feminist writers of a later period. Author Chris Kraus attributes the turn to autofiction in North America to the influence of queer and women writers of the 1990s like Kathy Acker, Eileen Myles, and, of course, Kraus herself, whose Native Agents Series at the publishing house Semiotext(e) was responsible for championing many of their works. When selecting these works for publication, Kraus recalls:

> What seemed most important to me was not the fact of the 'I' but the way it moved through the text and the world. It was an active, public 'I'—the 'I' of American realist fiction, from Mark Twain to Melville to Burroughs and Kerouac and Alexander Trocchi.[161]

Kraus extends the debate from focusing on the indexical qualities of the woman writing 'I' by strategically recasting the 'I' of autofiction written by authors like Myles, Cookie Mueller, and Ann Rower as the self-evident equivalent of the 'active, public "I"' of canonical American male authors like Twain, Melville et al. The auto-fictive mode employed by Heti, Nelson, and Tea can be understood therefore on a continuum with earlier North American fiction, but it also expresses to some extent impatience with the limitations of conventional fiction writing. As Jonathan Sturgeon remarked in 2014 in relation to recent autofictions by Lerner and Zink:

> [T]he rise or return of autofiction isn't the work of a movement, campaign, or vanguard: it's more of a murmur in the heart of the novel, one that lets us know that literature is alive, still-forming—a living hypothesis.[162]

The subtitle to Heti's autofiction *How Should a Person Be?*, for example, is *A Novel from Life*, neatly summarizing the blending of fiction and ambiguous autobiography Sturgeon praises. Heti's work draws on the lives of her circle of artistic friends based in Toronto, Canada, just as Michelle Tea's *Valencia* does with the author's friends

---

[160] Celia Lury, 'Reading the Self', p. 106.

[161] Chris Kraus, 'The New Universal', *Sydney Review of Books*, 17 October 2014, available at http://sydneyreviewofbooks.com/new-universal/ [accessed 23.02.2017].

[162] Jonathan Sturgeon, '2014: The Death of the Postmodern Novel and the Rise of Autofiction', *Flavorwire*, 31 December 2014, available at http://flavorwire.com/496570/2014-the-death-of-the-postmodern-novel-and-the-rise-of-autofiction [accessed 23.01.2017].

and lovers in San Francisco. Heti includes emails, recorded conversations, chunks of play script, essay-like passages and fiction. Whether in novel form or autofiction, then, the first-person voices in the literary works I discuss 'point to a new future wherein the self is considered a *living thing* composed of fictions'.[163]

As Kraus's comments suggest, quantitative and qualitative assessments of genres used by women authors today are not only made in alignment with the mores of an androcentric literary institution. The establishment of feminist literary criticism and a tradition of feminist fiction now entails that publishers, marketers, critics, and readers will also publish, market, critique, and read writing by women in accordance with their knowledge of previous genres employed by feminist writers. Helen Walsh's novel *Brass* (2004) for example, which I discuss in detail in Chapter 4, was positioned by one critic in relation to two cult pop writers of the 1960s and 1990s as well as one of the most important American consciousness-raising feminist authors of the 1970s: '[j]ust as Hubert Selby Jr in the Fifties [sic], Erica Jong in the Seventies and Irvine Welsh in the Nineties exposed worlds and attitudes never before represented in quality fiction, Walsh has blown the lid off hedonistic female sexuality in the 21st century.'[164]

This book also goes about constructing a tradition of feminist literary engagement on the basis of genre, aesthetics, and theme. Nevertheless, when I proceed to a discussion of the more recent literary fictions and their North American, British, and German authors, I make no general claim that all of their first-person narratives constitute 'feminist' texts. The problems surrounding the construction of such a generic category have been well documented.[165] Some of the writers I discuss have openly identified their work as feminist. Maggie Nelson, for example, whose work *The Argonauts* blends autofiction, quotations from feminist and queer theory, and commentary, views her text as 'a long tribute to the many feminist heroes that I had as teachers, men as well as women' (among them Sedgwick, Eileen Myles, and Wayne Koestenbaum).[166] Other authors express, somewhat strategically, public ambivalence towards being read exclusively through a feminist lens, although they, like the authors of the pop-feminist handbooks, often draw generically on the writerly strategies of second-wave feminist writers. The youth and social context of the contemporary authors—they were all born after 1970—place them moreover in the context of McRobbie's feminist 'aftermath', i.e. postfeminism.

There are moments when these authors' novels deviate from the generic expectations generated by any association with older feminist fiction. It is often at those moments that the texts enact their critique of certain strands of second-wave feminism. On a formal level, for example, Helen Walsh splits her narrative

---

    [163] Ibid.

    [164] Review by *Big Issue in the North*. Inside cover, Helen Walsh, *Brass* (Edinburgh: Canongate, 2004).

    [165] See Leslie Dick, 'Feminism, Writing, Postmodernism', in *From My Guy to Sci-Fi: Genre and Women's Writing in the Postmodern World*, ed. by Helen Carr (London: Pandora, 1989); Sarah Maitland, 'Futures in Feminist Fiction', in *From My Guy to Sci-Fi*.

    [166] Paul Laity, 'Maggie Nelson Interview: "People Write to Me to Let Me Know that, in Case I Missed it, There are Only Two Genders"', *The Guardian*, 2 April 2016, available at https://www.theguardian.com/books/2016/apr/02/books-interview-maggie-nelson-genders [Accessed 10.02.2017].

between two voices: the central protagonist Millie and Jamie, who is Millie's (male) best friend. Walsh thereby interrupts exclusive readerly identification with the female protagonist, allowing an alternative—often critical—perspective on Millie's behaviour. Thematically, it is Millie who acts as sexual predator and Jamie who functions as an ethical corrective. This strategy supports Walsh's claim that the novel was intended as 'an attack against Andrea Dworkin feminism and [...] its homophobic inference that there are only two genders or sexualities, and all men are perpetrators and all women are victims'.[167] Nelson inserts a whole passage written by her fluidly gendered partner, Harry Dodge, who passes as male but lives determinedly somewhere in between genders. Given that 2015–16 represented a threshold moment, ushering in a heightened visibility of trans*[168] issues generated by public figures like Caitlyn Jenner and TV shows like *Transparent*, the insertion of Harry's words into her text constitutes a challenge to transphobia in all its manifestations, in pop-culture and government policy, but also in the stance of some feminist thinkers on transgender women.[169]

Like *Brass*, the German author Charlotte Roche's novel *Feuchtgebiete* [Wetlands] draws on the genre of pornographic literature. This strategy inevitably activates long-standing debates about the nature of material appropriate for representation in literature and in literature written by women, in particular. In their explicit depictions of women engaged in transgressive sex or actively seeking sexual encounters, these writers also challenge preconceived notions about female sexuality. One of the most important questions that these novels raise, however, is the question of whether a novel can be pornographic and feminist. Walsh's public assertion that her text constitutes, in generic terms, a feminist novel, combined with its inherent critique of one aspect of feminist thought, resulted in varied textual reception. Following publication, the 'book tour and publicity saw Walsh both fêted and decried by feminists and grumbling old buffers alike'.[170] Equally, one newspaper review opined that in its 'unabashed exploration of female sexuality, *Brass* must be one of the few books I can imagine appealing to feminists and *Loaded* readers alike'.[171] *Brass*, then, has been read as both 'pro'- and 'anti'-feminist according to the values of the social groups receiving it. On the one hand, this is an example of the way in which narrative fiction opens up interpretive opportunities, rather than closing them down. These contrasting readings exist in tension with each other, generating a mental and social arena for reflection and productive debate. On the

---

[167] Katy Guest, 'Young Gifted and Bold as Brass', *The Independent*, 7 March 2008.

[168] The term 'trans*' is a catch-all term to refer to people, ranging from those who self-identify as gender queer to transgender men and women, who do not identify with traditional gender categories. The asterisk stems from a 'wild-card' search function commonly used in computing, meaning that every possible combination of characters attached to the prefix will be brought up in the results. Its use with the prefix 'trans' in both written and oral communication indicates the degree to which computer-mediated communication has influenced language usage across other media.

[169] See Tin Vasquez, 'It's Time to End the Long History of Feminism Failing Transgender Women', *Bitch Media*, 2 May 2016, available at https://bitchmedia.org/article/its-time-end-long-history-feminism-failing-transgender-women [accessed 19.02.2017].

[170] Katy Guest, 'Bold as Brass'.

[171] *Sunday Herald* review, printed in Walsh, *Brass*. *Loaded* is a popular men's magazine aimed at a young readership. Much of its copy is dedicated to sexualized images of women.

other, the anticipated positive reception of the text by readers of a misogynistic publication that sexually objectifies women (*Loaded*) also exemplifies the shifting signification of the radical, sexually transgressive gesture in fiction and pop-culture.

Scarlett Thomas's novel *The End of Mr. Y* (2008) is perhaps the most narrative driven and complexly plotted of the novels I discuss. Thomas nevertheless employs a mixture of familiar genres to construct what is ostensibly a novel concerned with the subjective development of its female protagonist. In general, the text owes much to the politically charged speculative fiction of writers such as Joanna Russ and Marge Piercy, whose work constitutes a touchstone for many of Thomas's characters. Partly due to the speculative quality of much of Thomas's fiction and partly owing to her foregrounding of complexly plotted narrative, Thomas is alone amongst the group of authors I discuss in escaping the conflation of her female protagonists with her in the public reception of her texts. Gwendoline Riley, on the other hand, whose novel *Cold Water* (2002) constitutes a forensic exploration of the central protagonist's reflective and cognitive processes, is frequently confronted with questions from journalists and critics concerning the degree of autobiography inherent in her novels. German authors Kerstin Grether and Alina Bronsky have also been exposed to such lines of questioning. Grether's *Zuckerbabys* (2004) and Alina Bronsky's *Scherbenpark* (2008) are written in a neo-realist pop mode and explore, through a process of mimetic experimentation with a selection of role models,[172] the array of unsatisfactory female identities available to young women in the twenty-first century.

In contrast to the critique, outlined by Lury above, that first-person narratives remain aesthetically orthodox, the German authors Antonia Baum and Helene Hegemann, like Nelson and Heti, disturb representation at the formal level. Their complex, self-reflexive novels question the possibility of 'self'-representation, eschewing mimetic representation and disturbing linearity. The almost relentless inner monologue from which *Vollkommen leblos bestenfalls tot* (2011) is constructed captures the muddled thought processes of its psychologically unstable protagonist. Like examples of experimental feminist writing before them, such as Acker's, Baum and Hegemann's novels question the terms in which the experience of women is represented and examine the possibility of coherent subjectivity. These two novels also foreground the act of writing as a means of claiming agency and of constructing the self on one's own terms in narrative form.

Nevertheless, Baum and Hegemann distance their protagonists from the feminist *grand récit* many of their literary forbears posited as a solution to crises in female subjectivity and agency. The authors subvert the linear development of consciousness inherent in many feminist novels of the second-wave, their characters disavowing the power of feminism or any form of socio-cultural critique to make a difference in their lives. Instead, the novels hurtle towards their protagonists' seemingly inevitable psychological and physical breakdown, offering them no system of belief or ideology on which to gain a purchase. Thus, Baum and Hegemann express ambivalence

---

[172] Kerstin Grether, *Zungenkuss: Du nennst es Kosmetik, ich nenn es Rock 'n' Roll. Musikgeschichten 1990 bis heute* (Berlin: Suhrkamp, 2007), p. 10.

towards feminism—an ambivalence Hegemann herself publicly identifies with—even while they draw in part on a tradition of feminist aesthetics and tackle the issue of female agency thematically.[173] Roche, on the other hand, understands her work to exist on a continuum with the tradition of literary feminist engagement, although she explicitly subverts certain tenets of second-wave discourse, as I will demonstrate in Chapter 5.

The subversion of a genre, however, entails its ghost remains present in the text, sustaining its original political impact. This occurs despite the initial act of resistance performed by genre subversions to previous dominant claims to representation. This means that the novels under discussion can still be read productively through a feminist lens, as, in most cases, they continue a dialogue with feminism on the level of genre as well as theme. The modifications they introduce gesture towards dissatisfaction with the representational claims of feminism as it stands, and with the legacy of second-wave feminism, in particular.

The (auto)fictional narrative thrives on forward propulsion towards resolution, an impetus that many of the writers I discuss seek to disrupt before capitulating to closure. Initially they depict the 'dissociation' their protagonists feel from their lives, the 'gaps, amputations, silences'[174] that separate them from the social contexts in which they live. These works therefore appear to contest the very demands of the form their authors employ.[175] Yet, as Sarah Maitland notes, '[f]orm requires (desires) conclusion, requires tidiness, requires the good ending, and the novel particularly thrives on that requirement'.[176] The pop-feminist guides certainly require formal construction, but the pressure of readerly expectation and desire for resolution is arguably reduced in comparison to (auto)fiction, where narrative progression becomes foregrounded. Moreover, the guides are organized according

---

[173] Helene Hegemann has publicly distanced herself from feminist debate, claiming: '[i]ch habe mich mit so etwas nie beschäftigt, weil ich in einer Generation—naja, verankert bin ich eigentlich in keiner Generation—aber in einem Jahrzehnt groß geworden bin, in dem sich Fragen nach Geschlechterrollen kaum mehr stellten.' [I've never really thought about stuff like that because I'm of a generation—well, actually, I'm not really rooted in any generation—but I grew up in a decade when questions about gender roles were no longer relevant.] Nevertheless, she acknowledges that members of the literary industry 'sind mit anderen Standards sozialisiert worden, da wird mir dann ab und zu dieses Biologie-Intuitions-Monster-Ding angehängt und jede Form von Rationalität aberkannt, mit der ich an meine Arbeit herangehe' [were socialized with different standards and so occasionally I get lumbered with this biology-intuition-monster-thing and denied the rationality with which I go about my work]. She is furthermore able to identify continuing gender bias inherent in literary institutions, acknowledging: '[t]rotzdem, wenn Hamlet auf die Bühne kommt, vertritt der ein Menschheitsproblem, und wenn Medea auf die Bühne kommt, ist sie eine Frau, die schwerstneurotisch ist.' [Nevertheless, when Hamlet comes on stage he embodies the human condition, whereas when Medea comes on stage, she's a crazy neurotic woman.] She nevertheless refuses to be drawn on the issue, claiming: 'ich rede da total ungern drüber, weil ich denke, je mehr darüber gesprochen wird, desto mehr bestätigt es einen darin, sich weiter in solchen Mustern wohlzufühlen.' [I don't like talking about it because I think the more it gets talked about, the more you feel justified in staying in those kinds of roles.] See Hegemann, in Cosima Lutz, 'Helene Hegemann beraubt ihre Freunde schonungslos', *Welt Online*, 10 February 2010 <http://www.welt.de/News/article6329626/Helene-Hegemann-beraubt-ihre-Freunde-schonungslos.html> [accessed 10.12.2012].

[174] Jeanne Perreault, 'Autograph/Transformation/Asymmetry', p. 191.

[175] D. A. Miller, *Narrative and its Discontents: Problems of Closure in the Traditional Novel* (Princeton: Princeton University Press, 1981).

[176] Sarah Maitland, 'Futures in Feminist Fiction', p. 199.

to thematic chapters, which encourages a more piecemeal and even non-linear approach to reading them.

The temporal dimension inherent in narrative fiction combined with its telos towards closure enhances narrative's suitability to the exploration of selfhood, particularly in the first-person (auto)fiction. Subjectification itself does not connote a static act, but a progression, a negotiation, through time. The depiction of a single, continually reflecting consciousness traces the processes of subjectification by exploring how subjects are constituted by discourse, but also how the subject may shape her choices and actions, without resorting to a rhetoric of personal choice that ignores social contingencies. As I argued above, narrative fiction sustains the ambiguity and tension inherent in this dynamic over a period of time, which highlights the element of flux and contradiction in the process of becoming. Yet the narrative drive to closure, which resonates with the diegetic subject's desire for coherence, can also reflect the reader's desire for subjective coherence. Quite apart from the diegetic representation of the protagonist's desire for coherence by means of a complementary intersubjective encounter, the reader herself can be conceptualized as a further 'other', who, through the imaginative and extrapolative act of reading, must acknowledge and complement the narrative of the fictional self (in the form of the protagonist or autofictional 'I'), in order for the process of becoming to be undertaken. The fictional character may be conceived of as an 'other' for the reading self, who undertakes a similar process of self-exploration, guided by the desire for coherence, through reading a fictional narrative. To some extent the reader/subject must relinquish elements of the self in order to enter the world 'proposed' by the text, just as the protagonists of the novels must acknowledge intersubjective dependency before re-entering the social.[177] This process, which appears at first to represent a capitulation, or acquiescence, provides the opportunity for a subjectively expansive experience. The first-person work may thus become an arena of intersubjective relations on both a diegetic and metafictional level.

---

[177] Lois McNay, *Gender and Agency*, p. 108.

2

Postmodern Literature in North America
Tracing Pop-Feminism's Narrative Arc

Kathy Acker and Mary Gaitskill, who function as particularly prominent examples of an innovative and transformative period of writing by women, represent two contrasting aesthetic points on a spectrum of influence that has filtered down not only to the works of a group of North American women authors but also to the writing of European women writers born post-1970.[1] As Jeanette Winterson observes in her introduction to *Essential Acker* (2002), Acker's formal experimentations were ground-breaking in the 1970s; placing her alongside authors Italo Calvino and Angela Carter, Winterson contends that hers was 'pioneer work of the kind that had hardly been attempted since Virginia Woolf's *Orlando* in 1928'.[2] Gaitskill is exemplary of a wave of urban postmodern feminist writing, emerging in the 1980s and greatly indebted to Acker, and her work has been read in relation to that of other New York-based ' "Bad Girl[s]" ' such as Tama Janowitz and Catherine Texier.[3]

The influence of these 'bad girls' can be discerned in a group of post-riot-grrrl, twenty-first-century North American, British, and European authors:[4] in North America, the queer and feminist creators of complex autofictions Maggie Nelson, Michelle Tea, and Sheila Heti; in France, the queer activist, writer and performance artist, Wendy Delorme; in Italy, the author Melissa Panarello; in Britain, the writers Gwendoline Riley, Helen Walsh, and Scarlett Thomas and in Germany, Charlotte Roche, Alina Bronsky, Kerstin Grether, Antonia Baum, and Helene Hegemann (for whom Kathy Acker functions as a direct point of reference). As

---

[1] Acker places herself firmly on a continuum with the 'other tradition', the Beat writers and The Black Mountain poets, whereas Gaitskill's greatest influence, Nabokov, suggests a lineage influenced by the European prose tradition. David Huddle also links her with the American short-story tradition (Hemingway, in particular) and southern gothic fiction. Admittedly, Huddle links Gaitskill with Flannery O'Connor less for formal reasons than due to their 'fiction's droll acknowledgment of just how truly dreadful human behaviour can be'. See David Huddle, 'Report from the Darkest Interior (of Us): The Fiction of Mary Gaitskill', *The Hollins Critic*, XXXVII.3 (2000), 1–16 (p. 2).

[2] Jeanette Winterson, 'Introduction', in Amy Scholder and Dennis Cooper, eds., *Essential Acker: The Selected Writings of Kathy Acker* (New York: Grove Press, 2002), p. viii.

[3] Elizabeth Young, cited in Joseph Wydeven, 'Mary Gaitskill', in *Dictionary of Literary Biography: American Short-Story Writers Since World War II*, ed. by Patrick Meanor (Detroit: Thomson Gale, 2001), p. 126.

[4] Kathy Acker, dubbed a 'riot girl ahead of her time', became an important figure for the 1990s riot-grrrl movement, working directly with riot-grrrl activists such as Kathleen Hanna. See Cynthia Carr, 'The Legacy of Kathy Acker, Theoretical Grrrl', *Village Voice*, 5 November 2002, p. 49.

this roll-call suggests, literary engagement with the issues pop-feminism raises, while extant in other European countries, has experienced a particular boom in Britain and Germany.

I am interested in these temporally and geographically distant writers' shared employment of the transgressive gesture, where transgression denotes the violation or infringement of the bounds or limits of established laws, conventions, or commandments. Discursive and physical acts of transgressing norms, in relation to both gender and sexuality, in particular, can be understood historically as one important element of feminist critique. Challenging normative boundaries also constitutes one strategy of assuming agency. My focus is directed towards recent authors' employment of similar tropes and aesthetic strategies to an earlier generation of female authors, albeit in a dramatically transformed cultural context where the transgressive gesture has been absorbed and re-signified by postfeminist consumer culture.

A parallel reading of Acker and Gaitskill's fiction reveals their mutual interest in '[c]ontesting conventional boundaries by closely investigating difference', an interest which activates both poststructuralist and feminist theory and exemplifies postmodern fiction.[5] 'Difference' here can be understood to emerge at the moment the female-authored text engages with questions of identity and agency and the mobilizing force of desire. In the fiction of Acker and Gaitskill, liminal positions become privileged as advantageous view-points both for investigating these questions and critiquing capitalism. Both authors explore transgressive sexualities, madness and neurosis, trauma and suffering, emphasize unstable, multifaceted identity and juxtapose the pop-cultural with the canonical literary archive, strategies which warrant the joint consideration of these authors' work. Their characters occupy de-privileged, marginal social positions as members of alternative, often nomadic communities, which allows for the exploration of subversive perspectives on normative society.

Acker's first literary productions were published by small, independent presses linked with the New York literary underground of the 1970s; her first major international publication *Blood and Guts in High School* appeared in 1984 (published by Grove Press in the US and Pan Books in Britain) and established her as an important voice in postmodern feminist experimental fiction.[6] Mary Gaitskill, who studied journalism and creative writing at the University of Michigan before moving to New York in 1981, first won critical attention with her 1988 short-story collection *bad behavior*. As well as writing fiction, both Acker and Gaitskill have worked with the essay form: Acker's essays were collected and published in 1997, the year of her death from cancer, while Gaitskill's essays are still published regularly in *Harper's*, *The New Yorker*, and *Village Voice*.

Acker began writing in a period when Anglo-American feminist literary criticism was still deeply biased towards the realist mode. Writing in 1985 about that context, Toril Moi observes that much feminist literary critique of that period still focused

---

[5] Martina Sciolino, 'Kathy Acker and the Postmodern Subject of Feminism', *College English,* 52. 4 (1990), 437–45 (p. 437).

[6] Ibid., p. 437.

on the 'study of female stereotypes in male writing' and, as a result, championed a form of writing by women that offered more 'authentic' representations of women's experiences.[7] This approach centred on a now outmoded conceptualization of what subjectivity and agency might mean in a feminist context: understanding women as objectified, i.e. written *about* and as a result prevented from assuming agency. This paradigm linked literature with life outside fiction and, in particular, the lived experiences of the reader. In that context, literature's function was thought to be geared towards aiding personal growth by raising readers' consciousness and as such its highest goal was to capture, in the most authentic manner, the lives reflected in literary form.[8] For some feminist critics writing in the late 1970s, such as Florence Howe, this was best achieved through autobiography because 'it is there, in our consciousness about our own lives, that the connection between feminism and literature begins'.[9] Yet as Moi observes:

> [T]he demand for realism clashes with another demand: that for the representation of female role models in literature. The feminist reader of this period not only wants to see her own experiences mirrored in fiction, but strives to identify with strong, impressive female characters.[10]

As a result of these dual impulses, Moi notes that feminist criticism remained 'hostile to non-realist forms of writing'.[11] Moi's repudiation of this stance reveals her pro-modernist position in the debate surrounding feminist aesthetics and textual politics, which echoed older and wider strands of theorizing about the emancipatory potential of modernist and realist modes among some of Europe's most significant socialist thinkers of the twentieth century.[12] For Moi, accusations that modernist writing lacks social relevance and risks ahistoricism (at a point in time when feminist critics were seeking to trace the historically-situated female subject) disregard the manner in which modernist aesthetic strategies such as multiple focalizations and fragmentation may effect critique on a formal level by questioning the capacity of language to express any notion of a unified self, thus undermining the masculine-humanist concept of 'essential human identity' per se.[13] Aesthetic representations of the shifting, self-contradictory processes of conscious thought reveal how the subject emerges from a complex web of psychological, material, social, and political factors rather than encountering them as a pre-existent entity.[14] Not only does this tactic foreground the socially constructed and gender-biased nature of the elements undergirding identity it reveals the gender bias inherent in the exclusionary, masculine-humanist framework by which identity has been conceptualized historically.

---

[7] Toril Moi, *Sexual/Textual Politics: Feminist Literary Theory* (London: Methuen, 1985), p. 42.
[8] Ibid., pp. 43–9.
[9] American feminist scholar Florence Howe, cited in Toril Moi, *Sexual/Textual Politics*, p. 43.
[10] Toril Moi, *Sexual/Textual Politics*, p. 47.   [11] Ibid.
[12] Ernst Bloch et al., *Aesthetics and Politics: Debates between Ernst Bloch, Georg Lukács, Bertolt Brecht, Walter Benjamin and Theodor Adorno* (London: NLB, 1977).
[13] See Toril Moi's discussion of Virginia Woolf, in Toril Moi, *Sexual/Textual Politics*, pp. 9–10.
[14] Ibid., pp. 9–10.

Drawing on Sandra Gilbert and Susan Gubar's influential study of nineteenth-century women's writing, *The Madwoman in the Attic* (1979), as well as Elaine Showalter's 'Towards a Feminist Poetics' (1979), Moi sketches the climate of late 1970s feminist reception, which still held sway well into the 1980s, as one still deeply influenced by Western patriarchal humanism. She observes that the dominant feminist aesthetics of that period place an emphasis on 'wholeness', implying that:

> women's writing can only come into existence as a structured and objectified whole. Parallel to the wholeness of the text is the wholeness of the woman's self; the integrated humanist individual is the essence of all creativity. A fragmented conception of self or consciousness would seem to Gilbert and Gubar the same as a sick or dis-eased self. The good text is an organic whole.[15]

The work of feminist thinkers like Rita Felski demonstrates that the politics of feminist aesthetics continues to be debated well into the era characterized as postmodern. Yet, as Fredric Jameson argued in relation to the advent of poststructuralism, postmodern critique has ostensibly shifted the parameters of the realist/modernist debate.[16] In 1989, for example, Felski perpetuates the Lukácsian bias practised by her mentor (and Moi's object of critique), Elaine Showalter, when she questions the potential of the radically experimental feminist text—either modernist or postmodernist—to subvert 'existing structures of representation' in the name of a progressive politics.[17] It is certainly the case that aesthetically, textual expressions of postmodernism share many features with the modernist text: self-reflexivity, textual fragmentation, which emphasizes the cacophonous processes of consciousness, disrupts temporality, and undermines linear narrative, as well as the juxtaposition of so-called high and low forms. The distinction lies perhaps in the scepticism inherent in postmodern textuality concerning the feasibility of the modernist notion of the 'new' and its ability to transform the major socio-cultural and political narratives governing turn-of-the-century culture.

This scepticism combines with the textual deployment of self-conscious ironizations of potential counter narratives in monolithic late-capitalist culture, through which may often be glimpsed a nostalgic yearning for the lost certainty of their existence.[18] If, as Georgina Paul has argued, modernist artists and intellectuals at the turn of the nineteenth to the twentieth century 'turned to a conceptualization of the "feminine" as the repository of values counter to the fragmentation and alienation of the modern male subject', the postmodern artist may be understood to doubt the existence of any available repository and, indeed, the validity of any

---

[15] Toril Moi, *Sexual/Textual Politics*, p. 66.

[16] See Fredric Jameson's afterword, in Ernst Bloch et al., *Aesthetics and Politics*, p. 199.

[17] Rita Felski, *Beyond Feminist Aesthetics: Feminist Literature and Social Change* (London: Hutchinson Radius, 1989), p. 156.

[18] Linda Hutcheon has challenged Fredric Jameson and Terry Eagleton's insistence on postmodernism's penchant for nostalgia. See especially, Linda Hutcheon, *A Poetics of Postmodernism: History, Theory, Fiction* (New York; London: Routledge, 1988), p. 39. She has, however, more recently returned to the topic in her essay 'Irony, Nostalgia and the Postmodern' (1998), published in *The History on Film Reader*, ed. by Marnie Hughes-Warrington (London: Routledge, 2009).

values to be stored.[19] The only repository becomes the field of representation itself, which, as Baudrillard and Deleuze have argued to contrasting conclusions, has become the only 'reality' available.[20]

The ongoing process of theoretical debate on the question of feminist aesthetics, however, often continues to revolve around the binaries of coherence/fragmentation and unity/difference, suggesting that more is at stake than the 'feminist critique of a traditional "male" aesthetic' that obtains despite some philosophers' attempts to theorize away a gendered world beyond representation. Continuing debate about feminist aesthetics emulates the wider theoretical 'difficulty of reconciling increasing demands for the recognition of cultural diversity [...] with a "coherent politics" ', and thus rehearses concerns about the future of feminism itself.[21] As Laura Marcus notes, the 'question then becomes less that of a feminist aesthetic than of what the aesthetic—the narrative form—of feminism might be'.[22]

Acker's work undermines any sense of either the text or the subject as an 'organic whole' and, as such, her work critiques the coherent universal subject of humanism and, by extension, the sovereign subject of late capitalism. Acker scholarship regularly aligns her work with the French deconstructive school, but Acker herself recalls how her early fictions emerged before she had discovered Foucault, or Deleuze and Guattari, writers who were to become central to her work. At that time she claims to have been fascinated by 'schizophrenia and the model of the centralized "I" ' and in her earliest pieces she attempted to 'see if, rather than trying to integrate the "I", [...] you could *dis*-integrate it and find a more comfortable way of being'.[23] Her interest in disintegration and fragmentation as routes to alternative modes of being results not only in a focus on the problems of signification but also a thematic preoccupation with liminal experiences and transgressing boundaries. This emphasis elicited a critical response from feminist quarters at the time, whose critics considered that Acker provided neither 'authentic' realist fiction nor what they considered to be positive female role models. Alternatively, they read her work literally.[24] Marilyn Manners notes that 'Acker's "pornography" and passive or

---

[19] Georgina Paul, *Perspectives on Gender in Post-1945 German Literature* (Rochester, NY; Woodbridge: Camden House, 2009), p. 13.

[20] See Jean Baudrillard, *Simulacres et simulation* (Paris: Éditions Galilée, 1985); Gilles Deleuze, *Différence et répétition*, 4th edition (Paris: Presses universitaires de France, 1981).

[21] Laura Marcus, 'Feminist Aesthetics and the New Realism', in *New Feminist Discourses: Critical Essays on Theories and Texts*, ed. by Isabel Armstrong (London; New York: Routledge, 1992), pp. 11–25 (p. 23).

[22] Ibid.

[23] Larry McCaffery, 'The Path of Abjection. An Interview with Kathy Acker', in *Some Other Frequency: Interviews with Innovative American Authors*, ed. by Larry McCaffery (Philadelphia: University of Pennsylvania Press, 1996), p. 23.

[24] Marilyn Manners' essay provides a useful overview of Acker reception which has succumbed to the pitfalls of reading literally. *Blood and Guts in High School*, for example, was banned in Germany and South Africa for its representation of paedophilia. Furthermore, Manners examines feminist scholarship which has read Acker's use of pornography literally. Colleen Kennedy, for example, argues that 'pornography written by women ultimately renders them victims of it'. Kennedy also critiques Acker's use of parody in her 'pornographic' writing: 'Clichés cannot be distinguished from their parody. To borrow from Toril Moi's analysis of Irigaray, "the mimicry fails because it ceases to be perceived as such; it is no longer merely a mockery of the male, but a perfect reproduction" '. See Colleen Kennedy,

victimized characters baffled or offended some feminists',[25] while Acker herself famously criticized British feminist writing of the time, claiming '[i]t's diary stuff and the diary doesn't go anywhere, and there's not enough work with language'.[26]

Both Acker and Gaitskill decline aspects of second-wave feminism that encourage absolute condemnation of prostitution and transgressive sex as symbols of female subjugation through patriarchal structures. Susan Hawkins has argued for a reading of sex in Acker's work as both a critique of patriarchal capitalism (as Acker writes: 'Having any sex in the world is having to have sex with capitalism'[27]) and as a site that, through desire, retains the potential for signifying identity and power differently. Gaitskill's fiction is peopled by sadistic men who act out fantasies of sexual domination upon vulnerable women who do not represent the positive role models required by some second-wave critics. However, the author never withdraws the aspect of transgressive sex that may allow for the productive articulation of elements of individual psychology. Gaitskill's interpretation, in particular, places sex in the realm of fantasy, an arena not suited to correction along socially progressive lines. Moreover, by including transgressive sexual elements in some queer relationships, Gaitskill complicates feminist debate about sadomasochism and its role in wider heteronormative structures that subjugate women. That is not to say that that critique is not present in Gaitskill's work, but it coexists in productive tension with an awareness of desire's role in identity construction.

Both Acker and Gaitskill have spoken publicly about working in the sex industry before they began to write fiction. Both have stressed the element of financial necessity that led to this work. They also draw on these experiences in their fiction. This autofictional blending merges with the thematic foregrounding of transgressive sex in both authors' work to produce a tension that highlights the issues involved when a women writer writes 'I'. While they often place fictionalized versions of 'themselves' in their work, Gaitskill and Acker should not be understood as autobiographical writers. Instead of existing on a continuum with earlier feminist writers who perceived autobiography as a strategy for rendering authentic female experience, Gaitskill and Acker question the notion of authentic experience, female or otherwise, examining instead the contradictions inherent in identity and the boundaries of expression. A key concept for Acker, in particular, is performance. Referring to her early engagement in the New York literary underground, she recalls: '[i]n those days, we did a lot with performance. We performed for each other [...]. Much of the women's art had to do with performance and identity. At art parties at the time, there was a lot of crossdressing, playing

'Simulating Sex and Imagining Mothers', *American Literary History*, 4.1 (1992), 165–85 (p. 175 and 183). Cited in Marilyn Manners, 'The Dissolute Feminisms of Kathy Acker', in *Future Crossings: Literature Between Philosophy and Cultural Studies*, ed. by Krzysztof Ziarek and Seamus Deane (Evanston, IL: Northwestern University Press, 2000), pp. 107–8.

[25] Marilyn Manners, 'The Dissolute Feminisms of Kathy Acker', p. 101.

[26] Ellen G. Friedman, ' "Now Eat Your Mind": An Introduction to the Works of Kathy Acker', *The Review of Contemporary Fiction*, 9.3 (1989), 37–49 (p. 19).

[27] Kathy Acker, *Blood and Guts in High School: Plus Two* (London: Picador, 1984), p. 135.

with gender and with identity.'[28] This comment might be a description of a scene from a Gaitskill short story and highlights the extent to which these authors' fiction anticipates and reflects discursive shifts in gender and queer theory that generated, most prominently perhaps, Butler's notion of pluralistic identity and performativity.

Despite Acker's interest in incoherence and disintegration in relation to subjectivity, my discussion of Acker and Gaitskill's fiction seeks to identify a conceptual trajectory that moves beyond fragmentation, suffering, and the risks of their aestheticization posited by Lynne Layton. Due to the formally experimental aspects of her work, my reading of Acker explores how she foregrounds language as the site of identity (de)construction. My analysis of Gaitskill's fiction complements this important feature of postmodern feminist writing by focusing on the thematic and ethical preoccupations exhibited by her work. Both authors depict the traumatically fragmented female self, exposed to the modalities of desire and suffering, but they also hint at a possible site of coherent identity, not in terms of an inner subjective core, but in terms of relational, intersubjective dynamics.

This chapter encapsulates the discursive concerns of North American postmodern writers of the 1970s and 1980s, like Acker and Gaitskill, which influence, albeit with important local distinctions, the contemporary works I have selected. The concerns taken up by poststructuralist gender theory—Butler in particular—become most keenly examined by German pop-feminist writers. Despite this shared legacy, however, the pop-feminist texts of which I am most critical often withhold or fail to envisage a site of successful intersubjective relations, locating agency in individual choice and responsibility for the self. This self is dependent for its existence upon a rebuttal of extant female identities often represented by the figure of the second-wave feminist. The influence of neoliberal individualism and postfeminism on contemporary pop-feminism has led to the co-option of notions of performative identity by consumer forces. As Felski has noted, the fragmented, transgressive textuality of the once radical experimental postmodernist text, may 'in this context merely reiterate rather than challenge the logic of hedonistic, consumption-oriented late capitalist society'.[29] What follows traces a literary and feminist arc that demonstrates how questions of female identity and agency have been invested with political meaning that signifies differently from Acker and Gaitskill's fiction.

MAKING FICTION WITH KATHY ACKER

For me writing is freedom. Therein lies (my) identity.[30]

In a discussion of gender published as part of Acker's late collection of essays, *Bodies of Work* (1997), Acker reflects upon her childhood certainty that 'as a girl,

---

[28] Kathy Acker in Ellen G. Friedman, 'A Conversation with Kathy Acker', *The Review of Contemporary Fiction*, 9.3 (1989), 12–22 (p. 15).

[29] Rita Felski, *Beyond Feminist Aesthetics*, p. 160.

[30] Kathy Acker, 'Preface' in Kathy Acker, *Bodies of Work* (London: Serpent's Tail, 1997), p. viii.

I was outside the world. I wasn't. I had no name. For me, language was being. There was no entry for me into language. As a receptacle, as a womb, as Butler argues, I could be entered, but I could not enter, and so I could neither have nor make meaning in the world'.[31] Nevertheless, Acker characterizes her first writing attempts as a search for 'a voice, a self'.[32] Placing what she calls '"true" autobiography next to "false" autobiography', she recalls her realization that 'in fiction, there is no "true" or "false" in social-realist terms. Fiction is "true" or real when it makes'. This autofictional process led her to conclude that 'if there is a self, it isn't Hegel's subject or the centralized phallic I/eye'.[33] Here, Acker demonstrates her interest in the deconstruction of the humanist subject, a project pursued by Butler in *Gender Trouble* when she provides a genealogy of how the Hegelian epistemological model led to the naturalization of compulsory heterosexuality, sex itself, and the concept of a 'global and globalizing subject'.[34] But, Acker continues: 'If there is a self, it's probably the world. All is real'.[35] The following explores Acker's exploration of subjectivity and identity in light of this comment.

The two essays by Acker mentioned above neatly demonstrate the productive tension at the heart of Acker's fiction between the drive to feminist critique and the subscription to a poststructuralist questioning of constative universalizing narratives. Acker's fiction, on the one hand, explores the social, linguistic, and material exclusions and hierarchies that perpetuate the subjugation of women by depicting women's victimization in, at times, graphically violent detail. On the other, she does not propose a model of the 'female subject as an absolute entity'[36] that might counteract the invisibility and voicelessness of the female characters she portrays, or that she herself claims to have experienced. Instead, as part of what Martina Sciolino considers a particularly postmodern project, Acker explores 'modalities of desire'.[37] But she does so with a hawkish eye trained upon the question of gender difference.

Acker's work and interviews provide evidence of her engagement with twentieth-century developments in critical theory, with Jacques Derrida, Jean Baudrillard, Michel Foucault, Gilles Deleuze, and Félix Guattari, in particular. But her work also engages directly with French poststructuralist feminist thinkers Luce Irigaray, Julia Kristeva and Hélène Cixous as well as the work of second-wave Anglo-American feminists such as Andrea Dworkin. Sciolino observes that Acker's literary dialogue with such diverse thinkers entails that she, thirty years before Maggie Nelson, 'creates fictions which are theories-in-performance, speculative fictions that act out the suppositions of both poststructuralism and feminism'.[38] The author's early work, in particular, seeks to deconstruct the myths constituting identity in late capitalism. The Oedipus myth—the repressive 'daddy-mommy-me

---

[31] Kathy Acker, 'Seeing Gender' in Acker, *Bodies of Work*, p. 161.

[32] Kathy Acker, 'A Few Notes on Two of My Books', *The Review of Contemporary Fiction*, 9.3 (1989), 31–6 (p. 33).

[33] Ibid., p. 33. [34] Judith Butler, *Gender Trouble*, p. 202.

[35] Kathy Acker, 'A Few Notes on Two of My Books', p. 33.

[36] Martina Sciolino, 'Kathy Acker', p. 438. [37] Ibid., p. 437. [38] Ibid., p. 438.

triangle'[39]—perpetuated by psychoanalysis forms the ground where her work dovetails with the investigations of Deleuze and Guattari. Acker's fictions constitute literary exemplifications of the attempt to 'schizophrenize' the (notion of the) unconscious and the socio-historical paradigm in order to 'shatter the iron collar of Oedipus and rediscover everywhere the force of desiring production'.[40] For Acker, as for Deleuze and Guattari, desire is not characterized by lack, as it is in the psychoanalytical model. As Claire Colebrook observes, '[d]esire, for Deleuze, is also positive and productive, and this allows for a radically new approach to politics and the relations between politics and the imagination'.[41] It is positive and productive because it:

> begins from connection; life strives to preserve and enhance itself and does so by connecting with other desires. These connections and productions eventually form social wholes; when bodies connect with other bodies to enhance their power they eventually form communities or societies. Power is, therefore, not the repression of desire but the expansion of desire.[42]

Acker's fiction demonstrates, first, how dominant social narratives have already laid down and thus limited the framework of female desire, how, in Deleuzian terms, female desire has been wrenched from its impersonal, connective origins and reinterpreted as 'interest'—or the fulfilment of a given lack—in the social domain. Using the language of machines in order to emphasize the impersonality of desiring exchange, Deleuze and Guattari suggest that social bodies retrospectively impose meaning on what begins as an impersonal connection between a 'desiring machine' and a 'partial object', for example, an infant and its mother's breast.[43] This exchange accrues meaning in the social sphere but in a reinterpreted form, coming to represent notions of 'family' or 'motherhood' that carry a symbolic weight absent in the original, impersonal interaction. For Deleuze and Guattari, there is no underlying being preceding what Colebrook calls the 'delusions and intrusions of power and imagery' whose genuine needs can be unequivocally determined.[44] Instead, Colebrook suggests that in *Anti-Oedipus*, desire itself becomes:

> power, a power to become and produce images. Desire also has the power to produce images that enslave it: images of a moral man obeying his social duty. But the task is not to get away from images so much as to reveal and intensify their production: why limit ourselves to the image of man and woman as social citizens, why not become other?[45]

In this way, Acker attempts to find the moment at which female desire may signify differently away from the parameters of its social coding, or what Deleuze and

---

[39] Gilles Deleuze and Félix Guattari, *Anti-Oedipus: Capitalism and Schizophrenia*, trans. by Robert Hurley, Mark Seem, and Helen R. Lane (London: Continuum, 2004), p. 58.
[40] Ibid., p. 60.   [41] Claire Colebrook, *Gilles Deleuze* (London: Routledge, 2002), p. 91.
[42] Ibid., p. 91.   [43] Gilles Deleuze and Félix Guattari, *Anti-Oedipus*, p. 50.
[44] Claire Colebrook, *Gilles Deleuze*, p. 93.   [45] Ibid., p. 95.

Guattari dub the 'yoke of daddy-mommy'.[46] Acker's project thus dovetails with Deleuze and Guattari's in their attempt to:

> renew, on the level of the Real, the tie between the analytic machine, desire and production[.] For the unconscious itself is no more structural than personal, it does not symbolize any more than it imagines or represents; it engineers, it is machinic. Neither imaginary nor symbolic, it is the Real in itself, the 'impossible real' and its production.[47]

Acker's own model of the self as 'the world' and contention that '[a]ll is real' can be productively viewed in light of this comment.

In *Blood and Guts in High School* (1978, first published 1984), Acker perpetually destabilizes the voice of her central protagonist, Janey Smith, who is ten years old and (in true Elektra style) views her father as 'boyfriend, brother, sister, money, amusement, and father'.[48] As Karen Brennan suggests, Janey should be read as a 'fluid entity-voice (not really a character) in Acker's novel'.[49] The author renders dialogue between Janey and her father, Johnny Smith, in the form of a play manuscript with stage directions, thus highlighting the pre-constituted artificiality of their interactions. (This is a strategy later adopted by Sheila Heti in *How Should a Person Be?*) This language becomes highly stylized, cliché-ridden, and repetitive but is interrupted by capitalized statements made by an ambiguous 'I', for example:

PLEASE ME NO LONGER MYSELF   (BG, 31)

Janey adopts the narrative I in the form of diary entries as soon as she is sent to New York from Mexico. Even then, Janey's voice is not stable: child-like and clichéd language (presumably Janey's) is juxtaposed with what appears to be an older, reflective, and more cynical 'Janey'. Compare:

> Daddy no longer loved me. That was it.
> I was desperate to find the love he had taken away from me.   (BG, 31)

And:

> Despite the restrictions of school, we did exactly what we wanted and it was good. We got drunk. We used drugs. We fucked. We hurt each other sexually as much as we could. The speed, emotional overload, and pain every now and then dulled our brains. Demented our perceptual apparatus.
> We knew we couldn't change the shit we were living in so we were trying to change ourselves.   (BG, 32)

These Janey voices are interspersed with deeply and humorously satirical passages emanating from an ambiguous narrator who also sometimes mimics the voices of

---

[46] Gilles Deleuze and Félix Guattari, *Anti-Oedipus*, p. 54.   [47] Ibid., p. 60.

[48] Kathy Acker, *Blood and Guts in High School: Plus Two*, p. 7. All subsequent quotes will be given within the body of the text, marked by BG.

[49] Karen Brennan, 'The Geography of Enunciation: Hysterical Pastiche in Kathy Acker's Fiction', *boundary 2*, 21.2 (1994), 243–68 (p. 263).

random other speakers. The reader is alert to the shifts in voice, which impede identification/immersion in the world of the text and highlight its fictional status and constant state of flux. For example, in this passage dealing with Janey's first abortion:

> It's all up to you girls. You have to be strong. Shape-up. You're a modern woman. These are the days of post-women's liberation. Well, what are you going to do? You've grown up by now and you have to take care of yourself. No one's going to help you. You're the only one. Well, I couldn't help it, I just LOVE to fuck, he was SO cute, it was worth it.   (BG, 32)

The general question Acker raises is not what female subject position may replace the phallogocentric 'universal' subject but how desire may function to 'reset' the Hegelian concept of subjectivity itself. Inserted into a section dealing with Janey's violent relationship with President Carter, the narrator observes:

> EVERY POSITION OF DESIRE, NO MATTER HOW SMALL, IS CAPABLE OF PUTTING TO QUESTION THE ESTABLISHED ORDER OF A SOCIETY; NOT THAT DESIRE IS ASOCIAL ON THE CONTRARY. BUT IT IS EXPLOSIVE; THERE IS NO DESIRING MACHINE CAPABLE OF BEING ASSEMBLED WITHOUT DEMOLISHING ENTIRE SOCIAL SECTIONS.
>
> (BG, 125)

But as the character Peter notes in Acker's later novel, *Great Expectations*, the 'mistake is believing that indulgence in desire a decision to follow desire isn't possibly painful'.[50] Acker's position is an ambiguous one when it comes to confronting the potentially violent/self-destructive consequences of desire (for example in the case of consensual S&M practice such as depicted between Janey and President Carter). It is this ambiguity that has drawn critique from feminist critics like Colleen Kennedy and Lynne Layton who accuse Acker of re-inscribing masculine models by writing pornography or glorifying/aestheticizing female victimization.[51] But Acker is interested in the potential of *all* kinds of extreme action to break through 'stable and socializable' subjectivity. Her continuous engagement with movement, madness, pain, violence—but also love—stems perhaps from the assertion that '[a]ny action no matter how off the wall—this explains punk—breaks through deadness' (GE, 219).

Her protagonists experience extreme physical and psychological torment and love with equal intensity. During her affair with President Carter, Janey observes that:

> One of the most destructive forces in the world is love. For the following reason: The world is a conglomeration of objects, no, of events and the approaching of events towards objects, therefore of becoming stases static stagnant, of all that is unreal. You get in the world, you get your daily life [...] you begin to believe what doesn't change is real, and love comes along and shows all these unchangeable for ever fixtures to be flimsy paper bits.   (BG, 124–5)

---

[50] Kathy Acker, *Great Expectations*, in Acker, *Blood and Guts in High School:Plus Two*, p. 211. All subsequent quotes will be marked within the text as GE.
[51] Colleen Kennedy, 'Simulating Sex and Imagining Mothers', p. 83; Lynne Layton, 'Trauma, Gender Identity and Sexuality', p. 108.

Dreams, too, offer a way of moving out of stagnation as they 'cause the vision world to break loose our consciousness' (BG, 36). But this particular contemplative narratorial passage is immediately undercut by Janey's observation that: 'I didn't have enough food, so I started working in a hippy bakery. [...] Working for money is the omnipresent fact of American life' (BG, 37). In this way, Acker never turns away from the material, be it the need to work to buy food, or the presence and relevance of the corporeal. Whether it is the rape and defilement of the female body by male agents, menstruation, pregnancy and abortion, sex and orgasmic rapture, Acker turns repeatedly to the material site of the body, and, in particular the female body (as Acker's graphic illustrations of genitals in *Blood and Guts* reinforce). After a period of imprisonment, when Janey is taught 'to be a whore' (BG, 65) and simultaneously begins to 'write down her life' with a pencil stub and scrap of paper found in a 'forgotten corner of the room' (BG, 65), Janey journeys with Jean Genet into the Algerian desert. Preparing to move into a state of complete abjection, Janey claims that it is 'my ugliness, my lack of femininity, my wounded body, earned minute by minute that is all that is left to speak' (BG, 139).

Thus, in her novels—or 'prose assemblages', as Larry McCaffery calls them—Acker's shifting voices echo the varying myths that constitute women's desires.[52] As Sciolino observes, these 'narratives of being' comprehensively 'inform the speaking subject even as she speaks', or in Janey's case as she writes.[53] Acker continues this project of deconstructing narratives that constitute female identity in her later works, *Don Quixote* (1986) and *Great Expectations* (1982). These novels, as their titles suggest, increase the degree of intertextual resourcefulness demonstrated already by her first works in order to enhance Acker's critique of the universal (male) humanist subject at the heart of Western canonical literature. The character Don Quixote, for example, engages with the social world at the cost of internalizing patriarchal discourse: 'BEING BORN INTO AND PART OF A MALE WORLD, SHE HAD NO SPEECH OF HER OWN. ALL SHE COULD DO WAS READ MALE TEXTS WHICH WEREN'T HERS'.[54] Commenting on her own writerly strategies, Acker notes how her initial solution to the difficulty of establishing a language of her own was to run 'into the language of others'.[55] Gesturing here towards her technique of what Sciolino calls '(auto)plagiarism' (placing others writers' works next to passages of autofiction, in this case versions of a fictitious authorial 'autobiography'), Acker's 1980s fiction often takes its starting point from other texts. Acker interweaves pre-existing texts into her own, borrows and modifies characters from classical myth, popular culture, and the political sphere. She places passages pirated from the literary canon next to snippets of contemporary journalese, advertising jargon, pornography, and lyrics. Acker modifies Ezra Pound's dictum 'MAKE IT NEW'[56] by juxtaposing already

[52] Larry McCaffery, 'The Path of Abjection', p. 14.

[53] Martina Sciolino, 'Kathy Acker', p. 439.

[54] Kathy Acker, *Don Quixote: Which Was a Dream* (London: Paladin, 1986), p. 58.

[55] Kathy Acker, 'Seeing Gender' in Acker, *Bodies of Work*, p. 161.

[56] Pound's invocation influenced the poet Robert Kelly, whom Acker knew when she lived in New York in the early 1960s. She remembers him painting Pound's dictum on stones and walls around the city. See Acker, 'A Few Notes on Two of My Books', p. 33.

extant texts in order to reveal something hitherto concealed within them. In response to criticism regarding the degree of violence portrayed in her fiction, for example, Acker comments: 'I make up nothing: I am a reader and take notes on what I read'.[57]

In a 1996 interview with Larry McCaffery, Acker claims that the period from *Great Expectations* to *Empire of the Senseless* (1988) constituted for her a time of increased deconstructive experimentation, that is 'taking texts and trying to see what they were really saying in a social, political and sexual context'.[58] Thus, in contrast to the Black Mountain poets (Acker studied with David Antin when she was in her early twenties) and Robert Creeley, in particular, Acker did not in the end subscribe to the tenet that 'a writer, a poet, is a real writer when he (or she) finds his own voice'.[59] Her motivation at this time was to 'see how texts that had already established themselves within our societal matrix worked or I wanted to destroy them, [...] I was tearing things apart'.[60] And yet in the same interview, Acker observes that during the process of writing *Don Quixote*, at the point of the narrative where she, like Helen Walsh twenty years later, engages with Andrea Dworkin's view that 'men are totally evil and responsible for all the shit that's ever existed in the world', she realized that the book was indeed about 'appropriating male texts and about trying to find your voice as a woman'.[61] Acker stresses, however, that her initial impulse had been to select and copy a book 'for no reason'.[62] Martina Sciolino contends that:

> Acker's (auto)plagiaristic technique foregrounds issues that are crucial to critical theory. One debate [...] attends the conflict between the deconstruction of the humanist subject (which demystifies authority as functional and fictive rather than absolute and essential) and the power of utterance desired by new subjects of history.[63]

In *Great Expectations*, Acker draws on the tropes of autonomy and dependence from Dickens's classic nineteenth-century tale, gendering these by having the decentralized central protagonist, Philip/Peter Pirrip, shift between genders uncommented upon. The name implies a male identity, but this is never explicitly acknowledged. Peter comments on strangers mistaking his/her mother for a sister, suggesting that he/she possesses female attributes (GE, 174). Moments of sexual attraction between Peter and other characters remain equally ambiguous. At some point, he/she/I refers to his/her 'cock' (GE, 182), but also registers an interest in sleeping with both men and women (GE, 178); this sexual ambiguity undergirds the uncertainty of Peter's gender. The text increases this ambiguity by shifting between focalized voices and narrators while moving between registers and source texts (from Dickens's *Great Expectations* to the novels of Pierre Guyotat to Keats). In the war scene at the beginning of the text (taken from Guyotat), the narrator comments: '...the passing wind immediately modulates the least organic noise that's why one text must subvert (the meaning of) another text until there's only

---

[57] Ibid., p. 36.   [58] Larry McCaffery, 'The Path of Abjection', p. 28.
[59] Kathy Acker, 'A Few Notes on Two of My Books', p. 33.
[60] Larry McCaffery, 'The Path of Abjection', p. 29.   [61] Ibid.   [62] Ibid.
[63] Sciolino, 'Kathy Acker', p. 442.

background music like reggae: the inextricability of relation-textures the organic (not meaning) recovered [.]' (GE, 177) While the notion of subversion, both political and textual, is an important one for Acker, it is a means to an end. Her project appears to be to reveal the 'inextricability of relation-textures', i.e. a multiple, non-hierarchical and rhizomatic nexus of machinic connections in a Deleuzian sense. By this I mean that Acker's model of self is not restricted to a single entity, but envisages an ultimately opaque being whose only knowable element is its place in a network of intersubjective dependencies and desires akin to Butler's model elaborated upon in the previous chapter.

Deleuze and Guattari's rhizome functions as an alternative model to what they call the classical hierarchical and binary model of thinking, which locates an origin—the root of a tree—at the beginning of all conceptual structures. A rhizome, on the other hand, 'ceaselessly establishes connections', much like a subterranean network of tubers or bulbs.[64] Acker's image of perpetual organic and textual modulation above resonates with Deleuze and Guattari's conception of a rhizome with 'no beginning or end'. Instead, it is:

> always in the middle, between things, interbeing, *intermezzo*. The tree is filiation, but the rhizome is alliance, uniquely alliance. The tree imposes the verb 'to be', but the fabric of the rhizome is the conjunction, 'and…and…and…'. This conjunction carries enough force to shake and uproot the verb 'to be'.[65]

The rhizome and indeed Acker's inextricable relation-textures resist assignment to conventional categories of value, i.e. 'good' or 'bad'. Much like the philosophers' desiring machines, the connections established by the machines or rhizomes are impersonal. This is why Acker refers to that which is 'recovered' through, in her case, the process of textual subversion as 'not meaning': for Deleuze and Guattari, the organizations formed through rhizomatic connections (be they social or political) attempt to 're-stratify', to attribute meaning retrospectively to those connections. However, '[g]ood and bad are only the products of an active and temporary selection, which must be renewed'.[66] As Colebrook notes, Deleuze and Guattari insist on an 'expanded point of view that sees all values as effects of the flow of life'.[67]

Empire of the Senseless seeks to locate a place beyond the binary of good and evil, beyond hell and utopia. The novel provides 'hints of a possibility or beginning: the body, the actual flesh, almost wordless.'[68] While continuing Acker's project to 'deconstruct, to take apart perceptual habits, to reveal the frauds on which our society's living', the work also connotes her 'first attempt' to 'find somewhere to go, a belief, a myth'.[69] The author describes the three sections of this text as functioning dialectically: in the first, 'Elegy for the World of the Fathers', she draws on Freud and the Marquis de Sade in order to describe a society 'defined by the oedipal

---

[64] Gilles Deleuze and Félix Guattari, *A Thousand Plateaus: Capitalism and Schizophrenia*, trans. by Brian Massumi (London: Continuum, 2004), p. 8.
[65] Ibid., p. 27. Original emphasis.   [66] Ibid., p. 10.
[67] Claire Colebrook, *Gilles Deleuze*, p. 96.
[68] Kathy Acker, 'A Few Notes on Two of My Books', p. 36.   [69] Ibid., p. 35.

taboo'.[70] There are loosely divided sections marked 'Thivai speaks' or 'Abhor speaks' (the two central protagonists, Abhor, female, 'part robot and part black'[71] and Thivai, male, pirate and drug addict). However, many other voices crowd into those sections and, most interestingly, Abhor's first section, entitled 'Rape by the Father', is recounted by Thivai, providing an interpretive frame for the first-person perspective of Abhor's original account. In the following section, located after the description of Abhor's rape by her father (a recurrent trope throughout Acker's fiction that provides the author's gloss on the oedipal dynamic), a narrator breaks in with the following polemic:

> The German Romantics had to destroy the same bastions as we do. Logocentricism and idealism, theology, all supports of the repressive society. Property's pillars. Reason which always homogenizes and reduces, represses and unifies phenomena or actuality into what can be perceived and so controlled. The subjects, us, are now stable and socializable. Reason is always in the service of the political and economic masters. It is here that literature strikes, at this base, where the concepts and actings of order impose themselves. Literature is that which denounces and slashes apart the repressing machine at the level of the signified. Well before Bataille, Kleist, Hoffman etc., made trial of Hegelian idealism, of the cloturing dialectic of recognition: the German Romantics sung brazenly brassily in brass of spending and waste [...] They tore the subject away from her subjugation to her self, the proper; dislocated you the puppet; cut the threads of meaning; spit at all mirrors which control.   (ES, 12)

Due to the general and deliberate unreliability of voice in Acker's fiction, the reader is at first wary of taking the narrator's outburst at face value. However, the passage might nevertheless function as an analogy for the author's own literary strategies, which, here, she places on a continuum with those of the German Romantics: her prose, for example, disturbs narrative linearity, perpetually juxtaposes logical and illogical statements and revels in ironic self-contradiction and word-play. The pointed employment of the feminine possessive pronoun in relation to the 'subject' further-more makes gender a visible aspect of this critique of logocentrism, activating not only poststructuralist but also feminist discourse. Indeed, following this passage, the female voice (Abhor's) is no longer transmitted through a male's (Thivai's), but is returned 'from her subjugation to her self' by narrating directly, without medi-ation or frame, in the first person.

Thus, this passage foreshadows the second part of the fiction, 'Alone', in which Acker seeks to describe a society not founded on the oedipal myth, that is, on 'phallic centricity and total domination on the political, economic, social and personal levels'.[72] Noting that for Westerners today, the 'other is now Muslim', Acker constructs an Algerian invasion of Paris.[73] Yet she discovered that 'it is impossible to have, to live in a hypothetical, not utopian but perhaps freer, society if one does not actually inhabit such a world. [...] The body does not lie. Language, if it is not

---

[70] Ibid.
[71] Kathy Acker, *Empire of the Senseless* (London: Pan, 1988), p. 3. All subsequent references will be marked within the text as ES.
[72] Kathy Acker, 'A Few Notes on Two of My Books', p. 35.   [73] Ibid.

propaganda or media blab, is the body'.[74] From this observation, Acker concludes that the conceptualization of any kind of utopia to counter, in this case, 'American postcapitalism' must perforce be a lie.[75] For, the 'body is real: if one, anyone lives in hell, one is hell. Dualisms such as good/evil are not real and only reality works'.[76]

Acker's interest in material bodies should not, however, be confused with the notion of *écriture féminine*, although the work of Cixous, in particular, was greatly influential on her work. In the essay 'Seeing Gender' Acker observes: 'I am looking for the body, my body, which exists outside its patriarchal definitions. Of course, this is not possible. But who is any longer interested in the possible?'[77] While she claims to be unable to 'separate language body and identity'[78] Acker does not subscribe to the notion of the body's essential and irreducible materiality. In 'Seeing Gender', Acker sides with Judith Butler against Irigaray's claim that, in Acker's terminology, 'men see differently than women'. Instead, Acker asks 'whether or not the body is and is only material'. She cites Butler: '*If the body signified as prior to signification is an effect of signification, then the mimetic or representational status of language, which claims that signs follow bodies as their necessary mirrors, is not mimetic at all.*'[79] If language is not mimetic, continues Acker, then 'the body, as Butler argues, might not be co-equivalent with materiality'. Instead, Acker suspects 'that my body might be deeply connected to, if not be, language'.[80] She continues:

> But what is this language? This language which is not constructed on hierarchical subject-object relations?
>
> When I dream, my body is the site, not only of the dream, but also of the dreaming and the dreamer. In other words, in this case, or in this language, I cannot separate subject from object, much less from the acts of perception.
>
> I call these languages, *languages of the body*.
>
> There are, I suspect, a plurality or more of such languages.[81]

Through its plurality of voice, Acker's fiction juxtaposes many of these languages in her multitudinous textual choirs. She draws on a fictionalized version of herself and texts from a wide variety of sources, both conventionally 'literary' and non-literary or popular. Sciolino notes that:

> Due to the simultaneity of plagiarism/autoplagiarism in Acker's fiction, identity is plastic. It mutates in Acker's innovative characterizations; gender is often, finally, in indeterminate relationship with identity. Moreover, both identity and gender are social constructions, works-in-progress whose very indeterminacy enables a politically motivated interruption.[82]

Acker is often considered to desire the deconstruction of the subject per se. Yet her work nevertheless reveals an interest in a model of subjectivity that while not in

---

[74] Ibid. [75] Ibid., p. 36. [76] Ibid.

[77] Kathy Acker, 'Seeing Gender' in Acker, *Bodies of Work*, p. 166. [78] Ibid., p. 167.

[79] Judith Butler, 'Bodies that Matter', in *Engaging with Irigaray*, ed. by Carolyn Burke, Naomi Shor, and Margaret Whitford (New York: Columbia University Press, 1994), p. 144. Cited in Kathy Acker, 'Seeing Gender' in Kathy Acker, *Bodies of Work*, p. 160. Original italics.

[80] Kathy Acker, 'Seeing Gender' in Kathy Acker, *Bodies of Work*, p. 166.

[81] Ibid., pp. 166–7. Original italics. [82] Martina Sciolino, 'Kathy Acker', p. 441.

any way traditionally humanist is also not entirely deconstructed. What emerges is a model of selfhood that is relational and contingent, which demonstrates the 'inextricability of relation-textures' (GE, 177). This subject is a being-in-process, and necessarily unstable, as it 'coexists in narrative relations to other subjects'.[83] Despite her aesthetic strategies designed to destabilize readerly identification with unified protagonists, Acker compels the reader to work hard to generate a narrative relation with a multiplicity of inextricably linked subjects. Indeed, Acker's texts resonate with the cacophony of multiple, shifting voices, with characters who blend seamlessly into others, swap gender, disappear and then reappear within the diegesis. The blurring of any sharply defined contours of character, plot, and voice result in narratives that are animated by the 'change' and 'rhythm' of a nexus of desiring, moving subjects.[84] It also gestures towards Acker's refusal to privilege a single, unified mode of being: the self becomes the world and all is indeed 'real'.

SHAPING ETHICAL NARRATIVES
WITH MARY GAITSKILL

In 1994 Mary Gaitskill's essay 'On not being a Victim: Sex, Rape, and the Trouble with Following the Rules' was published in the March issue of *Harper's Magazine*. Journalist Emily Nussbaum was to contend over a decade later that the essay exemplified Gaitskill's independent feminist view-point, characterizing her as a 'fiction writer unafraid to walk straight through the feminist battlefields of that very strange period, when debates over "victimology" and date rape dominated the landscape'.[85] Nussbaum places Gaitskill's essay on a conceptual continuum with the author's first collection of short stories, *bad behavior* (1988), which Nussbaum claims became a 'dorm-room bible' for her peers upon publication.[86] For those and other readers, Gaitskill's appeal lies not only in the simultaneously lyrical and acerbic quality of her prose, but in her morally ambivalent voice, her resistance to casting judgment upon the host of socially and psychologically dysfunctional characters populating her short stories: drug addicts, philanderers, prostitutes and their 'johns', neurotics, masochists, and sadists. These characters are depicted in the process of establishing or modifying their own internal ethical framework, or avoiding doing so; furthermore, the narratives themselves often focus on situations in which characters cast judgment upon the actions of others or themselves, even when the stories do not.

The author's interest in exploring the formless zone between moral absolutes in her fiction is recognizable in the aforementioned 1994 essay, in which she refuses to side either with feminists advocating stricter legal measures to prevent sexually motivated crimes against women or their critics, Camille Paglia and Katie Roiphe,

---

[83] Ibid., p. 443.   [84] Kathy Acker, 'Preface' in Kathy Acker, *Bodies of Work*, p. ix.

[85] Emily Nussbaum, 'Mary, Mary, Less Contrary', *New York Magazine*, 6 November 2005 <http://nymag.com/nymetro/arts/books/14988/> [accessed 13.03.2013].

[86] Ibid.

in particular. Gaitskill takes the latter authors to task for what she considers to be their absolutist stance, which Gaitskill equates with the drive of other feminists to legislate to protect women. Gaitskill notes that for postfeminists such as Paglia and Roiphe women who make themselves vulnerable to attack by placing themselves in precarious situations display a hardly credible ignorance, perpetuating thereby a damaging 'myth of false innocence'.[87] Gaitskill takes issue with the implicit assumption that 'everyone except idiots interprets information and experience in the same way. In that sense, they are not so different in attitude from those ladies dedicated to establishing feminist-based rules and regulations for sex. Such rules [...] assume a certain psychological uniformity of experience, a right way'.[88]

Gaitskill's fiction, on the other hand, acknowledges and explores the pluralistic nature of subjective responses to experience. Her narratives demur from locating achievement for her characters in acts or behaviours that conform to conventional and externally imposed criteria for success; instead, the narratives frequently foreground the moment when characters either take (or abdicate from) responsibility for their actions, thoughts and feelings, whatever they might be. Described by Matthew Sharpe as 'open systems', Gaitskill's narratives display fascination with the internal process of ethical reflection, but suspend any moral judgment of characters, a strategy which furthermore compels the reader to establish—and take responsibility for—their own responses to the text.[89] Much in line with Deleuzian ethics, Gaitskill seeks to reset the dualistic moral framework by gesturing towards an ethical system where 'we create and select those powers that expand life as a whole, beyond our limited perspectives'.[90] This comment resonates with my argument in Chapter 1 concerning the potentially expansive intersubjective encounter experienced by the reader of literary fiction. As I argued there, narrative provides the reader with the opportunity to consider her own subjectivity, testing the boundaries of self against those of another, permitting those boundaries to be modified through exposure to critique, and remaining critically and empathically engaged when she encounters intractable alterity.

In a 2009 interview, Gaitskill contended that '[m]ost of us have not been taught how to be responsible for our thoughts and feelings. I see this strongly in the widespread tendency to read books and stories as if they exist to confirm how we are supposed to be, think, and feel'.[91] Particularly troubling for the author is the manner in which people are 'brought up believing that to be responsible is to obey certain rules', resulting in an abdication of responsibility for the layout of their own ethical compass. Among the implicit social rules Gaitskill mentions in her 1994 essay are those that regulated her behaviour as a girl growing up in the 1960s: 'that good girls never had sex and bad girls did'. These were superseded by

---

[87] Mary Gaitskill, 'On Not Being a Victim: Sex, Rape, and the Trouble with Following the Rules', *Harper's Magazine*, March (1994), p. 38.

[88] Ibid.

[89] Matthew Sharpe, 'Interview with Mary Gaitskill', *Bombsite*, Spring 2009 <http://bombsite. com/issues/107/articles/3265> [accessed 14.03.2013].

[90] Claire Colebrook, *Gilles Deleuze*, p. 96.

[91] Matthew Sharpe, 'Interview with Mary Gaitskill'.

the less clear rules of 'cultural trend and peer example', which prescribed that to be 'cool' one should engage in intense sexual activity with multiple partners.[92] Gaitskill links this lack of opportunity to establish the layout of her own sexual landscape including her own sexual preferences, fantasies, and desires with an event she classifies as 'acquaintance rape'.[93]

It is not surprising, then, that Gaitskill's narrative strategy is designed to compel the reader to confront their own responses, often by thematizing experiences, behaviours and issues deemed taboo, sexually transgressive and beyond the pale of conventional social parameters. In relation to her portrayal of female characters, in particular, this strategy has elicited fierce debate among social commentators and feminists alike. The critic, James Wolcott, for example, notoriously stated that Gaitskill's female characters in *bad behavior* were 'dishrags and dickwipes, cold little biscuits slapped across Daddy's lap'.[94] Wolcott's troubling statement suggests disapproval of Gaitskill's depiction of submissive female characters and her failure to provide more positive female role models, implying in turn a set of rigid assumptions about the moral function of literature.

However, in a 1990 interview, Gaitskill questioned the validity of criticizing any literary work according to set of notional moral criteria, arguing that it is not 'morally wrong to create images of women in victimized or submissive roles'.[95] She stresses, however, that this 'doesn't mean that I'm insensitive to the type of pain that women suffer in this society. I think this is a very sexist society, a society in which women have suffered a great deal. Not just women personally, but a society in which a female spirit is not respected.'[96] Nevertheless, Gaitskill, like Acker, is uninterested in what she calls the 'artificial treatment of women's pain' in 'instructional didactic writing', by which she means depictions in which 'women are shown as being [...] Nautilus-machine strong, which is a type of strong that doesn't interest me because it's a strength disconnected from vulnerability and weakness'. In Gaitskill's view, strength that does not take vulnerability into account merely connotes a 'dislocated posturing which makes it possible to despise the vulnerability of others'.[97] Much like Acker's interest in following the consequences of female desire to painful as well as ecstatic conclusions,[98] Gaitskill's focus lies upon expressing experience in all its self-contradictory complexity, upon portraying the simultaneity of both the 'exalted' and the 'agonized face'.[99] It is through the

---

[92] Mary Gaitskill, 'On Not Being a Victim', p. 36.   [93] Ibid., p. 35.

[94] James Wolcott, cited in Emily Nussbaum, 'Mary, Mary, Less Contrary'.

[95] Stephen Westfall, 'Interview with Mary Gaitskill', *Bombsite*, Winter 1990 <http://bombsite.com/issues/30/articles/1290> [accessed 15.03.2013].

[96] Ibid. Gaitskill's reference to the 'female spirit' is surprisingly esoteric and at odds with the tone and materialism of her early fiction. However, later interviews, as well as her most recent collection of short stories, suggest a growing mythologizing tendency in the author's thinking, which pertains most frequently to notions of gender.

[97] Ibid.

[98] See Kathy Acker, *Great Expectations* in Acker, *Blood and Guts in High School: Plus Two*, p. 211. The 'mistake is believing that indulgence in desire a decision to follow desire isn't possibly painful'.

[99] Mary Gaitskill, 'The Agonized Face', in Gaitskill, *Don't Cry: Stories* (New York: Vintage Books, 2009), p. 57. All further references to this story given in the text as AF.

attempt to understand their own motivations in nuanced ways that take account of ambiguity and contradiction that Gaitskill's characters claim agency. For the author, agency does not reside in external expressions of strength, or in the act of critique alone; agency is predicated upon the attempt to understand why subjects take certain courses of action.

In its subtle and ambiguous negotiations of consciousness in all its self-contradiction, Gaitskill's fiction exemplifies the value of literature for the exploration of agency. Indeed, her preoccupation with the notion of simultaneous, discordant and multifaceted experience and the possibility of its coherent expression informs the author's recurring interest, both aesthetic and thematic, in the question of form and formlessness. Predominantly a writer of short stories, Gaitskill has also written two novels. This branching out makes sense when viewed in conjunction with the author's increasing interest, post *bad behavior*, in finding the most plausible linguistic and literary forms for expressing the inexpressibility of consciousness. In her attempt to render ontological experience in language, the author develops a repertoire of metaphors, analogies, imagery and voices that exemplify the very same strategies her characters use in their attempts to understand their own thoughts, feelings, and behaviour; both the author and her characters thus seek not only to open the 'door to the place where the huge things are' on a thematic level but to provide these formless 'things' with a tangible linguistic form.[100] At the same time, Gaitskill appears to revel in the difficulty of this process and the often tantalizing impreciseness of its results, for it is the process—the attempt—that ultimately holds significance.

Already in *bad behavior*, Gaitskill edges towards a language steeped in spatial metaphor, in images of interiors and exteriors and the construction and/or transgression of intangible boundaries between subjectivities. In the story 'Secretary', Gaitskill characterizes the relationship between Debby, the story's first-person narrator, and 'the lawyer', her employer, by means of a complex layering of spatial metaphors that gesture towards the oscillating power dynamic between the two. Upon their first meeting, Debby experiences an immediate loss of boundary integrity, the lawyer's handshake inducing the sensation that 'he could have put his hand through my rib cage, grabbed my heart, squeezed it a little to see how it felt, then let go'.[101] Debby's sudden sense of the permeability of her psychological boundaries contradicts her image of herself as 'closed up [...] like a wall' (S, 138), a perception shared by the lawyer and her family. Indeed, Debby enjoys 'feeling him impose his brainlessly confident sense of existence' on her. 'He would say, "Type this letter," and my sensibility would contract until the abstractions of achievement and production found expression in the typing of the letter. I was useful.' (S, 140) When the lawyer begins to find fault with Debby's typing, however, his encroachment upon her 'sensibility' becomes more sinister, an 'intimate

---

[100] Mary Gaitskill, *Veronica* (London: Serpent's Tail, 2007), p. 85. References to this novel will be made within the text as V.

[101] Mary Gaitskill, 'Secretary', in Mary Gaitskill, *bad behavior* (London: Hodder & Stoughton, 1989), p. 138. All other references to the story will be given within the text as S.

tendril creeping from one of his darker areas' (S, 141). His sudden desire to talk to her sympathetically about her 'problems' provokes a mixed response: 'it seemed, on the one hand, that this lawyer was just an asshole. On the other, his comments were weirdly moving, and had the effect of making me feel horribly sensitive. No one had ever made such personal comments to me before.' (S, 142) The novel intimacy of this exchange causes Debby to feel unusually exposed, affecting her response to the events subsequent to her next typing error, when the lawyer commands her to bend over the table to be spanked while she reads the letter out loud.

Conflicting emotions characterize Debby's response to this encounter: on the one hand, she appears passively accepting, unsurprised and numb, experiencing later an increased 'distance' from her family (S, 144). On the other, the memory of the event subsequently excites her sexually, forming the material of her sexual fantasies and recurrent sentimental dreams, in which she and the lawyer share intimate moments of mutual understanding while walking through poppy fields holding hands. Equally, when Debby decides not to return to work, she experiences relief, but also disappointment that the lawyer does not contact her. Furthermore, while Debby's acceptance of the spanking appears to be an extension of the pleasure she experienced when allowing her 'domineering' (S, 145) employer to impose his 'strong personality' (S, 142) on her, Gaitskill provides Debby with an important moment of reflection during which she internally debates her options; this passage suggests that this imposition is happening by choice: 'I thought, I don't have to do this. I can stop right now. I can straighten up and walk out. But I didn't. I pulled up my skirt.' (S, 145) While it is possible to construe Debby's decision as forced, as an action carried out under coercion or as a result of mental instability (Debby's history of mental illness is alluded to several times), what is really at stake in this passage is Gaitskill's representation of Debby's process of active conscious reflection. Gaitskill retrospectively provides Debby with a moment when she imagined an alternative course of action. Moreover, the repetition and syntactical placement of the subject pronoun 'I' emphasizes Debby's status as agent linguistically, implying that she at least does not abnegate responsibility for her subsequent actions.

Gaitskill resists the temptation to portray both characters—but especially Debby—in the clear-cut roles of victim and abuser, of exploiter and exploited, by depicting the self-contradictory and simultaneous multiplicity of Debby's responses both to her own and the lawyer's behaviour. Indeed, these highly stylized sexual encounters, in which Debby and the lawyer perform submissive and dominant roles respectively, appear to provide Debby with a sense of a structure in which an aspect of her being she had hitherto been unable to conceptualize can be both contained and expressed. Significantly, the structure is provided in the form of language. While being spanked, she observes: '[t]he word "humiliation" came into my mind with such force that it effectively blocked out all other words. Further, I felt that the concept it stood for had actually been a major force in my life for quite a while.' (S, 143) In this passage, Gaitskill portrays a situation in which a ritualized physical act triggers a linguistic response that provides shape to a hitherto incoherent and impenetrable aspect of Debby's subjective landscape. In this way, the pejorative concept, 'humiliation', is reconceived as part of a process of self-realization that functions as a potentially positive force.

Debby's part in her own sexual humiliation and punishment for perceived 'bad behaviour' constitutes both an attempt to attain a type of intimacy she is unable to gain in her family life and provides a tangible and controlled outlet for hitherto intangible emotions, freeing up her psyche for the contemplation of other aspects of her life. As a result, her feelings towards her family shift subsequent to her encounters with the lawyer. Debby's only memory of family intimacy is an event from when she was ten years old, during which her sister placed a coat around her shoulders when she was cold. However, listening to her family 'clumsily trying to organize itself for the day' from her bed after leaving her place of employment no longer induces 'irrational loathing', but 'despair and longing for them' (S, 147). This moment, while distressing, also connotes a long-denied acknowledgement of her emotional needs—for intimacy, in particular—and confrontation with her fears that this is unachievable.

The story's denouement subverts readerly expectations that Debby will feel sullied or exploited by her encounters with the lawyer by depicting her cheerful acceptance of a financial pay-off from him; the money will go towards a deposit on an apartment: 'I didn't feel like a whore or anything. I felt I was doing the right thing. I looked at the total figure of my balance with satisfaction' (S, 149). Indeed, the only occasion on which Debby feels 'uncomplicated disgust' (S, 149) for the lawyer is upon hearing he is running for mayor in Westfield, which Debby feels is an inferior town full of 'malls and doughnut stands' (S, 149). When she is approached by a journalist investigating accusations of sexual harassment against the lawyer, Debby does not talk. This moment is, however, deliberately ambiguous: Debby's 'I can't talk now' might suggest that she will at a later date; or it may evidence a conclusive unwillingness to provide damaging information about someone who remains at the centre of her sexual fantasies. Equally, Debby's descent into a seemingly dissociated yet highly self-aware state immediately after the phone call may connote a psychological break-down, or it may be Debby's attempt to express, using language she is familiar with from psychological assessments, the sensations involved in becoming self-aware, for self-awareness, after all, requires an element of 'being outside yourself' (S, 150). Debby's feeling that she is somehow outside her own body looking in at herself contrasts with the initial description of her as a hermetically sealed, impenetrable unit. Her assertion that 'it wasn't such a bad feeling after all' (S, 150) strikes a similarly optimistic note that further complicates the story's conclusion, leaving the reader with the task of navigating their own way through the complexity of Debby's thoughts, feelings, and actions.

In her first novel, *Two Girls, Fat and Thin* (1991), Gaitskill continues to employ the trope of sexual transgression and trauma as a means of exploring power, subjectivity, and agency. The novel focuses on the lives of Dorothy Footie (who renames herself Dorothy Never) and Justine Shade, central protagonists and dual focalizers. Their meeting and gradual friendship in the present tense constitute the framing narrative; flashbacks provide an account of their childhoods and, in particular, their experiences of being sexually abused. The novel's scope thus ranges from the 1960s to the 1990s, the novel form allowing for the construction of a more finely-drawn socio-cultural background than Gaitskill's short stories allow. The plot device of Dorothy's involvement in the 'Definitist' movement and her time working with the author and conservative political theorist Anna Granite (based on real-life author and founder of the politically influential Objectivist movement, Ayn Rand) allows the author to comment upon the political shift to the right and the rise of neoliberal individualism reaching its culmination, at least within Gaitskill's novel, in Reagan-era America. As Justine comments in the article she writes on Anna Granite: 'This cultural utopia of greed, expressed in gentrification and the slashing of social programs, has had its spokesperson and prophet for the last fifty years, a novelist whose books are American fantasies that mirror, in all its neurotic excess, the frantic twist to the right we are now experiencing.'[102] In this novel, sex reflects wider power dynamics in contemporaneous US politics and the economy. As William Deresiewicz notes of the period when Gaitskill wrote *Two Girls*:

> Sadomasochism became the master metaphor for human relations in the Ayn Randian dystopia of Reagan's America, a landscape of domination and persecution, littered with the broken and the homeless, where the ideology is winner-take-all and the only rule is fuck or be fucked. Sex, like everything else, was now about power.[103]

Dorothy's sections are narrated in the first person, Justine's in the third by a sympathetic, if slightly acerbic, narrator. This strategy functions to avoid confusion between the two voices as well as to privilege Dorothy's voice over Justine's. Gaitskill uses a similar technique of dual central protagonists in her second novel, *Veronica*, published in 2005. The titular Veronica Ross remains, however, a character without a direct voice as she is viewed through the eyes of the ex-model Alison Owen, who narrates the entire novel in the first person. Veronica nevertheless functions as a pivotal force in the novel, a stable, totemic figure against which Alison narrates in flashback the trajectory of her life, from her late adolescence when she was an egotistical super model to the last, meditative stage of her life, when she is alone and suffering from Hepatitis C. Both novels foreground their protagonists' search for adequate external formal structures that might contain and give shape to the 'sickening boundlessness' of their traumatized and/or dysfunctional interiorities (TG, 160).

　　While *Two Girls* provides a critique of the webs of familial silence and complicity that sustain the sexual abuse of children, the novel's main focus is the discontinuities and continuities between Dorothy and Justine's manner of dealing with the trauma of their childhoods. The novel can be read productively in conjunction with Lynne Layton's thoughts on traumatic fragmentation: the early transgression of the protagonists' physical and psychological boundaries results in both characters

---

[102] Mary Gaitskill, *Two Girls, Fat and Thin: A Novel* (London: Chatto & Windus, 1991), p. 288. All subsequent references will be marked within the text as TG.

[103] William Deresiewicz, 'When the Whip Comes Down: On Mary Gaitskill', *The Nation*, 11 May 2009 <http://www.thenation.com/article/when-whip-comes-down-mary-gaitskill?page=0,1> [accessed 11.07.2013].

experiencing themselves as both corporeally and psychologically boundary-less and seeking ways to compensate for their fragmentary psychological states. Justine and Dorothy's employment of spatial metaphors (often connected with the body) to capture ontological experience reveals the difficulties they encounter in relating intersubjectively and foregrounds the body as a site of psychological struggle to define or protect abstract boundaries. Justine's description of being repeatedly molested by a trusted family friend when she was five characterizes her understanding of the event as a violation of boundaries from which she has never recovered: 'this uncomprehended attack of invasive sensation had not felt like pleasure at all but rather like the long claws of some unknown aggression that had gripped her organs and her bones and never quite let go' (TG, 59). Dorothy's father's bullying behaviour had already induced the ability in Dorothy to 'divide' herself, 'a part of my mind separating from my body like a cartoon character' (TG, 119–20) and insulating the air around herself with 'numbness' (TG, 119). When he begins visiting her in bed at night, his fingers become 'hard implements inside my body' and 'with each visit my body seemed less mine and more his' (TG, 127). As she becomes older, Dorothy builds up a physical wall of flesh to function as an *Ersatz* for her psychological boundary-less-ness; while this makes her feel 'corporeally real' at times, she still feels as if her 'body had been turned inside out' (TG, 161). In fact, Dorothy feels entirely detached from her body, as if she were 'locked out', her consciousness merely a 'disembodied set of impulses and electric discharges, disconnected rage and fear' (TG, 162). Justine, the 'thin' girl of the title, instead winds a 'magic cloak' of 'aloneness' around herself as a form of protection (TG, 158). But when she thinks about the abuse, or about her own burgeoning sexuality, she feels her 'exposed pelvis constricted like an animal in a trap' (TG, 144). As Dorothy contends, ' "the body remembers everything" ' (TG, 44), leading her to live her adult life as a nocturnal, celibate recluse and Justine to engage in humiliating affairs with sadistic men.

One such affair, with the art director Bryan, allows Justine the opportunity to act out one side of her 'separated selves' (TG, 200), namely the side that, like Debby in 'Secretary', finds logical comfort in humiliation and cruelty. At one point, she contends that being humiliated makes her feel 'absolutely herself' (TG, 156). In a sadomasochistic mockery of the desire emanating from her other self for intimacy and 'human warmth' (TG, 199), Bryan and Justine have impersonal and cruel sex, 'touching as little as possible' (TG, 282). Bryan's descriptions and acts of sexual humiliation inflicted upon Justine cause the 'furniture of her internal self' to smash, make her feel 'split apart and boundary-less', her 'cunt and her heart utterly apart' (TG, 283). Images of fragmentation abound in the descriptions of Justine's sexual encounters, as if her response to that initial violation of her boundaries as a child were to walk further towards the 'eye of the storm' (TG, 282). Justine believes this kind of sex opens her up in a way she has no control over, functioning to dismantle the cloak of self-protection she is unable to shed herself (TG, 36–7).

Dorothy, on the other hand, seeks out definite structures with which to make her interior and exterior worlds cohere. She is drawn to the Definitist movement meetings as a young woman and works with Granite and the group's inner-circle; this earlier involvement brings about her meeting with Justine, who is writing a journalistic retrospective on the movement and its demise. For the younger Dorothy, still traumatized by the abuse she suffered, Anna Granite's appeal lay in the reassuring objectivity evoked by her name:

> She said reality was definable—no one was saying that in the sixties. She said you were important in reality, that you could control it. She was the first person to tell me I was important and that I could come out and say so [...] In school everything was disconnected, you were never supposed to discover the way things interlocked [...]. Evil comes from denying reality.   (TG, 32)

Through the concept of Definitism, Dorothy seeks to construct a comprehensive template of objective reality that will provide shape to the amorphous mass of subjective chaos constituting her inner life, allowing her to gain a sense of agency and moral clarity. While Dorothy's coping mechanism is to live according to rigid grids of moral absolutes (evoked by her adopted speaking name, Never), Justine Shade is drawn towards self-imposed disintegration, an equally dangerous, absolutist strategy; dark, masochistic sex allows her to leave her body and 'float away in empty air, turning somersaults in the contactless ease of space' (TG, 299). Importantly, Gaitskill portrays both characters' coping mechanisms as attempts to gain agency, albeit limited. Neither character is drawn as a passive victim, but as subjects seeking to discover some manner of claiming autonomy among the fragments of their damaged psyches. The final scene, when Dorothy intervenes in one of Justine's sadistic sexual encounters with Bryan, depicts a moment of mutual understanding between the two women, implying that each might provide a corrective to the other's extreme position. The novel's final tableau captures their embrace, which, to Dorothy, resembles a 'phrase of music', so perfect is the form their intertwined bodies make. The ending also suggests that Justine may not return to unsafe BDSM (bondage and discipline, sadism and masochism) relationships (without discounting the existence of safer ones) and that Dorothy may dismantle some of her self-protective yet self-isolating armour, implying conscious authorial emphasis upon the importance of intersubjective relations as a means of enhancing subject agency.

Intersubjective relations and their connection to selfhood and agency accrue greater ethical weight in Gaitskill's second collection, *Because they wanted to*, which was published in 1997 and confirmed the author's status as an important, if not prolific, literary voice. An air of bittersweet melancholy pervades the short stories as a whole; the protagonists are older, approaching middle-age, and frequently depicted reflecting on earlier periods of their lives and reassessing the actions and decisions of the past. Gaitskill maintains her focus on sexuality, sex, and personal responsibility as central motifs: in 'The Girl on the Plane', the central male character is compelled to reassess his role years before in the gang rape of a female friend at college, the father in 'Tiny, Smiling Daddy' confronts with regret and confusion his decision to cast his daughter out when she reveals her homosexuality; many stories deal with the role of fantasy in sex, asking whether role-play facilitates or prevents intimacy ('The Wrong Thing', 'The Dentist'), and enquiring after the relation between sadomasochistic sex and self-esteem and/or mental health ('Processing' and 'Stuff').

The collection's structure is noteworthy for its final cluster of four sequentially conceived stories gathered under the umbrella title 'The Wrong Thing'. The stories accompany Susan, a university lecturer and poet, through a series of affairs with a cocksure, immature younger man, a masochistic female partner turned dominant 'top' for the duration of their affair, and an older, male academic. The title is a reference to a line from T.S. Eliot's 'East Coker' section of *The Four Quartets*, the poem Susan's ex-lover, Erin, recites during the pivotal garden scene in the final story of Gaitskill's quartet. Like Eliot's composition, Gaitskill's stories each capture various lyrical moods: 'Turgor', 'Respect', 'Processing', and 'Stuff'. Linking these idiosyncratic and bathetic titles and the stories' provocative, distinctly urban subject matter with Eliot's spiritually meditative poem at first appears intended as an ironic comment on the irrelevance of such meditation in cynical postmodernity. In the stories themselves, moments of grandiloquent inner reflection are frequently undercut by juxtaposed moments of quotidian pragmatism, for example, when the clerk in the deli asks Susan how she is and she replies: ' "I have deep longings that will never be satisfied" ', the clerk frowns and asks: ' "Is it the weather that does that to you?" '[104] Further, immediately after Erin cites Eliot, one of her friends belches and the other asks: ' "Isn't Eliot that turd who made his wife think she was crazy?" ' (WT, 253). Nevertheless, the garden scene, in which Susan, Erin and their group of unconventional friends release ladybugs in the garden drops all pretence at ironic commentary and the relevance of Gaitskill's allusion to Eliot emerges:

> For a moment I felt I was in a limbo of shadows and half-formed shapes which would dissolve into nothingness if I touched them. I felt loneliness so strong it scared me. Then Jana laughed and Erin brushed by me, thoughtlessly caressing my spine with one hand. I was in a garden with my friends. I could not fully see what lay about me, but still, I knew it was there, abundant, breathing, and calm.   (WT, 254)

Susan, confronted with the 'terrible freedom of shapelessness' (V, 184), gains comfort from an awareness of her interconnection with others, her friends and the natural world around her. In fact, it is not awareness but rather faith in that interconnectedness: 'there is yet faith/But the faith and the love, and the hope are all in the waiting' (WT, 253).

This note of optimism, of faith in the redemptive potential of intersubjective connections, strikes a new note in Gaitskill's fiction. Whereas in *bad behavior* protagonists remain almost entirely stuck within the confines of their own consciousness, unable to connect with others, and in *Two Girls* the tentatively optimistic denouement remains ambiguous and brief, Gaitskill's later fiction adopts rather a Butlerian stance towards subject formation. On the one hand, this approach acknowledges the 'limits of self-knowledge', described by Gaitskill above as a

---

[104] 'The Wrong Thing', in Mary Gaitskill, *Because They Wanted To: Stories* (London: Picador, 1997), p. 191. All further page references will be included in the body of the text as WT.

'limbo of shadows and half-formed shapes'.[105] For, as Butler suggests, the subject emerges from a 'context of relations that become partially irrecoverable to conscious knowledge'.[106] On the other hand, the opacity of the self, the darkness and shadows of which Gaitskill writes, 'follows from our status as beings who are formed in relations of dependency'.[107]

Viewing the formation of selfhood in this light has consequences for agency. In the preceding discussion, I examined conceptualizations of agency in Acker and Gaitskill's fiction that included the act of critique from multi-vocal and/or fragmented positions of marginality, allowing the free-play of subjectivity; the subversion or transgression of discursive norms, especially those relating to sexuality; the mobilizing force of desire; and the accrual of an always incomplete and often ambiguous or self-contradictory reservoir of self-knowledge. In both authors' work, however, a further, inter-relational, model of agency emerges. In Acker's case, agency lies in the fluid movement of a multifaceted subject through the inextricable 'relation textures' of desire, body, language, world, other, and the elliptical string of 'and'. Gaitskill's model posits a subject perpetually negotiating who she is with other people and exploring her self—even if only momentarily—in the company of others who in some sense share themselves. This intersubjective dependency not only plays a role in subject formation and agency but also has implications for ethical action. This realization becomes a pivotal moment in Gaitskill's second novel *Veronica*. Alison gains insight into her own interior landscape only at the point when she acknowledges the similarities between her and Veronica. For Alison, this insight generates the potential for increasingly autonomous action through augmented self-awareness, echoing the dynamic between Justine and Dorothy in *Two Girls*.

Veronica becomes a meditation upon the various forms subjects impose upon feelings, thoughts and behaviours in an attempt to understand that which Butler argues must remain opaque and 'irrecoverable'. These forms might be productively conceived as identities. On the one hand, this pinning down of the contours of the self in the practice of identity performance connotes an attempt by Gaitskill's protagonists to augment an inevitably partial store of self-knowledge and increase their capacity for action. On the other, it possesses a social, communicative function. Alison, for example, observes that '[i]f you can't find the right shape, it's hard for people to identify you' (V, 16). Yet Gaitskill questions the efficacy of externally imposed forms/identities to capture the fluidity of consciousness and experience, and her fiction explores subjects' attempts to 'grab and hold something in place when nothing human can be grabbed and held in place'.[108] The author contends that some form, like fantasies, 'can be very good for people', a 'creative thing, a way to give form to something inchoate inside yourself [...]. The things that we experience as violent or destructive are huge formless forces that sometimes take form in us. Fantasy seems like a pretty harmless and creative way to express them.'[109]

In her most recent collection of short stories, *Don't Cry* (2009), Gaitskill continues to explore the connections between form and subjectivity, ethics and agency.

---

[105] Judith Butler, *Giving an Account of Oneself*, p. 19.   [106] Ibid., p. 20.
[107] Ibid.   [108] Matthew Sharpe, 'Interview with Mary Gaitskill'.   [109] Ibid.

The text deals with a wider range of issues and characters than previous works: from the emotional and psychological fall-out experienced by American soldiers after the Iraq war, to the issue of adopting a baby in Ethiopia, to serial killers and porn stars. Matthew Sharpe argues that this collection 'takes its place among artworks of moral seriousness'.[110]

In 'The Agonized Face', the narrator's term for specifically female pain and suffering, Gaitskill returns to the theme of victimhood explored in her essay 'On not being a Victim', discussed above. In this story, the reader gains access to the cognitive processes generated by identity's 'wounded attachments', in Wendy Brown's sense. In her essay of the same name, Brown reworks Nietzsche's concept of *ressentiment* to identify what she calls the 'logics of pain' constitutive of late modern politicized identity. Suffering endured at the hands of the reviled object— bourgeois male privilege—becomes a measure of moral superiority.[111] Identity forged in *ressentiment* thus becomes invested in its own subjection; it 'reverses without subverting this blaming structure'.[112] As a result, the politicized identity of the subordinated, which 'presents itself as a self-affirmation, now appears as the opposite: as predicated on and requiring its sustained rejection' by an antagonistic outside world.[113] Brown's thinking is not only useful for my reading of Gaitskill's short story, but foreshadows a recurring concern in the later first-person (auto)fictions I discuss in Chapters 3, 4, and 5. As I will show, their protagonists seek strategies to avoid forging identity at the sight of the 'wound', rejecting essentialist notions of female victimhood, which they often associate with their maternal forebears or with certain strands of second-wave feminism.

In Gaitskill's short story, the narrator connects suffering with an essentialist notion of 'the royalty of female nature' (AF, 71). Her belief in the existence and value of a mystical space of female pain, which brings suffering, but also a sense of pride and moral superiority, explains her sharp dislike of the 'feminist author' whose reading the narrator attends while covering a literary conference in her role as journalist. The feminist author challenges the narrator's firmly-held belief in the sacred nature of female suffering, which constitutes 'one of the few mysteries left to us on this ragged, gutted planet. It must be protected, even if someone must on occasion be "stoned". Even if that person is someone for whom we feel secret sympathy and regard.' (AF, 72) And indeed, despite the critical article she goes on to write about the feminist author, the narrator does feel sympathy for her views. The forty-year-old narrator identifies herself not as a feminist, but as a mother who agrees with a kind of feminism that seeks to protect young women and girls (AF, 54–5).

The feminist author, on the other hand, gives a speech in which she alludes to her experiences as a sex worker and an interned psychiatric patient but rejects readings of her work that focus on these aspects of her biography; she then reads her story, which is highly reminiscent of Gaitskill's 'Turgor' in *Because They Wanted To*: a middle-aged woman takes a young man back to her flat and fellates him. The

---

[110] Ibid.   [111] Wendy Brown, 'Wounded Attachments', p. 390.
[112] Ibid., p. 403.   [113] Ibid.

narrator is outraged by the story because the author 'spouted three heads and asked that we accept them all!' In other words, the author insisted upon a multiplicity of identities, one of which rejected outright being defined and contained by notions of suffering and, specifically, sexual victimhood: '[a]t first she was 'the girl who needed to be protected, and a woman standing to protect the girl. But then she became the other thing—the feminist who made girls into sluts' (AF, 55). What the narrator desires is clear categorization, precisely the moral absolutes that Gaitskill seeks to avoid, and a discrete juxtaposition between the two poles of intellectual agency and sexual determinism: 'intelligent words on one side, and mute genitals on the other. Between the poles, there was darkness and mystery' (AF, 58). The feminist author's 'glib acceptance' of her own difficult biography does not, in the narrator's view 'respect the profound nature of the agonized face' (AF, 59), revealing the narrator's continued investment in the 'wounded attachment' generating her own sense of self. While Gaitskill highlights the narrator's essentialism, the story neither judges the narrator, nor the feminist author. The pleasure of the story, in fact, inheres in the gradual manner in which the narrator comes to a point of notional agreement with the feminist author and acknowledges an alternative to the 'logics of pain' informing her sense of self and circumscribing her claim to agency:

> Wordless knowledge can be heavy and dark as the bottom of the ocean. Sometimes you want the relief of dryness, of light, bright, words. Sometimes you might be on the side of a smart-aleck middle-aged woman who thumbs her nose at the agonized face and fellates a snotty, sexy man, just for a dumb little thrill. Sometimes you wish it could be that easy.   (AF, 68)

Gaitskill's literary ethics require her to compose stories that pursue 'a couple of points of view'.[114] In her interview with Sharpe, Gaitskill suggests that in the writing of 'The Agonized Face' she deliberately adopted a view-point—the narrator's—that was at odds with her own. However, the narrator also represents that which Gaitskill has argued is a vital component of her strategy for portraying female characters: the creation of characters whose strength and vulnerability are both taken into account. Gaitskill's observation that 'when you go to what seems to be the opposite of your point of view, a whole gets created',[115] gestures towards her paradoxical desire to give full expression to 'those things that are always going to be outside our range of vision'.[116] This statement resonates with Cavarero's proposition that the desire for subjective coherence finds its full expression in the narrative impulse. But it also activates Butler's notion that conceptualizations of subjectivity should include an acknowledgement of the irrecoverability of the 'entire' self, and the role of the other in shedding some light on the opaque. In Gaitskill's view, literature can fulfil the role of the other by giving 'shape to rules, social mores, social attitudes, feelings' in a 'fluid way'.[117]

This desire to capture the complexity, ambiguity, and multiplicity of experience without casting judgment emanates from a deeply ethical place and from an aesthetic

---

[114] Matthew Sharpe, 'Interview with Mary Gaitskill'.
[115] Ibid.   [116] Ibid.   [117] Ibid.

drive to express the inexpressible in language. In her interview with Matthew Sharpe, Gaitskill quotes at length from Leslie Fiedler's introduction to Simone Weil's letters: 'This world is the only reality available to us, and if we do not love it in all its terror, we are sure to end up loving the "imaginary"'.[118] This quotation resonates with Acker's understanding of the self not as a discrete entity, but as the 'world' in its entirety: in both terror and pain as well as desire and love. It also gestures towards Gaitskill's belief in the importance of looking beyond the surfaces of socially constructed forms of understanding experience and taking responsibility for thoughts, actions, and behaviour, no matter how self-contradictory or ambiguous. This tenet echoes McNay's understanding of agency when she defines it as the generative configuration of self and as a process of 'active appropriation' of experience. Precisely this configurative process, which becomes 'immanent in the construction of narrative identity', emerges in the model of selfhood and agency in Gaitskill's fiction.[119]

MAINSTREAMING THE TRANSGRESSIVE

In 2002 the feature-length film version of Gaitskill's 'Secretary' was released in the US after initial screenings at domestic film festivals. Subsequent overseas releases followed in 2003 and 2004. The director, Steven Shainberg, who co-wrote the screen-play with Erin Cressida Wilson, had produced a short film based on the story six years previously. Shainberg selected the text because it originated in a 'well-known book of short-stories', which he felt could be made into an 'odd and interesting' film.[120] On approaching the major LA film studios in order to secure funding for a feature-length version, Shainberg was confounded by their requirement that Lee Holloway (Shainberg's version of Gaitskill's central protagonist Debby Roe) 'recover' from her predilection for BDSM.[121] The director observes that the film's depiction of BDSM as 'healing', instead of as a problem was 'entirely antithetical [...] to the Hollywood point-of-view [...] where everything turns out in a predictable way'.[122] As a result, the film was released independently (with New York-based producers) and proceeded to gross a total of $9,304,609, world-wide, rapidly becoming a cult classic.[123] The film won many prestigious awards; new-comer Maggie Gyllenhaal, who plays Lee, was nominated for a Golden Globe, while established actor James Spader, as domineering boss E. Edward Grey, secured a strong viewing public.[124] The soundtrack of the film was also released in 2002 to

---

[118] Leslie Fiedler cited by Mary Gaitskill, in Matthew Sharpe, 'Interview with Mary Gaitskill'.

[119] Lois McNay, *Gender and Agency*, p. 27.

[120] Interview with Steven Shainberg, in *Secretary*, directed by Steven Shainberg (Lionsgate, 2002), 0:23 and 3:12.

[121] Ibid., 0:57.   [122] Ibid., 1:40–1:54.

[123] *Box Office Mojo*, International Movie Database, 2013 <http://www.boxofficemojo.com/movies/?id=secretary.htm> [accessed 18.04.2013].

[124] *Secretary*, on IMDb.com <http://www.imdb.com/title/tt0274812/> [accessed 18.04.2013].

great success and special editions of the DVD have since been produced with cast interviews and behind-the-scenes documentaries.

The film *Secretary* shares some features with Gaitskill's short story but it is noteworthy for its tendency to divest its subject matter of the ambivalence—and distress—of its source. The relationship between the central protagonists remains one characterized by shifting power dynamics; and the issue of Lee's repressed emotions and stunted desire for intimacy, which is transformed through her relationship with the lawyer, continues to constitute a major element of her characterization. Nevertheless, the film smooths out much of the ambiguity at the heart of Gaitskill's story, instead laying down in clear didactic terms how the audience is supposed to feel about Lee's experiences with the lawyer, i.e. they constitute what Gaitskill has called a purely 'positive fantasy'.[125] The dictates of genre naturally play a large role in this process: the short-story form necessarily provides limited background, development, and perspective, allowing it to pivot on ambiguity and lack of resolution. A feature-length film of 111 minutes, however, requires precisely those elements in order to provide a coherent narrative arc. The discrepancy in financial outlay between cinematic and literary productions may also account for some of the adjustments in interpretation executed by Shainberg and Cressida Wilson: the film cost approximately $4,000,000 to make, a figure which had to be recouped upon release.[126]

Shainberg alleges that he desired to make a film that to some extent challenged Hollywood mores—a film in which not everything is 'predictable'. By marketing the film as a comedy romance and transforming the trajectory of the short story, Shainberg in fact produces a film that, despite its supposedly subversive content, becomes strangely normative. BDSM becomes connected with a neoliberal-inflected narrative of self-actualization and facilitates the successful coupling of two initially dysfunctional characters in a middle-class, gender-normative, monogamous union.[127] As Lee states at the film's close, they become 'like every other couple'.[128]

Gaitskill contends that Shainberg created 'the *Pretty Woman* version' of her story.[129] Lacking the complexity and hardness of Gaitskill's Debby, Lee's initial ineptitude and naivety are tempered by the charming billion-watt smiles of Gyllenhaal's Lee. The actor's patent physical beauty entails that the audience knowingly indulge the film's pretence that she is graceless and ugly, assured that the character will become increasingly well-groomed and advantageously lit (uncommented upon) as the film progresses. Shainberg and Cressida Wilson also introduce to Lee's background a recent stay in a psychiatric institution and a habit of self-mutilation. Gaitskill contends that these elements alien to her story become, in the screen-writers'

---

[125] Mary Gaitskill, 'On the Film *Secretary*. Victims and Losers: A Romantic Comedy', *American Zoetrope*, 7: 3 (2003) <http://www.all-story.com/issues.cgi?action=show_story&story_id=210> [accessed 19.04.2013].

[126] *Secretary*, on IMDb.com.

[127] One scene, in particular, taps into this narrative: Lee is pictured eating her lunch while listening to a self-help audio book with the title *How To Come Out as a Dominant/Submissive*. The scene is interspersed with brief scenes of Grey, who has not come to terms with his sexual preferences, destroying visual reminders of Lee back in the office. *Secretary*, 2002, 1:17:48.

[128] *Secretary*, 2002, 1:40:34.   [129] Mary Gaitskill, 'On the Film *Secretary*'.

hands, a visual abbreviation for the character's complex psychological conflicts, which they were otherwise incapable of portraying.[130] One of the film's clumsier moments is the exchange between Lee and Mr Grey after he discovers her self-harming. Grey forbids Lee from continuing her cutting and burning practices and she obeys, throwing her stylized kit of knives, sharpened ballerina figurines and iodine into the river.[131] The film thus presents a limited and sanitized view of BDSM: masochistic practices that do not take place within the context of stable, heterosexual coupledom become the truly transgressive act that must be 'recovered' from, in the sense used by McRobbie in her analysis of self-harm in a neoliberal climate.

In comparison with the scenes of self-harm, Lee's reaction to being spanked by Grey for the first time is rendered cinematographically with a fade-to-white signalling transcendence.[132] Her initial confusion is rapidly replaced by uncompli-cated acceptance. In contrast, the power of Gaitskill's employment of BDSM in her story resides in her refusal to resolve the paradox between misery and eroticism, between intimacy and absolute emotional isolation, which inheres in those practices. In the film, it is the character of Grey who is allowed the internal conflict denied Lee. A tightly framed head shot of Spader's character as he masturbates behind Lee's bared backside reveals 'sexual feeling that is deep enough to include sadness and vulnerability as well as furtive, guilty meanness, which he does not himself understand'.[133] Lee, on the other hand, never appears to be humiliated at all, an emotion that governs Gaitskill's Debby, and which she is finally able to externalize by adopting the submissive role in her encounters with the lawyer.

In fact, if the BDSM aspect were removed from the film, *Secretary* would resemble any quirky yet ultimately conventional rom/com in which the female pro-tagonist, having undergone a transformative process of some sort, wins the heart of the romantic lead. Lee, for example, at one point reads *Cosmopolitan* magazine in order to seek advice on how to 'snare her man'. When she finally confronts Grey with her love for him, the dialogue becomes trite formulae such as 'I want to get to know you', 'I love you', and 'I want to make love to you'.[134] The film's denouement even includes the classic bridal dash across town (with Lee in full white wedding dress), to win back Grey by means of a three-day test of endurance. She is ultim-ately carried across the threshold by the romantic lead where she is bathed and tended to by the once sadistic Mr Grey. Gaitskill wishes that the film had ended at the moment when Lee sits down at the desk after declaring her love. If it had, the film's one-dimensionality might have been 'leavened with ambiguity, an open place that allowed the viewer his or her own response'. Instead, '[w]e are made to realize that S/M here is not only painless, it's therapeutic: it's made both characters more confident, better looking, happier, freer, and self-actualized. Best of all, it's led them straight to marriage!'[135]

---

[130] Ibid.   [131] *Secretary*, 2002, 43:16 and 53:04.
[132] Ibid., 51:12.   [133] Mary Gaitskill, 'On the Film *Secretary*'.
[134] *Secretary*, 2002, 1:22:31, 1:27:19 and 1:28:30.
[135] Mary Gaitskill, 'On the Film *Secretary*'.

The sanitized adaptation of Gaitskill's story suggests two things: first, it resonates with the narrative about victimhood in the US. As Gaitskill contends:

> I believe that Americans are in fact profoundly, neurotically terrified of being victims, ever, in any way. This fear is conceivably one reason we just waged a grotesque and gratuitous 'war' in Iraq—because Americans couldn't tolerate feeling like victims, even briefly. I think it is the reason every boob with a hangnail has been clogging the courts and haunting talk shows across the land telling his/her 'story' and trying to get redress for the last twenty years. Whatever the suffering is, it's not to be endured, for God's sake, not felt and never, ever accepted. It's to be triumphed over. And because some things cannot be triumphed over unless they are first accepted and endured (indeed, some things cannot be triumphed over at all), the 'story' must be told again and again in an endless pursuit of a happy ending.

This is why Lee is depicted as increasingly in control throughout the film and why BDSM has to be redeemed by what becomes a self-optimization narrative about transcending suffering and victimhood through individual choice. An archetypal feminist character, who visits Lee during her self-abnegating marathon, is featured as part of a comic montage of the unenlightened who seek to persuade her to stop. She urges Lee to 'read about women's struggle first', a sentence that the film treats as misguided because it does not take romantic love into account.[136] This pivotal sequence of scenes, in which Lee follows the lawyer's orders and sits at a table for three days without eating or sleeping, must be clearly portrayed as denoting Lee's choice.[137] Lee's body is hers to do with as she wishes and feminism has no relevance in this personal realm.

Second, the film demonstrates how once transgressive sexual practices have become mainstream. As reviewer William Deresiewicz observes: 'When Gaitskill published her first collection, *bad behavior*, in 1988, sex, in the city or otherwise, was most certainly not on TV. Her blunt stories of prostitution, sadomasochism, and other flavors of sexual degradation came as a lash to the cultural system'.[138] Since the advent of what Ariel Levy has called 'raunch culture', transgressive sexuality has become increasingly aligned with an ethos of hedonistic consumption in late capitalism. As Andrew O'Hagan contends in his review of the first instalment of the S&M blockbuster series, *Fifty Shades of Grey* (2011) is as much about product placement and conspicuous consumption as it is about sex.[139]

Thus, subversive fragmented textuality and transgressive sexuality such as Acker or Gaitskill employed to cultural critical and political ends now represent a strategy available freely through pop-cultural channels—film, music videos, adverts, TV shows, popular fiction—and are therefore diminished in subversive impact. In the following, I trace the cultural process of mainstreaming transgression through an examination of 1990s riot grrrl, a distinctly non-mainstream feminist movement, whose activists deployed the transgressive gesture as a subversive political tool. After identifying the ways in which mainstream pop-culture assimilated a modified version

---

[136] *Secretary*, 2002, 1:33:09.   [137] Ibid., 1:31:20.

[138] William Deresiewicz, 'When the Whip Comes Down: On Mary Gaitskill'.

[139] Andrew O'Hagan, 'Travelling Southwards', *London Review of Books*, 34.14 (2012), 29 (p. 29).

of riot grrrl, I will consider the consequences of this shift for contemporary US pop-feminism and the recent North American literary narratives that engage its central issues.

RIOT GRRRL AND THE COMMODIFICATION
OF FEMALE TRANSGRESSION

Killing Ourselves is not Subversive.[140]

The twentieth anniversary of riot grrrl's ascendance prompted renewed media and academic interest in North America, UK, Germany, and Austria, adding to the already substantial body of scholarship on riot grrrl in feminist and Girl Studies.[141] The international media coverage of the incarceration in 2012 of three members of Pussy Riot also instigated debate about radical feminist protest and the possible resurgence of grassroots feminist activism.[142] In general, the anniversary provided the opportunity to reflect upon the state of contemporary feminism in the cultural contexts mentioned above; but accounts more often refer nostalgically to a lost spirit of radical feminist protest.

The emergence of riot grrrl in North America occurred at a time marked by unresolved social tensions that were reaching breaking point on American soil. In May of 1991, a Salvadorian man was shot by a white police officer during the traditional Cinco de Mayo celebrations in the Mount Pleasant neighbourhood of Washington DC.[143] Days of so-called 'race riots' ensued, which marked the beginning of a period of civil unrest and protest against ethnically motivated discrimination in impoverished urban centres across the US, culminating in the

---

[140] Fales Library and Special Collections, New York University Libraries: Johanna Fateman Riot Grrrl Collection, MSS 258, box 1, folder 64, correspondence between Kathleen Hanna and Johanna Fateman 1994–2000, Kathleen Hanna, *April Fools' Day*, 1995. The riot grrrl collection at Fales Library, opened in 2009, documents the evolution of the riot grrrl movement, focusing on the years between 1989 and 1996. The primary area of collecting is the personal papers of those involved in the creation of fanzines, music, and activism.

[141] Karren Ablaze!, 'Riot grrrl: Searching for Music's Young Female Revolutionaries', *The Guardian*, 18 March 2013; *The Punk Singer*, directed by Sini Anderson (opening band films, 2013); Olivia Laing, 'Grrrls Who Wanted More than Just Fun…', *The Observer*, 30 June 2013; Joe Pompeo, 'Original "riot grrrl" Kathleen Hanna meets the press, and this time it's happy', *Capital New York*, 31 May 2013; Rachel Smith, 'Revolution Grrrl Style, 20 years later', *NPR music*, 22 September 2011 <http://www.npr.org/blogs/therecord/2011/09/20/140640502/revolution-girl-style-20-years-later?sc=tw&cc=share> [accessed 04.10.2013]. See also, 'Riot Grrrl's not dead: Film- und Projekttage zu 20. Jahre Riot Grrrl', as part of *this human world* festival 2012 in Vienna; Christian Ihle, 'Who's That Grrrl? Eine Einleitung zu Riot Grrrl Revisited', taz.blog, 2 November 2011 <http://blogs.taz.de/popblog/2011/11/02/whos_that_grrrl_-_eine_einleitung_zu_riot_grrrl_revisited/> [accessed 04.10.2013]; Katja Peglow and Jonas Engelmann, eds., *Riot Grrrl Revisited: Geschichte und Gegewart einer feministischen Bewegung* (Mainz: Ventil Verlag, 2011).

[142] Pussy Riot is a Russian feminist punk rock group, three of whose members were incarcerated by the government in 2012 after they performed and filmed a song criticizing Vladimir Putin's regime and the Orthodox Church's support of it.

[143] The festival constitutes a celebration of American-Mexican relations, and marks a commemoration of the causes of freedom and democracy in the first years of the American Civil War.

LA riots of 1992. One of the most pervasive origin narratives for the punk feminist movement riot grrrl embeds its emergence in the unfolding of these riots, citing musician Jean Smith's letter to fellow Bratmobile band member Allison Wolfe, in which she wrote: 'We need to start a girl riot'.[144]

Riot grrrl's emergence can be traced to musicians and zine creators Tobi Vail, Allison Wolfe, Molly Neuman, and Kathleen Hanna (founders of the bands Bratmobile and Bikini Kill), and geographically to Washington State and Washington DC. Yet the movement soon became heterogeneous and spatially diffuse. Those involved in the initial stages were ideologically invested in the notion of a girl collective and resisted co-option as figure-heads, instead encouraging all girls to create their own music, art, writing, and forms of protest. Thus, young women who could not yet play instruments or who had never expressed themselves through the medium of writing picked up a guitar or a pen and 'did it themselves'. Riot grrrl co-opted the aesthetic discordance and counter-cultural energy of punk in order to scream feminist protest and give voice to female desire from stages on the East and West coasts of the US, in Canada, and in Great Britain. Word of riot grrrl only reached Germany in the late 1990s, but, in the second decade of the new millennium, the term and its associations retain great significance for many critical pop-feminists in the German-language context.

As Mimi Thi Nguyen notes: 'These women in each their own way refused to believe that the avant-garde, the revolution, and the work of art that challenged but also channelled both were only masculine provinces.'[145] In their musical and textual productions riot grrrls not only launched an attack against capitalism and consumer culture but also thematized feminist issues such as rape, assault, and the physical and psychological abuse of women. In order to do so, they drew on the repository of feminist theory developed over the previous two decades, challenging punk's premise that disciplinary power resided only in capitalism and authoritarian state control, as well as confronting the misogynistic tendencies within the punk movement itself.

In their textual undertakings, whether in song lyrics and performance poetry, or the modes most commonly found in zines, such as graphic art, poetry, short stories, and confessional autofiction, riot grrrls demonstrated an acute awareness of how identities arise from a nexus of social determiners such as gender, sexuality, class, and race—and how those factors impact upon the individual's encounter with authoritarian power structures. Drawing on one of the central tenets of second-wave feminist thought, riot grrrls linked the personal with the political, connecting individual lived experience to inequality and injustice perpetuated by dominant power structures. As the 'Riot Grrrl Manifesto' (1991) states, riot grrrl exists 'BECAUSE viewing our work as being connected to our girlfriends-politics-real lives is essential if we are gonna figure out how what we are doing impacts,

[144] Jean Smith, cited in Mimi Thi Nguyen, 'Riot Grrrl, Race, and Revival', *Women and Performance*, 22. 2–3 (2012), 173–96 (p. 173). Bratmobile was an American band synonymous with the riot grrrl movement; their DIY ethos and punk aesthetics functioned as a template for subsequent riot grrrl bands.
[145] Mimi Thi Nguyen, 'Riot Grrrl, Race, and Revival', p. 174.

Fig. 2. The front cover of *April Fools' Day* courtesy of Kathleen Hanna.

reflects, perpetuates, or DISRUPTS the status quo'.[146] This self-reflexive gesture characterizes much riot-grrrl engagement. Writing for an anthology of riot-grrrl creative work edited by Sheila Heti that went unpublished, Nina Aron and Beth Blofson, for example, claim that the movement constituted a 'call to arms, encouraging girls to revolutionize themselves and redefine themselves as punks, as girls, as individuals'.[147]

In *April Fools' Day* (see Fig. 2), a zine dedicated entirely to the issue of addiction (substance abuse was rife in the punk scene), Kathleen Hanna, singer in the band Bikini Kill and later Le Tigre, makes a connection between (her own) addiction issues and the inequities inherent in wider social structures. As shown in Fig. 3, she writes:

---

[146] This zine from 1991 is purported to have originated from the collaboration between members of the bands Bratmobile and Bikini Kill, whose aim was to spread a 'Revolution Girl Style Now'. See Fales Library and Special Collections, New York University Libraries: Kathleen Hanna Papers, MSS 271, box 1, folder 12, Kathleen Hanna et al., 'Riot Grrrl Manifesto', in Bikini Kill #2, 1991.

[147] Fales Library and Special Collections, New York University Libraries: Sheila Heti Riot Grrrl Collection, MSS 366, box 5, folder 8, Nina Aron and Beth Blofson, 'What a Riot!', in *Poised: An Anthology of Writing and Art by Young Women*, 1996. Random House dropped the anthology late in the editing stages when they realized that the actual product, with its overall tone of defiance and protest, defied their expectations of young girls' writing. They also calculated that the demographic constituting the anthology's intended readership would entail that they would make a financial loss on the project.

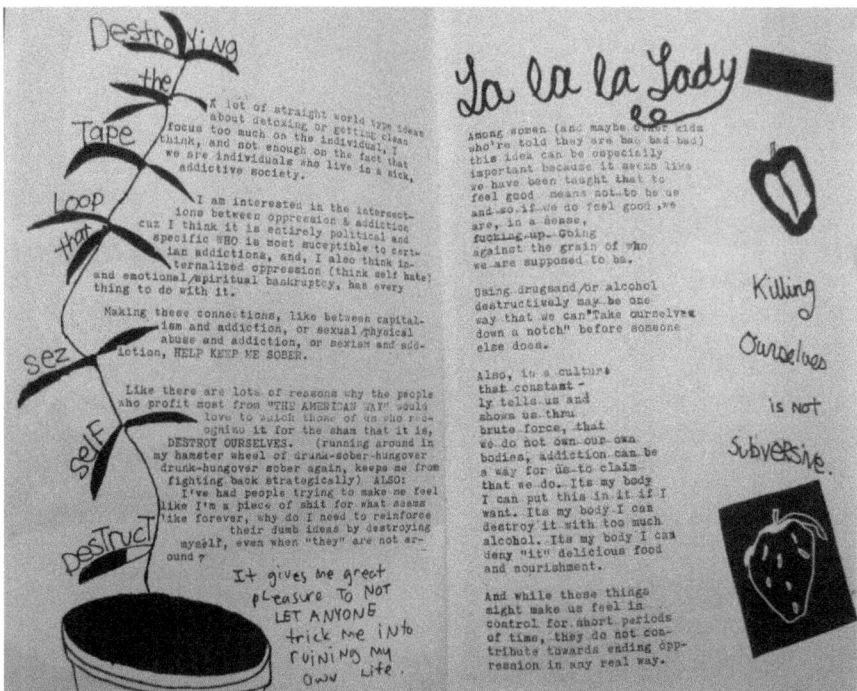

Fig. 3. Inside page from *April Fools' Day* courtesy of Kathleen Hanna. Note the playful mix of illustration, handwritten text, and type face typical of riot grrrl zines.

I am interested in the intersections between oppression and addiction cuz I think it is entirely political and specific WHO is most suceptible [sic] to certain addictions, and, I also think internalised oppression (think self hate) and emotional/spiritual bank-ruptcy has everything to do with it. Making these connections, like between capitalism and addiction, or sexual/physical abuse and addiction, or sexism and addiction, HELP [sic] KEEP ME SOBER.[148]

My interest lies predominantly in the nomadic community forged by the circulation of zines, which provided an alternative and complementary locus of riot-grrrl engagement from the radical public performances enacted by riot-grrrl bands.[149] These amateur publications initially functioned as fan magazines created by female punk enthusiasts, but quickly became an interactive forum for radical political debate as well as for subversive creative writing across genres by young self-identified riot grrrls. They often included autofiction, satirically humorous graphic art, epistolary

---

[148] Kathleen Hanna, *April Fools' Day*.

[149] At this time, zines would be passed around between groups of friends, or left in anonymous public spaces where women outside the scene might discover them. In order to receive a zine, or to order the next number in the series, readers would send postage costs and their address to the zine's creator. Zine creators often adopted pseudonyms, as personal prestige was considered secondary to the sense of collective their zines promoted.

exchange between creator and readers, and discussions of gender and nascent queer theory. Like the characters populating the fiction of Acker and Gaitskill discussed previously, members of this nomadic community (ranging on average between thirteen and twenty-five years old) experienced themselves as marginalized and alienated from mainstream society, from the cultures in which they were physically, socially, and geographically embedded. The mediated and mediating material culture of zines, which facilitated text-based, consciousness-raising encounters between zine and reader(s) that cut across regional and even national boundaries, engendered a sense of intimate solidarity (or to use riot-grrrl parlance 'girl love') among readers. This sense of intimacy was enhanced by the confessional tone dominating riot-grrrl textual productions, exemplified by the above quote from Hanna, in which she discusses her experience of addiction.

Social and political change was linked to an accrual of knowledge of oneself and of the other. Aron and Blofson, for example, observe that riot grrrl 'placed an emphasis on communication as a vital force, encouraging education through interaction'.[150] Lack of knowledge was therefore understood to form the basis for discrimination of all kinds, which engendered in zines what Nguyen calls an 'aesthetics of access'.[151] Understanding the experiences of the other as well as investigating one's own complicity in perpetuating discrimination accumulated an ethical dimension, for example, in this second point from the manifesto:

> BECAUSE doing/reading/seeing/hearing cool things that validate and challenge us can help us gain the strength and sense of community that we need in order to figure out how bullshit like racism, able-bodieism [sic], ageism, speciesism, classism, thinism, sexism, anti-semitism and heterosexism figures in our own lives.

Successful intersubjective relations, therefore, based on knowledge and reaching across '–isms', constituted the central impulse of the riot-grrrl ethos. But true knowledge could only be imparted if texts attained genuine 'authenticity'. The revelatory trope thus features heavily in much riot-grrrl writing: grrrls write about their most traumatic experiences, whether that is abuse, psychological instability or other mental health issues, self-harm, or addiction. The emphasis riot grrrl placed upon the revelation of true, lived experience as a means of assuring authenticity evinces a continuity with the mode of second-wave feminist thinking discussed at the beginning of this chapter, in which realistic writing, and above all, autobiography, features as the ideal mode of consciousness-raising feminist writing. In zines, the confessional mode, in particular, fostered a culture of pre-emptive self-critique or elective submission to public shaming, in which writers would expose themselves as 'flawed, processual beings [...] or, in the name of intimate love, allowed themselves to be publicly critiqued for their entitlements. Public shame, whether pursued through rigorous self-critique or delivered through the letters of an interlocutor, served as evidence of accountability'.[152] For those doing the shaming, following

---

[150] Nina Aron and Beth Blofson, 'What a Riot!'.
[151] Mimi Thi Nguyen, 'Riot Grrrl, Race, and Revival', p. 174.   [152] Ibid.

Myra Mendible, it can also be viewed as an important tool in building and maintaining a sense of community.[153] In *April Fools' Day*, for example, Hanna writes:

> In writing this stuff I have had to think a lot about how to share information without acting all bossy or being condescending. [...] Just cuz I'm an addict/alcoholic (what-fuckin-evah) doesn't mean I think I can speak for everyone in terms of addiction. It seems to me that each addict functions within his/her own context in terms of race, gender, location, class, personality, access, etc.... So it would be ridiculous for me to try and write a "manifesto" or a "universal account" of how addiction works.[154]

Here Hanna's 'etc.' pre-empts exposure to external critique that she speaks from a privileged and universalist position as a white woman, but importantly arrives after Hanna's revelation of her experience, indeed her expertise, in relation to addiction (her casual self-ironization '(what-fuckin-evah)' should be viewed similarly as a pre-emptive strike to evade accusations of assumed authority, self-righteousness, and privilege). The culture of privilege-checking fostered by riot-grrrl zines results, as Nguyen notes, in a 'troubling politics' in which traumatic experience reinterpreted as the result of systemic oppression 'enhances an authentic marginality, translating experience into expertise'.[155] In a later essay on her decision to distance herself from the riot-grrrl scene, for example, Hanna recounts the self-imposed transformation of one of her riot-grrrl colleagues from 'white middle class and straight' to a 'working class lesbian who, of all things, identified herself as "black"'. Hanna goes on: '[d]ay by day I watched as Jenny became more and more "oppressed". It actually felt like she'd thrown herself into a Miss America pageant in reverse. I.e. Instead of scrambling for a gold crown, she was scrambling for the title of Miss Least Enfranchised'. For Hanna, it was as if 'white middle class straight people [feel] entitled to everything, even other people's oppression'.[156]

Here a further reason emerges for Hanna's judiciously placed 'etc.' at the end of the list of possible identity determiners in the above quotation. The ultimately unsatisfactory if well-intentioned catch-all ellipsis recalls Butler's quibble, discussed in Chapter 1, with feminist identity politics that seek, but invariably fail, to encompass a fully situated subject. Furthermore, Nguyen has argued that the aesthetics of access practised by white middle-class riot-grrrl activists pivoted upon a sentimental impulse that created an illusory 'intimate public' in the sense used by Lauren Berlant.[157] In Nguyen's view, this desire for, and belief in, successful intersubjective intimacy entailed that in fact change was conceived of 'narrowly as the adjustment of the individual subject—recalibrating her capacity for love or

---

[153] See, Myra Mendible (ed.), *American Shame: Stigma and the Body Politic* (Bloomington: Indiana University Press, 2016).

[154] Kathleen Hanna, *April Fools' Day*.

[155] Mimi Thi Nguyen, 'Riot Grrrl, Race, and Revival', p. 179.

[156] Fales Library and Special Collections, New York University Libraries: Johanna Fateman Riot Grrrl Collection, MSS 258, box 1, folder 64, correspondence between Kathleen Hanna and Johanna Fateman 1994–2000, Kathleen Hanna, 'When the Words that once Liberated You Become Bars on Yr Cage—random notes on political depression'.

[157] See Lauren Gail Berlant, *The Female Complaint: The Unfinished Business of Sentimentality in American Culture* (Durham, NC; London: Duke University Press, 2008).

shame, for instance—to the structural determinations that constitute the historical present', i.e. race, class, gender, sexuality 'etc.'. This adjustment is less based on actual intersectional encounters, i.e. really 'knowing' the other and more in calibrating the individual to appear 'good', i.e. by acknowledging, and seeking to modify, their privileged positionality. This strategy, according to Nguyen, not only reifies those determiners, like class and race, but also registers 'how neo-liberalism and its emphases on the entrepreneurial subject shapes even progressive or feminist adjustments to [...] structural determinations.' According to Nguyen, the development of an ideal intimacy was 'confounded' by the question of race in riot grrrl, when white middle-class activists were forced to confront their own complicity in perpetuating racist power structures, and to acknowledge that their desire for knowledge or intimacy with the racialized other might perpetuate an coercive imperialist logic.[158]

For example in Ramdasha Bikceem's fourth issue of *GUNK* (see Fig. 4), she addresses the lack of racial diversity in riot grrrl and the matter of oppression-appropriation that not only ignored the genuine plight of the racialized other but ossified within language and thus in consciousness the discriminatory structures ostensibly intended as the target of riot grrrl. Bikceem is worth quoting at length as her comments, which are depicted in Fig. 5, summarize this issue:

> I used to laugh at this whole white bread punk rock scene, but now I'm not laughing as much as getting more annoyed. I swear every punk show I go to I'm usually the only person of colour in the joint and nobody seems to even question this or even seem to mind. I think my friend Beth was telling me that somebody said that punx [sic] were the 'white niggers'. What exactly does this mean? I guess it means that punx, like African Americans often reflect what alot [sic] of people don't want to see. They don't want to see the results of their oppressive society. Punx are revolting against a society that has repressed personal expression, which has intern [sic] resulted in the way alot [sic] of them (us???) dress and act etc.... Whereas in the case of African Americans their (our???) oppression has resulted in poverty, lack of education, and low self-images. But what this concept of 'white nigger' fails to realize is that white punx couldn't possibly come close to the stigma that is attached and associated with African Americans. White kids [...] can get away with having green mohawks [sic] and pierced lips 'cause no matter how much they deviated from the norms of society their whiteness always shows through.[159]

Thus zine culture in riot grrrl encouraged a tendency in some activists to brandish their credentials as marginalized subjects in order to gain credibility in the scene, which as I have shown generated rancour among those riot grrrls speaking from racialized or otherwise 'other-ed' positions. The cultural capital accrued through the assertion of disenfranchisement often became augmented by the exposure of the psychological consequences of oppression, understood by the zine creator as

---

[158] Mimi Thi Nguyen, 'Riot Grrrl, Race, and Revival', p. 180.
[159] Fales Library and Special Collections, New York University Libraries: Ramdasha Bikceem Riot Grrrl Collection, MSS 354, box 5, folder 23, Ramdasha Bikceem, *GUNK* #4, 1993.

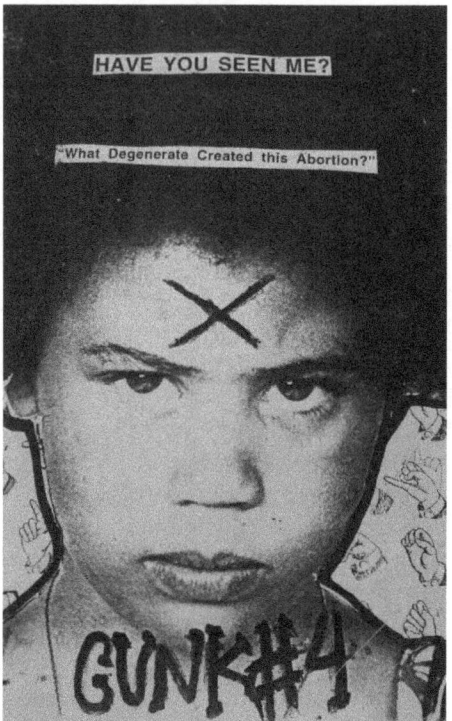

Fig. 4. The front cover of *GUNK* #4 shows how Bikceem intersperses the autobiographical (the photograph depicts her as a child) with a political commentary on the lack of racial diversity in riot grrrl. 'Have you seen me?' implies the answer 'No'. Photograph courtesy of Ramdasha Bikceem.

constituting a vital and cutting-edge violation of social taboos.[160] In the last edition of her zine *Alien* the creator, Whitney, reveals and reviles the practice of translating traumatic experience into cultural capital: 'The perpetuation of craziness is disguised in art, if I were to tell you I was cured (gasp!) you wouldn't read on... ☺ fuck you ☺ if i were to say i cut myself & my daddy hit me to smithereens you'd ask me when is the next issue coming out. You are reading and I am writing THE COMMODITY OF CRAZINESS in punk'.[161] This is perhaps why Hanna, in 1995, chose to create a zine based on addiction. She recognized the developing correlation between oppressive dominant social structures, the (sub-)cultural capital linked to marginality and processes of self-destruction: 'Recovery, to me, is about stripping my addictions of their false sense of glamour + rebelliousness in order to expose how they actually function in my life. [...] Like there are lots of

---

[160] Here I draw on Bourdieu's notion of cultural capital developed in Pierre Bourdieu, *Distinction: A Social Critique of the Judgement of Taste* (London: Routledge & Kegan Paul, 1984).

[161] Whitney, *Alien*, 1997, cited in Mimi Thi Nguyen, 'Riot Grrrl, Race, and Revival', p. 179.

Fig. 5. Bikceem's polemical passage is on the left side of the page. Observe how she juxtaposes her text with the graphic illustration, the statistics on the beliefs of white Americans about race, the dictionary definitions of 'black' and 'white', which she has annotated to reveal racism at the level of language, and with the image of emaciated black men behind a white man in uniform. The advert for a comedy show underlines the bleak irony at play in Bikceem's work more generally. Photograph courtesy of Ramdasha Bikceem.

reasons why the people who profit most from "THE AMERICAN WAY" would love to watch those of us who recognize it for the sham that it is DESTROY OURSELVES.'[162] It might be useful to recall at this point Lynne Layton's argument that trauma, and the consequent subject-splitting it may induce, had at that time become postmodernism's dominant mode. Hanna argues in a late essay that the 'mainst[r]eam has effectively appropriated certain tenets of post-modernist thought' so that now it is 'just another ruse' making her and others feel 'permanently House of Mirrors'd', indeed 'making certain people feel insane or lost'.[163]

Here Hanna anticipates Robin James's argument, made in 2014, that neoliberal narratives of 'resilience', whereby everything becomes measured by notions of 'health', depend upon 'crisis and trauma' as 'necessary, desirable phenomena': 'you

[162] Kathleen Hanna, *April Fools' Day.*
[163] Fales Library and Special Collections, New York University Libraries: Johanna Fateman Riot Grrrl Collection, MSS 258, box 1, folder 64, correspondence between Kathleen Hanna and Johanna Fateman 1994–2000, Kathleen Hanna, 'POSTMODERNIST DISCOURSE AS TRANSMUTATED THRU THE TELEVISION'.

can't bounce back without first falling'.[164] Yet, Hanna's decision to develop her own resilience, demonstrated by her recovery narrative and her contention that 'killing ourselves is not subversive',[165] provides an example of the way in which neoliberal resilience discourse in pop-culture has, since the 1990s, absorbed all kinds of 'damage and deficit', be it psychological, economic or physical, and turned it into 'surplus value'.[166] Damage is 'incited', 'spectacularly' and publicly overcome, and the person overcoming the damage, whose resilience mirrors that of wider society, is rewarded with 'human capital' and status.[167]

It would be a mistake, however, to read the textual productions of riot grrrls as mere symptoms of a culturally pervasive theoretical turn, or alternatively as unreflexive, self-indulgent outpourings. Many riot grrrls did, however, familiarize themselves with theoretical writing of all kinds, evidenced not just by the zines, but by accounts of discussions that took place among members of the riot-grrrl 'chapters' that arose across North America in the early 1990s and during the conventions that subsequently took place. Yet Kathleen Hanna's later essays, in particular, demonstrate uneasiness with the poststructuralist and postmodern theories informing her and others' initiation into riot grrrl:

> Aaaaah the '90s, a time when it actually seemed more progressive (and sexy) to be a barely functioning skitzophrenic than to have a viewpoint one could act from. Sure I know my 'inner voice' is shaped by my race, my class, my gender and my citizenship, I also acknowledge that I am an ever changing person and not a static identity. But I am angry with the 'post modernist' shit I learned (right about the time I started to think I had an identity in the first place) that told me having one was strictly akin to being a colonizer, a racist or male identified. That is a theoritcal [sic] trap I'd happily see conservative white males plunge into never to return but I just can't afford to wade thru that bullshit for the rest of my life.[168]

One cannot know for sure what works in particular Hanna refers to here, but she has spoken publicly about her admiration for Kathy Acker's fiction and essays. Indeed, she met the writer at a poetry performance and discussed her work with her, finding parallels between her own work and methodology and the work of the then established author.[169] Archive material from Hanna's contribution to the Fayles Library riot-grrrl collection, for example essays in which she embeds herself in the narrative reading a work by Acker, or the newspaper cutting of Acker's obituary, provide credence to the suggestion that Hanna may have been influenced by the theoretical sources Acker draws on in her fiction and essays, those discussed in the first part of this chapter. Taking Hanna's assessment of the psychological effects of reading postmodern and, presumably, poststructuralist theory, into account,

---

[164] Robin James, *Resilience and Melancholy: Pop Music, Feminism, Neoliberalism* (Alresford: Zero Books, 2015), p. 4.

[165] Kathleen Hanna, *April Fools' Day*, 1995.

[166] Robin James, *Resilience and Melancholy*, pp. 6–7.   [167] Ibid.

[168] Kathleen Hanna, 'When the Words that once Liberated You'.

[169] Fales Library and Special Collections, New York University Libraries: Lucy Thane Riot Grrrl Collection, MSS 287, 287.0027 (media), Kathleen Hanna interview, documentary footage of Bikini Kill concerts in Sheffield and Leeds, 13 March 1993, 12:08.

Fig. 6. The front cover of Sheila Heti's *Brillantine*. Photograph courtesy of Sheila Heti.

her and others' engagement with this discourse nevertheless yielded compelling aesthetic results.

As previously mentioned, zines are heterogeneous multimedia productions. Interspersed between what I have called autofictions, or the confessional passages recently discussed, zines often contain radically experimental creative work, both textual and graphic, using cut-and-paste techniques and collages to create meaningful juxtapositions. These creations attest to the self-reflexive and strategic writing practices exercised by the most accomplished riot-grrrl zine creators. They demonstrate the capacity for what Hanna calls 'writing strategically about a "subject" that is not outside myself'.[170] Sheila Heti's heteroglossic zine *Brillantine* (see Fig. 6), for example (created when she was eighteen), encompasses a snatch of absurdist theatrical dialogue, fantastical short stories, whose meiotic tone and demotic register enhance their grotesquery, satirical cartoons, poems, and a mock interview with a fictitious, egotistical male model entitled 'A Portrait of the Artist as a Young Stallion'.

The works emerge from a deeply political impulse, engaging in intertextual dialogues with canonical texts of literary history (as 'A Portrait' demonstrates) as well as the feminist movement in order to critique white-male privilege and strands

---

[170] Kathleen Hanna, *April Fools' Day.*

Fig. 7. The poem 'Lipstick' and the excerpt from Henry Miller's *Under the Roofs of Paris* are linked visually by the illustrations of women, which range from the hyper-feminine to the melancholic. Note how Heti's handwritten attribution appears to turn Miller himself into a faceless man in a bowler hat. With kind permission from Sheila Heti.

of contemporaneous feminist thinking. The short story 'I am Woman, Hear me Scream Rape' modifies the title of that famous women's movement anthem and engages with the victim-blaming debates discussed in relation to Mary Gaitskill's work above; the poem entitled 'Lipstick', depicted in Fig. 7, traces the thought processes of a young woman excited to wear make-up for the first time. Yet the poem ends with a sudden political thrust: 'Of course now I smell like a whore./ Lipstick smells thick and what's thicker than a whore?' This poem is juxtaposed with a cut-and-paste excerpt from Henry Miller's *Under the Roofs of Paris* (1941), in which a graphic and disturbing gang-rape scene takes place narrated from one male perpetrator's view-point. The contrast in perspective and tone between the two pieces creates an implied critical narrative of its own: the girl in 'Lipstick', due to her choice to begin wearing make-up, becomes 'fair game' for male sexual predators (viz. a 'whore') and slides down a slippery slope of logic to become the lifeless object of a gang rape, the piece of flesh evoked by the name of the lipstick in the poem: 'Hint of Flesh.'[171]

---

[171] Fales Library and Special Collections, New York University Libraries: Zan Gibbs Riot Grrrl Zine Collection, MSS 364, box 1, folder 20, Sheila Heti, *Brillantine*, approx. 1996.

The question of sex and, in particular the sex industry, took a prominent place in riot-grrrl discourse. Nguyen argues that some riot-grrrl feminists' decision to work in the sex industry as a transgressive, 'confrontational act', offended women who were economically dependent on such work.[172] No doubt in the spirit of that debate Kathleen Hanna sent a photocopy of Gaitskill's short story 'Something Nice' (from *bad behavior*) to fellow band member Johanna Fateman at some point between 1994 and 2000. The tale recounts the experiences of a middle-aged, married man during a period of visiting one particular, inexperienced prostitute working in a New York brothel. The man fantasizes about potentially dating the girl in the outside world, but realizes the intimacy he thought they shared was self-delusional when he sees her by chance in a café discussing with a friend her attempts to find a decently-paid job in the art world; she ignores her ex-client. The presence of the photocopy among the varied correspondence between the two riot grrrls is significant because it lies alongside an essay on Lizzie Borden's film, *Working Girls* (1986), a sympathetic portrayal of prostitution as an economic choice in the vein of the British *Belle de Jour* volumes I discuss in the next chapter. Furthermore, Hanna's riot-grrrl paraphernalia contain an essay of her own on prostitution in which she critiques Andrea Dworkin's prohibitive stance on the sex industry. Hanna met Dworkin in 1991 at a time when the former was working as a stripper, a choice she claims she made for economic reasons.[173] Draft manuscripts of Hanna's experimental writing demonstrate that she, like Gaitskill and Acker, drew on her experiences in the sex industry in her creative work. It is unclear whether Hanna had read *bad behavior* before this time, but the text—at whatever time she encountered it—clearly resonated thematically with her own writing practices. In terms of their form and interest in language as both a determiner and challenger of identity, Hanna's experimental prose narratives exist in a dialogic relationship with Acker's fiction (see Fig. 8). These prose fragments also negotiate similar thematic terrain: the idea of sex as a commodity ('When [...] a fuck is transposed onto survival in the figure of dollar signs'); violent abuse and incest ('My hands cupped my ears when you hit my sister when you fucked her with yr [sic] fists and i [sic] pretended not to notice because looking opened up the possibility that i'd be next') and desire ('desire, my desire, is not allowed within this economy').[174]

In the following passage, which is reminiscent of Acker's disjointed, paratactic descriptions of coitus, desire that is not enacted on the speaker's terms is likened to a cold military encounter with death. The narrator speaks to her lover (the first 'you') but the second 'you' may be glossed as representing Acker, whose fictions are littered with the metaphorical conflation of sex, death, hell, and the dyad of pleasure and pain:

(i fuck you like a soldier looks at a dead animal) You said (a girl said) you said that their is the place in fucking that is like hell, the way you imagine hell. It's the moment

[172] Mimi Thi Nguyen, 'Riot Grrrl, Race, and Revival', p. 179.

[173] Fales Library and Special Collections, New York University Libraries: Kathleen Hanna Papers, MSS 271, box 1, folder 25, Kathleen Hanna, 'Essay' and 'Customers', date unknown.

[174] Fales Library and Special Collections, New York University Libraries: Kathleen Hanna Papers, MSS 271, box 1, folder 25, Kathleen Hanna, un-named prose piece, date unknown.

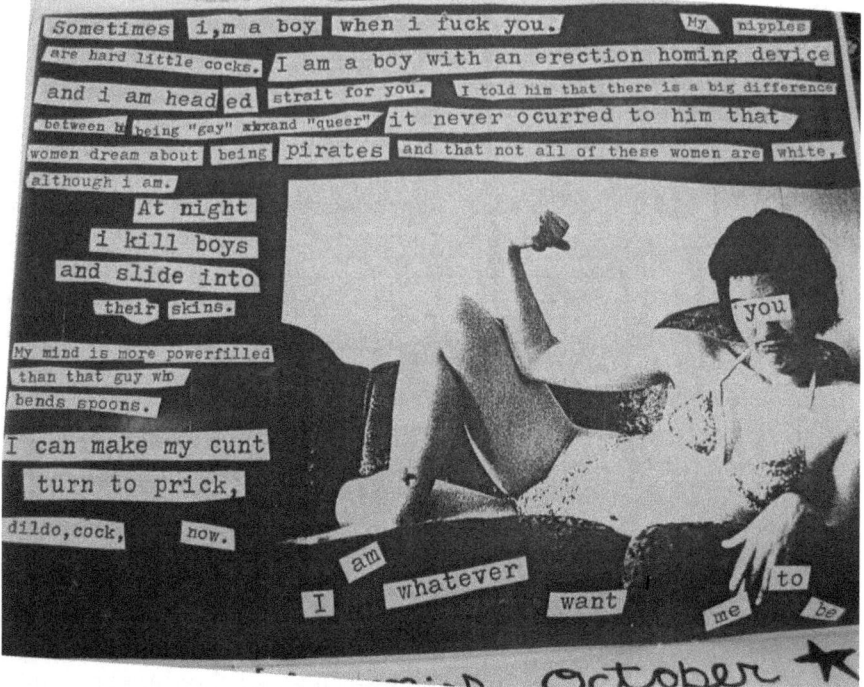

Fig. 8. This cut-and-paste calendar page by Kathleen Hanna demonstrates the thematic and aesthetic affinity between Hanna and Acker's work. Note especially the reference to pirates, that eminently Acker-esque theme. Photograph courtesy of Kathleen Hanna.

that is always their on the other side of his/her eyes where you are nothing but the word, dick or pussy and there seems to be nothing but the edge of bliss and the edge of death and our bodies skating along the edge of this.[175]

The inability to access the lover's consciousness despite physical intimacy resembles Acker's 'threshold' encountered during sex, where you must '[c]ommit yourself to not-knowing.' All that is available are '[r]ed eyes' that 'stare down on top of my eyes.'[176] In Hanna's piece, the speaker's inability to achieve psychological intimacy with her lover combined with the corollary placed around her own desires manifests itself in the sexual act being translated into a language that is not her own: 'you are nothing but the word, dick or pussy'. Speaking and being spoken through an ostensibly foreign language echoes Acker's narrator's observation about the central protagonist in *Don Quixote*: 'BEING BORN INTO AND PART OF A MALE WORLD, SHE HAD NO SPEECH OF HER OWN.'[177] Yet, like many of Acker's protagonists, in particular Janey in *Blood and Guts in High School*, Hanna's narrator

[175] Kathleen Hanna, un-named prose piece.   [176] Kathy Acker, *Great Expectations*, p. 235.
[177] Kathy Acker, *Don Quixote: Which Was a Dream*, p. 58.

rebels against this language and attempts to 'write down her life'.[178] She avers that 'the best place to start was paper because the only way i could destroy you [the incestuous father-figure/male lover] was by taking back language'.[179]

While I agree with Nguyen's assessment of the troubling aspects inherent in riot grrrl's aesthetics of access, especially its role in the alternating elision and reification of racialized power structures, it is vital to recognize zine work and other riot-grrrl creative writing as heterogeneous and, importantly, *mediated*. Nguyen's analysis does not pay enough attention to the ways in which confessional passages (which themselves constitute self-reflexively *constructed* texts) often lie alongside experimental creative pieces, either textual or graphic, which offer their own commentary on the 'autobiographical' aspects of the productions, as I have shown with Heti's work. Diana Fuss makes the point that the 'problem with attributing political significance to every personal action is that the political is soon voided of any meaning or specificity at all, and the personal is paradoxically depersonalised'. Fuss's insightful comment informs my contention that much riot-grrrl creative work channelled the personal into genres—fiction, poetry, graphic art—that avoid the collapse posited by Fuss, moving the personal into the mediating realm of imagination, where the political dimension may be preserved and extrapolated on the reader's own terms.[180]

In general, riot-grrrl texts connote constructed performances that cannot be read at face value but as modes of politicized self-fashioning (see especially Fig. 9). They deconstruct but also construct the creator's identity. The confessional passages pick apart layers of social conditioning, encompassing privilege-checking and public self-shaming, as well as traumatic and oppressive experiences, but the *act* of zine construction, of creating a multimedia, self-reflexively composed narrative constitutes a strategy of collaborative identity construction, which, as Hanna recognizes above, was threatened not only by conventional patriarchal forces but by strands of pervasive critical theory.

Riot-grrrl textual productions seek to create a nascent, and importantly collective, feminist consciousness through and despite discursive forces that posit the dissolution of the coherent subject per se, as Hanna observes, '... that's where writing comes in'.[181] The tension between the desire for the whole, recovered self and the work of deconstructing the self becomes especially visible in Hanna's work. Bikceem, too, claims: 'I think doing this fanzine in a way saved my life. [...] During high skool this fanzine was my only creative outlet.'[182] Zines and other riot-grrrl productions do not merely constitute a kind of therapy but provide a forum for creative self-expression in narrative form. As Kathy Acker observes: '[i]t's a common belief that something exists when it's part of a narrative. Self-reflexive consciousness is

---

[178] Kathy Acker, *Blood and Guts in High School*, p. 65.
[179] Kathleen Hanna, un-named prose piece.
[180] See Diana Fuss, *Essentially Speaking: Feminism, Nature and Difference* (London: Routledge, 1990), p. 101.
[181] Kathleen Hanna, *April Fools' Day.*   [182] Ramdasha Bikceem, *Gunk #4.*

Fig. 9. The front and back covers of *GUNK* #5, with kind permission from Ramdasha Bikceem.

narrational.'[183] Heti recognized the capacity for constructive and politically efficacious creativity in young riot-grrrls' writing when she appealed for contributions to the riot-grrrl anthology: '[w]e need, as a collective, to promote the art created by young girls. [...] We can be political, we can be intelligent and edgy and emotional without the requisite angst etc....'[184] Hanna recognizes the processual nature of this project when she observes that '[l]ike the recovery process itself, this writing will never REALLY be completed'.[185]

Riot grrrl, despite the fact that almost all commentators declare the movement to have dissolved by 1996, never was 'completed'. It is certainly the case that, as the 1990s progressed, the movement was exposed, justifiably, to increasing critique from within, which challenged the blind-spots of white middle-class riot grrrls, in particular. It is tempting therefore to round off the narrative with rhetoric familiar from popular accounts of the second wave in the late 1980s: with references to sectarianism and in-fighting around issues of race, class, and attitudes towards men. Yet that would be to add credence to a convenient, but over simplistic, feminist 'story', in Clare Hemmings' sense.[186] It would also establish an inaccurate periodization of feminist history that contains the long-term resonances of the movement,

---

[183] Kathy Acker, *Great Expectations*, p. 204.   [184] Sheila Heti, *Brillantine*.
[185] Kathleen Hanna, *April Fools' Day*.   [186] Clare Hemmings, *Why Stories Matter*.

and to ignore the role that the media and consumer culture played in appropriating riot grrrl as a profitable commodity within mainstream culture.

In riot grrrl's early days, media interest in the politics of the movement soon segued into trivializing, feminizing, and often downright condescending discussion of the protagonists' punk fashion sensibilities.[187] Of course, initial media coverage also helped to attract many young girls to the movement, but in order to ensure integrity and to protect the local, DIY ethos of the movement, many riot grrrls, including the band Bikini Kill, called for a media boycott in 1992. This decision piqued the press's interest and more coverage ensued.[188]

When the movement began to morph and diversify (around 1995), media reports attributed its 'failure' to internal schisms. A brief look at early twenty-first-century mainstream female recording artists in North America, however, reveals how punk characteristics, and in many cases the very term riot grrrl or grrrl, began to be appropriated by corporate institutions in order to market, but also contain, a neutralized, apolitical form of female protest culture. Writing in 2014, Robin James argues that the 'corporate music industry now profits from subcultural sounds and aesthetics that used to evade and challenge it', as well as the gesture of transgressive resistance encapsulated by those aesthetics.[189] As Dylan Siegler wrote in an introduction to his interview with Kathleen Hanna in 2000, 'an era of thriving musical experimentation and underground rock has come and gone, extinct largely because a music industry Grendel sank in his teeth and shook every indie scene until its neck snapped. Riot grrrl was no exception'.[190]

While riot-grrrl bands like Bikini Kill, Bratmobile, and Huggy Bear operated exclusively with small independent record labels, artists like The Spice Girls with their brand of 'girl power' in the UK, and in North America Avril Lavigne, Pink, Gwen Stefani, and the band The Donnas, among others, were signed to major mainstream record labels. All of the latter-day artists mentioned above have been linked in the press with the labels 'punk', or 'pop punk' or 'grrrl'.[191] As Anna Feigenbaum argues in her assessment of these post-riot-grrrl artists, the economics of production have everything to do with the politics of the product as 'both the punk and feminist movements have historically been grassroots, locally organized endeavours' and as such 'their emergence as "popular" may render them apolitical

---

[187] 'A Movement Begins in a Million Pink Bedrooms', *LA Weekly*, 10–16 July 1992, pp. 19–28, here p. 20; 'Meet the Riot Grrrls, a Sassy New Breed of Feminists for the MTV Age', *Newsweek*, 23 November 1992, pp. 884–6, here p. 84.

[188] *LA Weekly* published an article on Bikini Kill's refusal to engage with the press, including a photograph of Hanna hiding her face from the camera. *LA Weekly*, 9–15 October 1992, p. 58.

[189] Robin James, *Resilience and Melancholy*, p. 7.

[190] Dylan Siegler, *Ms magazine*, September (2000), 86–8 (p. 84).

[191] 'Avril Lavigne: Riot Girl', in *The Independent*, 22 May 2004 < http://www.independent.co.uk/arts-entertainment/music/features/avril-lavigne-riot-girl-6169362.html> [accessed 3.10.2013]; 'Gwen Stefani: Material Grrrl', Beauty Riot.com <http://www.beautyriot.com/fashion/gwen-stefani-style-evolution-g6362-page3> [accessed 22.08.2013]; 'Shy and Retiring Pink (Yeah, Right) is a Pop Punk Party Animal', 4Music.com <http://www.4music.com/artists/32/Pink> [accessed 19.10.2013]. The Spice Girls' catchphrase 'girl power' was originally used in a zine created by Kathleen Hanna.

or already co-opted'.[192] In the early 1990s, riot grrrls remained ideologically opposed to capitalism and corporate consumer culture as channels through which dominant oppressive power networks operated. These popular contemporary artists on the other hand represent what Feigenbaum calls 'corporate packaged girl power that morphed out of Riot Grrrl's success'.[193]

Pink is the only one of the mainstream 'punk' artists mentioned above who self-identifies publicly as feminist. The others operate in either ignorance of the term (Lavigne) or employ alternative descriptors, such as the gynocentric term 'pro-woman' (Stefani), or the neoliberal by-word 'self-empowerment' (The Spice Girls). All of them have taken part in multi-million-dollar advertising campaigns for the beauty industry or have launched their own line of products. Lavigne is linked with Sony, whose products appear regularly in her videos, as well as her own perfume range; Stefani has undertaken advertising campaigns for L'Oréal and Pink for CoverGirl; The Donnas have recorded advertisements for Levis and Pantene. The Spice Girls, famously, launched a lucrative range of dolls representing each band member and famously name-checked the Wonderbra in one of their songs.

Gathered together under the undifferentiated label 'punk', these artists' transgressive qualities become reduced to the trope of sexual and aesthetic transgression (hair colour or fashion sense)—especially in the mainstream visual media of video, television, and live performances—and are thereby contained, regardless of the actual content of their songs. Redirected to the realm of physical appearance (predominantly white, conventionally pretty) and sexuality (heterosexual, available, and sex-positive), pop-punk transgression becomes a vehicle for the marketing and sale of products to young women, an observation supported by the type of advertising these young women become linked with, and a non-threatening source of sexual fantasy for a heterosexual male audience. As Ariel Levy observes in her influential work *Female Chauvinist Pigs*: '[t]he glossy, overheated thumping of sexuality in our culture is less about connection than consumption. Hotness has become our cultural currency, and a lot of people spend a lot of time and a lot of regular, green currency trying to acquire it. [...] Hot can mean popular. Hot can mean talked about. But when it pertains to women, hot means two things in particular: fuckable and salable [sic].'[194] So when Avril Lavigne sings 'I don't care about my makeup/I like it better with my jeans all ripped up/Don't know how to keep my mouth shut/[...] Let's get wasted', her superficially transgressive gesture is absorbed and made meaningless by the politically neutralized, sexualized context in which she operates, i.e. corporate consumer culture that is driven by an ideal of conspicuous, raunchy female sexuality.[195] As Feigenbaum notes, 'the pathways of capital [...] inform and produce any feminist politics that is subsumed' in the artistic performances of these individuals.[196]

---

[192] Anna Feigenbaum, 'Remapping the Resonances of Riot Grrrl: Feminisms, Postfeminisms, and "Processes" of Punk', in *Interrogating Postfeminism*, ed. by Yvonne Tasker and Diane Negra, p. 138.
[193] Ibid., p. 139.   [194] Ariel Levy, *Female Chauvinist Pigs*, p. 31.
[195] Avril Lavigne, 'Rock and Roll', 2013.
[196] Anna Feigenbaum, 'Remapping the Resonances of Riot Grrrl', p. 140.

In her insightful work *Girls* (2002), Catherine Driscoll asks whether feminism can be a 'mass-produced, globally distributed product' and whether 'merchandized relations to girls' can be authentic.[197] In other words, can a product of capitalism critique capitalism in good faith? And can consumers of that product genuinely step outside the capitalist framework to understand that critique? In one of her spoken-word poems, Hanna provides a quote by Morgan Star taken from the literary journal *Sinister Wisdom*: '[t]he more a system expands to include what looks like change but essentially isn't, the harder it is to stand outside that system and criticize it.'[198]

When, in 2004, Hanna's band Le Tigre signed with the mainstream corporation Universal Records, many riot grrrls felt that the movement, in the form of one of its originators, had finally been fully absorbed by the capitalist system. Yet, the band argued that availing themselves of mainstream, corporate resources ensured the dissemination of radical feminist protest on a larger scale. Band member Johanna Fateman told reporters: '[t]here were no feminist voices at all in the mainstream and we felt like it would be really great if we could have some kind of a presence to a larger audience.'[199] In many ways, Fateman's comment anticipates the sentiment expressed just a few years later by many of the pop-feminist writers under discussion: that pop-feminism can and should work effectively within mainstream pop-culture in order to reach a new audience.[200]

---

[197] Catherine Driscoll, *Girls: Feminine Adolescence in Popular Culture and Cultural Theory* (New York: Columbia University Press, 2002), p. 272.

[198] Fales Library and Special Collections, New York University Libraries: Kathleen Hanna Papers, MSS 271, box 2, folder 2, Kathleen Hanna, un-named spoken-word fragment, date unknown.

[199] 'Le Tigre Talks Song-Writing, Politics and *Spin* Magazine', *The Huntington News*, 24 October 2004 <http://huntnewsnu.com/2004/10/le-tigre-talks-song-writing-politics-and-spin-magazine/> [accessed 19.12.2013].

[200] Sonja Eismann, 'Einleitung', p. 10.

3

North American Pop-Feminism
in the Post-Digital Era

Since the ascendance of 'cyberfeminism' in the 1990s, one response to the challenge of theorizing the post-human and the post-gender subject,[1] much feminist work on women and/in popular culture has occurred online. It is arguably here that the riot-grrrl ethos re-emerged towards the close of the 1990s, in an interactive subculture capable of avoiding the surveillance structures of the physical world and reaching a wider, younger audience.

The first wave of feminist digital theorists, who often focused on Multi-User-Domain technology (MUD) or computer-mediated communication (CMC), theorized the internet as an intrinsically 'female space' due to its function as a community-building tool resembling the practices of female sociality,[2] as a matrix of safe free-play disconnected from the millstone of the body,[3] and as a technology whose reliance on networks is analogous with the traditionally female craft of weaving.[4] Although the logic of these models is inflected with essentialist assumptions, the internet has also been construed by other feminist scholars as an ambiguously gendered and malleable realm suited to transgressing, subverting, or indeed dismantling gender binaries.[5]

Anna Feigenbaum uses the model of Deleuze and Guattari's rhizome to depict the non-linear pathways and networks first established by riot-grrrl zine culture and adopted by what she calls 'Web Gurls'.[6] Riot grrrl Rebecca Odes, along with Esther Drill and Heather McDonald, founded www.gurl.com in 1996, the largest website dedicated to teenage girls in North America at the time. Since then, feminist-defined websites for young women and teenagers created and moderated by women in North America, but also across the globe, have multiplied exponentially. Gurl. com still exists, as do the newer sites for teenage feminists *the f bomb* and *rookie*, conceived, produced, and moderated by two women under the age of twenty

---

[1] Rosi Braidotti, 'Cyberfeminism with a Difference', *New Formations* 29 (1996), 9–25.
[2] Dale Spender, *Nattering on the Net: Women, Power and Cyberspace* (North Melbourne: Spinifex Press, 1995).
[3] Anneke Smelik, 'Die virtuele matrix. Het lichaam in cyberpunkfilms', *Tijdschrift voor Genderstudies*, 3.4 (2000), 4–13; Jenny Sundén, 'What Happened to Difference in Cyberspace? The (Re)turn of the She-cyborg', *Feminist Media Studies*, 1.2 (2001), 215–32.
[4] Sadie Plant, *Zeros and Ones: Digital Women and the New Technoculture* (London: Fourth Estate, 1998).
[5] See especially, Rosi Braidotti, 'Cyberfeminism with a Difference'.
[6] Anna Feigenbaum, 'Remapping the Resonances of Riot Grrrl', p. 144.

(Julie Zeilinger and Tavi Gevinson). Such sites proclaim their feminist credentials to varying degrees, with a greater or lesser focus on fashion and beauty, but all pivot upon the notion of providing young women with a voice in a safe and interactive community forum and a progressive framework for navigating the realm of popular culture. *The f bomb*'s creator introduces the site as:

> a blog/community created by and for teenage girls who care about their rights as women and want to be heard. In this case the 'F Bomb' stands for 'feminist.' However, it also pokes fun at the idea that the term 'feminist' is so stigmatized—it is our way of proudly reclaiming the word. [...] The FBomb.org is for girls who have enough social awareness to be angry and who want to verbalize that feeling.[7]

Websites for 'older' younger women include *Jezebel*, *Bitch Media*, *Bust*, *Feministing*, and *Shakesville*, which generally contain greater political content. *Bitch* and *Bust* began as magazines at the height of riot-grrrl renown (in 1996 and 1993 respectively) with the aim of providing and encouraging an 'engaged, thoughtful feminist response to mainstream media and popular culture'.[8] The *Bitch Media* website claims that it attracts over 9,000 views a day and that the magazine has over 10,000 subscribers in over 46 countries. *Bitch* is a non-profit feminist media organization and *Bust*, which is not, nevertheless donates a percentage of its profits to breast cancer research.[9] Of all of these sites, *Feministing* and *Shakesville* are the only ones without an online shop in which products branded with the online community's logo can be purchased, or where related clothing and beauty products can be viewed from mainstream and/or independent fashion lines. *Bust* claims to provide 'an uncensored view on the female experience' and to tell the 'truth about women's lives', presenting a 'female perspective on pop-culture' by 'busting stereotypes about women'.[10]

Jessica Valenti, founder and executive producer of *Feministing.com*, wrote in 2007 of her love of *Bitch* and *Bust*. She locates these magazines and websites in the context of third-wave feminism, wherein she also situates riot grrrl and, in particular, Kathleen Hanna, 'scrawling SLUT across her stomach'.[11] Valenti's *Full Frontal Feminism*, indeed all of the pop-feminist texts under discussion, must therefore be viewed against the backdrop of a growing body of online feminist writing that works with the premise that young women can engage with popular culture in a reflective, critical manner and can locate a scene of agency in their negotiations without being duped by corporate consumer culture. Valenti states, for example: 'I do have faith that younger women can look at pop-culture and analyse it in a way that's positive'.[12]

By the end of 2014, seven years after the publication of Valenti's first volume, it seemed as if feminism had indeed fully permeated pop-culture, becoming what *Bitch*

---

[7] Julie Zeilinger, *The f bomb*, 2014 <http://thefbomb.org/about/> [accessed 04.10.2013].
[8] 'About Us', *Bitch Media*, 2013 <https://bitchmedia.org/about-us> [accessed 25.9.2017].
[9] 'Bust Boobtique', *Bust*, 2013 <http://www.bustboobtique.com/> [accessed 03.10.2013].
[10] 'About Bust', *Bust*, 2013 <http://www.bust.com/info/about-bust.html> [accessed 02.10.2013].
[11] Jessica Valenti, *Full Frontal Feminism*, p. 173.   [12] Ibid., p. 43.

co-founder Andi Zeisler terms 'cool',[13] in Rosalind Gill's terminology, 'luminous'.[14] In contrast to the earlier reticence of artists like Pink, Lavigne et al., artists and celebrities such as Beyoncé, Emma Watson, and Taylor Swift made public statements about their commitment to feminism; feminist micro-campaigns on social media were consistently challenging discriminatory practices or offensive statements by public figures and often had a tangible impact;[15] multiple consumer brands, media outputs and campaigns made explicit links to feminism;[16] and both celebrities and politicians alike donned the Fawcett Society's 'This is what a feminist looks like' T-shirt in 2014.

However, writing in 2016, Zeisler admits that she 'can't help worry that those of us who hoped that the marriage of pop-culture and feminism would yield deliciously progressive fruit might have a lot to answer for'.[17] Zeisler's admission is grounded in her observation that:

> Within a very short span of time, feminism has come to occupy perhaps its most complex role ever in American, if not global, culture. It's a place where most of the problems that have necessitated feminist movements to begin with are still very much in place, but at the same time there's a mainstream, celebrity, consumer embrace of feminism that positions it as a cool, fun, accessible identity that anyone can adopt. I've seen this called 'pop feminism', 'feel-good feminism' and 'white feminism'. I call it marketplace feminism. It's decontextualized. It's depoliticized. And it's probably feminism's most popular iteration ever.

Zeisler's 2016 textual intervention resonates with the arguments I make in this book. It is all the more striking due to her sense of complicity, her awareness of the ways in which the work she has been involved with for years has aligned with, if not contributed to, the assimilation and marketization of feminism. This is in part due to the strategy adopted by many commercial and media platforms, such as *Bust* above, to translate feminism into a 'lifestyle brand' thus offering it up to market forces. In relation to *Bust*, for example, the page welcoming prospective advertisers reads:

> Since 1993, *BUST* has been the groundbreaking [sic], award-winning, and original women's lifestyle brand that is unique in its ability to truly connect with over half a million members of the X and Y generations of female tastemakers. *BUST*'s brand value offers great integrated marketing platforms to strengthen your company's promotional strategies and add to your consumer base.[18]

---

[13] Andi Zeisler, *We Were Feminists Once*, p. x.

[14] See Rosalind Gill, 'Post-postfeminism?'.

[15] See Sherri Williams, '#SayHerName: Using Digital Activism to Document Violence against Black Women', *Feminist Media Studies*, 16.5 (2016), 922–5; Candi Carter Olson, '#BringBackOurGirls: Digital Communities Supporting Real-World Change and Influencing Mainstream Media Agendas', *Feminist Media Studies*, 16.5 (2016), 772–87.

[16] See Dara Persis Murray, 'Branding "Real" Social Change in Dove's Campaign for Real Beauty', *Feminist Media Studies*, 13.1 (2013), 83–101; Anita Brady, 'Taking Time between G-string Changes to Educate Ourselves: Sinéad O'Connor, Miley Cyrus, and Celebrity Feminism', *Feminist Media Studies*, 16.3 (2016), 429–44; Nosheen Iqbal, 'Femvertising: How Brands are Selling #empowerment to women', *The Guardian*, 12 October 2015. https://www.theguardian.com/lifeandstyle/2015/oct/12/femvertising-branded-feminism [accessed 06.02.2017]; Elisabeth Prügl, 'Neoliberalising Feminism'.

[17] Andi Zeisler, *We Were Feminists Once*, p. xv.

[18] 'Advertise with Bust', *Bust*, 2013 <http://www.bust.com/advertise-in-bust.html> [accessed 02.10.2013].

This move cynically transforms a feminist community, which promises its members—in bad faith—a toolkit for negotiating pop-culture to their advantage, into a marketing platform from which young women are offered up as consumers-in-waiting. As the advertisements these young women view emanate from a trusted, feminist source, they appear endorsed by the community, acceptable and desirable. The profits gained by the site allegedly flow back into its running, but this process is not transparent. When Valenti advised young women in 2007 not to 'believe the hype' when encountering pop-culture, urging them: 'roll your eyes when you see a sexist ad and point out its bullshittery [sic] to everyone around you', she overlooked the more insidious ways in which elements of pop-feminist media collude with corporate consumer culture to produce—and profit from—young women's desires.[19] It is important to note that *Maedchenmannschaft*, the German feminist website, does not host advertising but instead provides details to readers of where they can donate money to support the project.

It is worth returning to McRobbie's work on young women's melancholia and illegible rage at this point. She contends that subcultural entities like riot grrrl, the f word and Ladyfest provide young women with the opportunity to overcome melancholia by 're-attaching to social life' and to detach from the 'self-berating ego' coterminous with illegible rage.[20] But she also observes that no market is 'more precious to contemporary capitalism and its consumer culture than that of young women'.[21] Subcultures, like feminist websites or blogs, are 'almost instantly tracked, charted, documented and publicised', which process, alongside 'incessant discourses of female individualisation', transforms subcultures into spaces where young women's rage becomes 'once again illegible'.[22]

Just as early optimism regarding pop-culture's transformative potential for feminism has been exposed to scrutiny and invited more nuanced debate, recent research into feminist digital activism has emphasized the political potential of online protest, especially in its reconfiguration of local/global debates but also the entanglement of digital feminist and neoliberal economies.[23] On the one hand, Maria Stehle, Carrie Smith-Prei, and Christina Scharff highlight the 'challenge' made to 'neoliberal sensibilities' by digital protest culture.[24] Online protest stages this challenge by 'foregrounding wider social structures and thereby precluding the reduction of the political to the personal'.[25] Recent examples of this phenomenon include hashtag campaigns such as #YesAllWomen, #MeToo, #Aufschrei in the German language context, and #everydaysexism.

On the other hand, Stehle et al. also illuminate the ways in which neoliberalism may 'intersect with contemporary forms of protest'.[26] One way it does this is

---

[19] Jessica Valenti, *Full Frontal Feminism*, p. 239.
[20] Angela McRobbie, *The Aftermath of Feminism*, p. 121.   [21] Ibid.   [22] Ibid.
[23] Emily Spiers, 'Performing the "quing of berlin": Transnational Digital Interfaces in Queer Feminist Protest Culture', special issue of *Feminist Media Studies* 'Digital Feminisms: Transnational Activism in German Protest Cultures', 128–49.
[24] Maria Stehle, Carrie Smith-Prei, and Christina Scharff, 'Digital Feminisms: Transnational Activism in German Protest Cultures', 8.
[25] Ibid.   [26] Ibid.

through the potential overlap between the digitally active protester and the ideal entrepreneurial subject as constructed by neoliberalism. The links between online forms of communication, protest, and capitalist structures have been well documented.[27] Hester Baer has demonstrated how digital forms of protest can be commodified and deployed as marketing tools.[28]

Equally problematic are the politics of location in relation to online activism.[29] Rather than constituting a realm beyond difference, the virtual world may in fact make differences between women invisible, rather than more visible. The Twitter campaign of August 2013 entitled #SolidarityisforWhiteWomen and online responses to Courtney Martin and Vanessa Valenti's 2012 report on the future of online feminism represented a welcome challenge to what various digital feminists call 'Anglo-centric' online feminism, a seemingly deterritorialized, neutral zone that is in fact white, and culturally and politically North American.[30] These voices remain radical, staunchly opposed to cultural 'assimilation', staunchly resistant to mainstream feminism, which as one commentator puts it in relation to the UK is 'once again, Caitlin Moran'.[31]

What kind of feminism becomes visible across mainstream media is a question being asked both on- and offline. In their most recent publications, Jessica Valenti and Roxane Gay consider the disproportionate value placed on humorous and optimistic voices in contemporary pop-feminism. 'The feminism that's popular right now', Valenti argues, 'is largely grounded in using optimism and humour to undo the damage that sexism has wrought.' But, she continues, '[m]aybe it's okay if we don't want to be inspirational just this once'.[32] This statement marks a dramatic shift in tone from Valenti's humorous and largely optimistic 2007 volume, *Full Frontal Feminism*, which could not be further in tenor from her 2016 publication *Sex Object*. Valenti frames this latest volume, described as a memoir, with a statement that echoes remarks made by Mary Gaitskill in her 2003 essay on the film version of *Secretary*, discussed in the previous chapter: '[t]his inability to be vulnerable—the unwillingness to be victims, even if we are—doesn't protect us, it just covers up the wreckage. [...] Without a pat solution, silver lining, or happy ending, we're

---

[27] See especially Jodi Dean, *Democracy and Other Neoliberal Fantasies: Communicative Capitalism and Left Politics* (Durham, NC: Duke University Press, 2009) and my analysis of *Bust* above.

[28] Hester Baer, 'Redoing Feminism: Digital Activism, Body Politics, and Neoliberalism', special issue of *Feminist Media Studies* 'Digital Feminisms: Transnational Activism in German Protest Cultures', 17–34. See also the Twitter campaign #YesAllWomen and its feed @yesallwomen, where 'She's Someone' campaign T-Shirts are regularly promoted. They are sold via a linked online platform, Teespring, and it is unclear where the profits from the T-shirt purchases go.

[29] See Pinar Tuzcu, '"Allow Access to Location?" Digital Feminist Geographies', special issue of *Feminist Media Studies* 'Digital Feminisms: Transnational Activism in German Protest Cultures', 150–63.

[30] Mikki Kendall, '#SolidarityIsForWhiteWomen: Women of Colour's Issue with Digital Feminism', *The Guardian*, 14 August 2013. Courtney E. Martin and Vanessa Valenti, '#FemFuture: Online Feminism', *New Feminist Solutions*, 8.1 (2012), 1–34.

[31] Flavia Dzodan, 'US Centrism and Inhabiting a Non-Space in #femfuture', *Red Light Politics*, 10 April 2013 <http://www.redlightpolitics.info/post/47611939840/us-centrism-and-inhabiting-a-non-space-in-femfuture> [accessed 05.10. 2013].

[32] Jessica Valenti, *Sex Object: A Memoir* (New York: HarperCollins, 2016), p. 4.

just complainers.'[33] Valenti's book functions as a corrective to this tendency, by moving generically into the politicized personal, the memoir, and describing the author's experiences of sexual objectification, discrimination, and abuse. It ends with an uncommented upon index of graphically violent and abusive emails, Facebook messages, Tweets, and comments the author received between 2008 and 2015.

For Roxane Gay, the problem with humour in feminist texts is that it often comes at the expense of complexity and nuance. In her critique of Caitlin Moran's *How to Be A Woman*, which I discuss in Chapter 4, Gay asserts: 'There's so much in this book that demands we reconcile casual insensitivity and narrow cultural awareness for the sake of funny feminist (albeit dated) thinking.'[34] She continues: 'we need to overcome our deeply entrenched positions and resistance to nuance. We have to be more interested in making things better than just being right, or interesting, or funny.'[35]

In a move reminiscent of Mary Gaitskill's plea, made already in 1990, for the political importance of depicting women's vulnerability as well as strength, Valenti and Gay both advocate for the legitimacy of vulnerability and the importance of nuance in contemporary feminist thinking. In doing so, both Valenti and Gay turn to literature, specifically to writing by women, in their prose texts. Valenti does so through a selection of quotations from Joan Didion and Shakespeare, among others, which separate sections of her book, Gay through her nuanced and intelligent discussions of recent literary texts (she is also a writer of fiction herself). This emphasis on the literary aligns with both authors' understanding of the narrative qualities inherent in selfhood, identity formation, and the processes of subjective consciousness, as I laid out in Chapter 1. Yet, as Gay observes in relation to the wider socio-political sphere: '[r]arely do women get to be the center [sic] of attention. Rarely do our stories get to matter.'[36] Valenti also notes the role played by wider social forces on the 'stories' of self, constructed by and for women:

> A high school teacher once told me that identity is half what we tell ourselves and half what we tell other people about ourselves. But the missing piece he didn't mention—the piece that holds so much weight, especially in the minds of young women and girls—is the stories that other people tell about ourselves. Those narratives become the ones we shape ourselves into. They're who we are, even if so much of it is performance.[37]

An analysis of recent literary responses to the issues discussed by Gay and Valenti reveals a confluence of themes, aesthetics, and genre choice. Autofiction and the memoir, whether on- or offline, constitute the predominant generic vehicles employed by contemporary North American writers, like Michelle Tea, Sheila Heti, and Maggie Nelson, but also literary blogger and print author Kate Zambreno. Through their texts, these authors undertake the generation of self through narrative, drawing on the lived life, deeming it text-worthy in all its

---

[33] Ibid., p. 15.
[34] Roxane Gay, *Bad Feminist: Essays* (New York: HarperCollins, 2014), p. 103.
[35] Ibid., p. 108.   [36] Roxane Gay, *Bad Feminist*, p. viv.
[37] Jessica Valenti, *Sex Object*, p. 3.

aspects, including sexuality, desire, violence, despair, anger, awkwardness, narcissism, and so on. On reading Eileen Myles's influential autofiction *Chelsea Girls* (1994), Tea observes how the author was 'never afraid to reveal harshness, seemingly oblivious to how she came off in the text, narrating herself like a god looking down at a fascinating life'.[38]

By enacting radical openness and facilitating heightened visibility for marginalized subject positions through their memoirs and autofictions, these authors understand themselves to be undertaking a political act. They can therefore be placed on a continuum with riot-grrrl zine-makers as well as predecessors like Acker, Gaitskill, Myles, and Kraus, who, decades before, had radically opened up the possibilities for performing the self in print literature. Writing in 2012, Kate Zambreno argued that the online world of literary blogging offers similar opportunities, contending that the 'decision to write the private in public, it is a political one. It is a counterattack against [...] censorship. To tell our narratives, the truth of our experiences. To write our flawed, messy selves. To fight against the desire to be erased.'[39] Zambreno's statement resonates with Celia Lury's previously discussed defence of autobiographical writing by women authors made in 1991, when she viewed the employment by women writers of the first-person narrative 'positively as a space from which to construct a feminine position in opposition to that of the universal male position'. The continuing critical use of this mode well into the twenty-first century by the writers named above gives credence to Lury's twenty-five-year-old contention that this aesthetic would remain important so long as certain issues still retained their 'urgency for the women's movement as a whole: sexuality, subjectivity, self- and group-representation and political practice'.[40] Zambreno views her writing as negotiating the parameters of self, group, and political practice: '[t]his subculture of literary blogs, fluid, amorphous, non-hierarchical, functions as a community of solidarity, privately and publicly – fighting against feelings of illegitimacy and invisibility, of feeling like ghosts in the physical world.'[41]

Michelle Tea links her own 'self-writing' with the earlier practices of North American riot grrrl. In her memoir and putative 'self-help manual' for survivors of 'dysfunctional formative years' *How to Grow Up* (2015), Tea recalls zine-making parties in the 1990s: 'what [the girls] were all doing was creating culture—weird, underground culture—using their lives as the raw material'.[42] Both Tea and Sheila Heti cut their teeth making zines at the height of the riot-grrrl movement.

The corpus of autofictions I discuss here, written by queer and feminist writers engaging with the same issues of selfhood and agency in neoliberal postfeminism examined by pop-feminists, owes much to an earlier subculture of queer and feminist writing that predates riot grrrl. In part, the accessibility, archival quality, and rapid circulation inherent in internet technology and social media has facilitated a

---

[38] Michelle Tea, *Valencia*, 2nd edition (Berkeley, CA: Seal Press, 2008 [2000]), p. 8.

[39] Kate Zambreno, *Heroines* (Los Angeles: Semiotexte/Active Agents, 2012), p. 291.

[40] Celia Lury, 'Reading the Self', p. 106.

[41] Kate Zambreno, *Heroines*, p. 293. *Heroines*, published by Chris Kraus at Semiotext(e), emerged piecemeal on Zambreno's influential literary blog *Frances Farmer is my Sister*, which is now unaccessible.

[42] Michelle Tea, *How to Grow Up: A Memoir* (New York: Plume, 2015), p. vii and p. 227.

renaissance for writers like Myles, Kraus, and Acker. Decades of queer and feminist activism have also resulted in the current mainstream visibility of previously underground and/or marginalized queer, lesbian, and feminist communities, which has coincided with the increasing market viability of so-called transgressive identity performances in wider popular culture, attested to by recent commercially successful pop-cultural artefacts that focus on queer and trans* lives like the award-winning television series *Transparent* (2014–), *The L-Word* (2004–9), and *Orange is the New Black* (2013–). Drawing on a key concept of contemporary queer studies, the author Maggie Nelson refers to this phenomenon as 'homonormativity'[43] and observes:

> There's something truly strange about living in a historical moment in which the conservative anxiety and despair about queers bringing down civilisation and its institutions (marriage most notably) is met by the anxiety and despair so many queers feel about the failure or incapacity of queerness to bring down civilisation and its institutions, and their frustration with the assimilationist, unthinkingly neoliberal bent of the mainstream GLBTQ+ movement, which has spent fine coin begging entrance into two historically oppressive structures: marriage and the military.[44]

Ironically, then, the successes of queer feminist protest culture, the digital economy, and neoliberal economics have given rise to a renaissance for writers like Kraus, Acker, and Myles, whose works were highly influential for writers like Tea, Zambreno, Heti, and Nelson. Myles, who has recently embraced the visually poetic potential of Instagram, suggests that 'what social media has done is made us relish variables. [...] We're just living in these floating fragmentations.' According to Myles, the experience of fragmented existence brought the realization to many people that 'everybody's queer—everybody's wrongly shaped for a culture that requires conformity.'[45]

In her interview with Myles, Emily Witt claims that Myles's literary style in *Chelsea Girls*, first published over twenty years ago, feels 'as contemporary as the essayistic autobiographical fiction of Sheila Heti, Ben Lerner, and Tao Lin, who might be considered her literary offspring'.[46] The championing of Myles as a literary influence by such writers, as well as the rhizomatic spread of information online, has led to the republication of *Chelsea Girls* in both the US (2014) and the UK (2016), as well as a volume of new and selected poems aptly called *I Must be Living Twice* (2015).

Kraus experienced a similar renaissance when her epistolary autofiction *I Love Dick* (1997) was re-released in 2006, then released for the first time in the UK in 2015 and commissioned in adapted form as an Amazon TV series in 2016. The novel is based on actual events that happened between 1994 and 1995, when

[43] See Lisa Duggan, 'The New Homonormativity: The Sexual Politics of Neoliberalism', in *Materializing Democracy: Toward a Revitalized Cultural Politics*, ed. by Dana D. Nelson, Russ Castronovo (Durham, NC; London: Duke University Press, 2002), pp. 175–94.

[44] Maggie Nelson, *The Argonauts*, p. 32.

[45] Emily Witt, 'The Poet Idolized by a New Generation of Feminists', interview with Eileen Myles, *New York Times Style Magazine*, 15 April 2016, available at http://www.nytimes.com/2016/04/15/t-magazine/poet-eileen-myles-chelsea-girls.html?_r=0 [accessed 16.02.2017].

[46] Ibid.

Kraus and her husband began writing letters to an acquaintance, Dick, with whom Kraus's character becomes infatuated. The intimate letters function as a platform for Kraus's character to explore the contours of her own consciousness, selfhood and desires, while taking in critical and literary theory, the experiences of everyday life, marriage, and her own sexuality.

Writing in 2016, she recalls that when *I Love Dick* appeared in November 1997, it was received mostly with derision: ' "A book not so much written as secreted," as the reviewer for Artforum noted.'[47] However, when the book was re-released with Semiotexte in 2006, 'it enjoyed a much more welcoming reception. The world had changed. Women, by then, had utterly rejected the unspoken rule of feminine discretion. In a milieu of female blogs and third-wave feminism, *I Love Dick* was seen as prescient.'[48] Indeed, the recent volumes I now turn to continue the aesthetic and political explorations of works like Kraus's into the twenty-first century.

AUTOFICTION AND SELFHOOD: MAGGIE NELSON AND SHEILA HETI

So far as I can tell, most worthwhile pleasures on this earth slip between gratifying another and gratifying oneself. Some would call that an ethics.[49]

The two works I have selected for discussion here, Maggie Nelson's *The Argonauts* (2015) and Sheila Heti's *How Should a Person Be?* (2010), pursue a literary mode that melds autofiction, the novel, critical theory, and queer and feminist politics. As such, the authors are indebted to earlier writers like Kraus, Acker, and Myles. Nelson's hybrid work experiments with the fusion of direct quotations from critical theorists like Gilles Deleuze and Claire Parnet, Roland Barthes, Eve Kosofsky Sedgwick, Judith Butler, and Lee Edelman, among others, with a mode of autofiction that performatively explores the contours of self (the authorial voice at one point claims to be in 'drag as a memoirist'), but also the relationship between self and the other.[50]

Nelson plays continually with the trope of writing as self-construction and returns repeatedly to the central idea that the autofictive process reveals the profoundly intersubjective nature of articulating selfhood. Weaving Judith Butler's words from *Undoing Gender* (2004) into her own through the use of italics, Nelson calls this writing process 'the personal made public', by which she means 'writing that dramatizes the ways in which we are *for another or by virtue of another*, not in a single instance, but from the start and always' (TA, 59, original emphasis).

Nelson's text, which explores her relationship with artist Harry Dodge, an artist and writer who is fluidly gendered, explores Butler's premise of intense relationality

---

[47] Chris Kraus, 'I Love Dick Happened in Real Life, But it's Not a Memoir', *The Guardian*, 17 May 2016, available at https://www.theguardian.com/books/2016/may/17/chris-kraus-i-love-dick-happened-in-real-life-but-its-not-a-memoir [accessed 16.02.2017].

[48] Ibid.   [49] Maggie Nelson, *The Argonauts*, p. 120.

[50] Maggie Nelson, *The Argonauts*, p. 142. All other references are within the body of the text as TA.

being narrative based. Before meeting Dodge, Nelson claims to have been 'devoted to Wittgenstein's idea that the inexpressible is contained—inexpressibly!—in the expressed. [...] Its paradox is, quite literally, why I write, or how I feel able to keep writing' (TA, 3). Yet, when Harry expresses his feeling that an early version of the text with which the reader is immediately engaged does not 'behold' him, even when the author is writing about him, the narrator counters by paraphrasing American philosopher William James's account of subjectivity:

> Ok, but no mind can take the same interest in its neighbor's me as in his own. The neighbor's me falls together with all of the rest of things in one foreign mass, against which his own me stands out in startling relief.   (TA, 58)

Yet Harry's insistence that James's account falls short entails that Nelson's text goes on to probe further the relationship between 'writing and holding' (TA, 58). That is, she initially understands writing to be an act whereby one can find space away from the 'task of performing a self for others, [...] in response to a flow of projections and reflections ricocheting off us' (TA, 118). Yet, through her relationship with Harry, she comes to understand that the fundamental relationality of subjectivity continues even in the writing space.

In Shelia Heti's *How Should a Person Be?*, the character Sheila is first encountered in a state of paralysis as a result of a dilemma. Informed, as Nelson's character is, by her own understanding of performativity, i.e. that 'character exists from the outside alone', that 'inside the body there's just temperature', Sheila is nevertheless preoccupied by the question of how to 'build your soul'.[51] Sheila is an author and playwright attempting to make her life an object of beauty. Her frame of reference is twenty-first-century consumer and celebrity culture, meaning that when she asks '[h]ow should a person be?' she 'can't help answering like this: a celebrity'. She goes on:

> We are all specks of dirt, all on this earth at the same time. I look at all the people who are alive today and think, *These are my contemporaries. These are my fucking contemporaries!* We live in an age of some really great blow-job artists.   (HPB, 3, original emphasis)

At times, Sheila appears to be one of them. Referring to her friends, she complains: 'They like me for who I am, and I would rather be liked for who I appear to be, and for who I appear to be, to be who I am' (HPB, 3). This shame-faced admission lies behind her later observation that 'I see that I've done as little as anyone else in this world to deserve the grand moniker I' (HPB, 187).

Sheila can be understood as suffering from heterosexual melancholia and illegible rage, as I discussed in Chapter 1. The narrative's opening sections recount Sheila's early marriage to her now ex-husband and reveal a great deal about the normative frameworks in place that motivated her to marry in the first place:

> He didn't know my insides. There was something wrong inside me, something ugly, which I didn't want anyone to see, which would contaminate everything I would ever do. I knew the only way to repair this badness was devotion in love—the promise of

---

[51] Sheila Heti, *How Should a Person Be?* (London: Vintage, 2014 [2010]), p. 2. All other references are within the body of the text as HPB.

my love to a man. [...] I wanted to be an ideal. [...] Maybe it would correct my flightiness, confusion, and selfishness, which I despised, and which ever revealed my lack of unity inside.   (HPB, 22)

Sheila's comments reveal a subject who finds herself 'confined to the topographies of an unsustainable self-hood [...] and deeply invested in achieving an illusory identity defined according to a rigidly enforced set of feminine attributes'.[52] Marriage, at first seems the best option for securing a coherent, albeit illusory, identity. Yet after Sheila 'punches' through the 'brick wall' of her marriage (HPB, 44), she realizes that *she* will have to decide how to 'be', that marriage cannot prompt her vague idea of destiny to tell her how to 'behave', nor can it provide a sense of internal coherence. So the text itself charts this process of approaching coherence through self-narration in the mode of autofiction but also through the inclusion of stage dialogue with an 'other', marking an attempt to encounter being, both from the inside and in relational terms. In a wry side-swipe at the gendered and racialized politics of the literary scene Sheila is a part of, Heti implicitly valorizes the genre of autofiction as a more authentic as well as ethically preferable mode: 'All the white men I know are going to Africa. They want to tell the stories of African women. [...] They come at life from the outside, those white boys who went to Africa. To have to wear on the outside one's curiosity, one's pity, one's guilt...' (HPB, 168).

    In her attempt to 'come at life' from the inside, the character Sheila makes two important discoveries: the first is her growing friendship with the artist Margaux—allegedly her first female friendship, echoing the detrimental consequences for the melancholic self posited by McRobbie, resulting from a lacking feminist sociality. The second discovery relates to her voice and its relationship to self and other. Sheila finds an old tape recorder and begins using it to record her conversations with her close group of friends, all artists, and Margaux, in particular. The first time Sheila presses record marks a pivotal moment of self-reciprocity: 'I whispered low into the tape recorder's belly. I recorded my voice and played it back. I spoke into it tenderly and heard my tenderness returned.' The recorder becomes like a lover who would 'burrow into my deepest recesses, seek out the empty places inside me' (HPB, 57). Despite this moment of embodied self-reflexivity, Sheila spends most of her time recording Margaux, who confronts her greatest fear: having her words 'floating separate from [her] body' (HPB, 59).

    At first, however, Sheila merely uses Margaux's words verbatim in the piece of theatre she is trying to finish. She soon realizes, however, that:

[i]nstead of sitting down and writing my play with my words—using my imagination, pulling up the words from the solitude and privacy of my soul—I had used her words [...] and mixed it with the ugliness that was mine! [...] Unwilling to be naked, I had made her naked instead. I had not worked hard or at all. I had cheated.
                                                                        (HPB, 179)

Sheila's unwillingness to be 'naked' constitutes a symptom of the internalized drive for beauty and perfection in all areas of her life that is itself symptomatic of the

---

[52] Angela McRobbie, *The Aftermath of Feminism*, p. 120.

feminine 'masquerade' induced by postfeminist and neoliberal narratives of self-optimization. In an attempt to escape these drives, Sheila embarks upon a path of self-destruction consisting in her case of an all-consuming affair with a sadistic lover, Israel, for whom she 'castrates' her mind. Reflecting on the affair after she has finally ended it, she again reflects upon her motivations and the possibility of 'claiming life' again:[53]

> You missed it and the serpent slithered in. It is death coming, masquerading as life, and blessed is the man who can see the death drive in the woman. And blessed is the woman who can answer for herself, what about living? What is it about living that you want?   (HPB, 124)

The closing stages of the novel reveal that what Sheila in fact wants is to reject the internalized expectation of perfection that has dominated her search for 'how to be'. This decision is what ultimately allows her to write and to complete her work, the implication being that the work has become the text we are currently reading:

> If there can be no escape from who I am, then I ought to reach my end honestly, able to tell myself, at least, that I have lived it with all my being, making choices and deciding, walking the whole way. *Who cares?* [...] Aren't I human? Who am I to hold myself aloof from the terrible fates of the world? My life need be no less ugly than the rest.   (HPB, 274, original emphasis)

So Sheila starts to write and throws the 'trash and shit' of herself around: 'I made what I could with what I had. And I finally became a real girl' (HPB, 277). She reconciles with Margaux, who, simultaneously, has come to the conclusion that Sheila's recording, archiving, and reworking of her words denotes in fact the kind of 'beholding' that Harry Dodge desired from the central protagonist in Nelson's *The Argonauts*. 'All this time you've been recording me', Margaux reflects, 'you have been looking at me, really looking!' (HPB, 298). Heti's autofiction here echoes Nelson's through the emphasis placed on the relationality of selfhood. The novel's close brings this to a point when Sheila states: 'I had always believed that if I lost Margaux, I could go out and find another Margaux. [...] But I had never wanted to be one person, or even believed that I was one, so I had never considered the true singularity of anyone else' (HPB, 300). Both Heti and Nelson's autofictions thus illustrate the necessity of beholding the shape and definition of the other—their singularity—in the process of beholding the self.

'EXCELLENT DANGER' AND QUEER NORMALIZATION: MICHELLE TEA

In Miranda July's 2015 novel *The First Bad Man*, the central protagonist Cheryl Glickman, a repressed middle-aged employee of a non-profit women's self-defence organization, takes in the daughter of her employers as a house-guest. Clee, a sullen,

---

[53] Judith Butler, *The Psychic Life of Power*, p. 197.

self-declared 'misogynist' in her early twenties, begins to physically attack her host in her home. This horrifying behaviour quickly turns into a contractual 'adult game' that proves mutually satisfying and later forms the basis of their romantic relationship. The violent encounters constitute a particularly intense form of release for Cheryl:

> Our first tussle under the new agreement had been long and dirty and had taken us into all the rooms of the house. I can-canned and popped, not just to defend myself but out of real anger, first at her and then at people like her, dumb people. I popped her for being young without humility, when I had had so much humility at her age— too much. I bit and almost broke the skin on her forearm. [...] When we started up again my skin was tender; bruises were already forming, and every muscle was shaking. It was nice, deeper and more focused. I felt my face contorting with a wrath I didn't recognise; it seemed out of scale for my species. [...] I'd been mugged every single day of my life and this was the first day I wasn't mugged. At the end she quickly squeezed my hand twice: good game.[54]

That it is not only Clee but also the middle-aged Cheryl, the novel's focalizer, who embarks upon a consensual form of therapeutic violence entails that July extends the literary trope of the angry, often violent twenty-something seeking to discharge her 'illegible rage' and applies it to women who are also older, generally conservative, and professionally established. July's novel thus constitutes an ironic departure from the deployment of transgressive, sadomasochistic content in the works of Acker and Gaitskill, gesturing to a sense of normalization, in fact, of both a literary trope and a social phenomenon.

In Michelle Tea's 'memoir', *Valencia* (2000), however, the angry, violent woman is a twenty-five-year-old 'warrior' and an 'artist, a lover, a lover of women'.[55] The first-person narrator, named Michelle, lives in 'excellent danger' (Va, 250) in 1990s San Francisco, in a community that feels at times as if '[v]iolence could erupt at any minute like a big song and dance number, a musical of seething rage' (Va, 25). Michelle, awakened from the 'coma induced by [her] banquet of 70s flavoured feminism', arguing in bars 'about S/M and pornography' (Va, 96), lives excessively and 'uncompromisingly at the fringe of our culture'.[56] She drinks, takes drugs, organizes poetry events, and is briefly employed as a sex worker. The memoir traces her tumultuous, passionate affairs with several women over the course of a year or more. Tea's lyrical prose is at its most eloquent when describing the highs and lows of her feelings for these women. Seeing her new girlfriend at a party, Michelle explains:

> She didn't know that my heart was a sandstorm waiting to open her skin in a desert of cuts. She didn't know the animal that waited in my stomach, silently shredding the walls. [...] I wanted to shoot myself into her arms so she understood the need to crash cars with me, to tear up pavement because we were beautiful. (Va, 249)

---

[54] Miranda July, *The First Bad Man* (Edinburgh: Canongate, 2015), pp. 80–1.
[55] Michelle Tea, *Valencia*, p. 56. All other references are in the body of the text as Va.
[56] Michelle Tea, *How to Grow Up*, p. 232. All other references are in the body of the text as HGU.

The intensity of her feelings here becomes expressed through metaphors of violence, intoxication, and destruction, and the sex she has is equally marked with danger: knife play, violent fantasy, and the desire to be 'slapped around until I left my body, slid into an altered state of consciousness' (Va, 163). The desire for transcendence evoked by Michelle's search for extreme states of being is reminiscent of Gaitskill's protagonist, Justine Shade, whose experience of violent sex left the 'furniture of her internal self' smashed, making her feel 'split apart and boundary-less' (TG, 283). In *Valencia*, Michelle's desire for such violent transcendence runs parallel with romanticized depictions of squalor and hardship, of the beauty of friendship and community, and of the thrill of transgression.

Yet, in her 2007 introduction to the second edition of *Valencia*, Tea carefully distances herself from the heady affect evoked in the text. The author ends with this cryptic disclaimer: '*Valencia* is a bug trapped in emotional amber. It's a snapshot, more or less, of my twenty-fifth year on earth, written not how it happened but how I *felt* it happened, and how I felt about it happening. [...] Our lives make awesome stories, especially if you don't get too attached to the thread of your own narrative' (Va, 10, original emphasis).

This last statement, a warning of sorts, makes sense when considering the fact that *Valencia* is the second of five memoirs written by Tea; it was also the one to be selected as material for a film by a collaboration of queer filmmakers in 2013. Her latest memoir, however, *How to Grow Up* (2015), marks a departure from Tea's signature style and transgressive content and signals an attempt on the part of the author to detach from several key 'threads' of her own narrative that run through the previous memoirs. The introduction to *How to Grow Up* sets out the author's intentions:

> After a lifetime spent writing memoirs that detail the struggles that I and countless other girls experience when they're born broke, or weird, into tricky families and unsafe towns, it seemed like time to write a book about how that struggle can actually, with luck and grit, lead you straight into a life you didn't know you wanted and never thought you'd have.   (HGU, ix)

This statement throws light both on the disclaimer in the second-edition introduction to *Valencia* cited above and also the general tone and content of *How to Grow Up*. This last volume charts the period after the events woven into *Valencia*. It traces an unhappy relationship with a man, with whom she lives in poverty for many years; her continuing writing; her decision to stop drinking and identify as an alcoholic; her gradual accrual of stability in the form of wealth, professional reputation, and a home; and her relationship with and marriage to a woman named Dashiell, with whom she has a child. It is no surprise that the tone and language of this memoir differs starkly from earlier works like *Valencia*, as Tea revealed in an interview that the idea for *How to Grow Up* arose from a 'brainstorming session' with her agent, in which they tried to develop a 'non-fiction book' that would have more 'commercial appeal'.[57] *How to Grow Up* manufactures this appeal by

---

[57] Antonia Crane, 'Growing Up: The Rumpus Interview with Michelle Tea', 30 April 2015, available at http://therumpus.net/2015/04/growing-up-the-rumpus-interview-with-michelle-tea/ [accessed 16.02.2017].

focusing on the pathology of Tea's addictions in a somewhat proselytizing tone that evokes the language of the Twelve-Step programme the author embarked upon; it is also cleansed of the passages of breathless affect and lyrical imaginary identified in *Valencia* above.

The narrative arc embraces a rags-to-riches structure that foregrounds the narrator's recovery, growing wealth and material consumption. In this way, it reads less like a memoir and more like a self-help manual in the vein of, for example, Jen Sincero's 2013 *You Are a Badass: How to Stop Doubting Your Greatness and Start Living an Awesome Life*. As a result the fearless 'warrior' figure of *Valencia* becomes depicted retrospectively and almost exclusively as a scared, vulnerable addict, labouring under a false sense of agency while performing an identity characterized by overblown confidence and recklessness:

> [T]his urge to identify the most outrageous, slightly dangerous possibility and hurl myself into it—both daring the Universe and trusting that it would somehow hold me safe— has always been inside me. I think it's in a lot of addicts. Life can be scary. On some level it's scary for everyone and those layers of scary can really pile up when you're female, when you're sort of weird, when you're broke, when you're queer. [. . .] Acting fearless creates an understanding of yourself as sort of badass, which generates extreme confidence—which is super helpful when your individual battle to find your place in the world feels more than daunting.   (HGU, 63–4)

However, many of the dangerous events narrated in *Valencia* connect not only with self-destructive behaviours but also with politically conscious acts: Michelle attempting to protect a sex worker, who has just been raped, from being taken away forcefully by the police; breaking into the Communist press where she works briefly to make queer feminist zines with her friends; taking part in Gay Pride, and so on. The ardent commitment to political change evoked in *Valencia* by such passages as: '[w]hen the revolution came Iris would lift two rifles in the air, she would throw one to me and together we would run into the streets' (Va, 145) also becomes disavowed in *How to Grow Up*. Michelle's political consciousness, which is in *Valencia* 'very fresh and important' (Va, 96), now appears to have been merely a symptom of a fully pathologized past in which the 'excellent danger' becomes read as delusional, as the death-drive associated with addiction, not as something potentially transformative, politically or psychologically, but as an illness of sorts. Throughout *How to Grow Up*, recovery alone is valorized, and causally linked not only to financial stability and professional acclaim but also, more problematically, to normative practices of material consumption, beautification, and access to the heteronormative institutions of marriage and childbirth. Simultaneously, the grimy romanticism and experimental flashes of Tea's prose cede to formulaic and jargon-filled constructions filled with the clichés of the self-help genre.

When Michelle decides to begin dating again, for example, she states: 'I needed some rules. At first my Rules for Love were formulated to try and minimize heart break and embarrassment. Later they helped me not to waste my time' (HGU, 96). By wasting her time, Michelle in fact means dating people who are not 'marriage material' (HGU, 98–9). Her capitalization of 'Rules' and 'Love' provides an intertextual reference to the 1995 self-help book *The Rules: Time-Tested Secrets for Capturing the Heart of Mr Right* by Ellen Fein and Sherrie Schneider. The premise of this earlier book, which was a bestseller and frequently referenced on the TV show *Sex and the City*, contends that women should not pursue men, should retain an air of mystery, and should let men approach them with the goal of securing a marriage partner in the shortest time possible. Unsurprisingly, the book has since been criticized for its stereotypical depiction and cynical manipulation of gender roles.[58]

Nevertheless, Michelle embraces her set of Rules and finally meets Dashiell. Part of what attracts Michelle to Dashiell is how different she is from her. Michelle, who has just begun to take antidepressants at the time when she notes this conversation with Dashiell, recalls: 'On our first date, Dashiell actually told me how important it was to be happy—that she felt it should be a *choice*, and it was what she chose' (HGU, 113, original emphasis). Michelle's apparent admiration for such strong-willed decision contrasts with the evidence of her own life story, which traces her own and others' struggles to overcome often traumatic former lives— very material circumstances that might preclude happiness from being a straightforward 'choice'—through the empathy and support of the queer community in which they live. Dashiell's statement appears so removed from the realities of that life that Michelle's admiration for its sentiment itself borders on the delusional. The capacity to choose even complex ontological states like happiness implied by Dashiell's conviction evokes a neoliberal ethos of entrepreneurial self-optimization that increasingly informs Tea's memoir as it unfolds. The contention that such a choice can be made in a no-nonsense manner also evokes the fundamental premise of Sincero's *You Are a Badass* and the author's claim that there is 'no big mystery to this stuff: If you want something badly enough and decide you will get it, you will'.[59]

The growing endorsement of neoliberal values in *How to Grow Up* aligns, too, with a sense that Michelle's behaviour becomes increasingly homonormative over the course of the memoir. When Dashiell proposes to Michelle with a large diamond engagement ring, for example, Michelle comments:

> There was something surreal about that, about my weird life suddenly syncing up with the lives of countless normal people everywhere, that I couldn't help but love. [...] It was like that whole otherworldly moment of love and surprise and fantasy and reality all became crystallized in that sparkling mineral [...] looking like a crazy lady from some 1950s poster of womanhood. (HGU, 117)

The attribution of a sense of normality to her 'weird life' via the ring symbol betrays a profound yearning on Michelle's part to be considered 'normal'. The choice of simile here is also revealing, in that her idea of normality is instantly linked with a fantasy image of 1950s hyper-femininity. Indeed, the fantasy of femininity appears to be part of what attracts her to marriage; for example, she claims she does not

[58] See for example, Meg Barker, *Rewriting The Rules* (New York: Routledge, 2013).
[59] Jen Sincero, *You Are a Badass: How to Stop Doubting Your Greatness and Start Living an Awesome Life* (New York: Running Press, 2013), p. 195.

'care about its history of female oppression' (HGU, 98), but is thrilled by the prospect of the party and wedding veil (HGU, 98).

Self-defining as 'femme' in previous memoirs, Michelle in *How to Grow Up* appears nevertheless to jettison the non-normative elements of her queer femme sensibility and embraces a normative hyper-femininity that aligns with both heteronormative ideals and the kind of hedonistic capitalism Nelson critiques in *The Argonauts*. For example, with her newfound financial security, Michelle purchases contact lenses, finding that they make her a 'new woman' (HGU, 128). She practises a regime of 'self-care' and 'self-love' (HGU, 127) that appears based entirely on consumption and self-beautification. For example, when feeling down, or following a romantic catastrophe, Michelle advises her readers to 'get a facial', a 'new hairdo', a 'shot of Botox', a 'mani-pedi', an 'eye-brow wax', or to go to the gym because: 'You are made in the Universe's image and she likes to see you looking your best!' (HGU, 127–8). Michelle does not view these practices as contradicting her feminist principles. Instead, her thinking demonstrates a clear postfeminist instinct to redefine what feminism is according to both perceived personal preferences and the pleasure principle. 'When feminism felt like it was bumming out my reality', she avers, 'it was time to redefine what a feminist was [. . .]. So maybe I was the kind of feminist who gets Botox' (HGU, 269).

Apart from expressing wholehearted endorsement of normative, expensive, and dangerous beauty practices (Botox involves injecting a neurotoxin into areas of the face), Tea's memoir also charts her complicated relationship with and eventual acceptance of money. At this point the similarities between *How to Grow Up* and Sincero's *You are a Badass* become even more striking. Michelle uses an affirmation technique that could have been taken from Sincero's book in order to change her uneasy relationship with money, stemming on the one hand from her poor family background, but also from her earlier anti-capitalist stance. Michelle's affirmations consist of repeating the words 'I am a Money Magnet', 'Money comes to me', and asserting that money is 'sexually attracted' to her (HGU, 80). Sincero, in her chapter 'Money, Your New Best Friend', outlines precisely the predicament Tea found herself in: 'I was extremely poverty proud for so long, I felt I was so much nobler in my pursuit of art and fun and altruism than those people who wasted their lives just going after money.'[60] After describing the lengths she would go to to save money, Sincero's logic leads her to observe that, as she was spending so much time thinking about money anyway, she might as well be making some. Money, she claims, is not that bad; it is people's personal 'issues and anxieties' around money that are the problem.[61] Harbouring doubts about the ethics of capitalism becomes redefined as a 'silly'[62] personal problem, and, in this vein, Sincero suggests developing an equally personal relationship with money in order to overcome any ethical qualms:

> In order to bring money joyfully into our lives, we have to understand that we're having a relationship with it, and then treat it like any other important and meaningful

---

[60] Jen Sincero, *You are a Badass*, p. 207.   [61] Ibid.   [62] Ibid.

relationship: we need to pay attention to it, want it, nurture it, put effort into it, respect it, cherish it, love it, etc.[63]

This is 'if-you-can't-beat-them-join-them' logic concealed as a radical new approach to personal economics. In general, Sincero's book, published post-financial crisis, conceals the classic logic of post-crash neoliberalism: a harsh individualization of the economic system through the agency of media and print texts like hers that, to return to Negra, 'offer reassuring vignettes of individual agency as compensation to the ill-defined yet intensely valorized power of "the market"'.[64]

While in her latest memoir Tea disavows the persona of the 'badass' addict and gradually aligns with a homonormative sensibility of neoliberal entrepreneurialism, Sincero's self-help guide actively appropriates the term 'badass' in its title in order to portray orthodox neoliberalism as the edgy transgressive move. She takes advantage of precisely the cultural capital now imbued in the act of transgressing socio-sexual norms and applies it to personal economics, 'sexing up' the otherwise acquisitory tone and neoliberal ethos of her work. While Nelson argues that transgressive sexuality is now the domain of the straight world and of hedonistic capitalism, it could be argued that the sanitized transgressive gesture per se has become an intrinsic element of neoliberal rhetoric, even post-financial crisis.

Eventually, Michelle declares: 'Acting like I was somehow outside—or above—the money system was ridiculous. It was time to join the human race. *I am money*' (HGU, 83). This statement reads like a capitulation to—indeed full assimilation by—the forces of neoliberal normativity and concurrently a declaration of defeat on the part of the political principles that guided her earlier life. Yet, in the realm of her literary work, rather than her own personal life, her attitude towards money and the economics of cultural production ('the money system') still retains an element of her earlier thinking. Recalling her aspirations to set up an imprint at City Lights Booksellers and Publishers that would showcase the writing of her peers, she recalls her hope that the publishers 'would see that the bedraggled, upstart, underground literary voices I'd been championing for so long were in many ways the next wave of Beat literature—radical, experimental, written by people living uncompromisingly at the fringe of our culture' (HGU, 232). It is their uncompromising existence precisely outside the 'money system' that Tea appears to relate to their capacity to create radical, experimental work, worthwhile championing and publishing.

This returns us to the question raised at the end of Chapter 2 about the relationship between the economics of production and the critical cultural product, between the transgressive riot-grrrl gesture and its appropriation by commercial forces, between the desire to reach new audiences and the normatizing forces of the mainstream. The same shifts that prepared the ground for the re-release, heightened visibility and overdue critical acclaim of previously controversial or purely underground writing of the kind undertaken by Myles and Kraus can be understood to be part of a normalization and commercialization of queer and feminist protest

---

[63] Ibid.   [64] Diane Negra, 'Claiming Feminism', p. 275.

culture that coincides with the hedonistic embrace of transgressive behaviours, products, and practices in heteronormative North American pop-culture; both are profoundly connected to the market forces of entrenched neoliberalism.

Miranda July's novel, with which I opened this section, creates a humorously domestic and resolutely un-erotic setting for its consensual violence and queer sex, which acts as an ironic acknowledgement of that normalization. As Nelson argues, however, the acknowledgement of normalization should not act as a 'devaluation of queerness. It is a reminder: if we want to do more than claw our way into repressive structures, we have our work cut out for us' (TA, 32).

4

British Pop-Feminism on the Literary Marketplace

In this chapter, I explore some of the most significant cultural and literary developments informing pop-feminist writing in the British context from the mid-2000s. I discuss the appropriation by commercial forces of tropes of female transgression emerging from North American riot grrrl and its British manifestations, arguing that these tropes gained particular currency in late 1990s popular women's fiction, or 'chick-lit'. British chick-lit, as author Kate Mosse argues, was a product of its time, the literary legacy of the socio-political climate cultivated in Thatcherite Britain in which the individual's own social trajectory became the focus of attention and required a tireless process of self-optimization. Importantly, she links this phenomenon with that which she calls the concomitant 'collapse of analytical feminism', i.e. second-wave feminism, and the emergence of a distinctly postfeminist climate in the public sphere.[1]

As scholarship on 'chick-lit' is by now well established,[2] I focus on post-chick-lit debates concerning the 'democratization' of fiction that collide with claims that the UK's publishing industry inclines increasingly towards simplifying and sexualizing literary fiction written by women. Long-standing debates within feminist scholarship concerning the practices of reading first-person narratives written by women become compounded by the contemporary frameworks of market and genre within which those narratives are situated.

I examine three such textual examples by British writers Scarlett Thomas, Helen Walsh, and Gwendoline Riley, reading these against the corpus of British pop-feminist handbooks written by journalists Ellie Levenson, Caitlin Moran, Polly Vernon, and Hadley Freeman. My interest lies specifically in the contrasting models of subjectivity these textual groupings present: on the one hand, explicitly 'feminist' texts present an off-the-peg model of 'anything-goes' female identity packaged as a ready-made, celebrity-endorsed ontological product. On the other, the novelists

---

[1] Kate Mosse speaking on 'A History of Women's Writing (Part 4)', *Open Book*, BBC Radio 4, 31 July 2011. Available at <http://downloads.bbc.co.uk/podcasts/radio4/openbook/openbook_20110731-1630a.mp3>, 09:03–09:13.

[2] For an overview, see Cris Mazza, 'Editing Postfeminist Fiction: Finding the Chic in Lit', *symplokē*, 8: 1–2 (2000), 101–12; Cris Mazza, 'Chick-Lit and the Perversion of a Genre', *Poets & Writers*, 33. 1 (2005), 31–7; Imelda Whelehan, *The Feminist Bestseller: From Sex and the Single Girl to Sex and the City* (Basingstoke: Palgrave Macmillan, 2005); Suzanne Ferriss and Mallory Young (eds.), *Chick Lit: The New Women's Fiction* (New York: Routledge, 2006); Heike Mißler, *The Cultural Politics of Chick Lit: Popular Fiction, Postfeminism and Representation* (New York; Abingdon: Routledge, 2016).

I discuss problematize subjectivity by fragmenting any notion of coherent identity and deploying female transgression as a trope that both liberates and contains their protagonists' sense of agency. Lastly, I enquire after the effect that a literary climate allegedly tending towards simplification and sexualization has on the paratextual mobilizations (such as book covers' image and design, back-cover summaries, reviews, and point-of-sale advertising) of these writerly explorations of transgression and agency.

In her historical account of UK riot grrrl, Cazz Blase (pen-name Karren Ablaze!), zine creator and contributor to contemporary feminist website *The F-Word*, notes that British manifestations of the movement from 1992 were varied and widespread, emulating for the most part patterns of engagement in the US and initially ignored, then trivialized, by the mainstream UK press.[3] Julia Downes notes that in contrast to North America the UK's 'strong legacy of punk, protest and youth politicization' from the 1970s provided 'fertile ground for DIY feminist cultural subversions'.[4] However, Downes suggests that, despite this, 'issues of gender and sexuality were suppressed during this period and punk was experienced as an asexual space. This situation offered women cooperation as one of the boys or as sexless, which subsequently prevented a confrontational exploration of resistant femininities and sexualities within punk'.[5]

In the 1980s, as the punk sound was gradually replaced within the mainstream by the softer electronic sounds of commercially successful bands, the indie (independent) music scene became the site of DIY counter-cultural activism. Zine writing and distribution, in particular, remained an important element of forging networks and alliances in this underground scene as it had in punk. For those who had been affected by the recession of the early 1980s—especially those in the de-industrialized North—zines were 'cheaper [...] than the establishment music press', as well as 'more genuine'.[6] They were the 'backbone of a varied but connected scene of punk, hardcore, psyche, garage, skate and indie bands across the UK and an important link to mainland European bands.'[7]

Thus, it was often through zines or US record companies' newsletters crossing the Atlantic that British protagonists of the indie music scene came into contact with North American riot grrrl—as well as through the music itself. Young British women and girls first began engaging creatively and politically in the British riot-grrrl movement through zine culture: young women began interviewing bands after concerts for the zines they wrote and travelling across the country to distribute their zines at live music venues or at independent music retail outlets. Blase

---

[3] *But What of Us? UK Riot Grrrl (Part 1)*, The F-Word <https://www.thefword.org.uk/2004/09/but_what_of_us_uk_riot_grrrl_part_1/> [accessed 2.10.2017].

[4] Julia Downes, 'Riot Grrrl: The Legacy and Contemporary Landscape of Feminist Cultural Activism', in *Riot Grrrl Revolution Girl Style Now!*, ed. by Nadine Monem (London: Black Dog Publishing, 2007), p. 25. Reprinted in Germany as *Riot Grrrl Revisited: Geschichte und Gegenwart einer feministischen Bewegung*, edited by Katja Peglow & Jonas Engelmann (Mainz: Ventil, 2011), pp. 18–50.

[5] Ibid., p. 25.

[6] P6 from The Stretchheads, cited in Karren Ablaze!, 'Hey Zinesters! How Fanzines Empowered a Generation', *The Guardian*, 15 September 2009.

[7] P6 from The Stretchheads, cited in Karren Ablaze!, 'Hey Zinesters!'.

argues that from '1992 onwards, riot grrrl empowered the individuals that punk had not reached', such as women, people of colour, transgender, and lesbian communities.[8] She cites Simone Ivatts, producer of *Sawtooth* zine, who reflects: "'[w]hereas my punk/indie/goth roots had never really inspired creativity in me, riot grrrl came along and spoke to me as a female...I realised that I could write stuff too."'[9] Downes points out that the production of radical feminist magazines during the 1970s and 1980s, such as *Shocking Pink* and *Spare Rib*, also contributed to the 'emergence of a discourse, aesthetic and means of production, in which to conceptualize issues around gender and sexuality' within UK riot grrrl.[10]

In the late 1980s, previously underground bands began breaking through into the mainstream as the music industry realized the commercial potential of indie. As Downes observes:

> [S]hifts in the meaning of 'indie' in the United Kingdom began to emerge as bands like The Smiths broke through to the mainstream. As opposed to signifying a DIY mode of production, indie was reworked to refer to an increasingly popular sound, genre and style characterised as counter-cultural. British indie music cultures became dominated by music and culture produced by white men. Therefore, whereas punk, post-punk, and indie-pop allowed for the marginal involvement of women, this shift in the meaning of 'indie' as a popular commodity and genre led to a rigid reconstitution of a normative gender order in the indie public.[11]

In her article on zine creators, Blase/Ablaze! argues that commercial pressures not only affected musicians in that period but also writers and zine creators on the underground scene. She takes the example of James Brown, creator of the 'incendiary' Leeds zine *Attack On Bzag*, which was distributed in the early-to-mid-1980s.[12] By 1994 he had ascended through increasingly mainstream journalistic publications to launch *Loaded*, the original 'lads' mag', which publishes sexually-objectifying images of women, often celebrities and models, and in 2012 was sold to an adult film company.[13]

Commercial pressures such as those mentioned above combined with major structural differences between the US and UK music scenes to hinder the construction of a coherent riot-grrrl movement in the UK that might have countered gender normative representations in the mainstream indie music scene. As Downes notes:

> The character that the British riot grrrl would take [...] was to be dictated and shaped by dominant cultural industries whose mainstream concept of indie, pub-centred music venue circuit and nationalised music media restricted, distracted and hindered an underground independent riot grrrl community [from being] developed and expressed in the same ways as was possible across the Atlantic. Unlike America, with its DIY

---

[8] Karren Ablaze!, 'Hey Zinesters!'.
[9] Simone Ivatts, cited in Karren Ablaze!, 'Hey Zinesters!'.
[10] Julia Downes, 'Riot Grrrl', p. 25. [11] Julia Downes, 'Riot Grrrl', p. 26.
[12] Karren Ablaze!, 'Hey Zinesters!'.
[13] 'Loaded Mag Sold to Adult Film Company', *Press Gazette*, 30 April 2012 <http://www.pressgazette.co.uk/loaded-owner-paul-baxendale-walker-reveals-all-dont-worry-ill-keep-my-clothes/> [accessed 2.10.2017].

legacy of K Records, SST and Dischord enabling independent punk production, the United Kingdom lacked a coherent DIY punk infrastructure. British riot grrrl had to start from scratch, with a whole girl-orientated network and infrastructure to build.[14]

Disadvantaged from the outset in terms of the dominance of the mainstream music industry in such a comparatively small cultural context, British riot grrrl experienced greater difficulty in establishing a sustainable coherent movement. This is perhaps why the band symbolizing the commercial co-option of riot grrrl in both North American and British historical accounts of riot grrrl was a British band.

Both Downes and Blase echo Anna Feigenbaum when she makes the case that the appearance in 1996 of the manufactured band The Spice Girls marked the beginning of British and North American riot grrrl's appropriation by commercial forces within the corporate music industry. A de-politicized form of 'girl power' began being disseminated through wider pop-cultural channels.[15] Like Feigenbaum, Blase argues that riot-grrrl engagement continued post-2000 in textual rather than musical form, citing web- and zine-based feminist undertakings. These no longer necessarily carried the name 'riot grrrl', enacted as they were by women and girls too young to have participated in the initial stages of the riot grrrl movement yet who had access to a growing body of scholarship on the movement.[16] Writing of these activists from the early 2000s, Blase notes that:

> [...] the fanzine writers, ezine writers, and bloggers of today can be seen to be as influenced by 'No Logo' and the anti capitalist [sic] movement, by the anti war [sic] movement, and by direct action movements, as by feminism and riot grrrl. They also, frequently, have a strong desire to engage with and subvert mainstream mediums and media, as well as desires to stay outside such mainstream mediums and media.[17]

The question of how the mainstream affects progressive political movements such as feminism resonates with the manner in which 'girl culture' becomes translated into British literary culture in the mid-1990s. Terms connected with girlhood occupy a contested site from the mid-1990s onwards. They vary between the radical, ironically modified riot 'grrrl', conceptually linked with subversive third-wave feminist critique, and postfeminist deployments of related terms, which signify an illusory promise of agency contained within the disciplinary framework of mass consumer culture. These include, for example, Madonna's 1993–1994 'Girlie Show' concert tour; The Spice Girls brand of 'girl power'; the term 'ladette', inspired by the presenters of Channel Four's *The Girlie Show* (1996–1997), and the emergence of the term 'chick-lit'. As Hannah E. Sanders contends of the 1990s, 'discourses of female empowerment' began increasingly to focus on 'young women's and teenage girls' engagement with popular culture and reformulations of feminist

---

[14] Julia Downes, 'Riot Grrrl', p. 27.

[15] *But What of Us? UK Riot Grrrl (Part 3)*, The F-Word <https://www.thefword.org.uk/2005/01/but_what_of_us_uk_riot_grrrl_part_3/> [accessed 2.10.2017].

[16] *But What of Us? UK Riot Grrrl (Part 4)*, The F-Word < https://www.thefword.org.uk/2005/01/but_what_of_us_uk_riot_grrrl_part_3/> [accessed 2.10.2017].

[17] *But What of Us? UK Riot Grrrl (Part 4)*, The F-Word.

discourses regarding social behaviour and consumerism'.[18] For Sarah Projansky, 'whether it is in the form of [...] the linking of feminism and femininity, popularized feminism, glamour, mainstreamed feminism, or the commodified girl hero, since the 1990s postfeminist discourse has produced the conditions for the emergence of girl discourse and *girl discourse contributes to and sustains postfeminism*'.[19]

Barbara Mennel explores the transcultural resonances of girl discourse in her work on the 'global ghetto girl'. She argues that there exists:

> a current global phenomenon of literature and cinema by and about girls that validate[s] their experience and perspective, often, but not always, associated with the ghetto as a result of migration. Since the modern ghetto appears as a space of male criminality, the figure of the global ghetto girl appropriates signifiers of masculinity. This commodified and reified figure circulates in transnational media networks, intervening into national discourses and in that process changing gender configurations. The contemporary global presence of the figure of the girl speaks to an important shift from the singularity of the male as a paradigmatic figure to negotiate socio-historical shifts, such as transnational migration, the collapse of the Eastern Bloc, and the new global world order.[20]

The question of pop-feminism's relation, or rather lack of relation, to the migratory movements of cultural and ethnic groups will become an aspect of my analysis of German pop-feminist writing in the subsequent chapter. For now, I wish to focus on Mennel's contention that the 'increased digital and electronic communication that has accompanied globalization produces an intermedial exchange.' By this she means that representations of 'self-confident and independent girls from around the world circulate in transnational networks that cut across different media: girls produce and are produced by zines and blogs, music and videos, literature and film.'[21] Such widespread circulation across the channels of popular culture entails, as Mennel notes, that the girl figure becomes exposed to the forces of commodification.

UNPICKING THE LITERARY THREADS

The Intimate Adventures of a London Call Girl (2005), which originally appeared online as a blog in 2003, marked the beginning of a sequence of memoirs published by the pseudonymous Belle de Jour, which were adapted for an ITV2 television series in 2007. In aesthetic terms, the text draws on the continental cultural capital of Luis Buñuel's film *Belle de Jour* (1967), starring Catherine

---

[18] Hannah E. Sanders, 'Living a *Charmed* Life: The Magic of Postfeminist Sisterhood', in *Interrogating Postfeminism*, p. 76.

[19] Sarah Projansky, 'Mass Magazine Cover Girls: Some Reflections on Postfeminist Girls and Postfeminism's Daughters', in *Interrogating Postfeminism*, p. 44. Original italics.

[20] Barbara Mennel, 'Alina Bronsky, *Scherbenpark* (2008): Global Ghetto Girl', in *Emerging German-Language Novelists of the Twenty-First Century*, ed. by Lyn Marven and Stuart Taberner (Rochester, NY: Camden House, 2011), p. 163.

[21] Barbara Mennel, 'Global Ghetto Girl', p. 163.

Deneuve as the eponymous Belle. The modern-day Belle's print publications further optimize this capital through its formatting in cursive French; the hyper-feminized images of a scantily-clad female adorning the covers of the novels also read like an advertisement for French lingerie. As its origins suggest, the blog-turned-memoir-turned-series emulated the ascendance of 1990s chick-lit classics such as *Sex and the City*, the *Bridget Jones* brand, and anticipates, over a decade-and-a-half later, E.L. James's internet-fan-fiction-turned-novel/film franchise *Fifty Shades of Grey*. Yet its concept, consisting of the anonymously written confessional diary of a sex worker in London, exceeds even the sexually graphic content of *Sex and the City*, shifting the balance of narration even further towards sex. The books nevertheless intervene in the postfeminist debate concerning the relationship between sexual politics and romantic love familiar from earlier examples of chick-lit.

Joel Gwynne views the contemporary female-authored erotic memoir, as exemplified by the Belle de Jour publications, as a subdivision of chick-lit.[22] This sub-genre has become a profoundly profitable publishing phenomenon across Western contexts since the early 2000s.[23] Speculating about the extent to which these texts' popularity rests upon their thematic resonance with the actual desires and/or experiences of their consumers in the West (given chick-lit's predominantly identificatory mode) remains a fruitless exercise. Yet their popularity and profitability do lend credence to arguments made by Ariel Levy, among others, concerning the marked increase in sexualized content made available across most pop-cultural channels in the West.[24]

In these erotic texts, hedonistic sexuality and masculine-coded forms of social transgression, which subvert normative notions of femininity, constitute the central stage of female agency. The central protagonist is, to return to Angela McRobbie's terminology, the 'phallic girl'.[25] But Gwynne examines the 'conflict that arises' when the female-authored erotic memoir becomes co-opted by postfeminism or in Levy's terms 'raunch culture'.[26] On the one hand, the occupation of discursive space by accounts of 'authentic' female sexual experiences approaches parity of gender representation in the public sphere. Furthermore, the phallic girl appears to be 'liberated' or 'empowered' to pursue the neoliberal ideal of 'individual choice', to adopt freely the previously taboo habits of masculinity including 'heavy drinking, swearing, smoking, getting into fights, having casual sex [and the] consumption of pornography'.[27]

---

[22] Joel Gwynne, *Erotic Memoirs and Postfeminism*, p. 10.

[23] See for example in Italy, Melissa P., *One Hundred Strokes of the Brush Before Bed*, trans. by Lawrence Venuti (London: Serpent's Tail, 2004); in France, Wendy Delorme, *Quatrième Génération* (Paris: Bernard Grasset, 2007); in Germany, Sonia Rossi, *Fucking Berlin* (Berlin: Ullstein, 2008); in the US, Tracy Quan, *Diary of a Manhattan Call Girl* (New York: HarperCollins, 2001). E.L. James's *Fifty Shades of Grey*, although a work of fiction rather than authentic account, attests to the current popularity of postfeminist female-authored erotica.

[24] In Ariel Levy, *Female Chauvinist Pigs*. See my discussion of cultural sexualization in the introduction.

[25] Angela McRobbie, *The Aftermath of Feminism*, pp. 83–7.

[26] Joel Gwynne, *Erotic Memoirs and Postfeminism*, p. 7.

[27] Angela McRobbie, *The Aftermath of Feminism*, p. 83.

On the other hand, expressions of transgressive female sexual agency often remain on the level of rhetoric alone. Actual sexual encounters conform to regressive heterosexist frameworks of sexual interaction, in which male sexual pleasure takes priority or the female becomes subordinate in other ways.[28] As McRobbie contends, '[u]nder this pretence of equality which is promoted by consumer culture, such female phallicism is in fact a provocation to feminism, a triumphant gesture on the part of resurgent patriarchy'.[29]

This is because the socio-culturally endorsed licence to behave transgressively functions only as a 'strategic endowment to young women, a means of attributing to them degrees of capacity but with strict conditions which ultimately ensure gender re-stabilisation'.[30] McRobbie argues that this licensed transgression is 'facilitated not just by the fashion and beauty system but by the wider leisure industries which have responded vigorously to the possibilities opened up by women's disposable income'.[31] The transgressive girl is required therefore to retain certain aspects of feminine identity, especially in terms of appearance and product consumption. At the same time, being licensed to adopt certain masculine behaviours—including having sex with other women—not only challenges the 'repudiated' feminist, it also creates the illusion that diverse sexualities, or what Butler, in *Gender Trouble*, calls the 'phallicised dyke', may indeed be accommodated by the postfeminist social realm, provided these encounters remain 'visually coded to conform to the requirements of the fashion and beauty system, which [...] sits in judgement'.[32] Lastly, sanctioning transgressive masculine behaviours among young women by celebrating them as enactments of female empowerment discursively constitutes those behaviours as the ideal, strategically avoiding the need to interrogate the validity of the masculine heterosexist system in the first place.

It is precisely this terrain that *The Intimate Adventures of a London Call Girl* and Belle de Jour's subsequent texts navigate. They construct a protagonist who consistently perceives her work to be self-empowering, constituting a rational, autonomous choice, stating: 'I'm not selling out. I'm not getting paid for something I wouldn't do for free anyway.'[33] In fact, Belle's harshest criticism is reserved for women whose 'approach to the sexual double-standard is to accept that men can have stringless fun but you must martyr yourself on every loser attractive enough to dampen your knickers'.[34] Belle's sexual behaviour and refusal to pursue Brown's 'logics of pain' self-consciously align her with the male position in the sexual double-standard. Yet she is careful to adhere to certain standards of compulsory femininity, exemplified by the novels' continuous product voyeurism. For example, the texts feature forensic depictions of expensive clothing, especially lingerie, food and other luxury products associated with self-pampering. As frequently occurs in chick-lit,

---

[28] Joel Gwynne, *Erotic Memoirs and Postfeminism*, p. 11 and p. 27.
[29] Angela McRobbie, *The Aftermath of Feminism*, p. 85.   [30] Ibid., p. 84.
[31] Angela McRobbie, *The Aftermath of Feminism*, p. 84.   [32] Ibid.
[33] Belle De Jour, *The Intimate Adventures of a London Call Girl* (London: Weidenfeld & Nicolson, 2005), p. 101.
[34] Belle De Jour, *The Further Adventures of a London Call Girl* (London: Phoenix, 2007), p. 316.

Belle claims with ironic, if resigned, acceptance that the need to wax or shave is a 'statement of fact on the condition of being female'.[35]

The volumes position Belle as the epitome of twenty-first-century feminized labour and neoliberal entrepreneurialism:[36] she describes herself as a 'business woman', someone who recognized, and took advantage of, an opportunity that other less astute women have not grasped;[37] she continually itemizes the necessary soft skills and material tools required for successful execution of her work, remains flexible to the unpredictable patterns of work and retains an absolute moral relativism that enables her to satisfy all demands made of her without needing to jeopardize her career trajectory or her income.[38] Yet this portrayal depends absolutely on a refusal to engage with the question of sex work as anything other than a question of choice. Reflecting on the other non-white and/or non-British women working through her agency, Belle states, 'I don't ask about their motivations for doing the job. It's not my business. I wasn't forced into working for the agency and hope they weren't either.'[39]

Thus, the texts position Belle as an autonomous and highly intelligent being who prizes her capacity for un-impinged individual choice, viewing it, like the majority of the British pop-feminist volumes, as a universal given. The scene of agency upon which Belle acts remains a sexual one and the more transgressive the encounter, the greater her sense of empowerment. Yet Belle's own sexual satisfaction does not feature in her professional work as she does not allow herself to experience orgasm, stating 'this is a customer service position, not a self-fulfilment odyssey'.[40] This leads me to discuss the passages in the first memoir in which Belle enters into a sadomasochistic affair with a non-professional acquaintance. Upon attempting to describe the sensation she experiences on being hit repeatedly and systematically, urinated upon and whipped, she says that she feels:

> 'Nothing,' I said. There was only the moment when his hand would stop stroking my cheek and I knew the smack was coming; the first hard impact of his palm against the side of my face; the eye-wetting sting of pain; the warm glow of heat there afterwards. It was perhaps the only time when there was nothing else in my head. It hurt, but the pain was neutral: there was no hate or disgust behind it. It was pure and exhilarating, like any other physical experience. Like the moment of orgasm when you forget yourself, your partner, the world.[41]

It is tempting to view these S/M scenes as female-authored sublimations of the kinds of violent male fantasies endorsed by the pornography industry. Nonetheless, two decades of feminist scholarship on S/M and sexual coercion discourage contemporary scholars from viewing such practices as exclusively based on patriarchal power structures or as a manifestation of 'false-consciousness'—women

---

[35] Belle De Jour, *Intimate Adventures*, p. 61.

[36] For further discussion of 'feminized labour' see Angela McRobbie, *The Aftermath of Feminism*; Chandra Talpade Mohanty, *Feminism Without Borders: Decolonizing Theory, Practicing Solidarity* (Durham, NC; London: Duke University Press, 2003); Power, *One-Dimensional Woman*.

[37] Belle De Jour, *Intimate Adventures*, p. 10.   [38] Ibid., p. 8 and p. 14.

[39] Belle De Jour, *Intimate Adventures*, p. 268.   [40] Ibid., p. 94.

[41] Ibid., p. 56.

'eroticising the conditions of their own oppression'.[42] Such scholarship makes a critical distinction between 'real' and 'performative' sexual violence, where the latter connotes a productive 'acting out' of the transgressive potential and violence inherent in sexual desire.[43] Furthermore, S/M scholars often contend that, 'while the social structures of power that typify patriarchy are irrefutably institutionalized and rigid, the sexual practice of S/M remains a fluid and pluralised relation'.[44] Belle, for example, is depicted as pursuing a consensual scene of pleasure and self-empowerment. Nevertheless, the striking connection in this excerpt between consensual participation in sexualized violence with the apparently welcome transcendence of mind, body, and world by the female protagonist (seen in Mary Gaitskill and Michelle Tea's work) is one that I will pursue further in the section Literary 'Bad Girls' in Britain.

For now, I suggest that the Belle de Jour series straddles multiple sites of commercially successful postfeminist fiction. On the one hand, the novels activate a self-congratulatory attitude on the part of potential readers due to its uncompromisingly sex-positive stance. The 'finer points of feminism' no longer 'apply' in this realm of individual choice and sexual satisfaction.[45] In fact, the novels position themselves as overhauling outdated feminist notions concerning sex and body politics in general.[46] These notions include the contention that any desire for sexual violence on the part of women can be viewed as a type of sublimated male aggression and thus as an extension of patriarchal power structures. Texts such as Belle de Jour's make the case that female sexuality does not necessarily align with progressive feminist politics, and the realm of fantasy and desire does not always correspond with normative conceptualizations of 'healthy' sexual expression.[47] This implied feminist angle to the narrative in turn sanctions the re-reading of sex-work and sexual violence against women as questions of individual choice, provided that the sex trade depicted remains a sanitized and 'high-class' version.

Erotic memoirs such as Belle's connote ambiguous territory where female sexual autonomy is both actively celebrated and undermined.[48] The genre possesses feminist potential in terms of raising the profile of female sexuality in the public sphere and the opportunities for reconfiguring normative conceptualizations of sexual identity. However, it appears that within the paradigm of the phallic girl there exists little space for saying no to sexual encounters, surely an important aspect of the capacity of agency. Perpetual sexual availability and transgressive adventurousness constitute rival models of female sexuality and agency, which continue to correspond

---

[42] Joel Gwynne, *Erotic Memoirs and Postfeminism*, p. 92.   [43] Ibid., pp. 89–95.

[44] Ibid., p. 92. See also, Clarissa Smith, 'Pleasing Intensities: Masochism and Affective Pleasure in Porn Short Fictions', in *Mainstreaming Sex: The Sexualisation of Western Culture*, ed. by Feona Attwood (London: I.B. Tauris, 2009), p. 33.

[45] Belle De Jour, *Intimate Adventures*, p. 39.

[46] Those developed by prominent second-wave feminists Andrea Dworkin and Alice Schwarzer, in particular.

[47] See Chris Daley, 'Of the Flesh Fancy: Spanking and the Single Girl', in *Jane Sexes It Up: True Confessions of Feminist Desire*, ed. by Merri Lisa Johnson (New York: Four Walls Eight Windows, 2002); Naomi Wolf, *Promiscuities: A Secret History of Female Desire* (London: Vintage, 1998).

[48] Joel Gwynne, *Erotic Memoirs and Postfeminism*, pp. 115–19.

with notions of female selfhood emerging from patriarchal postfeminist and consumer-oriented frameworks. The following section examines the shifts in the literary and publishing industries that have influenced the emergence of this highly popular genre and the consequences for subsequent first-person literary narratives written by women.

MARKET-PLACE NARRATIVES

Scholarship on chick-lit has traditionally emerged from the same cultural and media studies departments where research into postfeminism is undertaken. This growing field complements the official history of Anglo-American literary trends of the 1990s, which often focuses on the confluence of commercially successful pop novels by male authors, such as Bret Easton Ellis's *American Psycho* (1991), Nick Hornby's *Fever Pitch* (1992) and *High Fidelity* (1995) and Irvine Welsh's *Trainspotting* (1993). Their commercial success, alongside their mostly positive critical reception, rekindled debate concerning the role and value of popular litera-ture in Britain. The notion that a process of democratization was occurring within literary and publishing practices and readers' tastes, while by no means new, never-theless regained currency. For example, the British author Matt Thorne, speaking of the period in the mid-1990s when his work was first published noted:

> I think a lot of the big eighties writers—I'm thinking of Rushdie and Amis—had a very limited political and social vision. They seemed to come out of a closeted, privileged position. I think a lot of our writers—even those who are financially well-rewarded—seem to have a better understanding of the world around them and don't see writing as this incredibly elitist thing.[49]

Thorne refers here to the literary movement he instigated with Nicholas Blincoe in the late 1990s, known as The New Puritans; an anthology of the same name was published in 2000. The movement, which has since fallen into obscurity, took its inspiration from the *Dogme 95 Manifesto*, published by Danish film-makers Lars von Trier and Thomas Vinterberg in 1995. Dogme 95 was intended to establish a new type of pared-down, authentic cinema as a counterweight to Hollywood's cinematic pyrotechnics. In the same way, Thorne and Blincoe formulated ten basic tenets to which the grouping of writers showcased in their anthology allegedly adhered.[50] Number seven asserts that '[a]s fragments of our time, all our texts are dated and set in the present day. All products, places, artists and objects named are real'.[51] In a 2003 interview, Thorne emphasized the continued importance of

---

[49] Richard Marshall, 'All Hail Matt Thorne: Matt Thorne interviewed by Richard Marshall', *3 am Interview*, 3ammagazine.com, 2003 <http://www.3ammagazine.com/litarchives/2003/nov/interview_matt_thorne.html> [accessed 11.05.2013].

[50] The fifteen authors featured in the anthology are Alex Garland, Bo Fowler, Toby Litt, Geoff Dyer, Anna Davis, Candida Clark, Tony White, Ben Richards, Nicholas Blincoe, Daren King, Matt Thorne, Matthew Branton, Rebbecca Ray, Simon Lewis, and Scarlett Thomas.

[51] Nicholas Blincoe and Matt Thorne, *All Hail the New Puritans* (London: Fourth Estate, 2000), p. xiv.

'feeling free to make reference to the current age and the modern media—film, TV, music—and not to be ashamed of those connections'.[52] This referencing connotes for Thorne a 'shared language', which establishes a 'connection' with readers foreclosed upon by the literary devices and poetic licence of writers Thorne singles out for critique, such as Salman Rushdie, Martin Amis, and Jeanette Winterson.[53] Thorne and Blincoe, on the other hand, emphasize the importance of 'textual simplicity'.[54] This emphasis on archiving the present, on name-checking real products or media phenomena is significant for the manner in which it dovetails with definitions of pop-literature in Germany at that time. The call for 'textual simplicity', for example, evokes the title of the German author Ingo Schulze's 1998 novel *Simple Storys*. But while the New Puritans' manifesto was received with mild interest and vague puzzlement by critics in Britain and America,[55] these issues, as I will argue in Chapter 5, were hotly debated in Germany throughout the 1990s as they were perceived to be symptomatic of a seismic shift in literature's social and political function.

The championing by Thorne et al. of democratizing processes within literary publishing in 1990s Britain, contrasts with other commentators' view of the ascendance and continued popularity of commercial fiction categories, such as chick-lit, as part of a process of deliberate 'dumbing down' within the publishing industry. Writing in 2009, Sarah Gormley argues that:

> The emergence of chick-lit as a category and the consequent proliferation of chick-lit novels from the mid to late 1990s onwards places chick-lit firmly within a period of flux within publishing; a period within which, as Claire Squires (2007) argues, a perceived shift has taken place from editorial-led to sales and marketing-led publishing. The structural changes which have taken place in the publishing industry: patterns of mergers and acquisitions which have resulted in the domination of the industry by a small number of large, international multi-media conglomerates, coupled with increasing competition and increasingly concentrated channels of distribution (Brown, 2006), have created a shift from a classed, raced and gendered ideology of publishing which found its expression in the figure of the 'gentleman publisher' associated with cultural guardianship yet disassociated from commerce, to marketing-led corporate publishing.[56]

Gormley goes on to discuss the transition within contemporary publishing from what Paul Delany calls ' "product differentiation" to "market segmentation"' leading to the formulation of markets according to gender, lifestyle, and interests instead of class or income.[57] Gormley contends that 'this shift has, for some within publishing, provoked micro-level conflict, expressed through the construction of a

---

[52] Matt Thorne cited in Richard Marshall, 'All Hail Matt Thorne'.   [53] Ibid.

[54] Nicholas Blincoe and Matt Thorne, *All Hail the New Puritans*, p. xi.

[55] James Wood, 'Celluloid Junkies', *The Guardian*, 16 September 2000. See also Lev Grossman, 'Man, oh manifesto! Brash Band of Young Writers Calls for Return to Storytelling', *Salon Magazine*, 22 November 2000.

[56] Sarah Gormley, 'Introduction: Chick Lit', Working Papers on the Web (2009) <http://extra.shu.ac.uk/wpw/chicklit/gormley.html> [accessed 19.03.2012].

[57] Paul Delany, *Literature, Money, and the Market: From Trollope to Amis* (Basingstoke: Palgrave, 2002), cited in Sarah Gormley, 'Chick Lit'.

culture/commerce dichotomy, which has fuelled criticisms of a "dumbing down" of the industry: a forgoing of diversity and quality in the pursuit of profit that has necessitated niche publishing'.[58]

Anecdotal evidence from female practitioners within the literary industry serves as a useful backdrop to my imminent contention that the aforementioned shifts in the structure and approach of the publishing industry have supplanted the old 'classed, raced and gendered' ideologies inherent in the figure of the 'gentleman publisher' with new ones. Speaking as part of a lecture series re-opening the question of 'Women's Writing' at Oxford University in 2013, the novelist and academic Clare Morgan recounted her experiences with agents and publishers, who, she claimed, were increasingly asking writers of literary fiction to be less demanding on readers. According to Morgan, readers are assumed to have a short attention span, which agents and publishers seek to extend by requesting their authors treat subjects such as sex and crime, which are perceived to sell well, and to combine them with a predictable and normative morality. Literary fiction, perceived by some publishers as a 'difficult' genre, is under pressure, Morgan contends, from self-publishing, and authors of literary fiction are likely to be dropped if their first two books do not make a substantial enough profit. Morgan was careful to state that many feminist writers welcomed the democratization implicit in self-publishing. Yet she claimed that the success of E.L. James's novel *Fifty Shades of Grey*, at that time a recent phenomenon, raises the question of the negative impact of self-publishing on literary fiction given the novel's formulaic reproduction of female masochism. In particular, she observed that women writers of literary fiction might find it difficult to resist pressure from publishers to reproduce profitable formulae featuring provocative, transgressive subjects and called for a 'robust criticism [...] in support of difficult novels' among academics and critics.[59]

Morgan's comments are thrown into perspective by the effects on the British publishing industry of the financial crisis of 2008 and the subsequent economic downturn. Sources at the leading publishing industry magazine *The Bookseller* published evidence in 2011 that a 'squeeze on consumer spending in supermarkets and the migration to digital are being blamed for the spectacular falls in sales suffered by many of the UK's biggest commercial women's novelists in 2011'.[60] Economic imperatives compel publishers to optimize the commercial viability of every book, even examples of literary fiction, which might a decade before have avoided exposure to such pressures.

In a 2012 interview, the author Scarlett Thomas reflected on an article she wrote for the *Independent* newspaper ten years previously that lends credence to Morgan's assessment of the pressures faced by young women authors, in particular. 'The Great Chick-lit Conspiracy' was an 'anti-chick-lit piece but it was really about how

---

    [58] Sarah Gormley, 'Chick Lit'.

    [59] Clare Morgan, *Gender, Literature and Culture Seminar* forming part of the 'What is Women's Writing?' Interdisciplinary Research Group, at the University of Oxford, 25 October 2013.

    [60] Benedicte Page, Felicity Wood, and Philip Stone, 'Women's Brands Hard Hit by Downturn', *The Bookseller*, 23 September 2011 <http://www.thebookseller.com/news/womens-brands-hard-hit-downturn.html> [accessed 30.05.2014].

the publishers force young women to write in a mode that doesn't come naturally to them. Nobody wants to write these cheesy romances; they come with a more interesting idea and then it gets edited into that.'[61] These pressures become most visible in the packaging, marketing, and paratextual information provided by publishers of much writing by women. In 2011, for example, the author Polly Courtney, who at the time was signed to the UK's fourth largest publishing conglomerate HarperCollins (specifically, their commercial women's fiction imprint, Avon), publicly critiqued the company for the incongruous 'fluffy', chick-lit packaging of her novels, which she claimed actually dealt with 'social issues'.[62] Furthermore, Philip Stone, writer for *The Bookseller*, revealed the results of a 2013 study into the most common nouns appearing in the titles of bestselling novels. He discovered that:

> Of the top 1,000 bestselling adult novels of 2013 with titles that contain male gender terms (and by this I mean specifically 'man' or 'men' and 'boy' or 'boys') 93% contain 'man' or 'men' with just 7% containing 'boy(s)'. Whereas, of the bestselling novels with titles that contain female gender terms, we see just 19% containing the adult 'woman'/'women' but an overwhelming 81% containing 'girl(s)'.[63]

Stone points out that this 'terminology bias rarely reflects the age of the characters involved. Countless bestselling novels feature an adult female character diminutively labelled 'girl' in the title'.[64] His observations dovetail with my previous point that the terminology of girlhood has gained currency since the mid-1990s, epitomizing postfeminist constructions of femininity across many Western contexts. Following Yvonne Tasker and Diane Negra, the splicing of girlhood with femininity per se has become a signifier of postfeminist liberation applicable to women of all ages. Girlhood offers a model of selfhood-as-process, akin to Catherine Driscoll's model of adolescence.[65] It connotes a 'fantasy of transcendence and evasion, a respite from other areas of experience'.[66] It also suggests, following Sarah Projansky, that 'turning toward girls is a way to keep postfeminism fresh in the context of corporate commodity culture. From this perspective, whether the obsession with girls marginalizes or privileges grown women is irrelevant as long as postfeminism continues to sell—ideally to both women and girls'.[67] Germany constitutes a particularly potent case-study of the intersections between language and girl discourse due to especially successful post-Second World War efforts to repeal strict legal constraints on modes of address to married and unmarried women (Frau/Fräulein [Mrs/Miss]). During the 1970s and 1980s, the German women's movement worked

---

[61] Scarlett Thomas, interviewed by Emily Spiers, 13 June 2012. Scarlett Thomas, 'The Great Chick Lit Conspiracy', *The Independent*, 4 August 2002 <http://www.independent.co.uk/arts-entertainment/books/features/the-great-chick-lit-conspiracy-638935.html>. [Source no longer available.]

[62] Alison Flood, 'Novelist Ditches Publisher at Book Launch for "Condescending" Treatment', *The Guardian*, 15 September 2011.

[63] Philip Stone, 'Boys to Men', *The Bookseller*, 24 June 2013 <http://www.thebookseller.com/blogs/boys-men.html-0> [accessed 19.03.2014].

[64] Philip Stone, 'Boys to Men'.   [65] Catherine Driscoll, *Girls*, pp. 5–6.

[66] Yvonne Tasker and Diane Negra, 'Feminist Politics and Postfeminist Culture', p. 18.

[67] Sarah Projansky, 'Mass Magazine Cover Girls', in *Interrogating Postfeminism*, p. 45.

consistently to drive the term 'Fräulein', in particular, into obsolescence.[68] Yet, the term 'Mädchen', like 'girl', became a pervasive pop-cultural descriptor and mode of self-reference for a generation of German 'Girlies' from the early 1990s onwards.[69] Its continued prevalence as a powerful postfeminist signifier is evidenced by the titles of the German pop-feminist texts I discuss in the next chapter, which are aimed at potential or established feminists up to the age of thirty-five or forty.

Returning to the question of literary markets and Polly Courtney's case, *The Bookseller* writer Jane Bradley contends that the problem touched on by Courtney's experiences and evidence such as Stone's extends beyond debates concerning chick-lit or commercial fiction by women in general:

> While authors will continue to face frustrations when it comes to creative input into their books' covers, publishers face their own frustrations with marketing fiction written by women, ones that may necessitate formulaic cover designs and simplistic marketing strategies. With last year's VIDA stats showing that only about 25% of the books reviewed in mainstream media were by women authors, there's more to this issue than chick-lit squabbling and snobbery: systemic sexism and gender stereotyping.[70]

Not only are, at the time of writing, merely a quarter of books reviewed in mainstream British media written by women, the publishing industry itself reveals a gender imbalance at the level where far-reaching changes to how books are marketed could take place. In 2011 *The Bookseller* examined the gender distribution within the top publishing companies in Britain. Their list of 'Rising Stars', or successful early career individuals consisted of two thirds women, while their 'Bookseller 100' (a list of the 'top brass in the book trade') depicted a ratio of 30 per cent female/70 per cent men.[71]

LITERARY 'BAD GIRLS' IN BRITAIN

Shortlists for literary awards such as the Baileys and Dylan Thomas Prizes over the last few years suggest that independent publishers rather than larger corporations are supporting writers of complex literary narratives.[72] Scarlett Thomas, for example, moved from multi-national conglomerates Hodder and HarperCollins to the independent publishers Canongate before publishing her 2006 novel *The End of Mr. Y*, which was long-listed for the Orange (now Baileys) Prize for Fiction in 2007.

---

[68] Luise F. Pusch, *Das Deutsche als Männersprache: Aufsätze und Glossen zur feministischen Linguistik*, 1st edition, (Frankfurt am Main: Suhrkamp, 1984).

[69] See 'Weil ich ein Mädchen bin', in Katja Kauer, *Popfeminismus!*, pp. 77–91.

[70] Jane Bradley, 'What's On the Inside', *The Bookseller*, 20 September 2011 <http://www.thebookseller.com/blogs/whats-inside.html> [accessed 21.10.2013].

[71] Tom Tivnan, 'Is the Future Female?', *The Bookseller*, 17 June 2011 <http://www.thebookseller.com/blogs/future-female.html> [accessed 25.04.2014].

[72] Katie Allen, 'Mantel, Kingsolver Make Orange Shortlist, as Indies Dominate', *The Bookseller*, 20 April 2010 <http://www.thebookseller.com/news/mantel-kingsolver-make-orange-shortlist-indies-dominate.html> [accessed 21.10.2013]; Joshua Harrington, 'All Indie Shortlist for Dylan Thomas Prize', *The Bookseller*, 7 November 2013 <http://www.thebookseller.com/news/all-indie-shortlist-dylan-thomas-prize.html> [accessed 12.04.2014].

Thomas, who began her career writing crime mysteries featuring a female central protagonist with a female editor at Hodder, remembers thinking when she began writing that 'all fiction was the same'.[73] She quickly learned that her field was considered to be a 'lesser form', for which publishers maintained a separate imprint. Speaking personally, Thomas claims to perceive a strong gender imbalance in publishing hierarchies constructed around assumptions of literary value: 'all the women work on the lower imprints and all the men work on the higher ones in every publisher in the country.' When Thomas ceased writing crime fiction and moved to HarperCollins (Fourth Estate) to write *Going Out*, she started working with a male editor, stating: 'The more literary you start to get, the more likely you are to then have a male editor.' Thomas found, however, that restrictions continued, despite having begun to make a name for herself as a writer of literary fiction, leading her to decide not to have children.[74] She contends that being 'young, relatively thin, without children, offset being female a bit'. She continues, however: the 'minute you start to get middle-aged, fat, or have children, as a female author, I think [...] unless you've become hugely successful doing a domestic thing and so that whole image fits, trying to be an edgy literary author [is hard]'.

Writing in 2014, Helen Walsh echoes Thomas's personal experiences, comparing the period when *Brass* was published with a decade later: '[a]s I reach my late 30s, I have come to understand that it is far more difficult to live an orthodox life while continuing to write about the kinds of worlds and characters that have always captivated me.'[75] When she published her first novel, she was able to 'give' her publishers 'what they wanted—a ballsy and sometimes brattish public face'. Having children changed that because strangers, acquaintances, and readers are often unable to 'distinguish between the transgressive anti-heroines of my novels and their originator'.[76] Such conflations in the public sphere of female author, subject, and protagonist are perpetuated all too often by the press as much as by those unfamiliar with the writing and publishing process.

The title of a 2014 article for *The Guardian*, for example, misleadingly compares the central protagonist of a chick-lit classic with a group of female authors, Helen Walsh among them. Its title, 'Farewell Bridget Jones—Hello Literary Bad Girls', resonates with the infantilizing term *Fräuleinwunder* deployed by the press in the German context to homogenize a group of diverse women writers.[77] But is also gestures towards the article's thesis that a 'cultural shift' has generated a crop of 'literary anti-heroines, who are more interested in drink, drugs and sex than finding the perfect man'.[78] Yet the ambiguous use of the word 'literary' enables a dual reading. One interpretation links the word to the literary characters in the novels

---

[73] Scarlett Thomas, interviewed by Emily Spiers. Further citations of Thomas in this section remain unmarked but also stem from this interview.

[74] The author Gwendoline Riley has also stated publicly that she will never have children. See Elizabeth Day, ' "The Buck Stops Here... I've got Bad Blood". Novelist Gwendoline Riley Talks about her Obsessive Need to Write, and Why She'll Never Have Children', *The Observer*, 18 May 2012.

[75] Helen Walsh, 'I'm a Writer. Just Don't Ask Me What I Write', *The Independent*, 23 February 2014.

[76] Ibid.   [77] See Volker Hage, 'Literarisches Fräuleinwunder', *Der Spiegel*, 12, 1999.

[78] Sarah Hughes, 'Farewell Bridget Jones—Hello Literary Bad Girls', *The Guardian*, 18 February 2014.

and the other to the authors of 'literary' fiction themselves, especially because the title is punctuated with two photographs of authors Helen Walsh and Zoe Pilger. The article seals this reading of the authors as 'bad girls', echoing the descriptor used in media discussions of Mary Gaitskill decades before, by emphasizing the elements of autobiographical borrowing finding expression in the novels. The conflation of author and protagonist in articles such as these occurs parenthetically, suggestively and cumulatively, achieved for the most part through journalistic interjections and comments rather than through direct quotations from authors. This excerpt from an interview with Gwendoline Riley exemplifies this strategy. The interviewer, using indirect speech, writes that a 'fair amount of real-life experience has gone into the writing, she says, though she's unwilling to go into details. But, as with Aislinn [the main character in Riley's fourth novel *Opposed Positions*], her parents divorced when she was young and her mother took her and her younger brother to live with Riley's maternal grandparents in the Wirral'.[79]

Awareness of how the publishing industry functions affects the writing process itself. Discussing work on her 2015 novel *The Seed Collectors*, for example, Thomas observes how she encountered certain obstacles when it came to creating a female character who she wanted to be a fashion stylist. She claims: 'I just couldn't make it work. [S]he just seemed so shallow. [H]aving a woman character interested in what things look like and clothes, I just—I just couldn't give her any depth.' Thomas attributes this creative impasse to an internalized awareness of literary values within the publishing world, claiming that 'there's a whole range of things that the minute you mention them, you've gone low-brow, and it's just because they're female things'. So, for example, a 'writer like me isn't allowed to write anything that the chick-lit authors write, because it's not cool and it's not feminist and it's not literary and it's not highbrow enough. So then what are you left with? You've got to actually do really different things to your female characters because they can't be too domestic, and they can't be worried about diets'. Helen Walsh, too, confronted comparisons of her work with chick-lit, such as the following review of *Brass*:

> It isn't chick-lit, as such, but it shares enough of the genes to make you realise how consummately awful chick-lit is—full of heroines waiting by phones, snogging the wrong man, taking their education/careers too seriously/not seriously enough [...], finding fulfilment in the arms of some milquetoast or other, mistaking shoes for independence of spirit. You forget how rare it is to find a heroine who acts the predator not the victim [...], whose character flaws are no less base than the rest of humanity's, and nothing at all to do with eating too much chocolate and letting herself be walked over.[80]

If genre can be understood as an active process of interpretation, then the selection of novels I discuss next cannot avoid being viewed as related, albeit subversively, to chick-lit and its legacy.

---

[79] Elizabeth Day, '"The Buck Stops Here...I've got Bad Blood"'.
[80] Zoe Williams, 'Survival of the Fittest', *The Guardian*, 20 March 2004.

In Sarah Hughes's article on Helen Walsh, Zoe Pilger, and Emma Jane Unsworth, discussed above, the journalist describes their forthcoming novels as 'full of women behaving badly'.[81] Hughes cites Unsworth, who claims that the reason for this 'crop of female anti-heroines' lies in the desire for 'alternatives'. She goes on: 'I felt as though there weren't many stories that featured women just dicking about'.[82] In the same article, Pilger observes that many reviewers categorize her central protagonist in *Eat My Heart Out* (2014) as 'unlikeable, damaged and lost' because of her tendency to 'live outside of society's boundaries'.[83] In fact, Pilger views her as 'strong' due to her dissatisfaction with the 'social facades' of 'daily life'.[84] Existential crisis, Pilger contends, remains the realm of male authors and literary figures, whereas a female character's concerns are 'dismissed as the petty stuff of personal life', a contention that resonates with Celia Lury's arguments concerning the indexical qualities of the first-person female narrative voice.[85]

Referring to the double standard experienced in the public sphere between misbehaving men, who retain social licence and a certain public affection, and women, who do not, Pilger claims to have been motivated to write a character who had the 'space to be free' but 'didn't feel she had to be good'.[86] The article's author understands these authors' shared literary interest in how women's bodies are viewed and represented as 'part of a wider cultural change in which the comfortable romantic lies of a Bridget Jones or a Carrie Bradshaw are replaced with something rougher, and perhaps truer'.[87] Yet the striking references made by Pilger and Unsworth to male standards, and male-centred language ('dicking about') and behaviour raise questions about the extent to which these 'bad-girl' characters merely emulate male-coded modes of behaviour and whether this strategy is necessarily subversive, empowering or, indeed, representative of a 'truer' paradigm.

Thomas, Walsh, and Riley create works of fiction that aspire to ask difficult questions about identity in a manner that self-consciously positions them at a distance from chick-lit fiction, even as they struggle to maintain that self-definition. Thomas describes herself as 'committed' to the realist project, but contends that it is difficult to show a woman's life objectively in fiction and still be classed as a writer of literary fiction. This is arguably due to the historically entrenched qualitative, gendered hierarchizations mobilized in wider culture by preconceptions linked to the author's gender, choice of subject matter, and characterizations. Thomas's words betray a feeling of being penned in, restricted: willing and unwilling to write with a feminist agenda, yet unable to portray objectively that which, culturally, has rarely been conceptualized objectively, i.e. women's behaviour and appearance. She asks:

> [D]o you have strong women as role models, or do you show the true horror of whatever you think is horrible, the workplace, domesticity, or—? But if you do that, how do you avoid it becoming an issues book. You know, if you're writing in a realist mode,

---

81 Sarah Hughes, 'Farewell Bridget Jones'.
82 Emma Jane Unsworth, cited in Hughes, 'Farewell Bridget Jones'.
83 Zoe Pilger, cited in Hughes, 'Farewell Bridget Jones'.   84 Ibid.
85 Ibid.   86 Zoe Pilger, cited in Sarah Hughes, 'Farewell Bridget Jones'.
87 Sarah Hughes, 'Farewell Bridget Jones'.

your job is just, as Chekhov says, to objectively show what's there, and then other people can be the judge, so is that feminist, is that humanist? I think if you go in with an agenda, you can't objectively show, and I think in that case feminism does become an agenda. On the other hand, as I've already said, there are things that you can't objectively show because they don't seem objective anymore.

When asked whether she thought it was more acceptable to create a female character that is 'sexily self-destructive' than it was to have a woman 'worrying about how much they weigh', Thomas agreed emphatically, adding:

> If we wanted to be all 1980s about it, we could say it's only acceptable to have women who are destroying themselves, but I think maybe that is what it is. When I had Ariel [the central protagonist in *The End of Mr. Y*] look in the mirror, I've created a picture of her that we don't think she's unattractive, she thinks she's unattractive but we don't. She doesn't look in the mirror and worry about, oh, my hair might not look that nice, she just thinks oh, I'm a bit of a fuck-up, never mind. You know, perhaps there's something slightly positive about rejecting that stuff, but it's not realistic at all, it's a picture of a woman that doesn't exist.

Thomas implies here that in order to avoid generic miscategorization, i.e. being read as a chick-lit writer, she is compelled to eschew certain elements of characterization (or 'stuff') that she perceives to be in fact a 'realistic' expression of female existence. Those elements relate to anxieties concerning physical appearance, in particular. Thomas's character Ariel maintains an insouciant attitude towards her own appearance, while Thomas ensures that she is nevertheless read as being attractive. In this way, the author negotiates a difficult path with regard to the representation of her female characters and their relationship to their own bodies, which is fraught with tension between the desire to depict a woman who transcends quotidian corporeal anxieties (while still remaining attractive in the reader's imagination) and to pursue an objective narrative methodology that might necessitate exploring such issues. In the character of Ariel, Thomas transforms these anxieties into their opposite: a sense of recklessness concerning bodily integrity. This recklessness borders on self-destruction but in a manner which sustains Ariel's sense of agency, mostly due to its connection with—once again—the expression of her sexuality. Thomas's fiction abounds with transgressive female characters like Ariel who defy a 'realistic' encounter with their mirrored reflection. They seek to transcend their bodies, indeed their gender, or like Julie in Thomas's *Going Out* are, according to the author, 'absolutely trapped' in the body and 'completely defined by it'. Thomas's female characters are usually risk-takers, their risk-taking bordering on a self-destructive impulse. For Thomas, this is 'about the body, whether you're stuck in your body, and I suppose perhaps your gender as well, and whether you can transcend the body'. Interviewed at the time of writing *The Seed Collectors*, Thomas reveals that its central protagonist is 'another one of these transgressive characters who, perhaps, does things that should harm you but doesn't really get harmed by them, but definitely tries to transcend the body'.

This behaviour constitutes, according to Thomas, a response to some second-wave feminist literature that depicts women as victims constantly at risk from the

'the threat of men'. Paradoxically, the transgressive behaviour manifested by Thomas's female characters becomes a method of writing a feminist dimension into her fiction by responding to elements of second-wave discourse. At the same time, self-destructiveness, or in Ariel's case, a full-blown pattern of self-harm through cutting, drinking, and transgressive sex, provides an element of social critique, depicting the female embodied experience in contemporary culture as challenging to the extent that agency and corporeal dominion become possible only in the twisted and negative paradigm of self-harm. This practice does not fully discount the possibility of agency because the characters harm *themselves*; they are, in Thomas's words, 'in control of it'.

Gwendoline Riley's debut novel *Cold Water* (2002), Helen Walsh's first novel *Brass* (2004) and Scarlett Thomas's *The End of Mr. Y* (2006) constitute the group of first-person narratives comprising my close reading in the following three sections. I have selected these novels because of their engagement with the feminist themes under discussion; these include, in particular, gendered cultural representations of subjectivity and agency as well as the use of transgressive tropes to subvert or modify those representations. They also constitute useful cultural artefacts in terms of their positioning on the literary market according to genre, aesthetic strategies, critical reception, and target audience. Unlike their German counterparts, all three have been awarded or shortlisted for prestigious literary fiction prizes. Both Riley and Walsh won the coveted Betty Trask Award for their debut novels, a prize given to exceptional new writers of literary fiction under the age of thirty-five. As previously mentioned, Thomas's *The End of Mr. Y*, a complex text that combines literary and science fiction, philosophy and adventure, was long-listed for the Baileys Women's Prize for Fiction in 2008. Riley publishes with Random House, whose Vintage imprint also publishes Mary Gaitskill in the UK; Thomas and Walsh are published by Canongate, which is part of the independent alliance of publishers that includes Serpent's Tail, Kathy Acker's UK publishers. As such, these novels are positioned by publishers, editors, and critics at the literary end of the genre spectrum, an analogy that gestures towards an entrenched set of distinctions between 'literary' and 'genre' fiction that, as Thomas's anecdotal evidence suggests, hold sway in the process of writing, editing, and publishing.[88] My interest lies specifically in the manner in which such literary works written by women engage with the issues mentioned above in a publishing world increasingly influenced by the demands of the market.

One of the many similarities between *Cold Water*, *Brass*, and *The End of Mr. Y* is the inclusion in all three novels of a sex scene in a public toilet, a disabled toilet to be precise. These striking passages constitute the starting point of my close reading for they illuminate how these examples of literary narrative intervene in the question of transgression, in this case sexual transgression, and its relation to the activation and foreclosure of agency. The consensual sexual encounter per se encapsulates a material-intersubjective moment involving two existents, each opaque to the other, who negotiate the process according to an internally generated set of

---

[88] Stuart Kelly, 'Is This the End of Fiction's Genre Wars?', *The Guardian*, 17 May 2013.

impulses equally impenetrable to the other. A site of potential pleasure and intimacy—but also power—the sexual encounter itself, as well as its depiction in literature, comprises an exploratory testing ground not only of the other but of the scope and limitations of the self's capacity for action. As Gwynne notes: '[i]n sexuality resides always the potential for both affirmative and transgressive experiences, concordant with the status of sex as a domain of restriction, repression and danger, as much as exploration, pleasure and agency.'[89]

Sex is constructed in these novels as an 'uncontrollable entity that cannot be constrained by either self or society' and thus sexual expression is understood automatically to be 'occupying a transgressive space'.[90] The transgressive quality of particular physical space (the toilet) raises the stakes, too, in that, in a realm beyond the constraints of social taboo, other behaviour becomes more unpredictable, the risks greater, and the costs potentially higher. In *Cold Water*, for example, the central protagonist, Carmel, is drunk and her ex-boyfriend, with whom she has sex in the disabled toilet of a bar, is intoxicated with drugs and alcohol. In *Brass*, the central protagonist, Millie, rapes a young girl, who is incapacitated by alcohol, in the disabled toilet of a club while she herself is intoxicated by alcohol and Class A drugs. She discovers the bruises inflicted upon the girl by her abusive father and proceeds with the perpetration regardless, afterwards taking a photograph of the young girl's exposed genitals. Scarlett Thomas's protagonist, Ariel, contacts her sadistic ex-lover to arrange the sexual encounter in the disabled toilet of a service station because she is in desperate need of money to escape her pursuers. She acquiesces to his demands for bondage and anal sex in return for cash.

While these novels as a whole do not fully represent examples of female-authored erotica, Gwynne's contention that in that type of text sexuality constitutes the scene of choice and agency for its female narrators remains nonetheless relevant to my close reading.[91] However, toilets denote an imperative physical function and the sexual encounters in these scenes become stripped of any romance by the grubbiness of the surroundings. The aesthetic strategy of juxtaposing these symbolic resonances with the sexual act throws light on these novels' interrogatory attitude towards sex as a potential site of agency and empowerment. The choice of the disabled toilet as the scene of action, while certainly practical for the purposes of achieving diegetic realism, emphasizes the transgressive quality of these encounters. As I have argued, the transgressive gesture in postmodern feminist fiction such as Acker's and Gaitskill's functioned historically to subvert norms pertaining to female identity and behaviour. Yet the novels currently under discussion, in their depictions of sex in a disabled toilet, simultaneously provide a commentary on the characters themselves as metaphorically 'dis-abled', paradoxically constrained to some extent in terms of their capacity for action even at the moment of transgressing the boundaries of convention. In *Cold Water* and *Brass*, the protagonists are also intoxicated with mind- and behaviour-altering narcotics; in *The End of Mr. Y*, Ariel is in dire need of financial support. These factors introduce the idea that these characters'

---

[89] Noel Gwynne, *Erotic Memoirs and Postfeminism*, p. 88.
[90] Ibid., pp. 98–9.   [91] Ibid., pp. 15–37.

capacity for action is, if not *incapacitated*, at least constrained. To some extent, the scene of action is already compromised.

All three scenes in the novels employ a carefully selected lexicon of subject/object relations, drawing attention to a potentially hierarchical nexus of power activated by the sexual encounter. The authors trace on the level of language the processes of reflection in their protagonists' consciousness, a characteristic of first-person narrative that highlights questions of choice, coercion, and responsibility in relation to action. In the scene preceding Carmel's encounter with Tony in the toilet, Carmel forensically recounts the sequence of actions leading up to the sex act in the past tense. Tony asks her to go outside to talk and she emphatically states: 'And I did. I did. I rose up, and went outside with him.'[92] In great detail, Carmel narrates the subsequent sequence of actions and events:

> And then I put my arms up around his neck. Easy as. We kissed for a while. I didn't close my eyes. I was drunk but he was wasted. He was gone. [...] He was fiddling with the fastener on my dress. We stood up and went back inside. I deliberately didn't look at Irene or Shelley. I stared at the floor as we walked past. [...] Tony unbuttoned his jeans. Then he took my hands and put them one by one on the plastic rail on the back of the door. He lifted up my dress.
>
> 'Bend over', he said.
> And I did.   (CW, 140–41)

The use of the past tense, combined with Carmel's slight amazement that she went outside with Tony, evoked by the repetition of 'I did', locates Carmel *qua* narrator outside Carmel *qua* actor, as if she were an observer with little influence on or insight into the motivations driving the act. Yet her easy instigation of the kiss and open eyes suggest, in comparison to Tony's drug-induced fumbling, a sense of heightened awareness and determination *in media res* as opposed to *post facto*. This sense is enhanced by her deliberate avoidance of her friends' gaze as they pass them, an act which implies an element of shame, but also a decision not to be diverted from the path taken, towards the toilets to have sex with Tony. The subsequent four narrated actions are Tony's and contain no mention of Carmel's thoughts or actions, merely the echo of the two words commencing the passage, 'I did'. This powerfully abbreviated and highly ambiguous conclusion echoes Debby's narration of the spanking in Gaitskill's 'Secretary'. It is ambiguous because the narrator provides only a truncated account of the act and not of the reflections or motivations behind it. This omission in a literary mode well-suited to interweaving narration and reflection upon action strikes me as deliberate in order to sustain ambiguity and reflect the impenetrability of consciousness to the self when it comes to ascertaining motivation and choice with any certainty. It also compels the reader to undertake a process of active extrapolation in order to plug the gaps left by the narrator, a process which includes acknowledging the elements that must remain unparseable. It is clear only that Carmel, like Debby, does not abnegate responsibility

---

[92] Gwendoline Riley, *Cold Water* (London: Vintage, 2003), p. 139. All further references will be provided within the body of the text as CW.

for acquiescing to Tony's command, which therefore does not foreclose on the possibility of agency.

However, there exists an alternative reading of this narrative silence around Carmel's thought processes. Gwynne might argue here that what appears to be a scene of action for Carmel collapses back into a scene of sexual passivity: the actual sequence of events inside the toilet is orchestrated and undertaken by an ostensibly incapacitated Tony, not Carmel, and her one action comprises her acquiescence to a command rather than the instigation of the act. The simultaneous existence of these multiple interpretations confronts the reader with an alterity that cannot be fully assimilated but that prompts a potentially expansive critical awareness.

In contrast to Riley's abbreviated style, the corresponding scene in Helen Walsh's *Brass* teems with narration, reflection, and moments of retrospective self-justification. The author's complex use of tense shifts allows for the narration of action in the present tense (simple and continuous) and Millie's reflections upon her actions in the past, and at times, past-conditional tense. Upon discovering the girl's bruised back and the realization that it was probably caused by the girl's father, Millie's thoughts are as follows:

> An ugly swill spills into my guts. I should go and get Jamie.
>   I would have.
>   If I had not been within such close proximity to her warm narrow arse, so perfect and inviting. If she hadn't turned round with tears in her eyes and said what she said. If she hadn't asked me not to stop. [...] That's what she said. I swear.
>   [...]
> Take me, her eyes were saying, take me. So with gentle hands I take her.[93]

Importantly, Millie is at that moment rubbing the girl's back and remembers that she learnt this method of comfort from her mother. But Millie, who McRobbie cites as a prime example of the 'phallic girl', interprets the girl's request not to stop as an invitation to sexual intimacy, an interpretation she constructs retrospectively ('her eyes *were* saying') alongside the self-justificatory passage concerning what she would have done had the girl not intervened.[94] Despite Millie's shift into the role of sexual agent, the description of her hands as 'gentle' resonates with Millie's prior memory of maternal comfort, a linguistic strategy that subverts conventional symbolic alliances between gender and sexual roles. Millie notes that the cocaine she has just taken 'has erased all reservations'. Nevertheless, she immediately supplants this observation of the drug's effects on her behaviour with the reflection that what she is doing feels 'right and natural' (B, 217). Unalive to the significance of her encroaching fantasy that she has taken the place of the girl's abusive father, Millie narrates the rest of the action in the present tense; she places great emphasis on the girl's complicity and imputed pleasure, becoming increasingly aroused by the girl's sexually transgressive behaviour as well as the consensual transfer of agency from the girl to her:

---

[93] Helen Walsh, *Brass*, p. 216. All further references will be provided within the body of the text as B.
[94] Angela McRobbie, *The Aftermath of Feminism*, p. 84.

And noiselessly she moves with my hand, rocking to and fro, swallowing it like it's the most normal, natural thing in the world. And this is what gets me. My whole cunt just floods at the sight of her, this young slag, loving it, *loving* the whole thing, just letting me do whatever the fuck I want. That's what gets me. She's part of this—she's letting me.

(B, 217)[95]

This final thought triggers Millie's orgasm, which, due to the drugs, is 'muted', leaving her feeling 'empty and cheated' (B, 218). A purported '*need*' to see the sight of this young girl's post-coital genitalia again leads Millie to take a photograph (B, 218). At this, the girl's face becomes 'wide open with terror and shock and hurt' prompting Millie to take recourse to internal emphatic self-justifications and reference to evidence that she made the girl orgasm: '*No!* She *loved* it! She did—she enjoyed it. You made her come. She *came*' (B, 218). The telling use of the second-person singular here reveals the dialogic nature of the internal reflective process and this authoritative first-person voice overrides the 'you' in Millie's consciousness that suddenly doubts the ethics of her actions. This split internal voice mirrors Millie's more fundamentally fragmented subjectivity, which I will go on to discuss. Once this voice has been quietened, Millie leaves the girl slumped on the floor, her own 'head [...] safe and calm once more' at the expense of the other girl's physical and psychological integrity (B, 218). The narrative grants unfettered access to Millie's reflective processes allowing the reader to observe the disconnection between the scene, Millie's actions, and her interpretation of them. The repetitive and italicized language, combined with the continual retrospective reconstructions of events, further enhance the mood of denial, desperate self-justification and avoidance of responsibility for her actions. In fact, she shifts responsibility almost entirely onto the girl, to whose internal perspective the reader is never allowed access. This latter strategy entails that the reader relies entirely on Millie's perspective in order to parse the girl's state of mind, sustaining a sense of ambiguity around the question of autonomy and consent in this scene. However, the alternating dual perspectives provided by Millie and her best friend Jamie throughout the novel ensure that the reliability of Millie's perspective has already been questioned.

This scene therefore depicts Millie's seizure of power at the expense of the other party's, an exploitation and violation of another in order to augment her own sense of agency, a gain she will not allow to be threatened by her conscience. She further constructs an unreliable image of the girl she is violating, convincing herself that the girl is enjoying, indeed has solicited, her own violation. The sexually transgressive scene of Millie's apparent agency becomes the scene of another's agency suppressed.

In fact, Millie's narration reveals that she feels powerless in the face of her own sexual drives, her 'unslaked' orgasm causes her to 'ache', 'burn', and 'sting', and causes her difficulty in walking. The intensity of her corporeal desire drives her to find solace immediately in a cubicle of the men's toilets where she can masturbate to the image of the girl's genitalia 'emblazoned' on her mind. She comments that this was 'not a very nice orgasm at all. Just a necessary purge' (B, 219). This ultimate

---

[95] All italics in this passage are from the original text.

word resonates with the basic functionality of her surroundings, an environment designed for the efficient and practical expurgation of human excrement, a process over which the body has little control.

In Thomas's *The End of Mr. Y*, Ariel is similarly portrayed as a woman at the mercy of her sexual drives towards 'darkness and violence'.[96] When, in the final stages of the novel, she requires money in order to escape the sinister forces pursuing her, she contacts Patrick, her sadistic ex-lover. In exchange for payment, Patrick is allowed complete access to Ariel's body; the transaction takes place in the 'grubby toilet' of a service station (EY, 323). Yet Thomas's already established depiction of Ariel as someone who derives pleasure from pain muddies the otherwise clearly unbalanced power dynamic between them in a manner that is reminiscent of Gaitskill's depictions of Justine Shade in *Two Girls: Fat and Thin*. In this scene, as in others depicting Ariel's sexual encounters with Patrick, the demands of narration entail linguistic expression of Ariel's actions. So when Patrick tells her to take down her jeans, we read the words: 'I do it'. Although this action presumably occurs silently, its rendition in language generates a subject 'I', who alone performs the verb 'do'. At this moment, Ariel *qua* narrator claims linguistic agency, signalling a moment in which Ariel the actor could have done the opposite but did not. Unlike in *Cold Water*, however, Ariel's internal monologue reveals to the reader the thought process behind the decision, which to some extent imposes an interpretation on an act that, in Riley's novel, remains ambiguous:

> And I'm thinking whatever he does next doesn't matter. It's only my body. I don't mind how fucked up my body gets as long as my mind's OK. And my body is up for this, anyway. However scared I am [...] my body recognises this feeling and wants more of it. It wants the familiar pain that's coming.   (EY, 324)

As this excerpt demonstrates, Ariel conceives of her 'self' by this point increasingly in terms of a Cartesian dualism of mind/body. Rather like Millie, she views her body as an entity entirely disconnected from her consciousness, with an independent will: her *body* 'wants the familiar pain' while *she* is scared. Her body is an entity imbued with unruly desires of its own that exist in tension with her cognitive response. Resigned to the consequences of existing within a corporeal form that seems intractably gendered, and thus discursively constructed as an entity that she cannot control and which others may possess, Ariel appears to value nothing about her body. Instead, she relinquishes it to Patrick's violent treatment (implied by the term 'fucked up') with the corollary that, cerebrally, she remains intact. The fact that Patrick ties up her hands creates a visual image of Ariel's figuratively constrained state; she becomes literally as well as metaphorically incapacitated. Significantly, after registering her body's desire for pain, there are no further descriptions of Ariel's physical sensations during the act, only of Patrick's genitals and his orgasm. The narrative silence around Ariel's perspective echoes the previous occasions when they have engaged in transgressive sex together: Ariel disappears into her mind and

---

[96] Scarlett Thomas, *The End of Mr. Y* (Edinburgh: Canongate, 2008), p. 112. All further references will be provided within the body of the text as EY.

observes herself from the outside, only later reflecting on the scars and burns those encounters have generated.

The arena of transgressive sexuality connotes for Ariel an area of complex negotiations around agency. On the one hand, transgressive sex corresponds with entrenched physical desires on her part, but on the other, they are desires for a violent erasure of self, which may connote the banishment of both desire and agency. This aspect of Thomas's depiction is reminiscent of Belle's description of her sensations when being hit by her lover. She describes it as a moment, similar to the moment of orgasm, when 'you forget yourself, your partner, the world'. It becomes a moment of transcendence in relation to the realm of rational thought, when agency becomes willingly abnegated and the complex negotiations of conscious reasoning cease. Reflecting upon a previous encounter with Patrick, in which he tied her up and subjected her to anal sex, she muses:

> Surely he hadn't meant to go as far as he did? Did he want me to tell him to stop? I don't know why I didn't. Except...I didn't tell him to stop because I didn't want him to stop, because, well, maybe I like the darkness and violence, too. Maybe I need darkness and violence like food, like cigarettes. Maybe...Maybe I should stop thinking about this. (EY, 112)

This striking passage activates the feminist debate outlined above concerning female sexual desire and violence that, on one side, positions the desire for sexual violence as a type of sublimated male aggression and, on the other, contends that female sexuality does not necessarily align with progressive feminist politics. On a formal level, the excerpt above encapsulates the difficulty of determining the self's motivations in relation to desires and actions. Ariel's repetition of 'maybe' combined with the ellipsis and sudden breaking off of thought evoke a sense of open enquiry, of probing, which is ultimately unsatisfactory and potentially disturbing; perhaps because the process of ascertaining the causes of desires and needs simultaneously links with the process of establishing the contours of the self.

All three protagonists are depicted as processual beings in continuous flux. The authors present the reader with characters whose subjective landscapes are fragmentary and incoherent. On the one hand, their subjective incoherence privileges them as liminal characters, nomads navigating and transgressing the borders of the social, psychological, and the symbolic. The act of transgressing the norms of these realms constitutes a scene of potential agency in the sense that the characters' behaviours intervene in the discourse on biological essentialism and representations of feminine identity and behaviour.

Yet the type of transgressive behaviour these characters engage in resonates with a climate of hyper-sexualized postfeminism, where agency all too often entails the adoption of male-coded behaviours, sexual promiscuity, and self-objectification. Although the novels interrogate the usefulness of those strategies for claiming agency, they circulate in a culture where sexual transgression has become licensed by postfeminist consumer culture. As a result, they become constructed by that context even as they seek to subvert elements of it and the novels' wider critique risks becoming absorbed and disarmed. Or, in Jameson's terms, the genres of erotic and pornographic fiction remain present even as the authors work from within to deconstruct them. As I pointed out in Chapter 1, *Brass* has been read as both a feminist novel and a pornographic text depending on the values of the social group receiving it. Influencing these interpretations still further are the publishing and marketing strategies discussed above, including the books' appearance, which combine with readers' interpretations and genre knowledge to affect how the text is read.

In their forensic aesthetic analysis of the chain of action and reflection, as well as their narrative trajectories, which are embedded in characters' personal history, social context, and individual psychology, the novels nevertheless seek to unpack the discourse that equates transgression unequivocally with female agency. They do this in part by examining the moments when transgression tips into self-destruction. In mining this seam of rich material, these three novelists reveal their indebtedness to the post-second-wave feminist climate in which they have been socialized. By this I mean the postfeminist discourse that problematized conceptualizations of women as victims of patriarchal oppression and aggression. I refer to Cris Mazza's contention that postfeminism connotes an empowering admission by women that they are '*part* of the problem instead of just a victim of it', as well as to Thomas's claim that she wanted to move away from second-wave literary models of female victimhood.[97] Yet the novels by no means celebrate self-destruction. Rather, they interrogate the socio-cultural conditions and normative systems that give rise to it. One of those conditions the novels interrogate is the model of subjectivity as fluid and fragmentary, combined with the notion of identity as unstable and decentralized, which, as I showed in Chapters 1 and 2, is the legacy of much poststructuralist thought.

The understanding of identity as performative and of subjectivity as fundamentally incoherent is one of the legacies of Butler's influential critical interventions, and constitutes the starting point for a great deal of pop-feminist writing. Renouncing the need for continual self-identity, an ethical project in Butler's later work, also finds fertile ground in consumer culture, where an outfit and matching accessories can be bought for every conceivable version of oneself. In Chapter 1, I argued that counter movements in critical thought such as those deployed by Paul Ricoeur, Lois McNay, and Adriana Cavarero observed the critical potential in considering the subject's *desire* for unity and coherence, rather than incoherence. McNay, for example, contends that a 'coherent sense of self is not just an illusion but fundamental to the way in which the subject interprets itself in time'.[98] Their philosophical work looks to narrative as a potential model for conceptualizing the subject's drive to understand itself as a temporally and socially embedded being:

As the privileged medium through which the inherent temporality of being is expressed, narrative simultaneously gives shape to identity and is the means through which selfhood is expressed. In other words, narrative is regarded not as determining

---

[97] Cris Mazza, 'Chick-Lit and the Perversion of a Genre', p. 31. Emphasis in the original.
[98] Lois McNay, *Gender and Agency*, p. 18.

but as generative of a form of self-identity which itself is neither freely willed nor externally imposed.[99]

The three novels under discussion dramatize precisely this narrative process of generating self-identity from the incoherent fragments of their protagonists' temporal existence. Their desire for a unified sense of self drives this process, which is depicted as neither wholly autonomous nor entirely socially determined. The first-person narrative navigates both the open terrain and the hard boundaries of the self's capacity for action.

HELEN WALSH'S *BRASS*

The sexual encounter in *Brass* discussed above constitutes a pivotal moment in the characterization of Millie's subjective state and forms part of the novel's wider political commentary. The text was heralded by some critics as one of the most important novelistic debuts of 2004.[100] Although Natasha Walter praised the novel as a 'striking coming-of-age story', it was condemned by other feminist writers in Britain for the depiction of its troubled central protagonist.[101] Critics were drawn to the unusual characterization and voice of the novel's young female protagonist, Millie, who was traumatized by the sudden disappearance of her mother some years before and develops increasingly transgressive and self-destructive behavioural patterns over the course of the novel.[102] Millie is drawn to the seedy underbelly of Liverpool, where she lives and studies, and to its underprivileged inhabitants rather than the milieu of middle-class privilege into which she was born. Millie's mother left when the former was seventeen after an (initially) unexplained event causing a rift between her parents; Millie has had no contact with her since then. A victim of circumstance in one sense, Millie nevertheless responds by adopting the role of perpetrator and is portrayed as a ruthless, opportunistic sexual predator. By refusing to depict her character exclusively as a vulnerable adolescent victim of trauma, Walsh engages in the ongoing feminist debate concerning agency and victimhood.

Despite Walsh's attempts to destabilize normative perceptions of female identity, sexuality and gendered power dynamics, she creates a protagonist whose behaviour appears to stem from a particularly traumatic experience and who, on a psychological level, experiences her 'self' as fundamentally fragmented. The author grapples with the tension between using traumatic fragmentation to explore the potentially productive aspects of malleable selfhood and criticizing the social conditions that give rise to Millie's disturbed, fragmented state, in this case her father's as yet still secret infidelities. The novel seeks to endow Millie with agency via the subversive behaviours of an incoherent self, while simultaneously

---

[99] Ibid., p. 85.   [100] For example, *Arena* magazine, quoted on the book cover.
[101] Walter is cited on the back cover of the 2005 edition of *Brass*. Katy Guest refers to the criticism the novel received from some feminist quarters in Katy Guest, 'Bold as Brass'.
[102] Millie says of her mother's departure: 'It was pure and instant shutdown' (B, 63).

offering a critique of the cause of her incoherence. Ultimately, Walsh secures a kind of resolution for Millie's pathologized self-destructive behaviour, at least on the level of narrative.

Throughout the novel, Millie adopts the signifiers of male-coded behaviour in order to augment her sense of agency, but in doing so finds herself perpetuating systems of oppression that impinge on other women's agency. In *Brass*'s opening scene, for example, she negotiates a sexual liaison with an under-age street prostitute with the 'spent constitution of a woman who has lived, breathed and spat these streets out all her life' (B, 1). Rapidly coming down from her cocaine and alcohol high, Millie registers 'elements of the old me lurking in my subconscious, urging me to turn on my heels and flee' (B, 2). Upon noting the prostitute's bruised body, she once again feels driven to 'run', but instead continues, resuming her 'role. Guiltlessly. As a punter' (B, 3). For Millie, the thrill of 'dangerous sex with a stranger who'll do anything, *anything* I want her to' redresses the 'balance of power' (B, 98) that the experience of her mother's departure abruptly upset. In contrast, Millie's sexual experiences with men are characterized by an immanent experience of herself as 'helpless', 'powerless', 'vulnerable' (B, 238). Her sexuality is thus situated firmly on an axis of power/powerlessness that sees her 'yearning for absolute depravity, to degrade and myself be denigrated' (B, 103). Returning to Lynne Layton's discussion of traumatic fragmentation, she observes of her own clinical studies that the traumatized subject's approach to social interactions can be characterized by their reliance on this very axis of power/powerlessness: victims of trauma and abuse are 'preoccupied with issues of power. These women exhibit a heightened desire or need for power as well as the need to see themselves capable of exerting power. But at the same time, they are frightened of power'.[103]

This oscillation between extremes also characterizes Millie's fragmented sense of self. At one point she claims: 'I decide that I adore the Me that a few sharp whiskies can conjure. She's bold, happy and depraved. The sober version is a fraud' (B, 77). This quotation reveals linguistically the split between at least two possible subject identities. She does not identify herself with either the drunk or sober 'version' of herself, as she refers to both in the third person. While the term 'version' gestures towards a model of the subject in process (a version being temporary, provisional, open to adaptation and development), the text depicts Millie's identity fragments as rigidly separate and mutually antagonistic. By splitting off the undesirable character trait into a separate fragment, she is able to distance herself from the negative consequences of her (self-) destructive behaviour. Looking into the mirror after raping the young girl in the club toilets, an act which was succeeded by her sleeping with Jamie's brother, Millie observes a person who 'has the same hair and the same face but it is someone else that inhabits this skin now...I swear, I look in the mirror sometimes and I'm terrified by the girl lowering back at me. I don't know her and I don't like her' (B, 127). While the act of splitting off undesirable aspects of the self serves to defend Millie's psyche from utter breakdown, it also increases her dissociative, fundamentally self-alienated state.

---

[103] Lynne Layton, 'Trauma, Gender Identity and Sexuality', p. 115.

As Layton notes, poststructuralist theories that employ fragmentation to connote fluid identity are challenged by clinical research: 'Rather than the flexibility postmodernists might see in a person whose gender identity is indeterminate, what I and other therapists and researchers see is fragments rigidly coded with cultural stereotypes of femininity and masculinity.'[104] Millie, for example, eschews feminine clothing, feeling that dresses 'render [her] feminine and vulnerable' (B, 178). Memories of her mother arguing with her father prior to her departure conjure images of 'fragile female tears heaving' from her mother's chest. After her mother has left, the 'feminine, the womanly, the motherly trappings' are literally stowed away in boxes, echoing the same psychological process occurring within Millie's psyche (B, 66). This is because Millie associates femininity strictly with a 'wounded attachment' to vulnerability and fragility. Thus, rather than offering a characterization of fluid subject identity, Walsh creates a character locked into ostensibly normative gender binaries.

Rather than empowering her, Millie's transgressions cause her to feel removed from a sense of autonomy, as if she were 'plunging into a desperate, dull, deadly vacuum' (B, 241–2). She in fact refers to her behaviour as a 'sickness', a comment that dovetails with Layton's contention that fragmentation and its effects on a psychological and social level in fact require attention (B, 282). The impetus for recovery is provided by a plot twist that signals the novel's denouement. Millie discovers letters from her mother that reveal that she left due to her father's multiple infidelities; she had never wanted to break off contact completely and, in fact, had continued to write to Millie, although her father hid those letters from her. The revelation of her father's deceit and her mother's exculpation jettison Millie at first into a cycle of binge drinking. Incapacitated, she allows herself to be helped by a stranger who watches over her as she lies unconscious on a park bench. At this moment of vulnerability, she experiences the 'fearful downpour of emotion' (B, 113) that her psychological defences have suppressed, yearning for '[h]umans. Warmth. Comfort' (B, 286). It is at this point that Millie claims she 'can recover from this sickness' (B, 282).

Brass's final scene depicts the reunion between Millie and her mother. This completes the narrative collapse of Millie's radically fragmented self into a subject made coherent through a moment of familial recognition. The final scene is written in an incongruent mode of pastoral idyll, in which her mother, 'so perfect and beautiful' (B, 295), is glimpsed by Millie through the kitchen window of her cottage engaged in domestic tasks. Critics were alert to the sudden shift in tone and credibility generated by the novel's ending. Taylor Antrim, however, argues that '[w]e can forgive Walsh an unconvincing family subplot and her ersatz happy ending' due to the overall clarity of Millie's voice.[105] On the one hand, this excessively retrograde conclusion smacks of the clumsiness of the debut novel, but may also lie with the kind of editorial demands discussed earlier in this chapter that could have been made in view of the novel's otherwise ceaselessly provocative material. The trajectory

---

[104] Ibid., p. 113.
[105] Taylor Antrim, 'First Novels: Rookie Sensations', *The New York Times*, 30 January 2005.

towards resolution driven by Millie's ultimate desire for coherence, however, remains present throughout the text, despite the awkwardness of the final pages.

GWENDOLINE RILEY'S *COLD WATER*

The sexual encounter between Tony and Carmel in *Cold Water* represents a rare moment of interpersonal intimacy. Carmel grew up in a household in which her mother was abused by her father, who died when she was fourteen. She eschews any notion of a career, working instead in a seedy bar in Manchester, spending her time getting drunk, taking drugs, and reading. Carmel creates a 'wall of ice' (CW, 66) between herself and others, believing that 'people should learn to spend more time in their own heads, they should come to their own terms' (CW, 81). Despite her efforts to 'keep everything remote as a matter of course' and passively 'feel the warm rush of things washing over' her (CW, 13), she continues to crave 'an answering call' (CW, 149) from another. This internal conflict between desiring intersubjective connection and the prevalence of the 'old, sad un-connection' somewhere in her chest (CW, 33) leaves her feeling like a 'loaded gun' or a 'spider that gets trapped in its own web' (CW, 32). These contesting impulses produce a character with a fragmentary and incoherent sense of self. On the one hand, she conceives of herself as 'temperamental, despite myself' (CW, 6), calling her feelings 'grotesque' (CW, 11). On the other, she configures herself as an aloof and omnipresent observer: 'I watch people that's what I am' (CW, 86). The result is a young woman who becomes a 'static, splintering explosion' (CW, 10), both preoccupied with and seeking to avoid the question of 'what I am. *What I am*' (CW, 86).[106] This occasionally produces in her:

> this desire, this strange desire, for somebody to really tell me, beyond argument and without mercy, exactly *what they know* about *what I am*, to ridicule my clothes, to tear apart my tastes, my pretensions, my sentimentality, to take me by the collar and lay it on the line. I want to *burn* with truth. It's an idle, narcissistic daydream I have.   (CW, 54)

This passage contains many striking elements in relation to the question of Carmel's subjective interior: first, the potential scene of recognition between the narrative 'I' and the other, which in the Hegelian-derived model of subject formation constitutes the self-conscious subject, abounds with violent imagery. The fantasized other in this excerpt is dominant and merciless, subjecting Carmel to ridicule and criticism according to an opaque yet specific set of norms connected with appearance, taste, and character. Exposure to such critical recognition excludes alterity, by which I mean the hitherto unassimilable aspects of her self, which simultaneously defines the contours of her self. Carmel's interpretation of her desire for this relentless exposure to censure as 'narcissistic' gestures towards her low expectations and isolated state, in which any encounter at all would suffice. This scene of discursive construction expresses Carmel's desire for an externally determined, passive

---

[106] All italics in this passage are in the original text.

subjective state.[107] The desire for recognition is not expressed as a wish to be *asked* the question '*who* are you?' but to be *told* unequivocally *what* she is by the other. The desire to know 'what' not 'who' she is implies a belief that the contents of the self exist in discrete and knowable categories connected with character and appearance. Being given rather than having to provide an account of herself enhances the sense of Carmel's desire to be a passive subject, who becomes discursively constructed through the revelations of the other. She subverts this desirable model, however, when she glosses the imagined encounter as merely fiction, implying an awareness that it does not correspond with the reality of things.

This daydream nevertheless gestures towards a desire on Carmel's part for a sense of coherence, of structure to her sense of self, which is currently lacking. On her way to visit the home of a musician who played an important role in her adolescent development, she observes:

> A room or a page or a cinema screen—you can take that space and charge it or configure it, give it its own laws and logic [...]. It's the same when you find a real friend [...]. Someone puts their arm around you. That seems like the most wonderful thing to me. Human beings are only this size and shape after all. Does that sound terribly bleak and small now I've articulated it?   (CW, 37)

Carmel in fact seeks to secure a capacity for autonomous 'configuration' in other areas of her life, which appear to function according to a set of impenetrable 'laws and logic'. Again, she introduces the analogy of an intersubjective encounter, implying that an other may also be capable of providing a sense of coherent structure around the edges of what she calls her 'dissolving' and palpably isolated self (CW, 13). Yet, as McNay argues, the 'coherence of the self is not conceived as an exogenously imposed effect, but as the result of an active process of configuration whereby individuals attempt to make sense of the temporality of existence. Narrative is the privileged medium of this process of self-formation.'[108] Carmel has to work to construct her own sense of self, a process of trial and error that the narrative, in its loosely-plotted form and excursive meanderings, reflects.

Apart from Carmel's relationship with her ex-boyfriend, Tony, the other relationships dominating Carmel's thoughts are those with her parents—her mother in particular—and an emotional link with the musician she followed as a younger woman. In flash-backs to when she lived with her parents, before her father's death, Carmel describes her father's abusive behaviour: 'I can't forgive him, even now. I just think of mum frightened, covered in bruises or all curled up on the floor and I can't stand it' (CW, 42). Other flash-backs recall Carmel's own cruel behaviour towards her mother after her father's death. She remembers making her mother cry with one particularly nasty comment. But, Carmel continues, '[a]ll of her crying sounded like singing to me. I thought cruel thoughts like maybe my dad had smacked her in the head once too often. She acted frightened all the time. And there was a petulance in there too, a martyrdom, that's what I couldn't take' (CW, 9). This distaste for her mother's vulnerability and her 'wounded attachment' resulting

---

[107] Lois McNay, *Gender and Agency*, p. 3.   [108] Ibid., p. 27.

in martyr tendencies resonates with Carmel's description of her own behaviour
when dealing with abusive customers in the bar where she works:

> I've screamed at people, I've thrown drinks in their faces. Bad behaviour, you'd better
> believe it. But more often I let them say what they like and then, later on, I get like a
> geisha on my hands and knees picking up broken glass and torn cigarette ends, sweep-
> ing up smashed bottles into a dustpan, mopping up spills and sick, and making them
> see me do it and look how young and pretty I am on my hands and knees in their shit.
>   (CW, 99)

This excerpt echoes the type of extreme oscillations in behaviour familiar from
Walsh's *Brass*; they are similarly gendered, in that an aggressive response towards
abuse in the workplace is deemed 'bad behaviour' when she enacts it, whereas the
alternative, the submissive role of a martyr, is that of a 'geisha', a female concubine.
The unpunctuated language in the last line evokes the same kind of petulance she
despised in her mother: 'making them see me do it and look how young and pretty
I am on my hands and knees in their shit.' But this language could also read ironically,
suggesting that she is conducting a self-conscious and strategic performance of a
female-coded behaviour.

The musician functions as a 'symbol of something important' for Carmel, despite the fact that now six years later he has left the band that made him semi-
famous and is living in a Macclesfield squat addicted to heroin. Carmel reflects
that the band's songs dealt with 'violence, frustration, claustrophobia, *escape*.
They never escaped though' (CW, 37). But at the time, Carmel felt the songs
made 'everything, everything, tauten with new significance' (CW, 59). One of the
central narrative threads concerns Carmel's 'pilgrimages' to Macclesfield to try to
find the singer (CW, 36). When she does find him, asleep on a camp bed in the
squat and in a very poor condition, Carmel feels 'the whole of [her] life stir'
within her (CW, 144). She climbs into bed with the man, pulling his 'frail arm'
around her and holding onto his 'gentle, cold hand' (CW, 144). The religious
symbolism and ecstatic metaphor connected with the musician develop greater
significance when, following this scene, Carmel reads from a prayer book given to
her by a friend. Reading the excerpt from the Nicene Creed concerning baptism,
resurrection, and the 'life of the world to come', Carmel reflects: 'Those words
meant something to me. I read them again and again' (CW, 145). This moment
signals a potential turning-point for Carmel: the words of the creed gesture
towards the 'remission of sins' and the 'resurrection of the dead'. By showing such
pity for the singer, who symbolizes Carmel's narrative other, she manages to
extend a similar sense of forgiveness towards herself for her cruel behaviour and
former transgressions; this process may allow her to feel 'resurrected' from the
dead, or rather from the self-alienated state that dominates the first parts of the
novel. The last few pages hint at a possible reunion between Carmel and Tony and
at the possibility, somewhat more ambiguously, of her escaping to Cornwall, a
place that the novel has established as the polar opposite of Manchester's 'worn
out' post-industrial landscape (CW, 146).

These scenes gesture towards a narrative impetus similar to that in Walsh's *Brass*. The drive towards reconciliation and resolution, often centring on the restitution of self through redeemed familial or otherwise interpersonal recognition, entails that the radically transgressive subject encountered at the novel's outset threatens to collapse into a normative model of coherent selfhood. While these two novels' final scenes in no way resemble the happy endings of chick-lit, with its trope of long-awaited union between the central protagonist and the 'One', the desire for resolution, even if it is only narrative resolution, imposes a sense of coherence that the novels initially set out to destabilize.

SCARLETT THOMAS'S *THE END OF MR. Y*

Thomas's central protagonist and first-person narrator, Ariel, is a PhD student of nineteenth-century English literature. In the novel's opening stages, she is portrayed as a woman consumed by an 'immense sense of disappointment' and loneliness (EY, 42; 73). Brief descriptions of her 'unhappy childhood' with her estranged, dysfunctional parents reveal a financially and emotionally unstable environment (EY, 42). As an adolescent, she attained a modicum of financial independence by selling sexual favours, which freedom granted her the opportunity to read as many books as she could. Her habit of self-harming, discovered by teachers while at school, proved insurmountable for local therapists, who could not fathom the concept of giving oneself 'pleasure through pain', as Ariel describes it (EY, 134). As she grew older, this tendency shifted to a liking for 'cigarettes and alcohol; [...] transgressive sex' and a preference for her 'own company to that of others' (EY, 128). Her relationship with the married university professor, Patrick, fulfils to an extent her masochistic fantasies: 'Our roles in bed are quite simple. I am the eager young student and he is the slightly sadistic professor. [...] I like it when he tells me what to do' (EY, 60). Significantly, Patrick finds her old scars attractive; Ariel, too, finds beauty in the newer injuries arising from an unanticipated bout of rough sex with him: 'My wrists and ankles have matching rope burns that glisten on my skin like little pieces of melted plastic.... I almost like them' (EY, 128).

Ariel's risk-taking behaviour connotes a strategy of working out the scope and limitations of her self, of penetrating the opacity of who she is: at one point she wonders whether these risks arise from a deep belief that she can 'survive anything', a belief that nevertheless remains in doubt because she is still 'looking for the definitive proof' (EY, 111). Marking her body, or having it marked, through cuts, burns, or bruises constitutes part of her search for such proof. But it also appears to provide Ariel with a sense of order imposed upon an unruly body, whose chaotic and unbiddable needs undermine the slick functioning of her mind. Observing the rope burns on her arms and ankles, she muses: 'There's something interesting about the grazed areas of flesh; something pleasingly symmetrical about them' (EY, 112–13). Her appreciation of aesthetic coherence co-exists in tension with a fascination for incoherence, expressed as a sense of internal fragmentation and dissolution. At moments of excitement, for example, Ariel states:

> [T]here's a feeling inside me like the potential nuclear fission of every atom in my body: a chain reaction of energy that could take me to the limits of everything. As I walk along, I almost desire some kind of violence: to live, to die, just for the experience of it. I'm so hyped up suddenly that I want to fuck the world, or be fucked by it. Yes, I want to be penetrated by the shrapnel of a million explosions. I want to see my own blood. I want to die with everyone: the ultimate bonding experience; the flash at the end of the world. Me becoming you; you becoming we; we becoming for ever. A collapsing wave function of violence.   (EY, 91)

Ariel's desire to 'fuck the world, or be fucked by it' echoes Millie's wish to 'degrade and be denigrated', a wish to occupy both active and passive sexual roles, to dominate and be dominated. But the excerpt above encompasses a scale that exceeds Millie's personal terms. Ariel's imagery is abstract and apocalyptic: self and other collapse into one, outside becomes inside in a violent intersubjective bond that divests each subject of their singularity—indeed removes the need for self-identity because the world no longer exists. The complexity and scale of the imagery gesture towards the ambitious scope of Thomas's novel, which combines the realist mode with passages of philosophical, especially poststructuralist, discourse and elements of science fiction. Nevertheless, the characterization of Ariel as isolated, fragmented, and self-destructive resonates with Walsh's and Riley's novels and therefore illuminates the presence of such female characters across a variety of types of contemporary fiction written by women.

As the above excerpt suggests, Ariel's desire for violence perpetrated against the self corresponds to a sense of fragmented interiority, like Justine's in Mary Gaitskill's *Two Girls*. For both protagonists, this phenomenon is profoundly connected with sex, a fundamentally corporeal act. Accepting pain directed towards their bodies elicits, with some relief and no small erotic charge, recognition that they are real material bodies, which dovetails with Nina Power's contention that self-harm constitutes 'an attempt to induce reality'.[109] But it also betrays a desire to control, and thus exceed the limitations of, the intractably embedded corporeal form, whose material has accrued an irreversible history of experience that functions as a constant reminder of contingent existence. Self-harm in this text may thus in fact be construed as a paradoxical expression of establishing the self as agent. As Scarlett Thomas observes, self-harm need not be interpreted as an expression of victimhood, for 'at least you're in control of it, you're doing it to yourself. You can decide.'[110] Nevertheless, the paradox inherent in this relationship between flexing the self's capacity for action and engaging in behaviour that puts the self at risk is not resolved by Thomas's observation. This expression of agency remains within a negative paradigm and, given the ubiquity of self-harming female characters in the texts I discuss as well as the ongoing debates concerning victimhood and agency in

---

[109] Nina Power, *One-Dimensional Woman*, p. 33.
[110] Emily Spiers interview with Scarlett Thomas.

contemporary feminist discourse, demands an investigation of the role that the gendered body plays.

The unequal power dynamic between Patrick and Ariel, for example, rests on gender and economics. Patrick is her senior both professionally and in terms of age but it is also his economic power that constitutes the coercive tool he employs most frequently to sustain his relationship with Ariel and to dictate its terms. She is extremely poor, living hand to mouth, and increasingly dependent on the food and cash gifts Patrick offers. This is an aspect of their relationship that both Patrick and Ariel exploit. Yet the freedom to make an ethical choice rests with Patrick, while Ariel's financial situation entails a drastic reduction in her choices.

Ariel finds her own sexuality 'dirty' and the further demands of her corporeal form inconvenient and messy. She prefers losing herself within the intangible world of the text because books are not 'real life':

> Real life is letting men fuck you over their desks (and enjoying it, which is somehow the worst thing). Real life is regularly running out of money, and then food. Real life is having no proper heating. Real life is physical. Give me books instead: give me the invisibility of the contents of books, the thoughts, the ideas, the images. Let me become part of a book; I'd give anything for that. (EY, 147)

As part of her research, Ariel discovers a copy of a rare nineteenth-century novel, thought to be one of only two remaining copies in existence, written by the obscure writer and intellectual Thomas Lumas; the book is supposedly cursed, because its author and all those who read it during the publishing process died. Lumas's novel, extracts of which appear within Thomas's novel, is narrated by the eponymous Mr. Y; both novels take *The End of Mr. Y* as their title. Lumas's novel contains the recipe for a hallucinogenic potion that appears to transport those who drink it through a rabbit hole of language and time to a strange realm, dubbed the 'Troposphere' by Lumas. This realm, consisting of surreal jumbled landscapes where corporeal sensations do not exist, provides access for those who travel there to the consciousness of all living beings. A console grid (like a computer screen), which appears across the vision of travellers in the Troposphere, functions as a guide to the connective possibilities available at each moment.

Over the course of the novel, Ariel realizes that the Troposphere connotes the realm of language, through which she may enter others' consciousness. Unlike other travellers to the Troposphere, Ariel is not only able to enter others' minds, but she can also manipulate their thoughts while her consciousness melds with theirs. This world endows her with a sense of agency she does not experience in her embedded corporeal and social existence, as the above quotation suggests. Before discovering the Troposphere, Ariel feels buffeted by the constitutive events of her life. Early in the novel, for example, she considers old friends who have moved away, married, had children, and developed careers. She wonders 'at what point' her life 'swerved to avoid that' (EY, 113), distancing herself linguistically from any autonomous directive force. In the Troposphere, however, which she at one point dubs 'this new world of poststructuralist physics', she claims she finally has 'free will'. However, this abundance of agency appears to her to entail that 'nothing means anything anymore' (EY, 448). Acknowledging the full extent of her capacity for action is terrifying. At this point, Ariel understands the function of narrative in relation to her understanding of herself as well as its more general cultural function. Occurrences become rationalized through the logic of narrative; its structure and impetus impose a sense of coherence on an otherwise chaotic constellation of events, desires, and sensations. Reflecting on her decision to have sex for money in the toilets with Patrick, Ariel states:

> To him, this is an affair with a downward spiral of logic—but it is logic. We start in hotels and end up in a service station café, drinking bad coffee and planning sex in the toilets. For him this is a story: Act One—glamorous sex. Act Two—violent sex. Act Three—we're going to do it in a grubby toilet, and he's going to pay me for it. I hope he realises that this is it now. Act Three. Game over. There'll be climax and catharsis, sure. And then the story will end. Of course in my world there is no such logic. For me this has been purely episodic and accidental, and this situation now means nothing at all. There is no game. I just need some money. But if something wants to be a story, it will be. (EY, 323)

Ariel presents narrative as an irresistible force, which she connects with the sociocultural function of religious faith: 'a higher power, even a cruel one, gives us meaning in a way we can't give meaning to ourselves' (EY, 59). The concept of an original creator or higher power, Ariel reflects, is 'narrative, pure and simple. There's a beginning, a middle and an end. And the middle is only there because the beginning is; the end is only there because the middle is. And in the beginning was the word, and the word was with God, and the word was God' (EY, 448). In this light, Ariel's desire for annihilation expressed at the beginning of this section constitutes a biblical, apocalyptic vision of 'the end'. Like Carmel, Ariel finds unexpected meaning in the Christian narrative, although in this case it relates to Ariel's death.

Ariel decides to stay in the Troposphere and fully relinquish her embedded body in order to be nothing 'but air', like her namesake.[111] She claims to be unable to achieve what she wants without transcending corporeal form completely. What she desires is to 'know how it all started, and what consciousness is' (EY, 500). At the novel's close, this turns out only to be another story—that of the beginning of the Judeo-Christian tradition, when Ariel walks into a place that resembles the Garden of Eden. The novel's final words are Ariel's: 'And then I understand' (EY, 502). Unlike Carmel's hopeful identification with the spirit of the Nicene Creed discussed above, Ariel's realization is that there is no ultimate transcendent spiritual experience, no final understanding; there is only narrative.

However, Ariel is not alone when she enters the narrative of the Garden of Eden. Earlier in the novel, the author introduces the character of Adam, a theology student with a speaking name who abandoned his training at a seminary. Adam's function in the text is to provide Ariel with a somewhat formulaic romantic love interest but also to make Thomas's point about the importance of intersubjective connections in general. Ultimately, 'meaning', to employ Ariel's term, is not located

---

[111] William Shakespeare, *The Tempest*, ed. by Stanley Wells and Gary Taylor (Oxford: Oxford University Press, 1988), V, 1, pp. 1167–91 (p. 1186).

in the closed system of language, nor is there an originary creator outside consciousness, but it arises instead in the emotional connections and transferences made through the encounter between one consciousness and another, like when Ariel travels through the Troposphere, or in her relationship with Adam.

When, for example, they perform what they construe as sexual intercourse in the Troposphere (but which connotes a type of necessarily non-physical merging of consciousness) Ariel remarks that 'it's as if I'm being turned inside out, and the whole world is penetrating me; and that means I contain everything' (EY, 467). She feels as if she were a 'void and he was everything real, and the sensation of him entering me was like the largest presence filling the smallest absence' (EY, 471). Although the problem of perspective entails that Ariel describes herself not unproblematically as the 'void' rather than the 'largest presence', these descriptions combine with previous portrayals of the intersubjective encounters occurring in the Troposphere as mutually enriching. The realm of language is where these encounters and transferences between consciousnesses occur, in much the same way as in the process of reading a book. Not only do these encounters function to enrich the self, they generate empathy and overcome alterity. By foregrounding the importance of language in this process, Thomas makes a case for narrative as a method not only for construing the self as a subject, but as an ethical model for the encounter between self and other.

My analysis of these three novels implies that the depiction of female protagonists who transgress normative conceptualizations of female behaviour, identity, and agency constitutes one mode of articulating feminist critique through literary fiction in a postfeminist climate. Such representations avoid depicting women as victims of male oppression and instead evoke some sense of gender parity: women adopt the signifiers of male-coded behaviour in order to extend the normative spectrum of conceivable female behaviours. Extreme representations of sexual transgression also respond to the literary legacy of chick-lit, whose protagonists' transgressions are often limited to a set of 'licensed' areas and are often resolved through gender-normative romantic conclusions. Furthermore, the complex narrative strategies employed by the novelists discussed above problematize the processes of conscious thought, highlighting the complex and often resolutely opaque processes of action, motivation, and reflection.

However, their novels also manifest a post-poststructuralist narrative drive towards the resolution of subjective fragments and unstable identities, often construed through the desire for or realization of intersubjective recognition, sometimes within a conceptual framework that incorporates religious thinking. This drive provides the protagonists I have discussed with some sense of coherent selfhood. The novels thus sustain an ambiguous relationship with the trope of self-destructiveness, which becomes at times the logical continuation of transgressive behaviour in these texts. On the one hand, self-harm or self-destructive tendencies further subvert or at least bypass female victimhood narratives, placing control of the scene of action in the female protagonist's hands. On the other, depictions of such behaviour write into fiction a desire to transcend gendered corporeality and to therefore escape culturally imposed restrictions on the experiences of the intractably embedded female. Agency therefore stays within the narrative paradigm and the potentiality inherent in transcending embedded existence remains suspended in fiction. This suspended potentiality becomes all the more pertinent when considering the climate in which these texts circulate. Due to their interest in transgression, and sexual transgression in particular, these novels' subtle navigations of social, psychological, and symbolic paradigms risk becoming read as provocatively sexual titillations, which coincide with the market-driven demands of consumer culture and the publishing industry. Yet it is the process of debate arising from contrasting interpretations of complex and ambiguous literary texts, the drive amongst readers and critics to establish a hierarchy of interpretive validity and authority, that lies at the heart of literary texts' capacity to provoke the practice of self-reflexive critique.

POP-FEMINIST GUIDES IN BRITAIN

In this section, I contrast the manner in which the fiction discussed above engages with questions of selfhood, identity, and agency with the strategies employed by pop-feminist essayists. Juxtaposing these textual groups in such a stark manner will reveal the extent to which narrative fiction functions as a medium offering a more complex and profound exploration of those questions.

Pop-feminist writing in Britain from the mid-2000s, such as Ellie Levenson's *Noughtie Girl's Guide to Feminism*, Caitlin Moran's *How to be a Woman*, Polly Vernon's *Hot Feminist* and Hadley Freeman's *Be Awesome*, was informed predominantly by the mainstream commercial manifestations of 1990s radical feminist activism such as riot grrrl. Pop-feminism in the UK therefore draws on the legacy of the politically neutralized, sexually transgressive 'bad girls' who, as I argued in Chapter 3, appeared on the music scene and in chick-lit.

The American writers of pop-feminist guides, Jessica Valenti, Ariel Levy, and Julie Zeilinger, as well as the authors of the earlier, highly influential volume *Manifesta* (2000), Jennifer Baumgardner and Amy Richards, emerge from an educational background incorporating gender or women's studies as well as English literature or journalism. Their professional histories demonstrate early feminist engagement in the academic context. As a result, their texts focus to a lesser extent on the authors' private lives and more on detailed discussions of feminist thought since the second wave. In contrast, the British texts I examine are produced by women who have experienced professional success in journalism without necessarily encountering gender or women's studies in their educational careers. This partly explains their pronounced bias against earlier academic feminist writing, although such distaste for specifically academic feminism could also be viewed as part of a broader trend towards the simplification of public discourse and the devaluation of academic expertise in the UK since the turn of the century. Instead, the British authors foreground how they arrived at their own view-points through professional and personal, rather than theoretical, encounters with feminism and popular culture.

In Caitlin Moran, Polly Vernon, and Hadley Freeman's case, the feminist touchstones they occasionally refer to are figures pre-dating third-wave feminist theory.

The American-born Freeman name-checks Gloria Steinem on a few occasions, citing her as a positive role model, whereas Moran and Vernon's main reference point is Germaine Greer. Ellie Levenson is the only author to provide a 'further reading' section in her book, which reveals that a large proportion of her thinking has been influenced by US third-wave writing, such as the Baumgardner/Richards volume mentioned above, as well as the works by Valenti and Levy I have discussed.

Levenson, Moran, Vernon, and Freeman are all well-known broadsheet journalists, who draw on their experiences working in that field to make their arguments. Levenson also lectures in journalism and Moran began her career writing for the music industry magazine *Melody Maker*. They seek to subvert the everyday problems they identify in their working lives, in pop-culture and in what Vernon calls 'classic feminism'[112] through the autobiographically inflected pop-essay compilation. Their texts utilize self-deprecatory humour and irony rather than political argumentation, use colloquial rather than academic language, and foreground discussions of relationships, sex, and personal appearance over debates concerning violence against women and large-scale structural or legislative inequalities, such as the wage gap. Celebrity functions as an important feature in the marketing of their texts and the version of feminism these authors mediate, as it has done frequently since the 1960s.[113] Readers are encouraged to think of their purchase as a guide not only to contemporary feminist thought but, in an aspirational manner, as a mode of emulative self-improvement. Moran's text, for example, features celebrity endorsements from Jonathan Ross, Lauren Laverne, and Nigella Lawson on the front and back covers.

Moran's, Levenson's, and Freeman's volumes are sexually explicit, employing their sex-positivism as a means of securing a kind of radical legitimacy. Even on a structural level, the texts foreground discussions of sex. Freeman provides an ironic disclaimer in her introduction that 'I've written the words "blow job" a number of times here, but it's purely for professional purposes'; Moran segues into a discussion of pornography and masturbation in the first chapter and, in Levenson's volume, the chapter entitled 'Sex' is placed third out of ten chapters.[114] This strategy stems from the authors' claims that sex constitutes a topic dominating women's lives, not only because 'sex is used to sell us numerous products or forms of entertainment' but also because women are judged on 'areas concerning sex' constantly.[115] Yet these volumes display a strange disconnection between explicit and implicit meaning: on the one hand, they critique the sheer wealth of 'clichés about sex and how it should feature in a woman's life' and on the other they perpetuate pop-culture's monomaniacal obsession with the sexualized female within their texts. Freeman's telling comment that this focus is 'inevitable (maybe)', alerts the reader to alternative explanations for such graphic sexual discussions, those which may emanate from publishers (and authors) with one eye firmly on the market.[116]

[112] Polly Vernon, *Hot Feminist* (London: Hodder & Stoughton, 2016), p. 7.
[113] See Anthea Taylor, *Celebrity and the Feminist Blockbuster*.
[114] Hadley Freeman, *Be Awesome*, p. 8.
[115] Ellie Levenson, *The Noughtie Girl's Guide to Feminism*, p. 37.
[116] Hadley Freeman, *Be Awesome*, p. 8.

Yet for all their championing of transgressive sex-related practices, such as anal sex (Levenson), pornography, and pole-dancing (Moran), their works appear strangely conservative due to their reluctance to engage in political feminist debate outside the realm of private corporeal practices and the effects of pop-culture on those practices. While Vernon's text is aimed at 'broaden[ing] the parameters on feminism a bit', the volume focuses predominantly on the author's take on fashion, relationships, and body politics.[117] What Vernon means by extending feminism's parameters becomes, in fact, showcasing a lifestyle, a brand of feminism that is 'politically incorrect [...], impure [...] naughty and sexy and fun'. Once again, sexuality—or 'hotness'—becomes foregrounded as the licensed scene of both female and feminist agency; fun becomes feminism's compulsory mode as the author seeks to present a type of feminist identity that is 'less angry; less judgey', capable not only of accommodating individual choice when it comes to choosing what to wear or how much importance is placed on how one looks, but actually *being* all about individual choice.[118]

As I stated in Chapter 1, Ellie Levenson's text also portrays feminism as a lifestyle choice, which is 'less based on political ideologies and more based on the experiences we [noughties girls] have in our day-to-day lives'.[119] Similarly, Moran contends that 'traditional' feminism is misguided when it focusses exclusively on the 'big stuff like pay inequality, female circumcision in the Third World, and domestic abuse'. In Moran's view, 'all those little, stupider, more obvious day-to-day problems with being a woman are, in many ways, just as deleterious to women's peace of mind'.[120] These problems consist predominantly of representations of women in pop-culture and the media, which they seek to subvert through humorous deconstruction. As Freeman notes, 'feminism has arrived at something of an awkward place in that while equal rights (if not equal pay) are, at the very least, expected, anachronistic expectations and depictions of women remain'.[121]

Ellie Levenson's 'guide to feminism' provides an image of 'noughtie' girlhood that draws explicitly on the conventions of chick-lit, from the cartoon cover, to the frequent name-checking of chick-lit texts, to her explicit statement that she is 'proud' her book 'looks like chick-lit' because that does not imply she is 'not making important points'.[122] In fact, the qualities of chick-lit that she praises and seeks to emulate include being 'an easy read', having 'a clear story arc' and characters to 'identify with'.[123] Her volume therefore maintains a deliberately simplistic discursive style, no doubt designed to reduce the potential alienation of readers new to feminist ideas. Yet this approach results in such a reduction of the necessary complexities of intersectional and inclusive feminist thinking as to become exclusionary and at times offensive. Her definition of feminism, for example, focuses on sex as the major category of oppression, and she suggests simply changing the word from 'sex' to 'race, class, sexuality or age if you wanted to have an equally good

---

[117] Polly Vernon, *Hot Feminist*, p. v.   [118] Ibid.
[119] Ellie Levenson, *The Noughtie Girl's Guide to Feminism*, p. 4.
[120] Caitlin Moran, *How to be a Woman*, p. 13.   [121] Hadley Freeman, *Be Awesome*, p. 3.
[122] Ellie Levenson, *The Noughtie Girl's Guide to Feminism*, p. 89.   [123] Ibid., p. 90.

definition of not being racist, classist, homophobic or ageist'.[124] This tendency to think in discrete categories of oppression and furthermore to prioritize the category of sex leads Levenson to include troubling disclaimers concerning her decision to exclude discussions of, as she puts it, 'foreign women', or 'women who are lesbians'.[125] Apart from such women, she hopes that her book is 'interesting to all women'.[126] Her use of the word 'all' reveals the slippage in her thinking. Seeking to find an inclusive terminology to represent a homogenous 'noughtie girl' identity, which is differentiated enough in terms of lifestyle choice not to alienate her narrow audience, she renders alternative experiences lived by other women *within her culture* invisible.

This effect is perpetuated in other passages. For example, in an attempt to describe the applicability of the term 'feminist' to 'all women', she blithely dehumanizes and objectifies sex workers. Citing the author Rebecca West's comment that being a feminist is when you 'express sentiments that differentiate [you] from a door mat or a prostitute', Levenson suggests that this problematic othering of sex workers constitutes a definition of feminism 'we'll all' enjoy.[127]

In fact the image of female identity that comes to the fore in Levenson's text could be taken from the most formulaic of chick-lit novels. Her depictions contrast drastically with the experiences of the isolated and troubled female protagonists in the novels by Walsh, Riley, and Thomas discussed above. Using the universal 'we' once more, she describes the bonds of female friendship: 'Our female friends are the people we turn to when we are worried about a job interview, the people whose shoulders we cry on when our hearts are broken, when we are excited about a date, when we need wardrobe advice, when we need an abortion.'[128] They are the partners of choice for 'having fun', which Levenson resists equating wholeheartedly with 'having sex' and shopping, while admitting that it involves predominantly 'going to bars and clubs to look for sex, or at the very least male attention, and going out for meals and shopping together'.[129] Female friends are moreover important because 'we can truly be ourselves with them', a contention that reveals Levenson's essentialist tendencies and her narrow conception of what that self might be. Being themselves in fact means that female friends are free to talk about 'love lives', 'careers', and 'recent shopping expeditions' without feeling the need to conform to the 'gender stereotypes' with which they would feel compelled to comply in the presence of men.[130] This belief in the necessity of gender segregation portrays the women in this scenario as helplessly determined. It also proposes a strategy of withdrawal from as opposed to confrontation with the learned behaviours and dynamics at play in a mixed-gender setting.

Yet Levenson's depiction of this allegedly free realm of unconstrained action—an all-female space—belies the extent to which her text promotes the central importance of accountability and self-imposed constraint for women. She contends,

---

[124] Ibid., p. 3.   [125] Ibid., p. 6 and xviii.   [126] Ibid., xviii.
[127] Author Rebecca West cited in Ellie Levenson, *The Noughtie Girl's Guide to Feminism*, p. 6.
[128] Ellie Levenson, *The Noughtie Girl's Guide to Feminism*, p. 8.
[129] Ibid., p. 10.   [130] Ibid., pp. 10–11.

for example, that part of being a 'noughtie girl is recognizing that we are all responsible for our own actions'.[131] Part of that responsibility includes, for example,
acknowledging that 'we' know that 'some behaviour can lead to an expectation of
sex' in men. If women are to become 'true feminists, that is, going about our daily
business with our eyes wide open to how society often operates rather than allowing the world and its wicked ways to wash over us, then we do have to take responsibility for the messages we give out'.[132] This 'true' feminist awareness, which results
in taking responsibility for one's actions in order to avoid becoming a victim,
therefore dictates, in Levenson's view, that we should 'never let people buy us dinner
if we don't intend to sleep with them'.[133] Again, shifting responsibility on to the
female protagonist problematically divests the male counterpart of any obligation—
or opportunity—to regulate his actions, reinforcing the entrenched cultural stereotype that women remain at some level responsible for men's violent actions.
Framing this 'taking responsibility' as feminist constitutes a pernicious strategy of
making women feel that they are acting as autonomous agents when they impose
a system of internalized disciplinary constraint on themselves. Levenson manages
this move once again in the passage where she discusses her 'choice' to give up her
brief foray into stand-up comedy after marriage:

> When I started stand-up I was single. I could get up on stage and include jokes about
> sex and poke fun at myself knowing that the only person I might upset was myself.
> I am sure my partner wouldn't mind if I wanted to carry on doing this. But now I have
> made a commitment to him I would feel awful putting myself forward for judgement
> by others. What is more, this has come entirely from me, not him.[134]

Reflecting on her decision, she wonders whether she now gets the 'attention' she
desired from stand-up from her husband: 'Perhaps I was hoping a member of the
audience would fall in love with me, or at the very least want to shag me. [...] Or
perhaps I am using him as a convenient excuse because actually I don't want to be
a successful comic, I want to curl up on the sofa with a duvet.'[135]

This passage echoes the scenes of reflection in *The End of Mr. Y*, in which Ariel
considers her motivations for allowing Patrick to inflict pain on her during sex and
mentally tests out the hypothesis that they might stem from her. One important
difference between those two passages is the ambiguity with which Ariel's musings
peter out inconclusively. In contrast, Levenson asserts a clear link between her
motivations for ceasing comedy and her husband's imputed desires. This occurs
when she describes one—highly sexual—joke she *believes* her husband would not
approve of her telling on stage. This self-imposed boundary, despite the joke being
her favourite, caps the potential horizon of motivations driving her actions and importantly, this demarcation has little to do with her desires but with a pre-emptive
perception of her husband's.[136]

In contrast, Moran's humorous rhetoric evokes an anything-goes conceptualization of female agency. Yet she falls foul of the same logic as Valenti when she

---

[131] Ibid., p. 17.   [132] Ibid., p. 58.   [133] Ibid., p. 59.
[134] Ibid., p. 88.   [135] Ibid., pp. 88–9.   [136] Ibid., p. 89.

argues for a model of autonomy based on 'genuine' or 'authentic' desire. Moran claims: 'You can be whatever you want—so long as you're sure it's what you really want, rather than one of two, equally dodgy, choices foisted onto you.'[137] Freedom to act based on complete self-awareness becomes the default setting for Moran's notion of agency. Yet the autobiographical passages in her text reveal that she has not always been able to achieve this level of self-awareness. This generates textual discontinuity between the self-ironizing anecdotal passages and the abstract polemical threads. For example, in Chapter 9 Moran writes convincingly about the structural and historical inequalities in Western society that prevent her from viewing strips clubs as anything but 'arenas of abuse'.[138] This passage, including the previous quotation is, however, laden with self-ironization. Moran is in fact satirizing her own principled stance because she then goes on describe her rapid ideological capitulation when she is promised free champagne if she joins a friend at such a club.

Further self-contradictions are at work in this passage. For example, she undermines her argument against the gender inequalities sustaining stripping as a cultural norm by pillorying middle-class women who strip in order to pay for their degrees, accusing them of 'letting us all down'.[139] Moreover, this theoretical passage is preceded by a description of her experiences in the club, where she enjoyed a private lap dance from one of the workers. Moran makes no comment on the apparent hypocrisy implied by her condemnation of those 'educated' women who strip and its juxtaposition with a wholly positive description of her own personal enjoyment of a lap dance. Importantly, the detailed description of this lap dance lies in an earlier anecdotal chapter on the topic of underwear, meaning that the focus of the portrayal appears to be restricted to the dancer's undergarments. But as the woman dances in front of Moran, the latter reflects: 'I was in some kind of Imperial Lingerie Swoon. Marina's incredible, Snow-White arse was wrapped, like a present, in the cerise coloured satin.'[140] Later, she remembers that this 'chick' had an 'arse like heaven'.[141]

Apart from Moran's use of objectifying language, her depiction of Marina, the dancer in question, is problematic in other ways: Marina, who is portrayed as 'drunk' and 'laughing', allegedly instigates the lap dance, which Moran construes as a moment of playfulness rather than the nature of her job. When Marina commands Moran to undo the ribbons of her underwear with her teeth, Moran interprets it as a moment of genuine sexualized intersubjective intimacy, removing it completely from the sphere of economics and trade. This moment of licensed lesbianism becomes entangled with the fetishizing of high-quality underwear, to the point that it is unclear whether Moran is more aroused by the lingerie products or by the dancer's body. In fact, the account of Moran's febrile state suggests that each element amplifies the other creating a potent hybrid of sexualized female form and luxury consumer product. Moran may intend the objectifying language she employs in relation to Marina to be understood ironically or as resignifying sexist language, but its alternative misogynistic signification still nevertheless circulates

---

[137] Caitlin Moran, *How to be a Woman*, p. 88.   [138] Ibid., p. 166.
[139] Ibid., p. 179.   [140] Ibid., p. 93.   [141] Ibid., p. 168.

in tension with her potentially subversive deployment. The emphasis on Marina's complicity and enjoyment also resonates with Helen Walsh's searing critique of Millie's fantasy that the prostitute she has paid 'loves being a whore' and in no way does it 'for the money'.[142]

Such self-contradictions crop up with increasing frequency throughout Moran's text. After critiquing the pressures of maintaining a youthful appearance to which older women become exposed, she continues:

> I love artifice and fantasy and escapism as much as the next person—I love drag and make-up and reinvention and wigs and make-believe and inventing yourself from the floor up as many times as you need to. Every day, if you want. At the very end of all this arguing, women should be able to look how they damn well please. The patriarchy can get OFF my face and tits. [...] But this is all under the provision that how women look should be fun, and joyful, and creative, and say something amazing about us as human beings.[143]

In this excerpt, Moran's argumentation has veered from condemning misogynist culture and its demoralizing effect on women to championing women's right to autonomous self-presentation, even if that does coincide with the image perpetuated by the beauty industries. From there she adds a final corollary, which piles still further pressure on women to comply with a vast array of expectations based on appearance, political integrity, and capacity for fun, by implying that women's appearance 'should' still remain a major feature of how women understand themselves and performs an important social function. Although the descriptors she deploys constitute a less toxic version of the standards upheld by the beauty and cosmetics industries, Moran imbues women's appearance with a social importance that appears to exceed other aspects of their being: not only must women's appearance 'say something amazing' about them, but about humanity itself.

The tension produced by such ideological meanderings results in part from Moran's reliance on the language of performance, which conceals an essentialist tendency in her thinking that ultimately re-inscribes gender binaries. The language of queer performativity deployed through her references to re-invention, wigs, and drag becomes short-hand for a model of fluid, temporary identity that Moran's subtext actually undermines. The following description of burlesque performance is a case in point: '[w]atching good burlesque in action, you can see female sexuality; a performance constructed with the values system of a woman: beautiful lighting, glossy hair, absurd [...] accessories, velvet corsets, fashionable shoes, [...] humour.'[144] Here, she links sexuality with performance, and even employs the poststructuralist buzz-word 'constructed'. Nonetheless, the reference to the 'values system of a woman' implies a belief that such a thing exists intrinsically in all women, and that the values include a highly feminized appearance combined with a non-threatening sense of humour.

Moran's description of performative sexuality involves normative, pre-feminist signifiers of femininity, but combines these with a sense of irony. Ironic deployment

---

[142] Helen Walsh, *Brass*, p. 103.   [143] Caitlin Moran, *How to be a Woman*, pp. 294–5.
[144] Ibid., p. 176.

mitigates the limited spectrum of traits, characteristics, and desires encompassed by this list of supposedly female values and performance options. Anything outside this arena of femininity becomes attached to masculine descriptors. For example, speaking up for equal rights is described as having the 'lady-balls' to say something.[145] Equal rights themselves are justified because '[w]e're all just, you know. The guys'.[146] Agency therefore becomes conceptualized within language by drawing on the signifiers of masculinity, the feminized female form becomes linked once again with sexuality.

In contrast to Moran, Freeman navigates a less self-contradictory line of argument when it comes to questions of female agency. She demonstrates critical awareness of how, especially in the arena of sexuality, practices, attitudes and products espoused as self-empowering often stem from consumer and/or misogynistic forces that have co-opted feminist language for their own profit. For example, she describes attending an educational class run by a 'sex expert' and porn actress. When one woman asks how to avoid becoming nauseous when fellating a male partner, the work-shop leader tells the woman to focus on the knowledge that 'HE LOVES IT', thus, in Freeman's terms, 'slipping over the surprisingly slender line that divides self-empowerment and self-abasement when it comes to discussions of female sexuality'.[147] She recognizes the postfeminist condition that maintains this slender and 'blurred' line, which makes any clear delineation between the respective territories difficult for the protagonist to ascertain.[148] In her introduction, for example, Freeman articulates her understanding of the limits of self-knowledge, which necessitate guidance in the form of another's experience: '[f]ew can understand why they believe or are doing something in the moment of believing or doing. That generally comes in the sentimentalized light of retrospect or—more brutally if more usefully—if someone else shines a shaming spotlight on it at the time.'[149]

Freeman positions her text as the provider of both retrospect and the 'shaming spotlight', claiming that 'this, in a sense, is what I've tried to do with this book: [...] point out that some things do not need to be. And as for the things that do unavoidably need to be, I'll suggest ways in which they can be made more bearable'.[150] Having thus established her authority as guide to those who are suffering from postfeminist false-consciousness (from which she herself appears to be free), the author mitigates any accusations of superiority by including herself in the circle of shame, which re-positions her as an unthreatening voice of experience: 'There is not a single word in this book that is not directed at myself. All the lessons in this book are lessons I learned by falling flat on my Semitic-nosed face. This has been

---

[145] Ibid., p. 309.   [146] Ibid.   [147] Hadley Freeman, *Be Awesome*, p. 29.

[148] I use the term 'blurred line' here deliberately to reference the R&B song of the same title by Robin Thicke and Pharrell Williams, which in 2013 attracted controversy and censure by lyrically condoning sexually predatory behaviour in men, who were urged to ignore the issue of consent and exploit precisely this fine line between self-empowerment and self-abasement. See Dorian Lynskey, 'Blurred Lines: The Most Controversial Song of the Decade', *The Guardian*, 13 November 2013, available at https://www.theguardian.com/music/2013/nov/13/blurred-lines-most-controversial-song-decade [accessed 21.02.2017].

[149] Hadley Freeman, *Be Awesome*, p. 5.   [150] Ibid., p. 7.

the way of my whole career.'[151] This strategic self-deprecatory move places Freeman on a continuum with Helen Fielding's central protagonist Bridget Jones, a character with whom Freeman, based on her analysis of the text which features in the volume, clearly identifies. This non-threatening, familiar authorial pose dovetails with the copious disclaimers scattered throughout Freeman's volume concerning every woman's right to prioritize individual choice, happiness, and confidence over collective politics. In a passage discussing the beauty industry, Freeman claims that she is 'very much of the belief that, as long as it's legal, a woman should be allowed to do pretty much anything if it makes her feel happy and confident in herself and, yes, that does include the styling of pubic hair'.[152] In fact, individual choice *becomes* the definition of feminism per se: '[i]t's about freedom, individuality and being allowed to enjoy yourself and not shaping yourself to a pre-existing stereotype [...] but rather to live as the individual you are.'[153]

Ultimately, Freeman argues herself out of the conviction that almost emerges at moments in her text, that many women have been duped into believing they desire certain products, practices and beliefs by misogynistic commercial forces. This *volte-face* occurs because of Freeman's conclusion that 'it is surely far more offensive to assume that women can't tell the difference on their own between being enslaved by western beauty ideals and enjoying themselves'.[154] Instead of pursuing the more ambiguous and to my mind more compelling line of analysis concerning the possibility of establishing the contours of one's own desires and motivations, her text collapses back into the trope of undifferentiated individual choice, which it portrays as feminism's, rather than neoliberalism's, highest achievement.

Having provided humorous vignettes of their encounters with the misogynistic representations of women in popular culture, the authors of these texts do not provide any concrete framework for systemic change. The pop-cultural status quo is treated as just that: inexorable. Freeman, for example, promises to provide ways to cope better with the 'things that do unavoidably need to be'. Thus, feminist transformation occurs not through revolution or collective action (for all Moran's frequent references to the 'revolution'), but it occurs within the reader herself, through hard work and learning how to negotiate the negative elements of pop-culture by optimizing her own responses to the status quo *within* the status quo.[155] Moran, in turn, emphasizes the amount of labour involved in self-optimization. When she was younger, she 'didn't have any notion about self-development, [...] or learning big life lessons'.[156] She did not realize she 'had to work hard to be a woman'.[157] In this excerpt, both self and agency become corralled once again within the realm of individual self-improvement. This hard work on the self as project runs alongside a wilful avoidance of the question of external factors. She states, for example, that 'if all the stories in this book add up to one single revelation, it is this: to just... not really give a shit about all that stuff. To not care about all those

---

[151] Ibid., p. 4.   [152] Ibid., p. 41.   [153] Ibid., p. 229.   [154] Ibid., p. 227.
[155] Moran frequently refers to 'the revolution', both drawing on and ironizing the language of radical Marxist feminism.
[156] Caitlin Moran, *How to be a Woman*, p. 299.
[157] Ibid., p. 300.

supposed "problems" of being a woman. [...] Yes—when I had my massive feminist awakening, the action it provoked in me was a...big shrug'.[158]

Instead of generating external, structural change in the ways in which society perpetuates inequality, readers are encouraged to behave like autonomous consumers of modes of being that have been endorsed by these celebrity figures. The authors employ the language of consumer capitalism in order to advise women how to act like self-reliant and self-aware consumers: 'be good to yourself' (Freeman),[159] be 'free to make your own choices' (Levenson), desire 'radical market forces' (Moran) that provide 'CHOICE', 'VARIETY' and 'MORE' of everything.[160] However, Moran's postscript reveals a striking disjuncture between the implicit and explicit functions of her book. Her title *How to Be a Woman* draws on the conventions of the self-help genre, rhetorically promising its readers ontological clarity via a step-by-step guide. This is a strategy shared by Levenson, Vernon, and Freeman's texts, too: 'being' awesome, 'being' a noughtie girl or a 'hot' feminist implies the availability of a ready-made identity slipped on with the purchase of the product. This tactic also helps to relegate pop-feminist discourse to the private realm of every-day embodied female experience.

Yet Moran's postscript reveals that the title is intended ironically, indeed subversively. She argues that her pre-feminist self spent more time worrying about what she should *be* rather than what she was going to *do*, and that the available identities ('A princess. A goddess. A muse') proved not only illusory but also destructive.[161] Nonetheless, the text still fulfils its generic expectations due to the fact that it is marketed as the memoir of a celebrity: Moran's identity becomes proffered as merely another available mode of 'being', trading on contemporary British culture's fixation on celebrity figures. Random House arguably undercut the author's own explicit message by placing a quote from Lauren Laverne on the book cover, testifying to the book's function and value: 'Ever since I was 18 I've wanted to be as cool as Caitlin Moran. Now this book has shown me how.'

Despite these texts' purported feminist intentions, they become positioned on a conceptual and generic continuum with the neoliberal narrative of self-improvement through enhanced self-esteem. These qualities are linked with the ways in which women engage with consumer pop-culture, i.e. what products they do and do not consume and what practices they do or do not consent to. In these texts, as Nina Power notes, 'the political and historical dimensions of feminism are subsumed under the imperative to feel better about oneself, to become a more robust individual. As a response to the "I'm not a feminist, but..." pose it's very successful. Almost everything turns out to be "feminist"——shopping, pole-dancing, even eating chocolate.'[162] Power goes on to identify what she argues is the 'remarkable similarity

---

[158] Ibid., p. 298.

[159] It is hard to ignore the fact that Freeman's platitude echoes an own-brand range of products sold by a popular supermarket.

[160] Hadley Freeman, *Be Awesome*, p. 8; Ellie Levenson, *The Noughtie Girl's Guide to Feminism*, p. 192; Caitlin Moran, *How to be a Woman*, p. 309.

[161] Caitlin Moran, *How to be a Woman*, pp. 299–309.

[162] Nina Power, *One-Dimensional Woman*, p. 27.

between "liberating" feminism and "liberating" capitalism, and the way in which the desire for emancipation starts to look like something wholly interchangeable with the desire simply to buy more things'.[163]

In this chapter I have shown how the three novels exist on a continuum with the radically transgressive literary modes of earlier authors such as Kathy Acker and Mary Gaitskill, as well as with the impetus of riot grrrl. More specifically, the novels interrupt pop-feminist models of female identity and agency by subverting gender normativity, a persistent subtext in pop-feminism despite superficial allusions to poststructuralist performativity. The novels counter the neoliberal narrative of self-improvement prevalent in the pop-feminist guides, whose model of the self connotes a work-in-progress where every step towards optimized existence requires a consumer investment of some sort, for example, in the books themselves. Pop-feminist essayists' notion of self-improvement become countered by literary exam-inations of its opposite, self-destructiveness, while the narrative of individual choice becomes destabilized by imaginative explorations of the socially embedded female subject's struggle to view with any clarity of vision the source of her motiv-ations, desires, and the causes of her actions.

The pop-feminist handbooks do of course approach the question of social and psychological constraints and the multiple forms they take, but they rarely probe beyond the surface. The question of genre expectation, their subscription to neo-liberal individualist ideologies, and their attempts to ameliorate the public concep-tion of feminism in a postfeminist climate prevent these volumes from offering anything more than a superficial engagement with complex issues. Positioned as they are on the literary market as humorous, sex-positive antidotes to the allegedly dry academic material their authors often associate with earlier Anglo-American feminist writing, the texts are prevented by their generic frameworks from contem-plating complicated questions too deeply. Each encounter with contradiction and ambiguity results in the authors defaulting to the rhetoric of individual choice, entailing that both everything and nothing can be understood as feminist.

The novels, on the other hand, thrive on the complexity and ambiguity gener-ated in the encounter between the social and psychological realms. Like Gaitskill and Acker's fiction, they probe the boundaries of self-awareness and autonomous action, problematizing, instead of simplifying, the processes of conscious thought and highlighting the complex and often resolutely opaque processes of action, motivation, and reflection. The protagonists in Walsh, Riley, and Thomas's novels are depicted as struggling through the tangled process of active configuration of the self, in McNay's sense. Their aggression, self-destructiveness and melancholic bleakness interrogate the impact of the social on the psychological, which forms the bedrock of the novels' wider critique. Their political dimension becomes pre-served in the realm of imagination, from which point the reader is able to extrapo-late on her own terms. The linear and discrete nature of the narrative form, combined with the alternating passages of reflection and narration inherent in the first-person voice, encapsulates the drive to configure a coherent understanding of

---

[163] Ibid., pp. 27–8.

the self through time, which process engenders a generative model of agency. In contrast with the pop-feminist guides, the novels construct this process as a difficult, and yet vital, aspect of being in the world. It is literary fiction therefore, and not the feminist guides, which constitutes a more self-reflexive and politically charged medium for contemplating questions of selfhood, female identity, and agency. In Chapter 5, the final chapter, I turn to the German context in order to develop this argument still further.

5

German Pop-Feminism and Generational Narratives

From the 1970s onwards many of the political goals fostered by the West German women's movement began to be enshrined in legislation and social practice, beginning the 'long march through the institutions' envisaged by the wider student movement of the late 1960s.[1] During this time, the journalist and feminist campaigner Alice Schwarzer came to occupy the position of West German feminism's figurehead and continued to embody the feminist movement in the public imagination of post-reunification Germany. In the mid-2000s, however, pop-feminists began questioning the continued relevance of Schwarzer's feminist politics and her ability to act as spokesperson for younger women in the early twenty-first century. Such contestations of established feminism—and of Schwarzer herself—appeared in pop-feminist guides and also emerged as a topos in examples of contemporary fiction by women.

Susanne Klingner, Meredith Haaf, and Barbara Streidl's *Wir Alpha-Mädchen* and Elisabeth Raether and Jana Hensel's *Neue deutsche Mädchen*, in particular, challenge Schwarzer's position and person while simultaneously advocating renewed engagement with feminism. These authors, who were in their thirties at the time of writing, seek to attract a younger readership, which explains to some extent their decision to self-identify as *Mädchen*. As 'girls' they distance themselves linguistically and ideologically from the *Frauenbewegung* [women's movement] and the negative stereotypes of second-wave feminists that have flourished in postfeminist popular culture.[2] Importantly, these new volumes eschew the term 'postfeminism', their authors reclaiming a fundamentally feminist identity while modifying it to suit their purposes.

German pop-feminist texts actively engage with the global channels of popular culture and wider Western feminist discourse, transcending their domestic context. Combining colloquial, often sexualized language peppered with Anglicisms, the authors justify their arguments in terms of their relevance for women between about fifteen and thirty-five years old, who have been socialized in a culture saturated by this language. Some German pop-feminists embrace globalized consumer

[1] This phrase, which came into circulation around 1967, is attributed to the student activist Rudi Dutschke. See Rudi Dutschke, *Mein langer Marsch: Reden, Schriften und Tagebücher aus zwanzig Jahren*, ed. by Gretchen Dutschke-Klotz et al. (Reinbek: Rowohlt, 1980).

[2] But it also infantilizes these thirty-something authors and their readers and aligns their feminism with wider commercial culture that idealizes female youth over maturity.

and pop-culture unreflectingly, name-checking certain brands and products that function as signifiers of contemporary cultural belonging. *Neue deutsche Mädchen*, for example, opens with Hensel's return from a press conference with Alice Schwarzer, 'einen Becher Kaffee von Starbucks in der Hand' [a Starbucks coffee in my hand].[3] Sonja Eismann, on the other hand, celebrates pop, but not uncritically. She seeks to challenge the misogynist tendencies and fetishization of consumer culture that thrive in pop-cultural discourse while utilizing its broad platform to bring feminism to those young men and women who have not engaged with feminism previously.[4] For Schwarzer, on the other hand, popular culture predominantly connotes a hegemonic patriarchal and above all profitable commercial domain that subjugates women through a process of sexual objectification, facilitates misogynistic porn culture, and reinforces stereotypical notions of female identity.[5]

After providing a brief overview of Schwarzer's feminist politics and her role in both West German and post-reunification *Neufeminismus* (what the Anglo-American tradition calls second-wave feminism), I assess the strategies employed by some pop-feminists to contest Alice Schwarzer's second-wave feminist politics. I enquire whether their championing of neoliberal individualism and freedom of choice, as undergirded by market-driven consumer culture, combined with their animosity towards the second wave, ultimately divests their writing of a coherent feminist politics.

The current tensions between established German feminism and its younger manifestations, arguably more pronounced than in Britain or North America, can be profitably viewed within a Foucauldian framework encompassing power relations, authority, and resistance. The perceived discontinuity between old and new, in particular, can be explored with the aid of Foucault's thoughts on institutions, which he situated in the intricate, all-encompassing web of power relations that envelops the social sphere. For Foucault, institutions are the macro-instruments or apparatuses through which the finer workings of power function. But, he argues, 'the term "institution" is generally applied to every kind of more-or-less constrained, learned behaviour. Everything which functions in society as a system of constraint and which isn't an utterance, in short, all the field of the non-discursive social, is an institution'.[6] In this model, institutions arise out of nexuses of power and not the other way around, allowing for feminism itself to be considered an institution. But an individual who functions as a 'system of constraint' may also be considered

---

[3] See Hensel and Raether, *Neue deutsche Mädchen*, p. 9.

[4] Sonja Eismann, 'Einleitung', p. 10. Sonja Eismann uses the term 'RezipientInnen' [recipients] with a Binnen-I [internal capital I], which orthographical emphasis makes the feminine plural visible within a mixed gender plural. This strategy highlights her willingness to express continuity with earlier feminist generations even on a linguistic level.

[5] Alice Schwarzer, *Die Antwort* [The Response] (Munich: Wilhelm Heyne, 2008), p. 114 and pp. 119–37. Schwarzer has dismissed pop-feminism as 'neues Mädchengeplapper' [new girl-prattle] (see the back cover of *Die Antwort*) and remains particularly critical of their allegedly unreflectingly positive attitude towards pop-culture.

[6] Michel Foucault, 'The Confessions of the Flesh', in Michel Foucault and Colin Gordon, *Power/Knowledge: Selected Interviews and Other Writings, 1972–1977* (Hemel Hempstead: Harvester Wheatsheaf, 1980), pp. 197–8.

as such. I begin, then, with the premise that Alice Schwarzer, who was still active at the time when the pop-feminist texts were published, constitutes an institution. As such, she becomes implicated in the workings of the grosser nexuses of social power and acts as a confrontational force on other social and political institutions that promote, perpetuate, or support discrimination against women. She constitutes, in short, an institution working to constrain systems of constraint directed at women.

In the mid-1960s Schwarzer began working as a freelance journalist; in 1969 she went to Paris, where she reported on the cultural and political consequences of the 1968 student barricades. Like many other women across European and Anglo-American contexts who were involved in the civil rights and student movements at the end of the 1960s, she found that leftist male activists perpetuated the misogynistic practices that were part of the bourgeois society they criticized.[7] This realization led Schwarzer, like many other feminist thinkers originally associated with the West-German New Left, to seek out autonomous groups dedicated to women's liberation.

Schwarzer's website demonstrates how adept she is at fashioning a narrative of West German feminism that situates her as the sole instigator of the movement, emphasizing her status as a Foucauldian feminist institution. The autobiographical details appearing on her website stress her role in establishing the Paris women's movement alongside Monique Wittig, before turning her attention to the situation in the Federal Republic. She traces the origin of 1970s West German feminism to the successful realization of the notorious media event 'Ich habe abgetrieben' [I had an abortion], for which she takes credit, stating: 'Ich exportierte die Idee nach Deutschland. Dort gab es zu dem Zeitpunkt weder eine Frauenbewegung und noch massiven Protest gegen den §218.' [I exported the idea to Germany. At that time there was neither a women's movement nor substantial protest against Section 218.] Her comments refer to the article dominating the June 1971 edition of *Stern* in which 374 women, among them celebrities such as Romy Schneider and Senta Berger, revealed that they had had an abortion. Schwarzer had been inspired by similar undertakings in France and the Netherlands and had sold the idea to *Stern*. The intention was to place pressure on the state to abolish Section 218 of the *Grundgesetz* [Basic Law], which made abortion illegal in West Germany.

Importantly, Schwarzer's account does not include the interventions already undertaken by women in the New Left in German-speaking countries as early as 1962. For example, Gunhild Feigenwinter, writer and editor of the Basel-based *Hexenpresse* [Witches' Press], was already campaigning for abortion rights at this time. The existence of the West Berlin *Aktionsrat zur Befreiung der Frau* [Action Council for Women's Liberation], however, which was formed by women active in

---

[7] All biographical information has been taken from Alice Schwarzer, 'Zwei, drei autobiografische Anmerkungen', Alice Schwarzer homepage <http://www.aliceschwarzer.de.> Alice Schwarzer's website as it appears in 2017 has a more professional appearance than in 2013, when I started researching her work and public persona. The blogs, too, have become shorter and less personal in tone. Many are written now in the third person, whereas the texts I quote here were written predominantly in the first person and clearly attributable to Schwarzer herself. The professionalization of her web presence is further testimony to her skilled public self-fashioning.

the SDS [German Alliance of Socialist Students] as early as spring 1968, constitutes a direct refutation of Schwarzer's statement. Helke Sander, the *Aktionsrat* delegate at the SDS convention in September of that year, accused alliance members of being 'ein aufgeblähter konterrevolutionärer Hefeteig' [pompous counter-revolutionary sponge-heads] for ignoring their concerns, while activist Sigrid Rüger pelted the men on the podium with tomatoes.[8] These are just two examples from a period of increasing engagement by women in German-speaking countries. Furthermore, Schwarzer records that she read Simone de Beauvoir's *The Second Sex* (1949) and Betty Friedan's *The Feminine Mystique* (1963), but suggests that she did so in Paris, implying that at the time Germany was a vacuum in terms of theoretical feminist literature. This plays down the importance of external textual influences on West-German feminism. For, in fact, there was an influx of Anglo-American theoretical feminist texts in West Germany from the mid-1960s onwards, including Friedan's influential volume and Kate Millet's *Sexual Politics* (1968), both of which were translated into German by the early 1970s.[9]

Nevertheless, Schwarzer functioned as a prominent activist in the campaign for women's rights from the 1970s onwards, engaging consistently with equality issues in her journalistic and sociological writings. She was responsible for the dissemination of works by de Beauvoir and Susan Sontag in Germany, wrote biographies of prominent figures such as Romy Schneider and Marion Dönhoff, a retrospective of the German women's movement, countless journalistic articles and several longer theoretical texts, from *Der kleine Unterschied und seine großen Folgen* [*The Small Difference and its Enormous Consequences*] (1975) to a volume on women and Islam, *Die große Verschleierung* [*The Big Cover-Up*] (2010). She began a longstanding campaign against pornography, known as PorNo, in 1987, and published her autobiography, *Lebenslauf* [*My Life*], in 2011. In 1977 Schwarzer founded the renowned feminist magazine *Emma*, whose first issue sold over 200,000 copies;[10] it is still being published every two months today. Schwarzer's regular appearances on television often provoked heated media debate. In February 1975 she accused the author Esther Vilar of being a fascist in a televised debate.[11] On her website, Schwarzer claims that this was the moment when she became German media's 'Parade-Feministin' [showcase feminist]. From that point, her comments continued to court media attention, especially her 2001 claim that beauty-pageant contestant turned television personality Verona Feldbusch was an 'Ohrfeige für Frauen'

---

[8] Edith Hoshino Altbach et al., eds., *German Feminism: Readings in Politics and Literature*, p. 5.

[9] Just some of the Anglo-American feminist publications which appeared in Germany from the late 1960s include Betty Friedan's *The Feminine Mystique* (1963; translated in 1966 by Margaret Carroux); Kate Millet's *Sexual Politics* (1968; trans. by Ernestine Schlant in 1971); Germaine Greer's *The Female Eunuch* (1970; trans. by Marianne Dommermuth in 1971); Juliet Mitchell's 'Women, the Longest Revolution' (1966) and Margaret Benston's 'The Political Economy of Women's Liberation' (1969) were translated by Erich Derschatta and Maxi Mohr as part of the collection of essays entitled *Frauenemanzipation: Antiautoritäres Missverständnis oder Beitrag zur Konsolidierung der Arbeiterbewegung* (Munich: Trikont, 1971).

[10] FrauenMediaTurm, Das Archiv und Dokumentationszentrum <http://www.frauenmediaturm. de/home/> [accessed 05.08.2013].

[11] Klaudia Brunst, 'Frau gegen Frau', *Die Zeit*, 16 June 2005. See also Klaudia Brunst, *Je später der Abend...Über Talkshows, Stars und uns* (Freiburg: Herder, 2005).

[slap in the face for women],[12] and her description of the minister for families, Kristina Schröder, as a hopeless case.[13] The advent of the internet allowed Schwarzer to publish open letters on her website, an opportunity she used to challenge perpetrators of misogyny in the public sphere, for example the hip-hop singer Bushido[14] and Jörg Kachelmann, a television presenter accused of rape.[15]

Schwarzer sought to exploit her position of high media visibility in order to challenge institutionalized misogyny and promote equal opportunities. In this light, she might be thought of as the embodiment of what Foucault saw as the ideal practitioner of social criticism: the 'specific intellectual'. In their account of Foucault's critique of institutions, John D. Caputo and Mark Yount describe this figure as 'operat[ing] her intelligence where she is already situated, at the precise points of her own conditions of life or work'.[16] Schwarzer arguably achieves that in her writings and television appearances, often explicitly setting her journalistic persona aside in order to speak 'als Betroffene: als Frau' [as somebody directly affected: as a woman].[17]

However, for Foucault, the specific intellectual is a 'destroyer of evidence and universalities, the one who, in the inertias and constraints of the present, locates and marks the weak points, the openings, the lines of power, who incessantly displaces himself, doesn't know exactly where he is heading nor what he'll think tomorrow because he is too attentive to the present'.[18] On the one hand, Schwarzer acted to destroy beliefs that patriarchal consensus once held to be 'true': that abortion connotes an immoral act; that essential biological differences dictate that women should be paid less than men; that pornography and prostitution are acceptable social phenomena stemming from men's 'natural' needs. On the other hand, Schwarzer's acts of 'destruction' were predicated on the construction of a set of universalities to replace them, precluding her from assuming the role of a self-displacing social critic who resides only in the present and the particular.

Schwarzer's tendency to create universalities of her own can in part be attributed to her political stance as a *Gleichheitsfeministin* [equality feminist], a term she employs interchangeably with *Universalistin* [universalist] in her writing. She associates her ideology with that of the radical feminists of the first women's movement in Germany and draws a sharp distinction between 'UniversalistInnen' [universalist

[12] 'Verona Feldbusch ist eine Ohrfeige für Frauen', in *Spiegel Online*, 10 April 2001 <http://www.spiegel.de/panorama/alice-schwarzer-verona-feldbusch-ist-eine-ohrfeige-fuer-frauen-a-127672.html> [accessed 05.08.2013].

[13] Alice Schwarzer, 'Offener Brief an Kristina Schröder', Alice Schwarzer homepage, 8 November 2010 <http://www.aliceschwarzer.de.>

[14] Alice Schwarzer, 'Antwort an den deutschen Rapper Nr. 1!', Alice Schwarzer homepage, 8 February 2010 <http://www.aliceschwarzer.de/index.php?id=blog_bushido_2010_02_08> [accessed 03.08.2013].

[15] See 'Alice Schwarzer muss Kachelmann-Prozess verlassen', *Der Tagesspiegel: Welt*, 3 February 2011 <http://www.tagesspiegel.de/weltspiegel/eklat-vor-gericht-alice-schwarzer-muss-kachelmann-prozess-verlassen/3793980.html> [accessed 29.07.2013].

[16] John D. Caputo and Mark Yount, *Foucault and the Critique of Institutions* (University Park: Pennsylvania State University Press, 1993), p. 8.

[17] Alice Schwarzer, 'Zwei, drei autobiographische Anmerkungen'.

[18] Michel Foucault, 'The End of the Monarchy of Sex', in *Foucault Live: Interviews, 1966–1984*, ed. by Sylvere Lotringer, trans. by John Johnston (New York: Semiotext(e), 1989), p. 155.

feminists] and 'DifferenzialistInnen' [difference feminists]. She claims the latter group cultivate 'den Unterschied: Je nach Kultur, Glaube oder Geschlecht sind Menschen eben "anders" von Geburt oder durch irreversible Prägungen bzw. Überzeugungen und gelten für sie unterschiedliche Maßstäbe' [the difference: that depending on culture, faith, or gender, people are simply born 'different', or become so due to irreversible influences or convictions, and that different standards apply to them]. Schwarzer contends that her position acknowledges the differences between people, but places greater emphasis on the 'grundsätzlich[e] Gleichheit aller Menschen' [fundamental equality between all people].[19] Due to Schwarzer's emphasis on the similarities between men and women (and the resulting need for equal treatment), much of her published work also demonstrates the belief that sufficient similarities exist among women to warrant speaking in generalized terms about 'women' as a unified category.

When Schwarzer published *Der kleine Unterschied* in 1975 she argued that the perpetuation of the socially and culturally upheld distinction between public and private spheres ensured the continuation of women's oppression in the home and in family life. The sharp separation of public and private worlds, she argues, prevents women from uniting in mutual recognition of their shared fate and taking collective action. While this argument is associated with early US second-wave feminism, the understanding that the private is political was common to early second-wave feminism across many cultural contexts, influencing both the thematic thrust and format of much second-wave writing. Indeed, its influence can still be felt in the most recent pop-feminist texts. Schwarzer's text consists of a series of transcribed interviews with female volunteers talking about their experiences of home, sex, and families. This same format was employed two years later by Maxie Wander in the German Democratic Republic (GDR) when she published *Guten Morgen, du Schöne* [*Good Morning, Beautiful*] (1977) and the pop-feminist scholar Katja Kauer argues that *Neue deutsche Mädchen* signals a return to a reflective, autobiographical narrative style that echoes the written interventions of many second-wave writers.[20] Thea Dorn's 2006 volume *Die neue F-Klasse* also consists of a collection of interviews with a variety of successful professional women, which, importantly, focuses more on their public lives rather than discussing family, home, and sex.

Like the American feminist Susan Brownmiller in her 1975 volume *Against Our Will*, Schwarzer emphasizes the role played by heterosexual sex in the perpetuation of gender inequalities, arguing that it represents the 'Spiegel und Instrument der Unterdrückung der Frauen in allen Lebensbereichen' [reflection and instrument of women's oppression in all areas of life].[21] The inability to recognize their common fate in the hitherto private realm of sex prevented women from recognizing the extent of women's oppression on a wider social level. *Der kleine Unterschied* was an attempt to banish the isolation experienced by many women and to clear the way for a progressive feminist movement dedicated to social and political change.

---

[19] Alice Schwarzer, 'Zwei, drei autobiografische Anmerkungen'.
[20] Katja Kauer, *Popfeminismus!*, p. 94.
[21] Alice Schwarzer, *Der kleine Unterschied und seine großen Folgen: Frauen über sich, Beginn einer Befreiung*, revised edition (Frankfurt am Main: Fischer Taschenbuch, 2007), p. 17.

Schwarzer's universalism draws criticism from pop-feminists for being elitist. They claim she ignores important differences among women—most importantly age—that influence the issues affecting them. However, in her written responses to such critique, Schwarzer remains sceptical about feminist ideologies that foreground differences between individual women based on class, ethnicity, education, sexuality, and physical ability. She also rejects feminist thinking that highlights difference between men and women in essentialist biological terms. Her reluctance to engage with difference discourse stems in great part from the recognition, common to much second-wave feminist thought, that socio-political and cultural change may be more easily achieved by a unified group than by disparate, uncoordinated factions. This position may, on the one hand, explicate her readiness to criticize female public figures who did not subscribe to her account of female experience. For example, Schwarzer often accused those who, like Verona Feldbusch, opposed her critical attitude towards the beauty industry of themselves working against women's interests. On the other hand, this confrontational strategy arguably served to undermine the very sense of solidarity between women in the public sphere she sought to secure, and only enhanced the impression touted in much of the popular media, which revelled in Schwarzer's 'clashes' with other female public figures, that the women's movement had, by the mid-2000s, disintegrated into sectarianism and bitter in-fighting.

The authors of *Wir Alpha-Mädchen* and *Neue deutsche Mädchen*, in particular, explicitly distance themselves from the universalist feminism they associate predominantly with Alice Schwarzer; even when discussing established feminism in general terms, their observations reveal the extent to which these authors often conflate Schwarzer with the movement as a whole. As a result, their initial sketches of the current state of feminism echo those, mentioned above, which are found in mainstream popular media. Haaf, Klingner, and Streidl present a movement scarred by authoritarianism, proscription, and the pursuit of power and personal interest:

> Dem Feminismus sind nicht die Füße eingeschlafen, weil er nichts mehr zu tun hat. Nein, er ist einfach nur den Weg so vieler eigentlich grandioser Bewegungen gegegangen: in die Grabenkämpfe und die Rechthaberei. Unter politisch Aktiven gibt es immer Menschen, die ihre eigenen Überzeugungen zu allgemeinen Wahrheiten erheben. [...] Und weil das zentrale Thema der Neuen Frauenbewegung letzlich das Privatleben war, schadete dieser Reflex der Entwicklung des Feminismus ganz besonders. Denn wenn ständig eine erzählt, wie alle anderen richtig zu leben haben, dann nervt das.

> [Feminism hasn't gone to seed because there's nothing left to do. No, it's just ended up the same way as so many other brilliant movements: scarred by sectarianism and self-righteousness. There are always some politically active people who extend their personal convictions to general truths. [...] And because private life was ultimately the New Feminism's central theme, that tendency became particularly damaging to feminism's development. After all, it's really annoying if somebody keeps telling you how to live properly.][22]

---

[22] Haaf, Klingner, and Streidl, *Wir Alpha-Mädchen*, p. 194.

Note how in this excerpt the non-specific and gender-neutral 'Menschen' [people] in the third line becomes a very pointed 'eine' [one female person] in the last sentence, presumably directed at Alice Schwarzer herself. For these writers, Schwarzer constitutes, following Foucault's definition of institutions, a 'system of constraint' privy to an ambivalent power/knowledge nexus that acts as both an instrument of persuasion and of discipline upon women's *private* lives. They contend: 'Da hatten sich die Frauen gerade von der patriarchalischen Bevormundung befreit, und schon wollten ihnen ihre eigene Weggefährtinnen wieder etwas vorschreiben.' [Women had only just freed themselves from patriarchal control and their feminist allies were already trying to tell them what to do.][23] Schwarzer is therefore no better than the patriarchal forces she seeks to challenge. Raether, on the other hand, refers to Schwarzer's decision to take part in an advertising campaign for *BILD*, a newspaper not known for its progressive position on gender equality, suggesting:

> [W]ahrscheinlich verhält es sich so, wenn man lange ausgeschlossen war und irgendwann doch dazugehört: Man selbst erinnert sich noch gut an die Zeit, in der man nicht mitreden durfte, und meint deshalb, gar nicht richtig zum Kreis der Mächtigen zu zählen. Und so lässt man für sich selbst andere Maßstäbe gelten als für die, die man zuvor die Mächtigen nannte.
>
> [It's probably just what happens after you've been excluded for a long time and then at some point you're suddenly included. You remember all too well being denied a voice and so you don't believe you number among the powerful. That's why you might apply different standards to yourself than to those you used to call the powerful people.][24]

The repetition of 'man' [one] here underscores Raether's view of Schwarzer as an extension of institutional patriarchy, as well as distancing her own language from the feminist linguistics of a previous generation (where 'frau' would replace the third-person singular 'man').[25] But apart from allegations of hypocrisy, Schwarzer becomes accused of elevating herself to the position of 'Oberboss des Feminismus' [feminism's head honcho] (another masculinist term), so that she divests the movement of its variety.[26] Haaf, Klingner, and Streidl cite the frequency of her appearances on the front cover of *Emma* as a reason to disbelieve her alleged modesty.[27] In fact, they continually insinuate that Schwarzer operates unethically and self-servingly and has a vested interest in maintaining the status quo in order to protect her position of power. Speaking of Schwarzer and her generation, Jana Hensel comments that:

> Die Zeit hat sie eingeholt, ihre Rhetorik ist oll, Alice Schwarzer und ihre Frauen sind Historie geworden [...]. Ihre Sache ist ihnen entglitten. Sie hat sich verselbstständigt, und Schwarzer wirkt oft so, als wolle sie mit aller Kraft verhindern, dass man ihr die Deutungsmacht aus der Hand nimmt.
>
> [Time's caught up with them. Their rhetoric is old hat. Alice Schwarzer and her women are history [...]. Their thing has slipped from grasp—because it's taken on a

---

[23] Ibid., p. 195.   [24] Jana Hensel and Elisabeth Raether, *Neue deutsche Mädchen*, pp. 23–4.
[25] 'Man' signifies 'one' but resembles 'Mann' [man]. German New Feminist writing often used 'frau' [from woman] as a replacement for the generic masculinist 'man'.
[26] Meredith Haaf, Susanne Klingner and Barbara Streidl, *Wir Alpha-Mädchen*, p. 196.
[27] Ibid.

life of its own. But Schwarzer often acts as though she'd rather die than give up inter-
pretative authority.][28]

Hensel's observation, which sketches Schwarzer as the commander of a feminist
entourage, resonates with Foucault's description of the supple dynamic between
power and resistance: 'between a relationship of power and a strategy of struggle there
is a reciprocal appeal, a perpetual linking and a perpetual reversal.'[29] Confrontation
between adversaries may at any moment cease in order to establish 'mechanisms of
power'.[30] In general, the pop-feminists discussed here imply that Schwarzer's strategy
of political resistance has reversed and become a strategy intended to uphold a
personal claim to power.

These accusations culminate most vociferously in the contention that Schwarzer's
form of feminism is irrelevant for young women in Germany today:

> Schwarzer tut so, als hätte sich die Situation der Frauen seit den siebziger Jahren kaum
> verändert – weil sie inzwischen vor allem eine strategisch handelnde Medienpersönlichkeit
> ist, die ihr Publikum sucht [...]. Und weil niemand merken soll, dass sie so vieles nicht
> weiß über Frauen, die heute jung sind.

> [Schwarzer behaves as if the situation for women had hardly changed since the 70s—
> mostly because in the meantime she's become a savvy media personality looking for an
> audience [...]. And because no-one is supposed to notice that there's a whole lot she
> doesn't know about young women today.][31]

Hensel and Raether decry Schwarzer's universalist rhetoric, stressing the disparity
between their experiences and those of the women for whom Schwarzer campaigns.
Her most recent initiatives concern prostitution, eating disorders, and the role of
women in Islam. But, according to Hensel, these issues have nothing whatsoever
to do with a thirty-year-old woman in Germany today.[32] This rather implausible
claim exemplifies one of the most troubling aspects of this generationally inflected
type of pop-feminist thinking: their indifference towards the above issues implies
an indifference towards the kind of women who might be affected by them. Indeed,
a group of young, white, middle-class, educated, heterosexual feminists who disregard the challenges facing women living in the same cultural context who do not
share those characteristics must face accusations of elitism and irrelevance themselves.

Christina Scharff and Hester Baer have argued that German pop-feminists all
too often rely upon the rhetoric of neoliberal individualism in order to distance
themselves from the perceived proscriptions of second-wave feminism.[33] More
specifically, this language emphasizes the importance of individual choice in order
to counter Schwarzer's universalist narrative. However, this strategy succeeds in
divorcing the private from the political and ultimately elides differences between

---

[28] Jana Hensel and Elisabeth Raether, *Neue deutsche Mädchen*, p. 14.
[29] Michel Foucault, 'The Subject and Power', in *Michel Foucault: Beyond Structuralism and
Hermeneutics*, ed. by Hubert L. Dreyfus and Paul Rabinow (Brighton: Harvester, 1982), p. 226.
[30] Ibid.   [31] Jana Hensel and Elisabeth Raether, *Neue deutsche Mädchen*, p. 25.
[32] Ibid., p. 14.
[33] Hester Baer, 'German Feminism in the Age of Neoliberalism', p. 364; Christina Scharff,
Repudiating Feminism: Young Women in a Neoliberal World (Farnham; Burlington, VT: Ashgate, 2012).

women in much the same way as Schwarzer's universalism. Initially, Haaf, Klingner, and Streidl engage critically with the climate of neoliberal individualism,[34] which has produced 'ein Heer von Einzelkämpferinnen' [an army of lone fighters].[35] Raether even broaches the matter of the social conditions that women face, arguing that they are not any less prevalent 'nur weil einige in der Lage sind, sich über sie hinwegzusetzen' [just because a few women are able to rise above them].[36]

However, they undermine their own critique by perpetually returning to an individualistic logic that dictates that ultimately everyone has to make their own decisions.[37] In this way, these texts underestimate the impact of socio-cultural and commercial forces on their brand of feminism and how those forces impinge upon agency. The clearest example of this tendency can be found in Thea Dorn's introduction to *Die neue F-Klasse*. She asks:

> Warum nicht zugeben, dass es in diesem Buch nicht um Frauensolidarität um jeden Preis geht, sondern um eine bestimmte Klasse von Frauen, die sich allerdings nicht durch priviligierte Herkunft definiert, sondern einzig und allein durch das individuell von ihr Erreichte und Gelebte?

> [Why not just admit that this book isn't about achieving female solidarity at all costs? Rather it's about a certain class of women, who aren't defined by their privileged background, but only by what they've achieved and experienced individually.][38]

But Dorn's meritocratic stance is based on the neoliberal illusion that background has no impact on that which the individual can achieve.

The devaluation of 'Frauensolidarität' [solidarity between women] distances Dorn's feminism from one of the fundamental tenets of the second wave. It also highlights the extent to which pop-feminism is influenced by Anglo-American critiques of the second wave that contend that differences between women along the lines of class, race, ability, and ethnicity, as well as gender, intersect to produce starkly contrasting experiences of oppression. As Dorn's comment demonstrates, however, F Class feminism, like that of the alpha or new German girls, translates intersectionality into a radical neoliberal politics of individualism, promulgating an ideology that privileges women's entitlement to exercise individual choice (because of their different experiences).

This emphasis, along with the accompanying antagonism expressed towards feminists of Schwarzer's generation, results in uncertainty concerning the actual nature of these pop-feminists' politics and emancipatory intentions. It is unclear precisely what they propose as an alternative to second-wave feminism apart from a policy of 'Selbstbestimmung' [autonomy].[39] These authors thus become implicated in a reciprocal Foucauldian dynamic of power/resistance inasmuch as their identity as a movement is thoroughly contingent upon a radical rejection of 1970s feminism, and of Schwarzer in particular. Declaring the ideology of 1970s feminism

---

[34] Meredith Haaf, Susanne Klingner, and Barbara Streidl, *Wir Alpha-Mädchen*, p. 19.
[35] Ibid., p. 197.   [36] Ibid., pp. 72–3.   [37] Ibid., *Wir Alpha-Mädchen*, p. 45.
[38] Thea Dorn, *Die neue F-Klasse: Wie die Zukunft von Frauen gemacht wird* (Munich: Piper, 2006), p. 37.
[39] Meredith Haaf, Susanne Klingner, and Barbara Streidl, *Wir Alpha-Mädchen*, p. 66.

redundant suggests that these new feminist protagonists have not sufficiently inter-
rogated the social constellations that gave rise to feminism in the first place,
although these writers' very engagement with feminist debate implies that they
must have done to some extent. Viewed in this way, the rhetoric of discontinuity
employed by some pop-feminists appears as a marketing strategy, designed to make
feminism palatable to the mainstream, but which results in the capitulation of
radical feminist politics to the demands of postfeminist neoliberalism.

While this new feminism's call for renewed attention to emancipatory politics
breaks with the postfeminist logic that rejects feminism out of hand, the repudiation
of second-wave feminism by many pop-feminists in the West forms part of what
Angela McRobbie calls a 'double entanglement':[40] on the one hand, German pop-
feminists aim to attract and reassure a younger generation of women who fear
association with the negative stereotypes peddled by postfeminist media concerning feminism. On the other, their ambivalence towards the achievements of
Schwarzer's generation combined with the continued reinforcement of pejorative
perceptions of feminism paradoxically entail that the pop-feminism at times col-
ludes with the anti-feminist rhetoric saturating the media and the public sphere.
On the first page of *Wir Alpha-Mädchen*, the authors re-inscribe precisely this
negative view of feminism when they claim that the 'problem' arises from the perception of feminists as ugly, anti-fun, anti-men, irony-free, and unsexy: 'Das alles
wollen wir uns natürlich nicht nachsagen lassen, und deswegen streiten die meisten
von uns lieber ab, irgendetwas mit "den Emanzen" zu tun zu haben.' [Naturally we
don't want people to think that about us and that's why most of us would rather
deny having anything to do with 'the bra-burners.']'[41]

As a result, these authors, like their British and North American counterparts,
seek to persuade the reader that being a feminist does not preclude fun, interaction
with men, or heterosexual sex. The fallacious belief, made popular by antifeminist
German media portrayals of the 'Emanze', that feminism equates with compulsory lesbianism feeds their insistence that heterosexual sex is compatible with
their brand of feminism. Thus, sex and sexuality once again play a pivotal role in
pop-feminism, as they did for the 1970s women's movement. The gesture, however, appears reversed. Far from analysing the ways in which sex, public/private
power, and women's oppression have intersected historically and continue to do
so, the position taken by many pop-feminists is unequivocal: being sexually active
is a marker of female liberation; partaking in transgressive sexual practices, such
as S&M, can be empowering, even when adopting the submissive role; watching
pornography can foster sexual creativity and enhance individual pleasure.[42]

All too often, sex and politics become uncoupled, and the private becomes private
once more. Indeed, agency withdraws from the wider social sphere and re-emerges

---

[40] See Angela McRobbie, *The Aftermath of Feminism*; Angela McRobbie, 'Postfeminism and
Popular Culture'.

[41] Meredith Haaf, Susanne Klingner, and Barbara Streidl, *Wir Alpha-Mädchen*, p. 13. Note on
translation: 'Emanze' derives from 'Emanzipation' [emancipation], but I sought to find a cultural
equivalent to highlight the term's perjorative tone.

[42] Ibid., p. 105. Cited in Chapter 1, p. 33.

in the realm of sexual preference and the concomitant consumer power to purchase the commodities associated with its practice: sex toys and pornography. Sex
thus becomes a marketing strategy, a tool for selling feminism (and its present-day
accoutrements) to women and avoiding any potential alienation of men. The
authors of *Wir Alpha-Mädchen* urge women, for example, to convince men of the
benefits they will enjoy once their female partners begin to explore new (sexual)
avenues. They suggest that their readers should 'den Männern erklären, warum es
auch für sie super ist, wenn wir uns weiterentwickeln' [explain to men why it's also
great for them if we keep on improving ourselves].[43] Their concern for men's
approval combined with the notable exclusion of the LGBTQ+ community from
their discussion of sex betrays a lamentable heteronormativity in many pop-feminist
guides. Schwarzer is less concerned with securing male allegiance, yet both Schwarzer's
and the pop-feminists' shared emphasis on heterosexual sex connotes an unrecog-
nized area of commonality between them.

The untroubled portrayal of sex as the source of limitless, unequivocal agency, as
well as an understanding of agency as inherently related to sexuality, resonates with
the trajectories of many of the North American and British volumes discussed
above. For example, one of the most important tenets for the authors of *Wir Alpha-
Mädchen* is that their feminism 'steht für sexuelle Selbstbestimmung' [stands for
sexual autonomy].[44] Being a feminist not only constitutes sexiness, but it leads to
'Knaller-Sex für Alle' [dynamite sex for everyone].[45] This emphasis proves to be
just as rigid as Schwarzer's insistence on the subjugating and oppressive nature of
heterosexual sex. The recent volumes fail to acknowledge a tradition of feminist
thought that examines the ways in which dominant patriarchal ideologies have
configured women as passive, sexual objects, and how the pornography industry,
for example, has been influenced by those ideologies. Instead, the subject's ability
to behave autonomously remains a given constant, a feature that constitutes an
almost wilful disregard of socio-cultural pressures. Curiously, many pop-feminists
acknowledge the influence of social contingency in other contexts, for example, in
their discussion of inequality in the workplace and the gender pay-gap. In the
realm of body politics, however, they disregard the influence of socio-political
forces, creating a flash point between generational perspectives.

The opening scene of Charlotte Roche's second novel *Schoßgebete* [Lap Prayers]
exemplifies this feeling of generational disjuncture on the subject of sex.[46] The narrative describes the attempts of a psychologically unstable young woman, Elizabeth
Kiehl, to secure the identity and concomitant lifestyle of 'eine brave Mutter und
Ehefrau' [a good mother and wife].[47] Apart from the narrative strands that deal

---

[43] Ibid., p. 15.   [44] Ibid., p. 66.
[45] See Haaf, Klingner, and Streidl, *Wir Alpha-Mädchen*, p. 63; Mirja Stöcker, ed., *Das F-Wort:
Feminismus ist sexy*. The preface to *Das F-Wort* plays on the multivalence of the term 'f-word', alluding
to the words 'ficken' [fuck], 'Fotze' [cunt] and 'Feminismus' [feminism].
[46] 'Der Schoß' can refer to the lap of a sitting person but can also be translated as 'womb'. 'Im
Schoß der Familie' signifies 'in the bosom of the family', for example.
[47] Charlotte Roche, *Schoßgebete* (Munich: Piper, 2011), p. 55. Further page references will be provided within the body of the text as SG.

with the familial trauma that led to Elizabeth's breakdown, the novel's general aesthetic is pornographic kitsch. On the one hand, the graphic depictions of Elizabeth's
sexual and other corporeal exploits tread ground familiar from Roche's first novel,
Feuchtgebiete [Wetlands] (2008), which I discuss in detail in the next section but
one. On the other, the character of Elizabeth is intensely conservative, driven by a
sense of nostalgia for a time when gender roles and familial duties were clear cut,
affording an equally unambiguous sense of identity. The novel therefore portrays
the pinnacle of wifely *and* personal achievement as Elizabeth's acquiescing to her
husband Georg's request to accompany him to a brothel to engage in a threesome
with a South American sex worker.

Roche name-checks Schwarzer several times over the course of the novel and the
majority of references occur whenever Elizabeth engages in sexual intercourse:
'Alice Schwarzer sitzt immer beim Sex zwischen mir und meinem Mann und flüs-
tert mir ins Ohr: "Ja, Elizabeth, das denkst du nur, dass du jetzt einen vaginalen
Orgasmus hast [...], um dich deinem Mann und seinem Machtschwanz zu unterwerfen."' [Alice Schwarzer always sits between me and my husband when we have
sex and whispers in my ear: 'Yeah, Elizabeth, you only think that you're having a
vaginal orgasm in order to subjugate yourself to your husband and his all-powerful
penis.'] (SG, 17) (The term 'unterwerfen' [subjugate] is a barely veiled allusion to
a particular passage in Schwarzer's *Der kleine Unterschied*.)[48] The press made much
of Alice Schwarzer's open letter to Roche, published in August 2011, which constituted a response to her being featured in Roche's text.[49] Schwarzer dubs the
novel a 'verruchte Heimatschnulze' [loathsome 'Heimat' tearjerker] featuring a
problematic and fully outdated relationship model.[50] In return, Roche claims that
she in fact never intended the novel to be a feminist manifesto and would never
encourage readers to copy Elizabeth's actions. Yet, in the same interview, Roche
confirms that she placed Schwarzer in her novel 'weil sie nicht abdanke und jahr-
zehntelang die feministische Diskussion in Deutschland bestimmt habe' [because
she's not stepping down and has dominated feminist debate in Germany for dec-
ades]. Roche finds that the time has come for younger feminists to find a voice.
However, 'die werden immer weggebissen von unserer Spitze' [they always get
chased off by our great leader]. Her comments suggest that she sought to spark
feminist debate about sexuality because, as she puts it: '[e]s ist noch nicht alles
darüber gesagt.' [There's still plenty to say about it.][51]

---

[48] Speaking on heterosexual sex, Schwarzer states: 'Hier liegen Unterwerfung, Schuldbewusstsein
und Männerfixierung von Frauen verankert.' [Women's subjugation, sense of guilt, and fixation on
men are rooted here.] Schwarzer, *Der kleine Unterschied*, p. 17.

[49] See Christian Buß, 'Schwarzer attackiert Roche: Häschen im Bett, Oma im Kopf', *Spiegel
Online*, Kultur, 15 August 2011 <http://www.spiegel.de/kultur/literatur/schwarzer-attackiert-roche-
haeschen-im-bett-oma-im-kopf-a-780345.html> [accessed 08.08.2011].

[50] Alice Schwarzer, 'Hallo Charlotte', Alice Schwarzer's blog, 15 August 2011.No longer available.
'Heimat' is a specifically German concept for which English has no cognate. It is often translated with
'home' or 'homeland'.

[51] Charlotte Roche quoted in 'Charlotte Roche geht auf Alice Schwarzer los', *Die Welt*, Kultur,
25 August 2011 <http://www.welt.de/kultur/literarischewelt/article13565397/Charlotte-Roche-geht-
auf-Alice-Schwarzer-los.html> [accessed 08.08.2011].

Yet it is not only Schwarzer who hovers figuratively over Elizabeth's bed in *Schoßgebete*: Elizabeth must struggle against the conflated internalized voices of her mother and 'führende Feministinnen' [leading feminists] as well as Schwarzer's. The combination of the mother's voice with Schwarzer's broadens Roche's critique as it becomes directed not just at one woman, but at a whole generation. The critique itself revolves around the content and delivery of second-wave sexual politics. As previously mentioned, Elizabeth claims that these feminist spectres disrupt climactic moments with her husband by whispering about the non-existence of the vaginal orgasm (SG, 16–17). These passages represent the moments when Elizabeth's 'feministische Erziehung meilenweit an der Realität vorbeigeht' [reality clashes with her feminist education] (SG, 17). The sinister feminist apparitions are portrayed as systems of constraint preventing the protagonist from experiencing the 'reality' of sexual pleasure in a depoliticized context.

Thus, when Elizabeth allows her husband to perform a sex act upon her that he has copied from a pornographic film and after that accompanies him to the brothel, her reaction is self-congratulatory because she has triumphed against the internalized voices of constraint who inconveniently insist on bringing politics into individual experience: '[i]ch muss innerlich lachen darüber, wie cool wir sind, wie cool ich bin, was für eine Angst ich vorher hatte und dass ich es geschafft habe, Alice und meine Mutter zum Schweigen zu bringen.' [I have to laugh inside when I realize how cool we are, how cool I am, how scared I was before, and how I've successfully shut Alice and my mother up.] (SG, 250) But Elizabeth's repetition of the keyword 'cool' is troubling. The term resonates tantalizingly with counter-cultural promise despite its co-option by mainstream, commercially driven forces that regulate identity by means of hierarchies of inclusion and exclusion. The former resonance thus elides the vital question of who sets the criteria for 'cool'. In *Schoßgebete*, as in *Feuchtgebiete*, pressure inheres in understanding female sexual (self-)objectification and pornographic role-play to be 'cool' and readers educated in postfeminist irony can congratulate themselves on avoiding the 'Sexfeindlichkeit' [anti-sex stance][52] allegedly promulgated by second-wave feminists.

As I argued in my discussion of postfeminist erotic fiction, strands of second-wave feminism viewed the concept of sexual pleasure inhering in self-objectifying or masochistic practices as representative of patriarchal structures undergirding women's subjugation. Roche, however, distinguishes between the social realm and that of private fantasy. In the novel, Elizabeth is so concerned with escaping the authoritarian feminist spectres of her imagination that she does not consider the ways in which both her sexual explorations, which she treats as a kind of neoliberal self-improvement project, and her nostalgic desire to perform the role of ideal mother and housewife, align with and reinscribe pre-feminist misogynistic stereotypes of idealized femininity. In fact, neither Roche nor the pop-feminists discussed above question how one's choice of sexual activity might be predetermined by the regulating forces of normative heterosexuality. The model of untroubled agency in the sexual arena matches the narrative of freedom of choice they employ

---

[52] Meredith Haaf, Susanne Klingner, and Barbara Streidl, *Wir Alpha-Mädchen*, p. 66.

when discussing young women's relationship to their personal appearance. While Dorn, Raether, Haaf et al. devote some time to criticizing ever more demanding beauty standards, they tend ultimately to undermine their own critique. They do this by making the individualist claim that every woman should ultimately do what she pleases with her body.

The narratives of neoliberal individualism and localism expounded by the pop-feminists discussed above mask the elitist universalism at work in their own volumes. They justify the paucity of pages examining international variances in women's corporeal, economic, cultural, and socio-political experiences by claiming to speak only to women in contemporary Germany. The texts offer a narrow understanding of these women, however. On the one hand, they insist their programme incorporates intersectionality by claiming to be aware of the differences between young women's lives in Germany.[53] On the other, the texts' autobiographical nature and their general exclusion of LGBTQ+ communities and migrant, non-white, older, non-middle-class perspectives elevate the experiences of a class of educated, heterosexual white women to a universal norm, precisely the accusation they levy at Alice Schwarzer. I can only concur with Christina Scharff when she argues that the privileging of white, heterosexual German women in mainstream endorsements of feminism 'resonate[s] with colonial discourses about the "other" where a knowing gaze asserts Western superiority, legitimizes civilizing missions, and overlooks differences between women.'[54] In the case of Roche's fiction, for example, women of a different class or ethnic background only ever feature as sex workers.

In the place of a coherent political agenda, the pop-feminists discussed here propose instead a withdrawal from feminist politics to that which Jana Hensel calls 'normality'. She observes that 'in den letzten Jahren wurde immer deutlicher: Längst ist es die Normalität, die zu unserer größten Sehnsucht geworden ist' [in the last few years it's become increasingly apparent that normality has long since been our greatest desire].[55] Indeed, Roche's protagonist, Elizabeth, demonstrates this yearning for 'normality' in the pleasure she takes in her daily encounters with domesticity and the pursuit of a slightly modified version of idealized femininity. This brand of feminism aligns itself with normative mainstream culture and circumvents the radicalism—and the concomitant exposure to censure—linked with Schwarzer's generation. These pop-feminist authors have been exposed to, and in turn impose, what Foucault might have called the disciplinary function of patriarchal institutions enacted by the power of the norm. For, as Caputo and Yount, glossing Foucault, note: 'Normalization keeps watch over the excessive and the exceptional, delimiting the outcasts who threaten the order of normalcy [...]. Institutions will form and well-adjust the young into supple, happy subjects of normalization. Institutions will reform the abnormal who stray beyond the limits.'[56]

---

[53] Ibid., p. 8.

[54] Christina Scharff, 'The New German Feminisms: Of Wetlands and Alpha-Girls', in *New Femininities*, ed. by Rosalind Gill and Christina Scharff, p. 269.

[55] Jana Hensel and Elisabeth Raether, *Neue deutsche Mädchen*, p. 15.

[56] John D. Caputo and Mark Yount, *Foucault and the Critique of Institutions*, p. 6.

Yet they are not only exposed to the normalizing force of patriarchal institutions. As their pop-feminist volumes suggest, they experience the institutional force of established feminism as an intolerable pressure on subsequent generations of women to continue the struggle for emancipation exclusively within the parameters set by second-wave feminism. Within this nexus of conflicting demands, the institution with a specific figurehead and high public visibility becomes a tangible point of resistance for some German pop-feminists, rather than the faceless, heterogeneous manifestations of neoliberal coercion.

These authors can be seen as both victims and perpetrators of the disciplinary mechanisms of postfeminist neoliberalism. Under pressure to conform and failing to interrogate the conditions and expectations generated by the economic, social, and cultural forces that influence their own withdrawal from the political arena, they equate the abnormal individual who threatens the status quo with the radical feminist. Certainly, second-wave feminists who are resistant to confronting ideologically transformative socio-cultural shifts would do well to remember that progressive political movements require continual adjustment in order to ensure relevance. However, some pop-feminists' employment of a neoliberal rhetoric of individualism discourages both politicization and collective action; paradoxically, they succumb to the postfeminist patriarchal norm even while proclaiming the need for a new type of feminism.

LITERARY GENERATIONS AND GERMAN POP-LITERATURE

The German literary scholar, Thomas Anz, notes that '[i]m Namen einer neuen Generation wurde seit Beginn der 90er Jahre entweder gezielt die 68er Generation verabschiedet oder die gesamte Nachkriegsgeschichte und Nachkriegsliteratur' [from the early 1990s it was either the 1968 generation in particular or post-war history and literature in general that were dismissed in favour of a new generation].[57] Reunification encouraged a demand for renewal in the literary sphere, too. Many prominent authors and critics announced the demise of both GDR and Federal Republic of Germany (FRG) literature, claiming that fiction had stultified and was, in terms of content, irrelevant to contemporary culture and also stylistically uninteresting. Fiction should no longer focus, they argued, on the German past, but look to realistic, Anglo-American models that foregrounded plot and characterization.[58] Public engagement with this so-called 'Neue Lesbarkeit' [new readability] was fierce after 1989,[59] while the 1990s also

---

[57] Thomas Anz, 'Konkurrenzen, Konflikte, Kontinuitäten', p. 24.

[58] Beth Linklater, 'Germany as Background: Global Concerns in Recent Women's Writing in German', in *German Literature in the Age of Globalisation,* ed. by Stuart Taberner (Birmingham: University of Birmingham Press, 2004), p. 69.

[59] See, for example, Uwe Wittstock, *Leselust: wie unterhaltsam ist die neue deutsche Literatur? Ein Essay* (Munich: Luchterhand, 1995); Frank Schirrmacher, 'Idyllen in der Wüste', *Frankfurter Allgemeine Zeitung,* 10 October 1989; Maxim Biller, 'Soviel Sinnlichkeit wie der Stadtplan von Kiel', *Die Weltwoche,*

witnessed a marked increase in Anglo-American publications appearing on the German-language market.[60]

On the one hand, calls for new readability in German fiction revealed the anxiety felt by German-language publishers at the time that domestic fiction would be unable to compete with its Anglo-American rivals; on the other, it expressed a genuine sense of discord, expressed in generational terms, in the literary community.[61] Thomas Anz argues that young writers were reacting to the perceived dominance of the 1968 generation, who had, at their peak, radicalized the demand that literature become more socially effective even to the point of renouncing art.[62] 'Neue Lesbarkeit' marked the returning pendulum: an equally radical attempt to liberate literature—as an aesthetically autonomous art form—from all social demands.[63]

Other voices expressed concern about the effects of emulating Anglo-American literary models, fearing the irrevocable trivialization of literature, and cultural homogeneity.[64] Frank Finlay notes that, in Germany, this debate touched on fundamental issues of national identity and internationalism that were not at stake in Anglo-American discussions of popular literature.[65] As I showed in my discussion of the New Puritans, similar debates occurring at the same time in Britain were also framed in generational terms, but did not touch on the questions of national cultural identity driving German discussions. Rather, generational dissent was framed by questions of elitism and class. This reduced concern for the representative qualities of cultural identity on a global stage is due in part to the dominance of (translated) English-language literature on the global market, mentioned above. Lawrence Venuti, whose study of global translation practices *Rethinking Translation* (1992) might have given credence to German concerns regarding Anglo-American literary hegemony, discusses the 'decisive mediation' performed by translated texts in global discursive transactions. He contends that translations are sites of 'multiple determinations and effects—linguistic, cultural, institutional [and] political'.[66] However, he points out that the appearance of a purportedly transparent international discourse (i.e. the presence of *some* translated foreign texts in distribution in English) actually 'sustains the grossly unequal cultural exchanges between the hegemonic English language nations, particularly the United States, and their others in Europe, Africa, Asia and the Americas'.[67]

Lawrence Venuti notes that the general trend among non-English-language publishers in the decades since World War Two has been to circulate vast numbers of translated English-language texts on their national markets. In contrast, the

---

25 July 1991; Matthias Politycki, 'Literatur muss sein wie Rockmusik', *Frankfurter Rundschau*, 7 October 1995.

[60] Frank Finlay, 'Literary Debates', p. 32.
[61] Ibid., pp. 31–6; Stuart Taberner, 'Literary Debates', pp. 5–10.
[62] Thomas Anz, 'Konkurrenzen, Konflikte, Kontinuitäten', p. 25.   [63] ibid.
[64] Frank Finlay, 'Literary Debates', p. 35.   [65] ibid.
[66] Lawrence Venuti, ed., *Rethinking Translation: Discourse, Subjectivity, Ideology* (London; New York: Routledge, 1992), p. 2.
[67] Ibid., p. 5.

circulation of translated foreign-language texts in Britain and North America has diminished since that period. In Venuti's view, this practice by non-Anglo-American publishers exploits the 'global drift toward American political and economic hegemony, actively supporting the international expansion of American culture by circulating it in their national cultures'.[68] This drift can be partly attributed to the establishment in the years following World War Two of multinational publishing conglomerates, which enjoyed greater editorial control due to increased financial stability.[69]

Venuti observes that West Germany's publishing industry kept pace with domestic production rates in the US and Britain in the late 1980s, yet his statistics for translations coming out of Germany versus Britain and America substantiate his claim that Anglo-American texts were translated more frequently. Using figures from the American journal *Publishers Weekly* and *Whitaker's Almanac* Venuti points out that between 1984 and 1990 'translations accounted for approximately 3.5 percent of books published annually in the United States, 2.5 percent in the United Kingdom'.[70] Figures for 1991 show that Germany and Great Britain published a comparable number of books: 67,890 and 67,628 respectively. Yet the number of translations among them was 3 per cent in Britain compared with 14 per cent in Germany. Most significant is the dominance of the English language among translations of this time period: 60 per cent of works translated in Europe were of British or American origin.[71] This figure leads Venuti to conclude that 'Anglo-American publishing has been instrumental in producing readers who are aggressively monolingual and culturally parochial while reaping the economic benefits of successfully imposing Anglo-American cultural values on a sizeable foreign readership'.[72] Even an American author such as Mary Gaitskill, who has never enjoyed mainstream success on the English-language market, was selected for distribution in Germany. (In 1989 *bad behavior* was picked up by Rowohlt, who published it under the title *Schlechter Umgang*.) This observation, as well as Venuti's statistics, supports my contention that the German pop-literary fiction I go on to discuss draws on the literary strategies employed by Anglo-American writers like Acker and Gaitskill.

In contrast, Agnes C. Mueller contends that the transnational circulation of discursive material pluralizes rather than closes down the 'meanings and pleasures of cultural commodities'.[73] Mueller prefers the term 'hybridization' to 'cultural imperialism', stressing that cultural transfers are not passive but active processes, in which cultures re-appropriate and fashion material to suit local purposes.[74] For

---

[68] Ibid.
[69] See Thomas Whiteside, *The Blockbuster Complex: Conglomerates, Show Business, and Book Publishing* (Middletown, CO: Wesleyan University press, 1981); Gayle Feldman, 'Going Global', in *Publishers Weekly*, 19 December 1986, pp. 20–4; Lawrence Venuti, ed., *Rethinking Translation*, p. 5.
[70] Lawrence Venuti, ed., *Rethinking Translation*, p. 6.
[71] Mona Baker and Gabriela Saldanha, *Routledge Encyclopedia of Translation Studies* (Abingdon: Routledge, 2009), p. 190.
[72] Lawrence Venuti, ed., *Rethinking Translation*, pp. 6–7.
[73] Agnes C. Mueller, 'Introduction', in *German Pop Culture: How 'American' is it?*, p. 4.
[74] Ibid., pp. 5–6.

example, Mueller points out that American popular culture appears to provide Germany's minority communities with a medium to articulate racial, ethnic, and economic difference from German culture.[75] Local identity, in some cases, can even be strengthened as a result of globalizing discourses and the 'struggle over the values of social or cultural experiences' that often ensues.[76]

In 2002, for example, Katja Kullmann published *Generation Ally: Warum es heute so kompliziert ist, eine Frau zu sein* [*Generation Ally: Why it's So Complicated Being a Woman Today*], which takes its inspiration from the American 'chick-TV' series *Ally McBeal* (1997–2002). Kullmann's volume, in its register and repository of transnational cultural references, is an important forerunner of the German pop-feminist handbooks I discuss here. The cover page of Kullmann's essayistic text appeals directly to '[d]ie Generation Ally' in Germany, who 'weiß vor allem, was sie nicht will: weder Karrieremonster sein noch Mutter Beimer' [above all know what they don't want to be: career monster or Mother Beimer].[77] Kullmann thus draws on the American character Ally McBeal, whose perpetual bafflement in the face of her career and romantic life was beamed around the world, but also a very different, well-known figure in German popular culture in order to express a locally specific sense of dissatisfaction with the role models available for women of the author's age.

Nevertheless, anxieties arising from arguments like Venuti's were particularly provoked by the boom in pop-literature in Germany in the mid-1990s, generating lively debate about the function of literature in German-language culture. According to the writer Kerstin Gleba and the academic Eckhard Schumacher, pop in Germany has always been a 'Störfaktor. Ein Fremdkörper, der für Unruhe sorgt' [disturbance. A foreign body stirring things up].[78] This is partly, but not only, because it connotes an international phenomenon.[79] German pop theorists, for example, unanimously place German pop authors on a continuum with American beat writers like W.S. Burroughs and British and American writers of the 1990s like Bret Easton Ellis, Irvine Welsh, and Nick Hornby.[80]

German pop-literature features as part of the post-reunification drive for new readability, but this latter term does not capture the full significance of pop, a designation that has been fiercely contested since its introduction to the German literary context in the 1960s.[81] The notion of 'popular' suggested by its prefix fails to define the term satisfactorily and pop's heterogeneous formal nature precludes the

---

[75] Ibid., p. 4.   [76] Ibid.

[77] Katja Kullmann, *Generation Ally: Warum es heute so kompliziert ist, eine Frau zu sein* (Cologne: Eichborn, 2002). 'Mutter Beimer' refers to the character Helga Beimer, played by Marie-Luise Marjan, in the long-running German soap opera *Lindenstraße* [*Lime Street*]. A maternal figure, 'Mutter Beimer' inherited the title of 'Mutter der Nation' [the nation's mother] from her television predecessor Inge Meysel.

[78] Kerstin Gleba and Eckhard Schumacher, 'Vorwort', in *Pop seit 1964*, ed. by Kerstin Gleba and Eckhard Schumacher, p. 12.

[79] Kerstin Gleba and Eckhard Schumacher, 'Vorwort', p. 14.   [80] Ibid.

[81] See Tom Holert and Mark Terkessidis, *Mainstream der Minderheiten. Pop in der Kontrollgesellschaft* (Berlin: ID, 1996), cited in Thomas Ernst, *Popliteratur*, p. 58. Many volumes on pop-literature trace the origins of German pop back to post-1968 beat and underground movements, mentioning authors like Rolf Dieter Brinkmann, Hubert Fichte, and Peter Handke.

dominance of one single style.[82] Attempts to define pop-literature along aesthetic lines, as Moritz Baßler and Hubert Winkels have done, therefore encounter resistance.[83] This is because, as Heinrich Kaulen notes, scholars generally seek to establish a distinction between highly complex, self-reflexive pop-literature (of the kind published by Suhrkamp) and mainstream pop-literature.[84] As Kaulen notes, this applies a 'Hochkulturschema' [high-culture model] to pop-literature that the latter explicitly challenges, and leads irrevocably to hierarchies or exclusions.[85] He concludes:

> An die Stelle einer normativen Ideologiekritik, die um jeden Preis das emanzipatorische Protestpotential von Literatur reaktivieren will und sich daran reibt, dass den meisten popliterarischen Werken eine eindeutige subversive [...] Botschaft im Sinne der 1968er Bewegung eben nicht mehr eincodiert ist, tritt tendenziell eine kaum weniger normative Popästhetik, die der inneren Vielfalt und Bandbreite der Popliteratur nicht gerecht werden kann.

> [A normative ideology critique, which seeks to reactivate literature's political potential at all costs, and which chafes at the lack of clearly subversive 1968-style subtext in the majority of pop-literary works, tends to be replaced with a similarly normative pop-aesthetics, which cannot do justice to pop-literature's variety and breadth.][86]

Instead, Kaulen focuses on pop-literature's most clear-cut characteristic: its focus on the everyday life of adolescents and young adults, as well as the pop-culture that shapes them, narrated from the protagonists' perspective.[87] Importantly, Gleba and Schumacher understand the 'reality' of these everyday lives, rendered in a mimetic neo-realistic style, as medialized; pop authors eschew any notion of authenticity residing beyond media and performance ('Inszenierung').[88] Gleba and Schumacher argue that pop should be defined by its very resistance to definition, for it is to be understood, above all, as 'eine Strategie, eine Haltung, eine Attitude' [a strategy, a pose, an attitude].[89] For them, as for Kaulen and Baßler, pop-literature's strategy is to operate with an 'aesthetic of ambivalence', drawing on material from the pop-cultural archive in order to play with the procedures of signification.[90] This view dovetails with Jörgen Schäfer's contention that pop-literature is conceptually situated exactly at the juncture of indifference located between social criticism and affirmation.[91]

Yet readings of pop-literature that stress its scepticism towards authenticity, its attitude, or political ambivalence fail to do justice to the overtly political dimension inherent in recent pop writing by women. As Margaret McCarthy argues:

---

[82] Heinrich Kaulen, 'Popliteratur als Generationsphänomen', pp. 138–41.

[83] See Hubert Winkels, 'Grenzgänger. Neue deutsche Pop-Literatur', *Sinn und Form*, 51. 4 (1999), 581–610; Moritz Baßler, *Der deutsche Pop-Roman*.

[84] Heinrich Kaulen, 'Popliteratur als Generationsphänomen', p. 142. Suhrkamp is a renowned literary publishing house in Germany.

[85] Ibid.   [86] Ibid.   [87] Ibid., pp. 142–3.

[88] Kerstin Gleba and Eckhard Schumacher, 'Vorwort', pp. 11–12.   [89] Ibid.

[90] Heinrich Kaulen, 'Popliteratur als Generationsphänomen', p. 141.

[91] Jörgen Schäfer, cited in Thomas Ernst, *Popliteratur*, p. 7.

[I]f one considers the kinds of gendered variations that often fall outside of official histories – and indeed Baßler's volume and many others feature solely or largely men – it becomes clear that some writers clearly do have larger aims in mind when they tamper with signifying processes: they seek to expose or even blunt the effects of traditional social divisions.[92]

Indeed when Kerstin Grether's pop novel, *Zuckerbabys* [*Sugar Babies*], was published in 2004, it was welcomed by critics for its unflinching portrayal of young women's complex desires within a discourse dominated by male perspectives.[93] The journalist Elke Buhr claims *Zuckerbabys* compensates for the numerous portrayals of young men's troubled lives constituting the bulk of post-reunification pop-literary productions.[94] She celebrates Grether's provision of a subjective voice to a demographic of young women who otherwise feature as the objects of mass popular culture. The author Thomas Meinecke has observed that a woman who writes 'ist eigentlich schon Pop, das ist das Problem. Damit stellt sie sich eigentlich auch als Beschriebene hin' ['is in fact already pop; that's the problem. By writing, she puts herself out there as the object of representation'].[95] Here Meinecke alludes to gendered critical practices that neglect the text under discussion in favour of an assessment of the author herself, her gender and personal appearance.[96] But his comment also reflects a wider cultural prejudice concerning women's ready compliance with mass cultural imperatives, as well as attributing a lack of ironic detachment from the status quo to women pop authors. Most importantly, however, his comment gestures towards the processes that ensue when the female pop writer, upon taking up the pen, assumes the position of subject, as well as object, of mass culture. Given the gender dynamics at play when women assume *author*ity, pop writing by women always manifests a political dimension. For this reason, my reading of *Zuckerbabys* and Charlotte Roche's *Feuchtgebiete* in the following section draws on recent developments in German feminism, a strategy which provides greater insight than employing a theoretical framework that discounts the political in pop.

McCarthy's work forms part of a current surge of interest in women writers of pop feminism and pop fiction in Germany. Researchers in this field observe that the work of women writers of pop-literature has often been relegated to the category of mainstream 'popular' fiction along the lines of the 'Hochkulturschema'

[92] Margaret McCarthy, 'Feminism and Generational Conflicts', pp. 56–7. See also, Emily Spiers, '"Mädchen haben keine Lobby im Pop": Writing the Performative Popfeminist Subject,' in *German Pop Literature: A Companion*, ed. by Margaret McCarthy, pp. 143–65.

[93] Elke Buhr, 'Weil ich ein Mädchen bin: Kerstin Grether ist Zuckerbaby', in *Frankfurter Rundschau*, 23 April 2004 http://www.fr.de/kultur/literatur/weil-ich-ein-maedchen-bin-a-1201298- [accessed 2.10.2017]. Note that Buhr employs the word 'Mädchen' [girls] here, which resonates with the discourse of girlhood activated by the titles of many pop-feminist volumes.

[94] Recent examples of scholarly engagement with pop-literature do much to confirm—and reproduce—the gender-based exclusions operating within pop to which Buhr alludes. See for example Moritz Baßler, *Der deutsche Pop-Roman*. Baßler's is not the only pop volume to feature almost exclusively men.

[95] Thomas Meinecke in conversation with Benjamin von Stuckrad-Barre, Eckhard Schumacher, and Kerstin Gleba, 'Protokoll eines Gesprächs', in *Pop seit 1964*, p. 366.

[96] Thomas Meinecke et al., in 'Protokoll eines Gesprächs', p. 365.

[high-culture model] mentioned above. Many feminist scholars seek out a political dimension within contemporary German pop-writing by women, both literary and journalistic; they contend that this dimension draws on international (Western) feminist debates that overarch discrete cultural contexts. The American scholar Brenda Bethman, for example, seeks to reclaim a subversive (post)feminist space for chick-lit, which, since its initial boom in Britain and North America in the 1990s, has diversified and become a global phenomenon. Bethman makes the case for reading a group of contemporary German novels as examples of chick-lit, including Karen Duve's *Dies ist kein Liebeslied* [*This is not a Love Song*] (2000) and Marlene Streeruwitz's *Jessica, 30.* (2004). She points out that many chick-lit titles from authors such as Helen Fielding and Sophie Kinsella, among others, were being translated into German by the mid-1990s, at a speed that contrasts significantly with the sluggish transmission to Germany of less mainstream work by Anglo-American riot grrrls.[97] In Bethman's view, the group of women writers collected under the title 'literarisches Fräuleinwunder' [literary wonder girls] in 1999 by the critic Volker Hage, which included among others Judith Hermann and Karen Duve, can be understood as responding to this influx of chick-lit titles, as their work often conforms to some of chick-lit's generic conventions while transgressing, and thus extending, the boundaries of others.[98]

The German novels I discuss can be viewed as responding to the legacy of Anglo-American chick-lit, revealing a corresponding interest in all three contexts in producing popular books aimed at young women. But they are also influenced by the work of a preceding generation of German-language pop-literary authors like Sibylle Berg, Alexa Hennig von Lange, and Elke Naters,[99] as well as renowned German-language forerunners such as the author and playwright Elfriede Jelinek, and film-maker Monika Treut. In particular, Jelinek and Treut's sustained and continuous interrogations of female sexuality, agency, and the gendered terms of representation, which become achieved through satire, textual sampling, or visual montage, and the ironic citation of clichéd language, prepared the ground for the most recent authors' explorations under discussion here.

Elfriede Jelinek's 1989 novel *Lust*, for example, can be understood as an important forerunner of Roche's *Feuchtgebiete*. It has become common for commentators to refer to *Lust* as Jelinek's 'Anti-Porno'.[100] While Jelinek creates a world in which sex and sexuality are employed to realize the total subordination of women, she is also in constant dialogue with literary predecessors working within the genre of pornographic literature, and is thus involved in a struggle to find a language to discuss sexuality. Like Gerti, the central protagonist in *Lust*, Jelinek recalls struggling against becoming assimilated by patriarchal sexual discourse. Writing about her project, embodied by *Lust,* to find a new language to describe the aesthetic of

[97] Brenda Bethman, 'Generation Chick', p. 137.   [98] Ibid., p. 149.

[99] Key texts include: from Sibylle Berg *Ein paar Leute suchen das Glück und lachen sich tot* (1997) and *Sex II* (1998); *Relax* (1997) from Hennig von Lange; *Lügen* (1999) from Elke Naters.

[100] Wolfram Schütte, *Frankfurter Rundschau*, 6 May 1998.

the 'obscene',[101] Jelinek describes how important it was to her to find a female language for the obscene and to portray obscenity from a female, rather than male, perspective. Her work on *Lust* made her feel that it was, in fact, impossible to talk about sexuality without falling back into the language of men.[102] Part of the problem lies in how male dominated the literary pornographic canon is. *Lust* was conceived as a response to Georges Bataille's *Histoire d'Oeil*, published in 1928, one of a handful of French pornographic works dealing with graphic violent sex and female subordination considered to have literary value (Jean de Berg's *L'Image* and 'Pauline' Réage's *Histoire d'O* being two others published in the early 1950s). All were written by men.[103] *Lust* is thus a textual question mark gesturing towards the difficulties involved in writing about sexuality from a woman's perspective without capitulating to the gendered conventions of the sexual status quo. Charlotte Roche's *Feuchtgebiete* pursues the question posed by Jelinek twenty years before, but in a climate transformed by the aesthetics and ubiquity of porn-culture, in particular online.

The above overview thus characterizes the literary climate informing the publication of the pop-literary fiction I now turn to. The female protagonists in these novels are depicted transgressing conventional gender roles in terms of their appearance, behaviour, and sexuality; however, they are frequently deeply disturbed individuals who have suffered traumatic experiences in childhood or adolescence. These traumatized individuals perceive themselves as fundamentally fragmented, possessing no cohesive sense of identity. But far from connoting a playful process of autonomous identity selection, this lack of cohesion interferes with their sense of agency, and they feel helplessly buffeted by social circumstance, their lives determined by events even as they seek to gain purchase on their own sense of selves.

These narratives' protagonists do not tally with the image of the self-possessed, culture-savvy contemporary female, who ostensibly represents the target audience of the pop-feminist guides. This is the case despite sharing many of their concerns regarding the role of feminism in contemporary culture and also interrogating the value of intergenerational feminist exchange.

CHARLOTTE ROCHE'S *FEUCHTGEBIETE*

Both Charlotte Roche and Kerstin Grether worked for many years in pop media before writing their first novels. Roche gained notoriety as a long-standing presenter on the German music channel Viva and Grether worked for many years as a journalist for *Spex*, *Intro*, and *frieze*. Roche's internationally successful début *Feuchtgebiete* was both praised and criticized by reviewers for its subversive take on

---

[101] Brigitte Lahann, Elfriede Jelinek im Gespräch mit Brigitte Lahann: 'Männer sehen in mir die große Domina', *Der Stern*, 8 September 1988, p. 78.

[102] Ibid.

[103] It has been suggested that 'Pauline Réage' was the pseudonym of Jean Paulhan.

personal hygiene and beauty practices directed at women. The novel secured a prominent place for Germany on the international publishing stage in 2008 by becoming the world's best-selling novel in March.[104] It was adapted into a full-length German-language film in 2013, which has grossed $10,560,478 worldwide.[105] Grove Atlantic (Acker's publishers in the US) bought the rights to the English translation soon after, making *Feuchtgebiete* one of the highly visible translated texts circulating on the English-language market, of which Venuti contends conceals long-term disparities.

The novel depicts the experiences and inner thoughts of 18-year-old Helen Memel during her stay on a proctology ward. An infected anal wound, incurred when trying to shave around her haemorrhoids, instigates her admission to hospital. Narrated in a humorous, first-person confessional mode, the novel allows access to Helen's consciousness, her memories, desires, and insecurities. Flash-backs focus in graphic detail on her past sexual exploits, drug and alcohol excesses, and transgressions of socially sanctioned hygiene norms. Roche certainly depicts Helen's hygiene habits and sexual proclivities non-judgementally, but the novel's wider critical dimension should not be ignored. The journalist Jenni Zylka, for example, called the novel a 'Schleimporno gegen den Hygienezwang' [mucus-porn against hygiene fanaticism].[106] Carrie Smith-Prei contends that *Feuchtgebiete*, indeed German pop-feminism in general, 'positively embraces the negatively coded female body, whether raunchy, pornographic, sick, injured, or otherwise unruly'.[107] In an interview with the British press in 2009, the author herself contends that:

> The feminist angle to the book is this: I think women, now, have to have this clean, sexy, presentation side to their body. At any time, you must be available for sex, and you can just strip naked and look super. That's a high pressure, and the joke in this book is saying, 'Women shit, too, you know'.[108]

Thus, Helen subverts conventional notions of feminine beauty standards, 'testing' new lovers by forcing them to physically negotiate her haemorrhoids, which she linguistically redefines as her 'Blumenkohl' [cauliflower].[109] In one parodic rendition of femininity, Helen dabs her own vaginal secretions behind her ears like perfume (F, 19–20). Importantly, then, Helen does not reject all forms of body modification per se—she revels in her mascara-encrusted eyelashes and daubs her vagina in make-up. Instead, Roche de-naturalizes normative beauty practices by depicting

---

[104] 'Fiction in German Makes it to Pole Position', *The Economist*, Books and Arts section, April (2008) <http://www.economist.com/node/10952281> [accessed 21.08.2014]. Figures were taken from Amazon websites in America, Britain, Canada, France, Germany, and Japan.

[105] See Box Office Mojo, available at http://www.boxofficemojo.com/movies/?id=wetlands.htm [accessed 22.02.2017].

[106] Jenni Zylka, 'Schleimporno gegen Hygienezwang', *Die Tageszeitung*, 28 February 2008 <http://www.taz.de/!13560/> [accessed 23.06.2012].

[107] Carrie Smith-Prei, ' "Knaller-Sex für alle": Popfeminist Body Politics in Lady Bitch Ray, Charlotte Roche, and Sarah Kuttner', in *Studies in 20th and 21st Century Literature*, 18–39 (p. 18).

[108] Charlotte Roche, in Ed Caesar, 'Charlotte Roche is an Unlikely Shock Artist', *Timesonline*, 1 February 2009. [Article no longer available online.]

[109] Charlotte Roche, *Feuchtgebiete* (Berlin: Ullstein, 2009), p. 9. All further references will be provided within the body of the text as F.

exaggerated or non-standard manifestations of them. Yet Roche demonstrates how Helen remains susceptible to the pressures, like shaving, that the author seeks to criticize. Thus, in Helen, Roche creates a paradoxical character allegedly intended to represent her 'brave, freed alter-ego', but who simultaneously reacts to social pressure.[110]

According to Nina Power, Helen 'promises a certain kind of liberation'.[111] Her qualification gestures towards the tensions inherent in Roche's novel. Helen at first appears to be a self-assured agent, capable of revelling in playful body performances at will. She narrates acts of sexual self-objectification humorously and non-judgmentally. For example, in the passage where Helen recalls her ex-partner Mattes stretching her labia, securing them with eyelash curlers and taking a photograph, Helen's complicity and the pleasure with which she observes Mattes clap his hands joyfully undercut any straightforward interpretation of the act as sexual victimization. On the other hand, the scene resonates with the images and language of violent pornography. Helen's 'Feuchtgebiete' function synecdochically, replacing Helen, the person, with a 'Loch' [hole] (F, 67), and her comparison of the act to the scene in *A Clockwork Orange* (in which the Ludovico Technique is performed upon Alex) evokes images of torture. Whether intentional or not, this scene performs a critique of neoliberal and self-fashioning narratives: to return to Judith Butler, Helen's belief in her role as self-fashioning agent furthers the notion that her identity performances are manufactured internally, from a sovereign subjective core, and not externally as part of the wider sexist structures that undergird what Butler calls the 'regulation of sexuality within the obligatory frame of reproductive heterosexuality'.[112] For Butler, performance is the external fabrication, through acts, gestures or desires, of an appearance of internal 'essence or identity'; for her, performance is engendered by social contingency and is precisely *not* autonomous, as neoliberal self-fashioning narratives imply.[113]

In an interview with Thea Dorn, however, Roche foregrounds the playful, performative aspect of sex:

> Jede coole Frau kann damit spielen, sich in der Sexualität auch mal zu unterwerfen. [...] Die Frau, die eine selbstbewusste Sexualität hat, fühlt sich bei den Sachen, wo die Feministin sofort „erniedrigend" kreischt, nicht erneidrigt. Blümchensex braucht nur die, die nicht cool genug ist, Sex als Spielwiese zu begreifen.

> [Every cool woman can experiment with sexual subordination. [...] Some sex acts cause feminists to shriek 'humiliating!' immediately, whereas a woman who is confident in her sexuality doesn't feel humiliated by them at all. It's only those people who aren't cool enough to see sex as a playground who need vanilla sex.][114]

Roche's insistent repetition of the keyword 'cool' is reminiscent of her protagonist in *Schoßgebete*, Elizabeth. Again, the term resonates tantalizingly with counter-cultural promise despite its co-option by mainstream, commercially-driven forces

---

[110] Charlotte Roche, in Nina Power, 'The Dirty Girl. Nina Power Interviews Charlotte Roche', *Salon*, 4 April 2009 <http://www.salon.com/2009/04/04/charlotte_roche/> [accessed 16.07.2013].
[111] Nina Power, 'The Dirty Girl'.   [112] Judith Butler, *Gender Trouble*, p. 186.
[113] Ibid.   [114] Charlotte Roche, in Dorn, *Die neue F-Klasse*, p. 142.

that regulate identity by means of hierarchies of inclusion and exclusion. These dual resonances thus elide the vital question of who sets the criteria for 'cool'. In *Feuchtgebiete* as in *Schoßgebete*, pressure is applied to understand female sexual objectification as ironic and 'cool', constituting the successful avoidance of the anti-sex stance allegedly maintained by second-wave feminists, while tradition is simultaneously restored for misogynist readers.[115] Helen functions as a cipher for this playful postfeminist subject who is cool enough, in Angela McRobbie's terms, to 'get the joke'.[116]

Significant, too, is Roche's repetition of the word 'spielen' [play] in conjunction with transgressive sex. This playful, permissive stance is shared by the authors of *Wir Alpha-Mädchen*, who contend that women may do whatever they like doing, adding that contemporary feminism stands for sexual self-determination.[117] Many second-wave feminists viewed the concept of sexual pleasure inhering in politically incorrect, that is, masochistic practices as representative of patriarchal structures undergirding women's subjugation, whereas Roche distinguishes between the social realm and that of private fantasy. Thus, neither Roche nor many pop-feminists question how one's choice of sexual activity might be predetermined by the regulating forces of normative heterosexuality. Butler of course views the disconnection of performance from contingency to be a malignant and normative tool: '[i]f the "cause" of desire, gesture, and act can be localized within the "self" of the actor, then the political regulations and disciplinary practices that produce that ostensibly coherent identity are effectively displaced from view'.[118] Butler suggests that the subject's belief in the autonomy of its identity performances is vital for both the perpetuation and the invisibility of the public and social discourses that regulate identity.

However, Roche clearly seeks to find the moment at which performances could signify differently through Helen's parodic renditions of femininity and sexuality.[119] Some resonate with postfeminist re-enactments of sexism, but others, such as Helen's habit of using vaginal secretions as perfume, escape this alignment due to their explicitly opposing misogynist narratives, in this case that female genitalia and bodily effluvia constitute objects of disgust. But the question remains whether highly individual performances such as Helen's in fact alter anything for women in the wider social field.[120] Roche has argued for the self-empowering potential of female sexuality. She claims, for example, that sexually explicit performances by female pop artists connote a clear demonstration of power.[121] Thus, Helen's rejection of passivity and the epicurean pleasure with which she consumes her body's

---

[115] Meredith Haaf, Susanne Klingner, and Barbara Streidl, *Wir Alpha-Mädchen*, p. 66.

[116] Angela McRobbie, 'Postfeminism and Popular Culture', p. 33.

[117] Meredith Haaf, Susanne Klingner, and Barbara Streidl, *Wir Alpha-Mädchen*, p. 66.

[118] Judith Butler, *Gender Trouble*, p. 186.

[119] Margaret McCarthy argues just this in Margaret McCarthy, 'Feminism and Generational Conflicts'.

[120] In her discussion of *Relax*, McCarthy also questions whether performance advances integrated selfhood and gender equality or whether it merely articulates individual needs and 'strategic theatrics'. See Margaret McCarthy, 'Feminism and Generational Conflicts', pp. 66–71.

[121] Charlotte Roche, in Dorn, *Die neue F-Klasse*, p. 141.

secretions like a gourmet might be construed as an expression of self-empowerment, or 'self-guided sexual potency' (F, 51).[122] After all, her body imbues her with a clear sense of identity: in moments of uncertainty, she touches her genitals, which she calls her 'Zentrum' [centre] (F, 36). Her strategy of devising special names for parts of her body demonstrates, too, the drive, both exhibited and denied in Jelinek's *Lust*, to gain agency through linguistic control of her body.

However, her language also betrays a sense of compulsion, an almost pathological desire to police the borders of her body: 'Helen überlässt nix dem Zufall' [Helen leaves nothing to chance] (F, 51). This desire arises from a fundamental mistrust of her environment and other people. Helen does not like to rely on others, claiming that '[s]elber machen klappt am besten. Mir selbst ist am meisten zu trauen' [d.i.y. always works best. I trust myself most of all] (F, 188). Her decision to keep the television switched off in her hospital room highlights her mistrust of external media influence and her desire for autonomy, but the novel suggests that Helen cannot escape outside influence, either from her family or peers, or advertising slogans (which she is able to cite), or from the religious artefacts (a bible and a cross) that furnish her hospital room. Helen nevertheless construes her corporeal performances to be emanating from an internal core, thus imbuing them with an autonomy that is, according to Butler, illusory. Her belief that she selects her performances at will, indeed her continuing insistence on corporeal autonomy, displaces from view the external forces that compel her behaviour.

Helen's confidence in her corporeal autonomy belies a certain fatalistic mistrust that extends to her individual psychology. She believes that she, like her mother and grandmother before her, will suddenly experience a severe and debilitating deterioration of mental health (F, 215). This leads Helen to break what she perceives to be a congenital cycle of female madness by being sterilized soon after her eighteenth birthday. This generational legacy mocks any sense of control that Helen attempts to assert and, because it passes down the maternal line, suggests that for women there is no escape from predetermination. The issue of determination invests Helen's subversive acts of body play with new weight: they become the acts of an individual desperate to assert control over an unpredictable body in order to create the illusion of coherent identity and a sense of agency.

Indeed, Helen's body becomes the site of a struggle for self-determination in the face of familial influence. Her transgressive behaviour often constitutes a response to her mother's actions and opinions in order to establish, as Kauer argues in her reading of the novel, 'a different female identity'.[123] Helen's refusal to wash her face for fear of ruining her mascara (which she never removes) can be connected with a childhood event when her mother allegedly cut off her eyelashes while she was asleep. Roche also links Frau Memel's pedantry regarding Helen's genital hygiene as a child (her brother's was ignored) to Helen's predilection for wiping public toilet seats with her vagina.

---

[122] Carrie Smith-Prei, ' "Knaller Sex für alle" ', p. 30.
[123] Katja Kauer, *Popfeminismus!*, p. 123.

As Smith-Prei notes, the mother's suicide attempt, veiled in family secrecy since Helen was a child, contributes to the feeling that Helen's sexual investigations might be traumatically induced. Smith-Prei contends, furthermore, that they 'also connote power or mastery of that trauma in self-guided and controlled eroticism'.[124] However, the pathological extremes of Helen's corporeal performances make it difficult to imbue them with as much 'power or mastery'. Power confronts Roche with the argument that *Feuchtgebiete* cannot be read as a feminist novel because 'Helen isn't totally strong…; she's not fully mentally sound'.[125] Roche's response is worth reproducing in full as it highlights the fundamental tension underlying her novel:

> The problem with political ideas like feminism is that you are not allowed sometimes to say the truth. In Germany we have lots of older, very famous feminists. And it is not allowed for me as a young feminist to say that women are masochistic. I am and all my female friends are. We stand in front of the mirror, we are naked, and we feel ugly as fuck. We see everything as wrong. We try and fight our body to become prettier and work on it. It's not at all free and self-confident. I don't want it to be like that, but I see that it is.[126]

Roche's comments suggest that individual psychology connotes an arena unsuited to regulation by progressively political forces, that, indeed, feminism remains unable to penetrate this realm.[127] In *Feuchtgebiete*, transgressive sexuality constitutes an extension of this private sphere, equally resistant to correction along social lines because it reflects private pleasure and not social conditioning. On the one hand, the novel creates in Helen an ideal representative of contemporary pop-feminist selfhood, 'free and self-confident'. Social factors and cultural taboos influence Helen to an extent, but she takes pleasure performing her identity in ways which overtly subvert social norms, celebrating her body and sexuality as a site of agency. However, as Butler suggests, performance per se does not automatically result in subversion and Helen's performances often reinscribe postfeminist mobilizations of sexism or reveal the dysfunctional workings of a traumatized psyche. In this way, Helen's mental instability constitutes a greater determining factor than the social and cultural influences she mockingly subverts and destabilizes the representation of autonomous pop-feminist performances. Ultimately, Helen remains trapped in a binary model that, as Butler argues, conceptualizes free will and determinism as the only two options for identity.[128] The strains of neoliberalism in Roche's form of pop-feminism emanate from her emphasis on individual choice and pleasure, which provide the impetus for action. However, in Helen these generate an extreme individuality that merely reflects Helen's own psychological needs as opposed to a desire to change the social field in progressive ways. Roche's individualism represents

---

[124] Carrie Smith-Prei, '"Knaller Sex für alle"', p. 30.   [125] Nina Power, 'The Dirty Girl'.
[126] Charlotte Roche, in Power, 'The Dirty Girl'.
[127] Here I draw upon Margaret McCarthy's reading of *Feuchtgebiete*. She suggests that '[s]econd-wave forms of feminism would do well to understand women's choices in psychological terms that often resist change, no matter how revolutionary the battle cry', in Margaret McCarthy, 'Feminism and Generational Conflicts', p. 64.
[128] See Judith Butler, *Gender Trouble*, p. 201.

an alternative to a collective feminist politics that does not take account of individual psychology/fantasy but it also undermines Roche's critique of the wider social pressures placed upon women.

KERSTIN GRETHER'S *ZUCKERBABYS*

In *Zuckerbabys*, polemical passages from Grether's journalistic articles find expression through her characters, who function as mouthpieces for as well as objects of her critique of gender inequalities in what the twenty-three-year-old central protagon- ist Sonja calls 'die Scheißgesellschaft der Männer' [this shitty men's society].[129] *Zuckerbabys* constitutes the product of Grether's professional engagement, spanning over a decade, with pop-culture and, as such, reflects the debates around pop that were circulating from the 1990s through to the mid-2000s.

One of these involves pop's close ties with consumerism. Grether targets the cultural obsession, sustained by commercial forces in the media and music indus- tries, with what she calls holy commodities (Z, 31). She critiques the negative impact on women's psychological and physical health through exposure to media images of corporeal perfection (Z, 68). Grether levies criticism through Sonja's laconic tone, yet with ambivalence, due in part to her championing of the very medium that produces the focus of her criticism. The reviewer Tobias Rapp con- tends that Grether is unconditionally loyal to the notion of pop she mobilizes on behalf of her protagonist and Grether herself admits to being addicted to pop.[130] Her novel suggests, on the one hand, that pop can create and sustain bohemian utopias; but she is also critical of the gender-based exclusions traversing pop- cultural channels and pop's symbiotic relationship with neoliberal consumerist culture (Z, 21).[131] Grether's strategy dovetails with Sonja Eismann's, as she under- takes what the scholar Linda Hutcheon calls a 'challenge from within'.[132]

Zuckerbabys depicts a constellation of young female characters attempting to realize this bohemian lifestyle in twenty-first century Hamburg. Sonja is the pro- tagonist in crisis around whom these variously ironized models of modern female life rotate, presenting her with versions of womanhood she alternately aspires to and rejects during her descent into and recovery from anorexia. Grether constructs aesthetically that which she claims to have experienced personally: a process of mimetic experimentation with a selection of role models.[133] Flashbacks to her unstable childhood intimate an absent father and an antagonistic relationship with her mother, a constellation familiar from *Feuchtgebiete* (Z, 102).

Images of female perfection surround Sonja in her job as a media designer. The women Sonja associates with in her non-professional life become three- dimensional versions of these: the model Melissa Melloda, described as 'ein bisschen

---

[129] Kerstin Grether, *Zuckerbabys* (Berlin: Suhrkamp, 2006), p. 120. All further references within the body of the text as Z.
[130] Kerstin Grether, *Zungenkuss*, p. 9.   [131] Ibid., p. 19.
[132] Linda Hutcheon, *A Poetics of Postmodernism*, p. xiii.
[133] Kerstin Grether, *Zungenkuss*, p. 10.

magersüchtig' [a little bit anorexic] and the elite group of musicians' girlfriends she meets, whose studied indifference stems from their subsisting on crisp bread (Z, 224). The pop-journalist Allita, who is ten years older than Sonja, acts as a cipher for a form of second-wave feminism that Sonja initially rejects, calling her a 'feministisches Monster' [feminist monster] (Z, 174). Kicky, Micky, and Ricky, members of the band Museabuse, represent positively-coded models of pop-feminism. Their characterization draws noticeably on Grether's journalism on the North American riot-grrrl movement of the late 1990s: they emphasize, for example, the importance of female creative spaces and criticize the music industry's exclusion of female artists who do not correspond to the commercial image of pop divas.[134] These themes echo many of those broached in Sonja Eismann's *Hot Topic*.[135]

Sonja, who maintains the first-person narrative voice throughout her sections of the novel, resents these musicians' ability to maintain 'Luxuskörper' [luxury bodies] and still have the energy to be creative and to have fun, a combination Sonja feels only men can attain (Z, 44; 216). By allowing all three musicians a first-person narrative strand, however, Grether grants access to their own insecurities. In fact, this connotes her general strategy: through Sonja's eyes, the reader makes assumptions about the characters she imitates or resents; by providing them with a voice, Grether problematizes any ideal mode of being and underscores the unreliability of Sonja's perceptions of other characters.

Initially, then, Sonja desires nothing more than to fit in, to comply with the social narrative that demands that young women seek: 'Liebe und Nachtleben, Freundschaft und Shopping, Diät und Kunst' [love and night-life, friendship and shopping, diets and art] (Z, 55). Justifying her eating disorder to herself, Sonja argues that all the 'cool' women are anorexic, a reminder of the pernicious forces inherent in the pressure to be cool (Z, 186). Pressure inheres, too, in the form of Sonja's dream of becoming a 'wild' and creative girl pop singer (Z, 119). These conflicting forces precipitate Sonja's fantasies of a 'selige Kindheit' [blissful childhood], which she associates with freedom from all existential concerns (Z, 138; 76). By representing Sonja's fantasies as restricted to a binary (pop star or child), Grether provides an implicit critique of the limited choices available for women in the wider social field. By equating Sonja's eating disorder with a fantasy of childhood, Grether suggests her anorexia connotes a regressive response to pressures experienced by young women. But it also constitutes a form of protest. On the one hand, her disciplined programme of starvation and exercise provides a single focus that relieves her from confronting the myriad overwhelming pressures of adult life. On the other, her emaciated physical form functions in a Butlerian sense as a grotesque parody of idealized female corporeality and masochism, which in its extremeness questions the nature, terms, and consequences of the ideal. Sonja's starved body thus becomes emblematic of both her silent compliance with

---

[134] Kerstin Grether, *Zungenkuss*, pp. 48–9.

[135] See Bettina Mooshammer and Eva Trimmel, 'Ladyfest can save your life! Ladyspace als Strategie feministischer Raumproduktion', in Sonja Eismann, *Hot Topic*, pp. 184–9; Clara Völker, 'Platten statt Schminke auflegen: HipHop und Feminismus', in Sonja Eismann, *Hot Topic*, pp. 254–63.

and 'illegible rage' against the demands placed upon women's appearance. Her hatred of what she perceives to be society's authoritarian conditions becomes re-routed and inflicted upon herself.

By reproducing scenes from popular television shows, children's books, journalistic articles, and celebrity interviews, Grether deftly depicts how pop-cultural channels disseminate a melange of competing narratives concerning female identity that can lead to psychological instability. On a TV chat show, neoliberal individualistic logic rubs against postfeminist thinking about a 'woman's place'. A male celebrity claims, citing evidence in the form of successful female media personalities, 'dass Frauen heute alles erreichen können, was sie wollen, wenn sie nur mit beiden Beinen fest auf dem Boden der nackten Tatsachen stehen' [that women today can achieve anything they want to as long as they just face up to the bare facts of life] (Z, 104). Sonja's psychological and physical return to childhood appears all the more striking against this backdrop.

On the other hand, Grether demonstrates how a popularized notion of Butlerian performativity has been absorbed and modified by pop-culture to give the impression that women can make autonomous choices about identity performance while the spectrum of female role models remains limited. Butlerian language and concepts permeate Sonja's friends' conversations and Butler herself is name-checked during a conversation about gender inequality at Micky's birthday party (Z, 100–1). Sonja refers ironically to 'Kulturkritiker in schlauen Büchern' [cultural critics in smart books] who argue that identity must be continually re-invented (Z, 185). At the same time, she observes that television hosts interview only the thinnest and youngest women, providing they are not intellectually threatening. Sonja's juxtaposition of theory and reality here reveals her scepticism towards the potential of performance to signify identity differently. She furthermore characterizes performance not as playful but as a concept hijacked by commercialized popular culture, modified along gendered lines and implemented as a rigorous disciplinary tool designed to increase consumption: 'Immer wieder neu muss die Puppenidentität von allen Frauen in der westlichen Welt immer wieder neu hergestellt werden' [Time and time again, every woman in the Western world has to re-fashion her doll-identity time and time again] (Z, 185).

Initially, Sonja believes she chooses her identity freely, gaining individual 'control' in terms of her appearance and consumer habits, aspects which become conflated with identity per se. Through the metaphor of Sonja's eating disorder, Grether demonstrates how this initial sense of becoming and agency actually becomes an erasure of self: 'Will ich wirklich so werden wie alle anderen? Meine Gestalt in den Spiegeln dieser Stadt: Je schlanker ich werde, desto kleiner und mickriger sehe ich aus. Ich bin so komisch unvorhanden' [Do I really want to become like everyone else? The shape of my body in this city's mirrors: the thinner I become, the smaller and more pathetic I look. I am so strangely absent] (Z, 63). As she descends further into illness, Sonja begins to perceive herself as already intractably determined. She contrasts her experiences to those of male rock stars, who behave as if it were possible to choose how one lives. Viewing her personal experiences and those of other women in relation to broader socio-cultural structures, Sonja claims: 'Keiner macht es uns leicht, einfach nur frei zu sein. Denn wir träumen davon, uns für die Träume anderer zu eignen [...]. Wir sind die Musen des Neoliberalismus—an uns sieht man, was man Menschen alles antun kann' [Nobody makes it easy for us just to be free. For we dream of being suitable for other people's dreams [...]. We are the muses of neoliberalism—look at us, and you'll see just what you can put people through] (Z, 215).

Here, Grether critiques a culture that profits from and thus perpetuates the objectification of women, who then become unable to distinguish between physical appearance and sense of self. But Sonja's comment also suggests a degree of complicity on the part of women and that they must take responsibility for improving their own circumstances. As she begins to recover from her eating disorder, she contends that she has been her 'eigener schlimmster Feind, eine Kriegerin, die eine Schlacht gegen sich selbst gewonnen hat' [her own worst enemy, a warrior who has won a battle against herself] (Z, 246). Grether's critique of the socio-cultural factors impinging upon her protagonist's identity and agency remains powerful, but this conclusion suggests that, while eating disorders connote a societal problem, women must acknowledge their complicity and take responsibility for their own recovery. The matter of 'taking responsibility' for oneself resonates with neoliberal individualist narratives of self-optimization, which allows Sonja's self-guided recovery to be read as a renunciation of protest and capitulation to the neoliberal status quo. The penultimate scene supports this reading: Museabuse obtain their long-awaited record deal, but on the condition that they lose weight. In an ironic twist, Grether portrays how the once radical performers capitulate to this demand in exchange for the opportunity to gain mainstream exposure, commenting, '[w]ir regen uns über gar nichts mehr auf' [we're not getting worked up about anything anymore] (Z, 245).

Grether's continued championing of pop exculpates the neoliberal consumerist culture on which it depends. For example, Sonja's recovery is motivated in part by the desire to exercise her creativity through the medium of pop once more (cartoon design and writing pop songs). Sonja writes a song called 'Träum den übernächsten Traum' [Dream the Next Dream but One], modifying her comment about women's readiness to become the object of others' dreams. In her song, Sonja envisages the possibility of women dreaming a different kind of dream, of imagining identity in new creative ways, of becoming the subject as well as the object of the dream, artist not muse. This is why, despite the prerequisites, the aptly named Museabuse accept the record deal: it will provide them with a platform for their feminist project. Thomas Meinecke's comments, cited on p. 204, confirm that this strategy is not straightforward, but Grether still affirms pop's potential to provide a platform that will reach many people, young women in particular. On the one hand, then, Grether clearly aligns herself with second-wave critique by associating Sonja's eating disorder with images generated by pop-culture, an aspect of the novel that has clear didactic intent. On the other, she claims that pop remains amenable to correction along progressive feminist lines and insists on its potential for imagining identity differently.

STRATEGIES OF RESISTANCE IN ALINA BRONSKY'S
SCHERBENPARK [BROKEN GLASS PARK]

Like Helen Walsh's *Brass*, Charlotte Roche's *Feuchtgebiete* and Kerstin Grether's *Zuckerbabys*, Alina Bronsky's *Scherbenpark* was read as a 'coming-of-age' novel upon publication in 2008. Critics focused on what they perceived to be the unusual characterization and voice of the novel's adolescent protagonist, Sasha. One critic claimed her 'schnodderig-forsche[r] Ton' [brashly forceful voice] prevented the novel from lapsing into 'Mitleidsprosa' [pity prose].[136] Reviews also highlighted the author's unflinching exploration of gender roles in a community of Russian migrants living on a ghetto-like estate near a large city sometime after 1989. Indeed, some critics labelled the novel 'männerfeindlich' [anti-men], while others considered the work to be in fact 'frauenfeindlich' [anti-women].[137] These contrasting assessments are due in part to Bronsky's subversive interpretation of the relationship between gender, violence, and victimhood, a line of questioning the novel shares with Walsh's *Brass*. Bronsky's novel levels critique not only at those gender inequalities experienced in Sasha's immediate environment, but also highlights the specific issues and multiple exclusions faced by young female migrants in contemporary Germany. As I argued above, the frequent failure to address the particular circumstances of Germany's ethnic 'others' constitutes one of pop-feminism's most troubling omissions.

Sasha's mother, Marina, was murdered by her stepfather, Vadim, after trying to protect Sasha and her half-brother from his violence and sexual abuse. In the novel's opening passages, Sasha outlines her intention to attain retribution by murdering her step-father and writing a book about her mother's life. Yet over the course of the novel Sasha's unstable and at times violent behaviour worsens until she undertakes a series of increasingly self-destructive acts, only increasing her sense of isolation from the community in which she continues to live. Sasha can be read as a 'phallic girl', in McRobbie's sense, or perhaps more appropriately, as Barbara Mennel's 'global ghetto girl'. Sasha's socially displaced environment certainly 'appears as a space of male criminality' and Sasha's strategy for survival consists of appropriating the 'signifiers of masculinity', including the use of aggressive language, violence, sexual promiscuity, and drug use.[138] Bronsky's strategy resembles Walsh's in that she refuses to depict Sasha as a passive victim of trauma and social circumstance, exploring the ways in which Sasha rejects the 'wounded attachment' to victimhood she associates with her mother and seeks instead to gain a sense of agency through acts of social and sexual transgression.

Sasha's sense of identification with the rap artist Eminem and his music further destabilizes normative perceptions of female victimhood as Sasha creates her own

---

[136] Rainer Moritz, 'Und alles riecht nach Zimt', *Die Welt*, 28 August 2008 <http://www.welt.de/welt_print/article2342417/Und-alles-riecht-nach-Zimt.html> [accessed 27.09.2012].

[137] Carsten Schrader, 'Literatur statt Russendisko', *umagazine.de*, 10 October 2008 <http://www.umagazine.de/artikel.php?ID=107601> [accessed 27.09.2012].

[138] Barbara Mennel, 'Global Ghetto Girl', p. 163.

violently threatening lyrics aimed at Vadim to Eminen's raps. But her affinity for American rap music also connects her with a transnational subculture that provides her with a form with which to express her sense of disenfranchisement and anger in her local context. As Agnes C. Mueller contends, American pop-culture offers 'great opportunities for Germany's minorities to articulate ethnic and racial difference from German culture'.[139] But listening to Eminem also allows Sasha to differentiate herself from her immediate migrant community, most of whose members listen to Russian music.

Sasha is portrayed as severely dissociated from her surroundings, her community, and her self. The traumatic events of her past have resulted in an extremely unstable and fragmented psychic landscape, which produces a black-and-white view of the world. When she looks in the mirror, Sasha is disappointed by the lack of resemblance to her mother, who Layton might describe as the 'idealized other' by whom Sasha has been 'traumatically disappointed'.[140] Even her eyes are not the 'right' colour.[141] Yet Sasha oscillates between idolizing and disparaging her dead mother, who at times she calls a 'dumme dumme Frau' [stupid, stupid woman] for not seeing the extent of Vadim's abusive behaviour. Negotiating the act of separation from her mother combined with her own sense of guilt that she never revealed the fact of her own abuse to her results in Sasha's fragmented subjective state: she frequently speaks of herself in the third person, and employs other distancing techniques such as relating the story of her mother's death in the style of a fairy tale.

Sasha's black-and-white world-view relates predominantly to her perception of the male and female genders. She perceives men and women according to a rigid gendered framework, identifying identity 'fragments rigidly coded with cultural stereotypes of femininity and masculinity'.[142] Sasha's professed hatred of men (S, 19) stems from her overwhelmingly negative encounters with absent or abusive male care givers such as Vadim and her absent biological father, who, she is told, never wanted her to be born. Sasha thus declares her intention to remain self-sufficient and to adopt the role of masculine carer for herself, stating 'Ich bin mir selber ein Mann' [I'm a man for myself] (S, 19). Yet masculinity is not only associated with self-sufficiency, but also violence and aggression, behaviours Sasha also adopts. Her violent disgust at the behaviour of the women in her community is an example of this. Sasha's repulsion stems from her perception of these women as weak and helplessly dependent on men, which, like Carmel in Gwendoline Riley's *Cold Water*, she describes in terms of an essential female masochism (S, 88). Maria, the Siberian aunt who comes to care for the children after Marina's death, and Angela, Sasha's adolescent neighbour, are reviled for their fearfulness, their docility, and their unwillingness to defend themselves against aggressive men. After one such event, Sasha notes that 'mir kommt der Gendanke, dass ich nicht nur Männer hasse. Sondern auch Frauen' [it occurs to me that I don't just hate men, but women

---

[139] Agnes C. Mueller, 'Introduction', p. 4.

[140] Lynne Layton, 'Trauma, Gender Identity and Sexuality', p. 108.

[141] Alina Bronsky, *Scherbenpark* (Cologne: Kiepenheuer & Witsch, 2008), p. 111. All subsequent references will be given within the body of the text as S.

[142] Lynne Layton, 'Trauma, Gender Identity and Sexuality', p. 113.

too] (S, 110). While depictions of allegedly 'dusselige Frauen' [gormless women] were in part responsible for the book's negative reception by some German commentators, aesthetically they function as the foil against which Sasha's rebellion against gendered expectations stands out.[143] Intellect, violence, and fearlessness are the 'masculine' features Sasha seeks to develop, fearing all the time that she is just as vulnerable as Maria, Angela, and her mother. As a result, Sasha closes down emotionally, eschewing feminine clothing, as does Millie in *Brass*, who is equally inclined to view gender roles in rigid binaries. Sasha, like Millie, associates femininity with victimhood and her transgressive behaviour thus functions as a direct and subversive response to a community in which the women around her, like her mother and neighbour, are often exploited, beaten, disrespected, and abandoned.

But her rage also stems from a deeply traumatic incident, the memory of which frequently plunges her into a melancholic state, inducing lethargy and dissociation. In order to combat this uncomfortable passivity, Sasha employs the tools learned from her masculine role models: violence and confrontation. Her tendency to fall into a kind of frozen state ('erstarren' S, 67) in the period following her mother's death echoes her disconnected response to earlier moments of physical abuse. When, for example, Sasha recounts an occasion when Vadim struck her, she describes how she felt the blow to be 'völlig natürlich und überhaupt nicht schockierend, es war der Lauf der Dinge, ebenso wie der stechende Schmerz quer über mein Gesicht' [completely natural and in no way shocking. It was just business as usual, like the piercing pain across my face] (S, 178). This frozen state, which I interpret as a form of withdrawn melancholia in McRobbie's sense, becomes so unbearable to Sasha that she seeks out potentially dangerous situations and confrontations as a mode of inducing a state of rage. She realizes that '[w]enn ich mich wieder richtig ärgern kann, dann geht es mir schon besser' [if I can get really annoyed again, I'll be fine] (S, 217).

When she attempts to goad Volker, a young stranger, into having sex with her, the act is clearly connected with a desperate drive to escape a 'grauer Nebel' [grey fog] that threatens to consume her (S, 217). She states that she would 'jetzt mit jedem gehen, der mich anspricht, und ich würde alles machen, je schlimmer desto besser' [right now I'd go with anyone who spoke to me and I'd do anything—the nastier the better] (S, 217). Superficially, Sasha's sexual initiative endows her with a sense of agency, but the apparent autonomy with which she acts becomes undermined by the self-destructive consequences of her actions as well as the element of masochism these acts contain. For example, Volker reveals that he is a member of the far-right group, the NPD (*Nationaldemokratische Partei Deutschlands*), and, unaware that Sasha is a Russian migrant, he launches into a xenophobic tirade against migrant communities in Germany. The increased thrill that Sasha experiences at that moment suggests an element of masochistic self-degradation in her motivations for her sexual conquest, emulating the more general pattern of oscillation between 'self-depreciation and grandiosity' she experiences daily, as well as echoing the very behaviour she despises in other women.[144]

---

[143] Carsten Schrader, 'Literatur statt Russendisko'.
[144] Lynne Layton, 'Trauma, Gender Identity and Sexuality', p. 108.

Drawing once again on McRobbie and Butler, Sasha's behaviour constitutes on the one hand a withdrawal from the expectations of the community around her, a rebellion against 'the violence of social regulation'. On the other hand, the rebellion does not result in productive 'unilateral action', but in a process whereby the 'psyche accuses itself of its own worthlessness'.[145] Sasha's symbolic double-exclusion, first from wider German society as a result of her migrant status and second, from her immediate community of fellow expatriates, identifies her as precisely the kind of individual in need of access to a feminist network like pop-feminism. Yet, all too often, pop-feminism, as I have demonstrated, only repeats the process of exclusion and isolation by failing to address the specific oppressive structures experienced by young 'ghetto girls' like Sasha.

As a result, Sasha, like Millie, constantly oscillates between feelings of power and powerlessness with no underlying sense of a coherent self. Her attempts to gain a sense of agency result in an increased sense of self-alienation. When she has sex with Volker, she claims that 'das Gefühl dabei ist, als würde es mich nicht wirklich betreffen. Das ist nicht das, was ich erreichen wollte' [I had the feeling it had absolutely nothing to do with me. That's not what I wanted to achieve] (S, 230). At that moment, Sasha recalls two school friends, one of whom is anorexic and the other who engages in self-harming practices. She is critical of what she considers to be their attention-seeking behaviour. But it is striking that these young girls appear in her thoughts at the very moment that she has sex with a stranger she hates. This juxtaposition reveals Sasha's behaviours to be equally self-destructive. Despite her grandiose claim that she is 'etwas völlig anderes' (S, 125) [something completely different] from the women around her, Sasha is merely more active in her search for self-destruction. After leaving Volker to the violent retribution of a local Russian gang, she rollerblades down the middle of the road, high on drink and drugs, and seeks out a collision with a car. Her outwardly directed rage is calculated to reap a violent response, exemplified towards the end of the novel when, after discovering that Vadim has died in prison, she throws stones through the windows of her apartment block and provokes a retaliation from her neighbours that almost kills her.

The traumatic experiences that Sasha has undergone result in a psychological defence mechanism—fragmentation—that is ultimately self-destructive. Like Millie, Sasha interprets her own actions and character according to a rigid binary of good and bad. Her interactions with others are also both characterized and limited by such rigid perceptions. Because the trauma is connected with the parental caregivers the rigid binaries run along the axis of gender. Therefore, rather than offering a characterization of fluid subject identity, Sasha becomes locked into a rigid and debilitating 'acting out' of gender roles. Fragments are alternately suppressed and allowed free rein, often with the aid of alcohol and drugs, and Sasha cannot fully comprehend the motivations for her actions after the event, only that '[e]s fühlt sich schlimmer an als vorher' [it feels worse than before] (S, 230).

---

[145] Judith Butler, *The Psychic Life of Power*, p. 116.

Like Walsh, Bronsky creates a protagonist who subverts conventional gender roles by adopting explicitly masculine-coded behaviour. Yet these moments of transgression bring no respite from suffering. Instead Sasha feels even more removed from any sense of her self as a coherent subject, capable of autonomous action. As in *Brass*, the turning point for Sasha occurs at the moment that she allows somebody to help her. In a sense, she is brought to accept the fact of her own dependency on others and in doing so acknowledge her own vulnerability. Sasha accepts help from a disabled neighbour, Oleg, who taught her chess as a child. His proclivity for reciting scenes from pornographic literature and film to the children on the estate—an act that is connected with his diminished mental capacities—entailed that Sasha cut off all contact with him, viewing him as just another predatory male in her community. After her night of sex, violence, and self-harm, she seeks him out, and they are reunited over a chess game in which Sasha allows him to help her to win. This signifies a moment of transformation for Sasha, who at first cannot accept his help. However, once she has won, she admits: '[e]s fällt mir schwer, mir einzugestehen, wie unendlich stolz ich bin und wie nah an dem Gefühl, dass mir von nun an alles gelingen wird' [It's really hard for me to admit to myself how incredibly proud I am and how close I am to feeling that, from now on, I'll succeed] (S, 255).

This moment of intersubjective recognition also coincides with a more nuanced reconfiguration of femininity. In the process of forgiving Oleg, Sasha comes to view her mother's tolerance and compassion as a positive attribute—indeed an act of strength—and not as masochism (S, 249). The symbolic implication of this shifting perception is that Sasha reviews her conception of the feminine as associated exclusively with victimhood, and the enactment of resistance to femininity loses its urgency. Drawing once again on Butler, Sasha becomes compelled to abandon her sense of autonomy and accept the social realm from which she has withdrawn. Sasha's survival does not occur because an 'autonomous ego exercises autonomy in the face of a countervailing world (i.e. autonomy is not the solution)'. Instead, Sasha attains a sense of coherent self through the 'animating reference' to the social world from which she had withdrawn.[146] *Scherbenpark* thus offers a counter-model of subjectification that contrasts with the relentless bolstering and exposure of the female ego occurring so frequently in pop-feminist texts.

The question remains as to the character of the social world to which Sasha returns after the capitulation of her radically transgressive self. Throughout *Scherbenpark*, Sasha's encounters with the newspaper editor Volker and his son, Felix, reveal a desire for a domestic tranquillity that Sasha has not experienced since childhood:

> So ein Gefühl hatte ich, als ich mit fünf Jahren einmal bei meiner Großmutter übernachtet hatte – pures ungetrübtes Lebensglück, wenn jede Wahrnehmung noch mehr Freude verheißt. Das Klappern des Geschirrs, das Licht, das Summen der Hummeln, die Stimmen in der Küche und der Geruch frisch gekochten Kaffees und warmen Zimts. Auf den Brötchen, die meine Oma gerade aus dem Ofen geholt hat.

---

[146] Judith Butler, *The Psychic Life of Power*, p. 195.

[I felt like this when I stayed over at my grandmother's once when I was five—pure undiluted happiness, when every new sensation promised more joy. The dishes clattering, the light, bumblebees humming, voices in the kitchen and the smell of freshly brewed coffee and warm cinnamon. On the bread rolls gran had just taken out of the oven.]

(S, 111)

This nostalgia for a lost domestic idyll echoes the sentimental closing stages of *Brass* and evokes the desire for 'normality' expressed by Hensel and Raether, discussed above. In *Scherbenpark*, Bronsky offers up almost exactly the above scene in the novel's closing stages when Sasha's family, along with Volker and Felix, meet up in the kitchen after Sasha is released from hospital. The normative resonance of this domestic scene risks undermining the subversive work the novel has achieved up to that point. Yet Bronsky cleverly sidesteps this sense of closure by creating a different ending, one in which Sasha slips away from the family scene, which now at least remains anchored in a sense of stability, and sets off on a journey abroad on her own.

HELENE HEGEMANN'S *AXOLOTL ROADKILL* [AXOLOTL ROADKILL] AND ANTONIA BAUM'S *VOLLKOMMEN LEBLOS BESTENFALLS TOT* [PERFECTLY LIFELESS PREFERABLY DEAD]

Published a year apart, Hegemann and Baum's debut novels warrant joint consideration due to their striking aesthetic and thematic resonances. Both novels are formally experimental, self-reflexive works, existing on a continuum with earlier German-language pop-literary works but evoking the 'prose-assemblage' style and ironic tone of Kathy Acker, in particular. Hegemann's text is a complex, intertextual hybrid, combining song lyrics, advertising slogans, email exchanges, and letters. Its fragmentary, non-linear first-person narrative draws on the work of German blogger Airen but also many English-language authors and film-makers such as Jim Jarmusch, Malcolm Lowry, and David Foster Wallace. Hegemann's central protagonist, Mifti, is sixteen years old. The novel is assembled from a diary of her thoughts and exploits in Berlin, although the line is often blurred between dream or nightmare worlds and what might be considered 'reality'. In her literary style and methodology, Hegemann draws heavily on Acker's technique of auto-plagiarism, involving interlingual transpositions of other authors' works (especially Acker's) into her own 'patchwork' story.[147] Like Acker, Hegemann fragments the narrative voice, plays with 'true' and 'false' autobiography, and embeds unacknowledged textual passages from literary sources, music, and advertising in her own work. When it was first published, *Axolotl Roadkill* was read as an authentic coming-of-age tale, in other words, a coherent account of a single—albeit

---

[147] Helene Hegemann, *Axolotl Roadkill: Roman* (Berlin: Ullstein, 2010), p. 10. All further references will be included in the body of the text as A.

disturbed—consciousness.[148] This critical reception became the consensus despite the novel's, albeit self-ironizing, disclaimer that '[d]as alles hat nicht das Geringste mit dem Begriff des "Coming of Age Dramolettes" zu tun'[all of that hasn't the least to do with the notion of the coming-of-age-mini-drama] (A, 199). The German press predictably made links in their headlines between Hegemann and the term *Fräuleinwunder* [wonder girls], neatly categorizing the then seventeen-year-old author, film-maker, and playwright with a discrete and successful cohort of women writers.[149]

When the extent of Hegemann's intertextual strategies was uncovered, the scandal that ensued led to rapid critical re-calibrations that, among other accusations, saw her condemned by leading literary commentators in Germany as a mouthpiece for her famous theatre director father's literary aspirations (Carl Hegemann). In both scenarios, both pre- and post-scandal, Hegemann was denied any agency or recognition of literary skill. Antonia Baum suffered a similar fate when she was invited by Hubert Winkels to read from her debut novel during the Tage der deutschsprachigen Literatur in Klagenfurt in 2011.[150] The panel of critics dismissed her work as derivative, suggesting that Baum had created a simple emulation of Thomas Bernhard's style and voice. In this way, the author's creative autonomy, as well as the novel's compelling political dimension and innovative aesthetics, were overlooked.

Hegemann's central transgression was to wrong-foot the literary elite when they miscategorized her work as an authentic rites-of-passage novel. Instead, they were confronted with a highly crafted comment on the inauthenticity of coherent selfhood that challenged deeply entrenched notions of the function of literature in Germany. Iris Radisch observed at the time that Hegemann's true transgression was in fact to subvert—through her cut-and-paste intertextuality—what Radisch calls 'unsere alte Literatur der bürgerlichen Subjektivität mit ihren subtilen Nöten' [our traditional literature of bourgeois subjectivity with its depictions of under-stated distress].[151] She also aggravated well-rooted anxieties among that elite group about the growing influence of Anglo-American literary styles on the German literary tradition.

Axolotl Roadkill and *Vollkommen leblos bestenfalls tot* present the reader with two young female protagonists, Mifti and Rosa Sperrlich, whose aggressive self-awareness, acerbic commentaries, and ironic attitudes place both themselves and the reader at one remove from their otherwise palpable existential distress. Like Sasha in *Scherbenpark*, both characters have experienced traumatic childhood events: Mifti was physically and psychologically abused by her mother, who died two

---

[148] '*Axolotl Roadkill* kann man als großen Coming-of-age-Roman der Nullerjahre lesen.' [*Axolotl Roadkill* can be viewed as the big coming-of-age-novel of the 2000s.] See Mara Delius, 'Mir zerfallen die Worte im Mund wie schlechte Pillen', *Frankfurter Allgemeine Zeitung*, 22 January 2010. For an overview of this initial reception, see also Thomas Ernst, ' "The Author is a DJ!" '.

[149] Marc Reichwein, 'Helene Hegemann, das Fräuleinwunder im Medienzoo', *Die Welt*, 20 August 2013; Lisa Sonnabend, 'Blogger entlarvt Fräuleinwunder', *Süddeutsche Zeitung*, 17 May 2010.

[150] A renowned literary festival and awards ceremony.

[151] Iris Radisch, 'Die alten Männer und das junge Mädchen: Warum das männliche Kulturestablishment auf Helene Hegemann einschlägt', *Die Zeit*, 18 February 2010.

years before the novel begins. There is also some intimation—never confirmed—that she was sexually abused by her father.

Rosa grew up with a depressed, alcoholic mother, whose unhappy marriage led her to leave her husband and child in order to return to her studies, which she had broken off when pregnant with Rosa. Afterwards she took up with a new partner in Italy. Both characters' families are materially wealthy, but dysfunctional. Rosa describes her family as 'ein asozialer Familienrest mit Geld' [the anti-social remnants of a family with money].[152] In fact, families connote for them the most dangerous thing in the world (V, 2), engendering a fear of adulthood (resonating with Sonja's in *Zuckerbabys*), which expresses itself in Mifti's desire never to grow up (A, 15) and in Rosa's rejection of what she calls the 'Zukunfts-Krankheit' [the scourge of the prospective] (V, 5). By focusing on the stalled and troubled transitions from adolescence to young adulthood of two disruptive female protagonists, the novels pose important questions about the political implications of subscribing to the available 'substantializations of identity', in Lee Edelman's terms, within contemporary neoliberalism and the notion of 'history as a linear narrative [...] in which meaning succeeds as revealing itself—as itself—through time'.[153] By refusing to partake in this 'narrative movement toward a viable political future' the protagonists and their textual vehicles enact a queer resistance to the socio-political status quo.[154] They also critically illuminate the troubling trajectories invoked by the pop-feminist guides under discussion, which are based on normative ideas of progress. In contrast, the novels' young, disoriented protagonists and the fragmented form of the novels themselves embody what Judith Halberstam has called a postmodern rupture in the 'stability of form and meaning', which, according to Halberstam, constitutes both a 'crisis and an opportunity'.[155]

The scourge of the future, then, can be understood in terms of the narrative of neoliberal self-optimization that, in McRobbie's thinking, exposes young women to relentless pressure to aspire and succeed. The protagonists' families constitute one source of this pressure and yet the unhappy and dysfunctional biographies of the parental generation in Baum and Hegemann's novels function as a mode of critiquing those expectations, as well as echoing Acker's literary strategy of deconstructing the oedipal myth. In fact, a striking point of continuity between the German pop-feminist guides and the novels is the foregrounding of intergenerational discord. In *Wir Alpha-Mädchen* and *Neue deutsche Mädchen*, the generational metaphor functions rhetorically as a means of ensuring 'das Absterben der Position des Gegners' [the demise of the opposition], i.e. Schwarzer's generation. In the pop-literary fiction, the metaphor functions on a metafictional level to signal aesthetic divergence but also on a thematic level as a means of levelling socio-cultural

---

[152] Antonia Baum, *Vollkommen leblos bestenfalls tot* (Hamburg: Hoffmann & Campe, 2011), p. 2. All further references are provided within the body of the text as V.

[153] Lee Edelman, *No Future: Queer Theory and the Death Drive* (Durham, NC: Duke University Press, 2004), p. 4.

[154] Ibid.

[155] Judith Halberstam, *In a Queer Time and Place: Transgender Bodies, Subcultural Lives* (New York: New York University Press, 2005), p. 6.

critique. Through their characters, both Hegemann and Baum practise the 'Attitüde des arroganten, misshandelten Arschkindes, das mit seiner versnobten Kaputtheit kokettiert und die Kaputtheit seines Umfeldes gleich mit entlarvt' [attitude of an arrogant, abused arsehole of a child, who flirts with her snobby fucked-up-ness, exposing the fucked-up-ness of her surroundings in the process] (A, 47).

As this citation demonstrates, Mifti (and Rosa) appear remarkably self-aware; they wield the language of psychoanalysis with dexterity, displaying a firm under-standing of the ways in which their experiences have informed their current self-destructive drives. Yet this knowledge—deployed predominantly in an ironic manner—seems unable to help them overcome their distress, or to alter their behav-iour. At one point, Rosa theorizes her dilemma by imagining a conversation with the implied reader shot through with the language of self-help: 'Was fehlt einem in sich drin?, frage ich und Sie mit Ihrem Verständnis antworten: wahrscheinlich man selbst.' [What's missing inside?, I ask and you, with your sympathetic insight, reply: probably yourself.] Rosa responds: 'Oh Gott, verpissen Sie sich mit Ihrem Scheißvokabular, gehen Sie ein Buch schreiben, oder sonst was' [Oh Jesus, fuck off with your crappy vocabulary. Go and write a book or something] (V, 106).

In fact, the authors' narrative technique, which involves their characters' voices shifting between inner-monologue to addressing the reader directly, enables them to employ this self-awareness to satirize the reader's voyeuristic motivations, but also implicitly the authors' writerly endeavours. Hegemann's novel begins with the television station Pro7's tagline 'We love to entertain you' before executing a move of reversed bathos that plunges the reader into a depiction of the detritus of Mifti's drug-fuelled night and her feverish sleep (A, 7). Later, in a line of Jelinek-like satirical intonation, Mifti asks the reader: 'Ist es das, was ihr für Wahnsinn haltet? Fürchtet ihr euch davor, verrückt zu werden? Jagen euch Leute, die durchdrehen, einen wohligen Schauer über den Rücken?' [Is that what you all class as insanity? Are you scared of going insane? Do people who go crazy send nice warm shivers down your spine?] (A, 64). Despite its resemblance to a moment of Jelinek-like provocation, this passage is sourced and translated from Acker's *Blood and Guts in High School*. In Acker's text, the line runs: 'Is that what you think craziness is? Are you scared you're going crazy? Do people who go crazy freak you? Look sweetheart.'[156] What strikes me as interesting is the manner in which Hegemann's translation transforms Acker's lines from being a one-to-one interaction between the narrative voice and the implied reader, and becomes instead directed at a 'you' plural ('ihr'). This intertext enhances Hegemann's critique of a voyeuristic readership, but by slightly modifying the line, Hegemann extends the breadth of her critique.[157]

By ironizing their disorders, and the reader's desire to read about them, both Mifti and Rosa reclaim some agency in their otherwise chaotic lives, and are able to offer a critique of the society in which being anything other than the sum of

---

[156] Kathy Acker, *Blood and Guts in High School*, p. 68.

[157] I use Katy Derbyshire's English translation of Hegemann above because she captures my point about mode of address. See Helene Hegemann, *Axolotl Roadkill*, trans. by Katy Derbyshire (London: Corsair, 2012), p. 42.

their disorders seems impossible. There are no longer any grand narratives intact to which these characters can subscribe in order to find gain a coherent sense of self. According to Mifti and Rosa's inner reflections, psychology becomes an ineffective intellectual exercise, love remains a narcissistic illusion, left-wing cultural criticism is merely a means to assuage bourgeois guilt (V, 100–1), or remains ineffectual (A, 148). Feminism has failed (V, 17), and consumer culture, superficial and insidious, has become all-pervasive.

Although the protagonists remain cynical about the efficacy of cultural critique, the strong undercurrent of criticism and anger inherent in both texts remains apparent. Rosa rails against what she calls 'nationalsozialistisch[e] Popkultur' [national-socialist pop-culture] (V, 116), a homogenous postmodern culture, in which identity has become a lifestyle commodity, the pivotal consumer product concept driving neoliberal economics, or as Rosa puts it 'I.C.H. inc.' [M.E. Inc.] (V, 57). Rosa satirizes a culture in which individual self-responsibility has become the dominant narrative, what she calls 'Werde-Pflicht' [compulsory becoming] (V, 132), and citizens exist in solitary units, protecting themselves from intersubjective encounters with headphones (V, 114). The consequence of freedom of individual choice and self-empowerment is that '[l]etzlich ist jeder für sich selbst verantwortlich' [ultimately everybody is responsible for themselves] (V, 32), a line which echoes the rhetoric of many pop-feminist handbooks discussed earlier in this chapter. Such a climate has no patience for those who are relentlessly exposed, buffeted, and subsumed by the weight of social expectations. Instead, Mifti's family remind her constantly: 'Du sollst das einfach durchziehen' [you've just got to see it through] (A, 77).

The novels simultaneously express and thwart the yearning for an alternate mode of being, countering longing for a better future with cynical posturing, intoxication, rage, self-harm, and the rejection of the future in the form of adulthood. Mifti, for example, claims:

Ich wollte aufhören zu denken, weil Wörter bedeutungslos waren, weil Bedeutungslosigkeit bedeutungslos war, weil das Leben nichts wert war, weil meine komplette Physiognomie Teil des In sich stimmigen Organismus eines belebten Himmelskörper ist, von dem ICH mich abgrenze.

[I wanted to stop thinking because words were meaningless, because meaninglessness was meaningless, because life was worth nothing, because my entire physiognomy is part of the inherently consistent organism of a populated celestial body from which I keep distancing myself.]   (A, 166)

Mifti and Rosa thus withdraw from a social world they view as culturally and politically bankrupt, seeking even to escape the body and the psyche, which proves impossible. They are portrayed as symbolically fragmented individuals, experiencing themselves as alienated from their own bodies and disconnected from any sense of personal agency. Mifti often dreams of her mutilated body, where only '[d]as Gesicht ist übrig geblieben, ein paar Fetzen an den Fingerknöcheln auch. Hände und Füße baumeln, weil sie im Gelenk getrennt wurden' [my face is left, also a few shreds hanging off my knuckles. Hands and feet are flopping around because they've been severed at the joint] (A, 40). Mirrors, which feature heavily in *Axolotl Roadkill*, function as a tool for Mifti's attempts to overcome the association of her body with abuse and weakness.

> Nur noch die grenzenlose Schwäche ist sichtbar und diese daraus entstandene Unschuld. Ohne den Blick von mir selbst abzuwenden, versuche ich mir in Erinnerung zu rufen, dass die Haut oberhalb meine Kniekehle, das Narbengewebe zwischen den Schultern und das Sommersprossenfeld auf meinem Oberschenkel zu mir gehören.
>
> [I can only see limitless weakness and the innocence it generated. Without taking my eyes off my reflection I try to call to mind that the skin above the back of my knee, the scar tissue between my shoulders and the sprinkle of freckles on my thigh belong to me.]   (A, 110)

Her body has become a cipher for those abstract qualities of weakness, but also innocence, a vehicle onto which can be projected intolerable experience. As long as the body remains something '[d]er eigentlich nichts mit dir zu tun hat' [that has nothing to do with you] (A, 96), that is, remains disconnected from consciousness per se, Mifti is able to retain, to use Layton's terminology, some element of good affect, in this case pride in her mental resilience: 'weil mein Körper im Gegensatz zu mir selbst ein auf körperliche Schmerzen reagierendes Reflexbündel ist' [Because in contrast to my self, my body is just a bundle of reflexes reacting to physical pain] (A, 84). This observation resonates with Gaitskill's depiction of Dorothy in *Two Girls*, who feels entirely detached from her body, as if she were 'locked out', her consciousness merely a 'disembodied set of impulses and electric discharges, disconnected rage and fear' (TG, 162).

But Mifti despises the way that her body continues to experience sensations despite being 'disconnected' from her consciousness. For example, she becomes disgusted with her body's ability to experience orgasm during sex with a stranger despite the sensation that her consciousness remains disconnected from the event (A, 113). The world of sex, which becomes connected with corporeality and abuse, entails the loss of language (A, 113), a capacity Mifti equates with her 'self'. Like many of the protagonists in the novels I have discussed so far, Mifti's sense of self is fragmented, but rigidly divided into binaries: the female body is associated with victimhood and language equates with consciousness or 'self'. For example, after being attacked by her sister, Mifti observes that '[s]elbst das Schreien hat nichts mit mir selbst zu tun, sondern mit der unvermittelten Reaktion eines Organismus auf einen bestimmten Reiz. Ich bin nicht meine Schreie, ich bin nicht mein physisches Schmerzempfinden, ich bin kein Tier' [even the screaming has nothing to do with my self, only with an organism's sudden response to a certain stimulus. I am not my screams. I am not my physical experience of pain. I am not an animal] (A, 84). The inability to integrate body and mind leads only, in Mifti's case, to the degradation of her body in an attempt to prove the superiority of *ratio*, the capacity she associates with agency.

At the beginning of *Vollkommen leblos*, Rosa views her imminent move to the city as an opportunity to shape her own life: 'Man kann alles machen. Ich will was werden' [Anything is possible. I want to become something] (V, 6). However, once in the city, Rosa experiences difficulty in establishing relationships, theorizing that, due to her traumatic childhood, something has been 'ripped out' of her and never replaced (V, 21). Like Mifti, she begins to perceive herself as fatally determined, a product of social construction that prevents her from truly autonomous action. These reflective passages constitute the interrogatory dimension inherent in these works of fiction that remains lacking in the pop-feminist handbooks. For example, in her relationship with Patrick, her controlling boyfriend, she feels unable to be anything but 'ferngesteuert' [remote-controlled] (V, 17), a victim of the 'seit Jahrhunderten überlieferten Schlamm' [legacy of centuries' old sludge] of social convention and fixed gender roles, which react violently with the 'Propaganda-Durchsagen' [propaganda announcements] inherent in a postfeminist climate. They demand that women become 'total befreit. Sei weiblich und sei dabei wie ein Mann. Sei auch sexuell befreit [...] lass' dich krass überall rein ficken und wirke dabei möglichst selbstbewusst' [totally liberated. Be feminine and, at the same time, be like a man. Be sexually liberated, too [...] let yourself be fucked like crazy in every conceivable hole, but make sure you look as self-confident as you can while you do] (V, 19). This passage resonates strikingly with the thrust of my critique of many pop-feminist volumes, which, as I have demonstrated, often foreground confident sexuality as the site of agency.

Having attempted to gain a purchase on life through two (failed) romantic relationships and a tedious job in new media, with which she copes by numbing herself with drugs, Rosa becomes pregnant. After taking her mother's advice to abort, Rosa realizes she has undertaken that which her mother wishes she had done when she was pregnant with Rosa, increasing Rosa's sense of being socially alienated. She isolates herself still further, experiencing herself as trapped in a 'Kopfgefängnis' [mind prison] (V, 130), eventually developing an eating disorder, which further alienates her from her body. This development echoes McRobbie's observation that the figure of the sick girl withdraws from the social in an act of rebellion that paradoxically requires the destruction of the object—the body— placed under so much scrutiny and so many demands. Rosa describes her illness as a 'Leistungssport' [competitive sport], satirically inverting the social demands placed upon her to succeed (V, 117). As McRobbie notes, the call to agency and activity aimed at young women all too often continues even during the period of sickness and rebellion. She 'who suffers (along with her fellow-sufferers) is no longer passive, indeed she is expected to be highly active in her struggle to overcome her afflictions'.[158]

Rosa even views her disorder with ironic detachment: 'Ich fand es nicht sehr originell essgestört zu werden, das störte mich tatsächlich, aber man braucht irgendein Geländer, irgendetwas was einem sagt, was man ist' [I didn't find it very original to develop an eating disorder. In fact, that really disturbed me. But you need some kind of handhold, something that tells you what you are] (V, 117).[159]

---

[158] Angela McRobbie, *The Aftermath of Feminism*, p. 98.
[159] Note the use of 'what' rather than 'who' in this citation, which is reminiscent of Carmel's desire in *Cold Water* for someone to tell her brutally 'what' she is, i.e. to impose identity on her.

When her attempt to find this point of purchase at university fails, viewing the education offered there as an extension of her intellectual cage, Rosa begins to open herself up in other ways ('sich öffnen' V, 130). She cuts herself because '[r]ot zeigt dir an, wo du im Raum stehst, Rot zeigt dir, dass du dich nicht irrst, Rot macht dich sichtbar, Rot schafft Ordnung, Einheit, Unterschied, ein Oben, ein Unten, einen Anfang und ein Ende' [red shows you where you are in space, red shows you that you're not mistaken, red makes you visible, red creates order, coherence, difference, an above, a below, a beginning, and an end] (V, 130). This passage echoes the comfort Scarlett Thomas's Ariel takes from the symmetry of her own self-inflicted scars and also gestures towards Rosa's desire to attain some concrete sense of subjective coherence. Without the red blood, Rosa would be a free-floating, amorphous entity, echoing Alison's fear, in Mary Gaitskill's *Veronica*, of 'the terrible freedom of shapelessness' and Justine's sense of 'sickening boundlessness'.[160]

As an alternative to cutting, Rosa attempts to write down her experiences in order to find the structure and coherence she desires. This is perhaps why she states: 'Erst versuchen wir was Ganzes, eine Erzählung' [First, let's try something whole: a story] (V, 131). For Rosa, a story represents something necessarily coherent due to the conventions of narrative structure and the telos propelling it. However, the procedure produces only distress:

> Denke ich, fällt mir sofort das Gegenteil dazu ein, denke ich, sehe ich immer die eine und die andere Seite, gibt es niemals etwas ganzes, gültiges. [...] Aber so denkt man heute, dachte ich, als sich Alles in mir zerlegte, alles falsch war und nichts stimmte. Unverschämt, anmaßend, überheblich fand ich es von mir zu denken, es könne überhaupt einen *ganzen Satz* oder gar eine *ganze Geschichte* geben.
>
> [I think and then the opposite thought occurs to me immediately, I think and I always see both sides, there's never anything whole and valid. [...] But that's how people think today, I thought, as everything in me fragmented, everything was wrong and nothing added up. I found it shameless, presumptuous, arrogant of me to think that there could ever be a *whole sentence* let alone a *whole story*.]   (V, 131)[161]

This passage echoes Kathleen Hanna's angry reflections on the legacy of certain poststructuralist and postmodern theories, which made her feel that it was 'more progressive (and sexy) to be a barely functioning skitzophrenic [sic] than to have a viewpoint one could act from'.[162] Hanna calls this a 'theoretical trap', which Rosa, in the above passage, views as the dominant mode of thinking, 'so denkt man heute' [that's how people think today].[163] Although Rosa claims towards the novel's conclusion that she never succeeded in writing, the narrative ends with the inscription 'Rosa Sperrlich, Marcialla im Sommer 2011' (V, 133), suggesting that writing did in fact present one reason for her stepping back from the edge of the building she is about to jump off when the novel ends. For Mifti, too, writing provides a sense of coherence where it is subjectively lacking and represents an externalized connection of sorts. It becomes clear that the novel the reader is reading is

---

[160] Mary Gaitskill, *Veronica*, p. 184; Mary Gaitskill, *Two Girls, Fat and Thin*, p. 160.
[161] Original italics.   [162] Kathleen Hanna, 'POSTMODERNIST DISCOURSE'.
[163] Ibid.

Mifti's diary, which she views as 'die Ausdruckswaffe gegen meine Angst' [the weapon of expression against my fear] (A, 38) and as an attempt to make whole and permanent that which might otherwise disappear (A, 67).

It is worthwhile recalling here the arguments made by Lois McNay and Adriana Cavarero concerning the role played by the narrative medium in the 'active process of configuration whereby individuals attempt to make sense of the temporality of existence'.[164] Through their explorations of two characters struggling against the effects of social circumstance and psychological damage, Hegemann and Baum foreground the 'retentive dimension of the sedimented effects of power on the body'.[165] Yet the authors also develop a generative logic that imagines a more creative and imaginative stratum to action. As McNay contends, it is 'crucial to conceptualize these creative or productive aspects immanent to agency in order to explain how, when faced with complexity and difference, individuals may respond in unanticipated and innovative ways which may hinder, reinforce or catalyse social change'.[166] In this case, the narrative impulse experienced by Mifti, Rosa, and to some extent, Sasha, can be understood as what Cavarero calls the subject's desire for unity of the self in the form of a story. The subjects who emerge coincide with the 'uncontrollable narrative impulse of memory' that produces the story the reader has before her and are also 'captured in the very text itself'.[167]

As suggested by the narrative models mentioned above, as well as by Butler's in *Giving and Account of Oneself*, a fundamental element of the narrative impulse remains the other to whom the narrative is related or who relates the subject's narrative to her. In both novels, the desire for coherence in the form of narrative does not exist in a vacuum but in conjunction with a process of intersubjective recognition that signals a return to the social from which they had withdrawn. For Mifti, it is her relationship with her former lover, Alice, which makes her feel 'so als wäre das, was ich bis jetzt gewesen bin, vor ihr zu einem "Wir" erwacht [...]. Ich bin etwas mehr, etwas weniger als ich' [as if that which I was up to now is becoming a 'we' in her presence [...]. I am a little bit more, a little bit less than me] (A, 201). The location given by Rosa's inscription suggests that she has joined her mother and step-father in Italy. These moments of narrative closure, which highlight a desire for intersubjective connection, resonate with those in much of Mary Gaitskill's later fiction and in *Valencia*, *The Argonauts*, *How Should a Person Be?*, *Cold Water*, *The End of Mr. Why*, *Zuckerbabys*, *Feuchtgebiete*, *Brass*, and *Scherbenpark*.

The novels I have discussed in this chapter highlight the challenges facing contemporary feminist critique in a climate of postfeminism, neoliberalism, and intergenerational unrest. They reflect the paradigmatic turn to narratives of freedom of choice and individual responsibility perpetuated by neoliberalism and underscored by popular consumer culture. They imaginatively represent young women's struggle to assert a sense of authentic identity in place of the unsatisfying options offered by a matriarchal legacy, the regulating forces of neoliberalism, and misogynistic popular culture. In contrast to many of the essayistic pop-feminist texts, the novels

---

[164] Lois McNay, *Gender and Agency*, p. 27.   [165] Ibid., pp. 4–5.
[166] Ibid., p. 5.   [167] Ibid., p. 35.

explore the social, cultural, and familial factors that constitute identity and affect agency. However, they also underscore the role played by individual psychology in, for example, the perpetuation and cessation of self-destructive behaviour.

Zuckerbabys underscores the scale of the challenge facing German feminism upon its encounter with popular culture. Grether challenges individual agency that relies on consumerism as the foundation of identity. Suspicious of interpretations of Butlerian performance that align with consumerism as well as postfeminist neo-liberal individualism, Grether shows how the array of female identities available remains limited by the forces that regulate identity. She sets out to challenge the neoliberal mandate that states that individuals may transcend social contingency through individual endeavour and responsibility, yet concludes that Sonja must take responsibility for her own recovery. In Sonja, Grether creates a character cap-able of reflexive mediation, of overcoming the factors regulating her identity and selecting the aspects of pop-culture that benefit her. Problematically, agency relies upon the ability described by Valenti to distinguish between 'good' and 'bad' per-formances; in Butler's view this is not always possible. Ultimately, Grether carves out a site of agency for Sonja in creative self-expression through pop, sparing the medium from rigorous critique.

Feuchtgebiete enquires after the efficacy of applying feminist correction to the private sphere of sexual fantasy, yet Roche oscillates between claiming a private, autonomous performative space for Helen and depicting the factors that constitute and regulate her. Despite attempts to locate an alternative site of agency for their protagonists (parodic performance and pop), Grether and Roche's novels still demonstrate an ultimately limiting oscillation between the alternatives of free-will and determinism as denoting the parameters of selfhood and agency. In *Feuchtgebiete*, Roche addresses the shortcomings of Butler's early thinking by foregrounding the role of the corporeal in identity construction and agency. She presents a spectrum of subversive corporeal performances that potentially signify female identity differently. As in *Zuckerbabys*, *Axolotl Roadkill*, and *Vollkommen leblos bestenfalls tot*, Helen's body becomes the site of struggle between the exercise of free will and the consequences of pre-determination. In *Zuckerbabys*, Sonja real-izes that her body alone does not constitute identity, that agency can be sourced through creativity and engagement with one's social environment instead of by pursuing unrealistic dreams of corporeal perfection. Helen does not seek corporeal perfection, but *Feuchtgebiete* does suggest that performance identity can be selected autonomously by a coherent sovereign subject, who, by patrolling the body's borders, attains agency; this stance aligns troublingly with postfeminist consumer culture. The novel also demonstrates how the pop-feminist strategy of performative iden-tity does not always result in the subversion of gender norms or in progressive re-significations of female identity. Performance may also reveal the contours of an unstable psyche or re-inscribe the gender norms it appears to subvert.

The aesthetic depiction of traumatic fragmentation and incoherent selfhood, as well as the transgressive behaviours they generate, constitute the basis of social cri-tique in *Scherbenpark*, *Axolotl Roadkill*, and *Vollkommen leblos*. These novels explore the social, cultural, and psychological factors that determine and regulate identity in a more detailed manner than many of the pop-feminist handbooks published around the same time. *Scherbenpark*, in particular, foregrounds the specific socio-cultural factors experienced by Germany's ethnic minorities. The telos of these novels implies that trauma must be recovered from in order to attain a coherent sense of self. Yet the attainment of coherence is predicated on the reintegration of the raging or melancholic subject into the social realm and is attained through an acceptance of the subject's impenetrability to her self and her consequent reliance on others. The conclusions reached by these novels contrast significantly with those proffered by the less reflective pop-feminist volumes. These posit an always already sovereign subject, who selects identity performances at will. This pop-feminist subject relies upon individual strategies for self-empowerment, disavowing any dependency on others, just as the authors disavow any sense of commonality with older feminist protagonists. For the pop-feminists critiqued above, the most frequently featured strategy for attaining a self-empowered state remains the arena of sex, which, as my work has demonstrated, has become a field of 'licensed' transgression.

Conclusion
Pop-Feminism and the Future

The central concerns of this book included first, the models of subjectivity and agency in pop-feminist essayistic writing and pop-literary (auto)fiction and second, possible lines of literary and discursive influence from North America, to Britain and Germany. My primary question was whether the notions of subjectivity and agency proposed by pop-feminist and pop-literary authors differed and how, in turn, those differences, mediated by particular genres, impacted upon the degree of tangible socio-cultural and political critique.

My analysis confirmed, however, that it remains important to pay attention to the precise qualities of the feminist narratives that get recounted. This is particularly the case now, in a climate where many varieties of feminism have become increasingly visible across mainstream local and global contexts. Pop-feminism, therefore, does not connote a single, unified discourse but includes a range of aesthetic, generic, and critical strategies. What unites pop-feminist texts, however, is their 'awkward' entanglement with the neoliberal structures that enable them, and which may impinge upon the articulation of coherent feminist politics. Close readings of the pop-feminist guides unpicked at least two distinct strands of pop-feminist thinking across North America, Britain, and Germany. By focusing on the authors' various representations of female identity, agency, consumer culture, sexuality, difference, and second-wave feminism, I revealed the extent to which some pop-feminist thinking in fact relies heavily on the logic of postfeminism and neoliberal individualism.

In volumes like Valenti's *Full Frontal Feminism*, Levenson's *The Noughtie Girl's Guide to Feminism*, Moran's *How to Be a Woman*, Freeman's *Be Awesome: Modern Life for Modern Ladies* and Vernon's *Hot Feminist*, Streidl, Haaf, and Klingner's *Wir Alpha*-Mädchen, Hensel and Raether's *Neue deutsche Mädchen*, and Stöcker's edited work *Das F-Wort: Feminismus ist sexy*, the authors all too often retain the implicit assumption that, underlying playful or at times ironically executed identity performances, there remains a sovereign subject capable of and responsible for mediating reflexively and maintaining full autonomy over such performances. This occurs despite the fact that most pop-feminist accounts of subjectivity draw heavily upon poststructuralist notions of pluralistic, unstable identity and Butler's concept of subversive performativity. But theirs is an interpretation of Butlerian performance that aligns with hedonistic consumer practices, in which identities can be selected, with matching accoutrements, as easily as a pair of shoes. As a result, the forces of social construction, conditioning, and constraint disappear into the background. Apart from the assumption of consumer autonomy, sexuality also becomes foregrounded as a scene of agency. This strategy, viewed against a theoretical background that posits the sexualization of contemporary Western culture as a result of the continuing sway of postfeminist narratives and neoliberal consumerism, further attests to the danger that pop-feminism may end up colluding with narratives of postfeminism and neoliberalism, withdrawing entirely from the political arena. Despite the appeal to a collective, an implicit or explicit 'we', this pop-feminism in fact leaves the individual quite alone with the obligation to make her own choices and deal with her own problems. The call to self-accountability strikingly still obtains in some pop-feminist guides, or in memoirs like Michelle Tea's *How To Grow Up*, that were published after the global financial crisis, particularly in the US and in Britain, attesting to the adaptability of neoliberalism's incursions into feminist discourse.

What I deem to be a more reflective variety of pop-feminism, on the other hand, constitutes an expression of resistance, albeit 'awkward' resistance, to the misogynistic elements of mainstream pop and consumer culture, the dominant discourses of neoliberal individualism, and postfeminist disparagements of the second wave. Their attempts remain awkward in their articulation due to the neoliberal economy that enables them. Yet despite this symbiosis, these pop-feminists continue to critique the systems in which they are entangled rather than be assimilated by them. In doing so, they draw on the aesthetics and critical strategies inherited from third-wave feminism and social movements like riot grrrl but they also seek to build bridges with their feminist predecessors. While I identified a relatively small field of such reflective pop-feminist writing among the essayistic texts (from Eismann, Levy, Zeilinger, Gay, Redfern, and Aune), the continuing work of the German-language *Maedchenmannschaft* community online, the American website *Bitch Media* and the British site *The F-Word* demonstrates that local and transnational pop-feminist thinking is occurring via multi-authored platforms that analyse pop-culture, politics, and neoliberal economics critically; these sites, for example, have been paying particular attention to the gendered dimensions of the financial crisis and subsequent austerity politics. Furthermore, the recent publication in North America of Valenti's *Sex Object* and Zeisler's *We Were Feminists Once* intimates a new stage of self-critique within pop-feminism, at least in North America. Given that these two authors were involved in the early, optimistic stages of North American pop-feminism, their present-day reflections on the pitfalls of the originally optimistic union between feminism and pop-culture evidence a more sober approach to the potential of pop-feminist politics.

Indeed, I located the most coherent interrogation of the issues dealt with by the pop-feminist handbooks in a corpus of pop-literary fiction and autofiction written in the first-person voice, demonstrating that pop-literature can indeed align with feminist critique, albeit one beset by the pitfalls of the postfeminist neoliberal status quo. My investigations revealed that examples of pop-literary writing by women explore the possibility of securing a coherent sense of identity beyond the surfaces of the pop-cultural archive. My chosen authors' foregrounding of trauma, transgression, and subjective incoherence constitutes a strategy for critique and also contrasts strikingly with the model of sovereign subjectivity and individual self-empowerment ultimately proposed by the pop-feminist handbooks. While I acknowledge the risks, posited by Lynne Layton, involved in aestheticizing traumatic (female) fragmentation, a theme so visible in pop-literary fiction and autofiction, I conclude that the opposite strategy, as characterized by the a priori sovereign subject, abnegates responsibility for interrogating new and old forms of discrimination, inequality and oppression, resulting in a withdrawal from social critique. This suggests that some value is retained for identity from suffering—at least within the literary paradigm.

Subjective incoherence in the literary narratives co-exists in productive tension with a desire for coherence and unity that in no way resembles the model of pre-discursive sovereign subjectivity uncovered in many of the pop-feminist handbooks, as it fundamentally relates to an ethics of intersubjective relations. I also demonstrated how the role-play undertaken by the reader of these first-person narratives activates a critical sensibility within the reader that can potentially be applied to the extra-diegetic world.

The first-person voice in the (auto)fictions allows the complexity and opacity of interiority, as well as moments of complicity with structures of power and oppression, to be revealed. The forensic representations of the narrator's self-reflexive puzzlement in the face of her own self-destructive behaviours or relationships, the probing of motivations so prominent in the disabled toilet scenes, emerges first in Mary Gaitskill's fiction (and is precisely what is lost in the film *Secretary*) and remains a thread throughout all of the fictions subsequently discussed.

The portrayal of psychological complexity and opacity as the narrator grapples with those postfeminist neoliberal constellations that impinge upon female agency generates a more multi-faceted—and honest—representation of individual psychology than the glib urging to self-assertion characterizing many of the handbooks. The probing first-person voice and the consciousness it seeks to articulate also functions as the reader's fictional other, prompting an extrapolative and self-reflexive process in the reader that holds the potential to activate nuanced critical thinking. This complex, fluctuating diegetic/extra-diegetic intersubjectivity is part of what makes the literary fiction more politically charged and valuable to feminist critique. In contrast, the incitement to self-empowerment proffered by many pop-feminists, combined with the absent 'I' in the 'we' of their accounts, leaves the reader alone with the compulsion to succeed in self-empowerment without the critical tools or the platform for self-reflection.

The teleological structure of this book enabled me to trace as yet undiscussed lines of feminist discursive and literary influence as I moved from the early 1980s in North America, through riot grrrl, to the current moment as characterized by intensely self-reflexive autofictions by queer and feminist writers that recall the self-probing undertakings of many second-wave feminists; I then moved through riot grrrl's arrival in Britain in the late 1990s, to the literary debates characterizing that post-chick-lit period in Britain and Germany, which so informed the climate in which pop-feminist authors have been writing. I revealed the extent of indebtedness to poststructuralism inherent in the work of the literary authors, a theoretical legacy they share with the earlier postmodern authors, Acker and Gaitskill, thus revealing a critical pop-literary interest, spanning approximately three decades and shifting across cultural contexts, in subjectivity, female identity, and agency in the face of late-capitalist and neoliberal manifestations of social constraint.

By beginning my investigations with Acker and Gaitskill, I was able to demonstrate, through the lenses of riot grrrl, homonormativity, and aspects of pop-feminism, how radically transgressive feminist and queer gestures became appropriated and disarmed by postfeminist consumer culture from the 1990s onwards. The mainstreaming of the radically transgressive trope led to a shift in its cultural significance. By this I mean that its impact as a politically subversive tool in the fictions of Acker and Gaitskill, as well as in the riot-grrrl movement and in texts by Myles and Kraus, contrasts with its normative ubiquity in popular commercial culture and hedonistic heteronormativity, where transgression all too often becomes contained within certain 'licensed' arenas, such as the realm of sexuality. This shift results in a precarious predicament for the writers of pop-literary (auto)fictions. On the one hand, the contemporary authors I have discussed all use representations of transgressive sexuality as a method of subverting norms, or questioning the capacity of sexual transgression to generate a scene of agency. On the other, their foregrounding of transgressive sexuality aligns with the demands of consumer culture and an increasingly market-driven publishing industry in North America, Britain, and Germany.

The comparative methodology of this study did reveal some striking commonalities between North America, Britain, and Germany, such as the shifts in publishing practices mentioned above. The presence of pop-feminist volumes in all three contexts, as well as the number of theoretical, aesthetic and thematic characteristics they share, attests to the strong transnational circulations of feminism, commercial pop-culture, neoliberalism, and postfeminism. The impact in all three contexts of performativity on pop-feminism, as well as the presence of third-wave and riot-grrrl references in the more reflective pop-feminist volumes, speaks of the continuing impact of Anglo-American feminism on German feminisms. Not only German, but also British and American pop-feminist essayists register difference and/or dissent from established feminist discourse in their local context by drawing on the aesthetics and ideologies of global popular consumer culture and elements of poststructuralist or third-wave Anglo-American feminisms. My comparative framework thus illuminated a line of feminist influence from the Anglo-American context to Germany and a line of literary influence from North America to Britain and Germany. But in each case impact was inscribed with culturally-specific characteristics.

Local specificities emerged in terms of the cross-cultural traffic of transnational pop-feminism, which highlights how a global discourse generates important local differences. The figure of Butler, for example, is invoked particularly often in the German pop-feminist volumes, due in part to the lateness of German feminism's encounter with third-wave feminism and pop-culture, but also due to the inevitable temporal patterning of transnational discursive transmissions. The wave metaphor, so common in Anglo-American feminist discourse, remains absent as a referent to domestic feminist developments in Germany. Instead debates become framed through discursive constructs such as 'generation', or 'new' and 'old'. The generational metaphor in German pop-feminism resonates with the rhetorical language employed during the literary debates of the 1990s discussed in Chapter 5 and gestures towards the longevity of this popular motif in the German socio-cultural imagination.[1]

The tendency to represent shifts and gradual developments in the social and cultural fabric with the discrete categories common to the generational metaphor contrasts with the British context where, as I demonstrated, feminist disjuncture becomes expressed in terms of the dichotomy between academic and popular discourse, where academic feminism, often implicitly conflated with the second wave, is portrayed as elitist and disconnected from 'real life'.[2] Ironically, those British pop-feminists like Caitlin Moran and Polly Vernon who make the case for depictions of 'real life' are unique in the three cultural contexts for their shared status as celebrity media figures.

A common feature of the less reflective German pop-feminist handbooks was the degree of animosity expressed towards individual feminist predecessors, Alice Schwarzer in particular. While the British and American texts allude to the need for fresh, relevant feminist voices, this is achieved (with the exception of Vernon and Levenson's texts, which name-check Germaine Greer) without repeatedly singling out individual second-wave feminists for personal critique, a result perhaps of the particular media presence enjoyed by Schwarzer over the last forty years. Indeed, my analysis of the German pop-literary fiction also revealed more pronounced dissatisfaction with the legacy of German (but also Anglo-American) feminism than in the British context. There, disagreement becomes expressed in terms of character and plot, as in the case of Walsh's *Brass*, but rarely through direct diegetic reference to feminist forebears (as in *Schoßgebete*, *Feuchtgebiete*, *Axolotl Roadkill*, and *Zuckerbabys*), or in passages of detailed reflection on the minutiae of feminist discourse (as in *Vollkommen leblos*).

Despite the characterization of pop-literature by many theorists discussed in my introduction and in Chapter 5 as self-consciously apolitical, the broad and swingeing cultural critique levied at both thematic and formal levels by Hegemann and Baum's texts, in particular, may lie precisely in the authors' awareness of their embattled position as young female debut authors in relation to the competitive, literary-prize dominated, male literary establishment.[3] (Recall Baum reflecting on

---

[1] For more on the specificity of the generational motif in German feminisms, see Emily Spiers, 'Split Infinities: German Feminisms and the Generational Project', *Fractured Legacies: Historical, Cultural and Political Perspectives on German Feminism*, 5–30.

[2] Ellie Levenson, *The Noughtie Girl's Guide to Feminism*, p. 210; Moran, *How to be a Woman*, p. 12.

[3] See Iris Radisch's thoughts on the 'threat' Hegemann posed to the male elite of literary critics in Germany in Radisch, 'Die alten Männer und das junge Mädchen'. On the competitive dynamics ascribed to both German-language literary prize culture and authorial achievement and how authors respond to the commodification of their authorial bodies, see Rebecca Braun, 'Embodying Achievement: Thomas Bernhard, Elfriede Jelinek, and Authorship as a Competitive Sport', special

her reading at the prestigious Bachmann Prize festival in 2011, known as a 'Wettlesen' [competitive reading], during which she imagines her chair, placed before the jury of literary critics, turning into a death row electric chair.)[4] Indeed, while the Anglo-American and German contexts have all produced pop-feminist essayistic texts in the last decade, my study revealed fascinating local specificities in the degree of literary engagement with pop-feminist issues, as well as in the generic and aesthetic choices of the literary authors. The wealth of German-language pop-literary fictions uncovered, for instance, suggests that Germany constitutes a highly active scene of pop-literary engagement with the issues raised by pop-feminism. One consequence of such visible activity has been the rapid publication of Hegemann's *Axolotl Roadkill* and Roche's *Feuchtgebiete* in English translation and their distribution in both Britain and the US, a rapidity that speaks of the active industry strategies at play that form a part of consolidating German-language literature's presence on the global publishing stage.[5] The high number of German-language pop-literary productions discussed here is due in part to the continuing tradition of pop-literature as a distinct literary category per se in Germany. Yet the German-language works discussed here owe their formal and thematic qualities not only to the influence of North American authors like Acker and Gaitskill, but also to the literary feminist tradition set by local women writers and cultural producers like Berg, Jelinek, and Treut, who have continually drawn on the pop-cultural archive of the moment to explore issues of transgression, sexuality, selfhood, and agency. In comparison, literary engagement with this discourse in North America demonstrates a strong inclination to the mode of autofiction. This inclination is due not only to the example set by previously underground authors like Acker, Kraus, and Myles and their recent renaissance owing in large part to the internet's circulatory archival system, but it is also reflective of the prevalence of literary blog culture in North America. This medium lends itself to the weaving of the private self into a public persona and, as Zambreno contends, has become a popular medium of writerly engagement with feminist debates concerning identity and agency in North America.

One commonality between the literary works across all three contexts, specifically *The Argonauts*, *Valencia*, *How Should a Person Be?*, *The End of Mr. Y*, *Vollkommen leblos bestenfalls tot*, and *Axolotl Roadkill*, is their emphasis on the role played by narrative in the generation of coherent selfhood, securing a scene of agency and intersubjective relations. The importance of narrative, however, lies not only in its capacity to capture a sense of self, to express the desire for subjective coherence or

issue of *Austrian Studies, Elfriede Jelinek in the Arena: Sport, Cultural Understanding and Translation to Page and Stage*, ed. by Allyson Fiddler and Karen Jürs-Munby, 22 (2014), 121–38; Braun, 'Prize Germans?: Changing Notions of Germanness and the Role of the Award-Winning Author in the Twenty-First Century', special issue of *Oxford German Studies, Post-War Literature and Institutions*, ed. by Sean Williams and Daniel Wilson, 43.1 (2014), 37–54.

4 See Antonia Baum, 'Wie ich einmal vorlas', *Frankfurter Allgemeine Feuilleton*, 10 July 2011, available at   http://www.faz.net/aktuell/feuilleton/buecher/autoren/bachmannpreis-in-klagenfurt-wie-ich-einmal-vorlas-13739.html [accessed 16.02.2017].

5 See *Axolotl Roadkill*, trans. by Katy Derbyshire; Charlotte Roche, *Wetlands*, trans. by Tim Mohr (New York: Grove Press, 2009).

to underscore the profoundly intersubjective quality of selfhood. How we anticipate the future is directly linked to the aesthetics and structure of narrative form. The achievement of many of the literary texts discussed in this book is that they stage an imaginative break with the probable futures of their protagonists, a break experienced simultaneously by and through the reader.

This is because the encounter with the other's consciousness in the realm of narrative (auto)fiction generates a continual and fluid process of self-reflexive assessment, reconsideration, and self-adjustment on the part of the reader. As Maggie Nelson observes, 'I like to think that what literature can do that op-ed pieces and other communications don't do is describe felt experience, the flickering, bewildered places that people actually inhabit.'[6] Engaging with another subject who is reflecting upon the complex systems of lived experience, the reader embarks upon a succession of creative extrapolations based on cognitive and affective comparisons with her self. These are characterized by moments of identification, but also difference. This encounter may augment the self, as the reader steps into the shoes of the fictional character even for a moment, or as dissolving the contours of the self as the reader confronts alterity and is compelled outside the boundaries of the 'self-up-to-this-point'. This imaginative space is profoundly linked to the anticipatory domain of thinking the future. For it may hold a challenge to the 'self-up-to-this-point', to think differently, to acknowledge alterity, to consider what a 'self-from-this-point' might be like. To put it another way, these works invite us to think the feminist future differently, to imagine a space where things do not merely go on as before. While the pop-feminist handbooks purport to do the same thing, what in fact follows in most cases is precisely a regurgitation of postfeminist and neoliberal thinking, and a feminist future confined to the limitations of that logic. Let's think the future differently.

---

[6] Paul Laity, 'Maggie Nelson interview'.

Bibliography

MANUSCRIPTS

New York, Fales Library and Special Collections, New York University Libraries: Ramdasha Bikceem Riot Grrrl Collection, MSS 354, box 5, folder 23. Bikceem, *GUNK* #4, 1993.

New York, Fales Library and Special Collections, New York University Libraries: Johanna Fateman Riot Grrrl Collection, MSS 258, box 1, folder 64.

– Kathleen Hanna, *April Fools' Day*, 1995.

– Kathleen Hanna, 'When the Words that once Liberated You Become Bars on Yr Cage random notes on political depression'.

– Kathleen Hanna, 'POSTMODERNIST DISCOURSE AS TRANSMUTATED THRU THE TELEVISION'.

New York, Fales Library and Special Collections, New York University Libraries: Zan Gibbs. Riot Grrrl Zine Collection, MSS 364, box 1, folder 20. Sheila Heti, *Brillantine*, approx. 1996.

New York, Fales Library and Special Collections, New York University Libraries: Kathleen Hanna Papers, MSS 271, box 1, folder 25. Kathleen Hanna, un-named prose piece, date unknown.

– Kathleen Hanna, 'Essay' and 'Customers', date unknown.

New York, Fales Library and Special Collections, New York University Libraries: Kathleen Hanna Papers, MSS 271, box 2, folder 2. Kathleen Hanna, unnamed spoken-word fragment, date unknown.

New York, Fales Library and Special Collections, New York University Libraries: Sheila Heti Riot Grrrl Collection, MSS 366, box 5, folder 8. Heti et al. *Poised: An Anthology of Writing and Art by Young Women*, 1996.

New York, Fales Library and Special Collections, New York University Libraries: Lucy Thane Riot Grrrl Collection, MSS 287, 287.0027 (media). Kathleen Hanna interview, 13 March 1993.

PRINTED SOURCES

Primary Sources

Acker, Kathy, *Blood and Guts in High School: Plus Two*. London: Picador, 1984.

Acker, Kathy, *Don Quixote: Which Was a Dream*. London: Paladin, 1986.

Acker, Kathy, *Empire of the Senseless*. London: Pan, 1988.

Acker, Kathy, 'A Few Notes on Two of My Books', *The Review of Contemporary Fiction*, 9.3 (1989), 31–6.

Acker, Kathy, *Bodies of Work*. London: Serpent's Tail, 1997.

Baum, Antonia, *Vollkommen leblos bestenfalls tot*. Hamburg: Hoffmann & Campe, 2011.

Bronsky, Alina, *Scherbenpark*. Cologne: Kiepenheuer & Witsch, 2008.

Dorn, Thea, *Die neue F-Klasse: Wie die Zukunft von Frauen gemacht wird*. Munich: Piper, 2006.

Eismann, Sonja, 'Einleitung', in *Hot Topic: Popfeminismus heute*, ed. by Sonja Eismann. Mainz: Ventil, 2007.

Freeman, Hadley, *Be Awesome: Modern Life for Modern Ladies*. London: Fourth Estate, 2013.

Gaitskill, Mary, *bad behavior*. London: Hodder & Stoughton, 1989.

Gaitskill, Mary, *Two Girls, Fat and Thin: A Novel.* London: Chatto & Windus, 1991.

Gaitskill, Mary, 'On Not Being a Victim: Sex, Rape, and the Trouble with Following the Rules', *Harper's Magazine*, March (1994), 35–44.

Gaitskill, Mary, *Because They Wanted To: Stories.* London: Picador, 1997.

Gaitskill, Mary, 'On the Film *Secretary*. Victims and Losers: A Romantic Comedy', *American Zoetrope*, 7.3 (2003) <http://www.all-story.com/issues.cgi?action=show_story&story_id=210> [accessed 19.04.2013].

Gaitskill, Mary, *Veronica.* London: Serpent's Tail, 2007.

Gaitskill, Mary, *Don't Cry: Stories.* New York: Vintage Books, 2009.

Gay, Roxane, *Bad Feminist: Essays.* New York: HarperCollins, 2014.

Grether, Kerstin, *Zuckerbabys.* Berlin: Suhrkamp, 2006.

Grether, Kerstin, *Zungenkuss: Du nennst es Kosmetik, ich nenn es Rock 'n' Roll. Musikgeschichten 1990 bis heute.* Berlin: Suhrkamp, 2007.

Haaf, Meredith, Susanne Klingner, and Barbara Streidl, *Wir Alpha-Mädchen: Warum Feminismus das Leben schöner macht.* Hamburg: Hoffmann und Campe, 2008.

Hegemann, Helene, *Axolotl Roadkill: Roman.* Berlin: Ullstein, 2010.

Hegemann, Helene, *Axolotl Roadkill.* Trans. by Katy Derbyshire. London: Corsair, 2012.

Hensel, Jana and Elisabeth Raether, *Neue deutsche Mädchen.* Reinbek bei Hamburg: Rowohlt, 2008.

Heti, Sheila, *How Should a Person Be?* London: Vintage, 2014 [2010].

Levenson, Ellie, *The Noughtie Girl's Guide to Feminism.* Oxford: One World Publications, 2009.

Levy, Ariel, *Female Chauvinist Pigs: Women and the Rise of Raunch Culture.* New York; London: Free Press, 2005.

Moran, Caitlin, *How to be a Woman.* London: Ebury, 2011.

Nelson, Maggie, *The Argonauts.* London: Melville House, 2015.

Power, Nina, *One-Dimensional Woman.* Winchester: O Books, 2009.

Redfern, Catherine and Kristin Aune, *Reclaiming the F Word: The New Feminist Movement.* London: Zed Books, 2010.

Riley, Gwendoline, *Cold Water.* London: Vintage, 2003.

Roche, Charlotte, *Feuchtgebiete.* Berlin: Ullstein, 2009.

Roche, Charlotte, *Wetlands.* Trans. Tim Mohr. New York: Grove Press, 2009.

Roche, Charlotte, *Schoßgebete.* Munich: Piper, 2011.

Stöcker, Mirja, ed., *Das F-Wort: Feminismus ist sexy.* Königstein/Taunus: Ulrike Helmer, 2007.

Tea, Michelle, *Valencia*, 2nd edition. Berkeley, CA: Seal Press, 2008 [2000].

Tea, Michelle, *How to Grow up: A Memoir.* New York: Plume, 2015.

Thomas, Scarlett, 'The Great Chick Lit Conspiracy', *The Independent*, 4 August 2002 [source no longer available].

Thomas, Scarlett, *The End of Mr. Y* Edinburgh: Canongate, 2008.

Valenti, Jessica, *Full Frontal Feminism: A Young Woman's Guide to Why Feminism Matters.* Berkeley, CA: Seal Press, 2007.

Valenti, Jessica, *Sex Object: A Memoir.* New York: HarperCollins, 2016.

Walsh, Helen, *Brass.* Edinburgh: Canongate, 2004.

Walsh, Helen, 'I'm a Writer. Just Don't Ask Me What I Write', *The Independent*, 23 February 2014.

Warnecke, Jenny, ' "Das ist mir zu extrem!" Eine Generationen-Studie', in *Das F-Wort: Feminismus ist sexy*, ed. by Mirja Stöcker. Königstein/Taunus: Ulrike Helmer, 2007.

Secondary Sources

Ablaze!, Karren, 'Hey Zinesters! How Fanzines Empowered a Generation', *The Guardian*, 15 September 2009.

Ablaze!, Karren, 'Riot grrrl: Searching for Music's Young Female Revolutionaries', *The Guardian*, 18 March 2013.

Alice, Lynne, *What is Postfeminism? Or, Having it Both Ways: Feminism, Postmodernism, Postfeminism*. New Zealand: Massey University, 1995.

Altbach, Edith Hoshino, Jeanette Clausen, Dagmar Schultz, and Naomi Stephan, eds., *German Feminism: Readings in Politics and Literature*. Albany, NY: State University of New York Press, 1984.

Antrim, Taylor, 'First Novels: Rookie Sensations', *The New York Times*, 30 January 2005.

Anz, Thomas, 'Generationenkonstrukte: Zu ihrer Konjunktur nach 1989', in *Konkurrenzen, Konflikte, Kontinuitäten: Generationenfragen in der Literatur seit 1990*, ed. by Andrea Geier and Jan Süselbeck. Göttingen: Wallstein, 2009.

Ashby, Melaine, 'Beyond the New Feminism?', *Sibyl*, 8. May–June (1999), 34.

Attridge, Derek, 'Innovation, Literature, Ethics: Relating to the Other', *PMLA*, 114.1 (1999), 20–31.

Attwood, Feona, 'Sexed-Up: Theorising the Sexualisation of Culture', *Sexualities*, 9.1 (2006), 77–94.

Baer, Hester, ed., 'Contemporary Women's Writing and the Return of Feminism in Germany', special issue of *Studies in Twentieth and Twenty-First Century Literature*, 35.1 (2011).

Baer, Hester, 'German Feminism in the Age of Neoliberalism: Jana Hensel and Elizabeth Raether's *Neue deutsche Mädchen*', *German Studies Review*, 35.2 (2012), 355–74.

Baer, Hester, 'Redoing Feminism: Digital Activism, Body Politics, and Neoliberalism', *Feminist Media Studies*, 16.1, (2016) 17–34.

Baer, Hester and Alexandra Merley Hill, eds., *German Women's Writing in the Twenty-First Century*. Rochester, NY: Camden House, 2015.

Baker, Mona and Gabriela Saldanha, *Routledge Encyclopedia of Translation Studies*. Abingdon: Routledge, 2009.

Baldauf, Anette and Katharina Weingartner, eds., *Lips Tits Hits Power? Popkultur und Feminismus*. Vienna: Folio, 1998.

Baßler, Moritz, *Der deutsche Pop-Roman: Die neuen Archivisten*. Munich: Beck, 2002.

Baudrillard, Jean, *Simulacres et simulation*. Paris: Éditions Galilée, 1985.

Berlant, Lauren Gail, *The Female Complaint: The Unfinished Business of Sentimentality in American Culture*. Durham, NC; London: Duke University Press, 2008.

Bethman, Brenda, 'Generation Chick: Reading *Bridget Jones's Diary, Jessica, 30.*, and *Dies ist kein Liebeslied* as Postfeminist Novels', *Studies in 20th and 21st Century Literature*, 35.1 (2011), 137–54.

Biller, Maxim, 'Soviel Sinnlichkeit wie der Stadtplan von Kiel', *Die Weltwoche*, 25 July 1991.

Blincoe, Nicholas and Matt Thorne, *All Hail the New Puritans*. London: Fourth Estate, 2000.

Bloch, Ernst, Georg Lukács, Bertolt Brecht, Walter Benjamin, and Theodor Adorno, *Aesthetics and Politics: Debates between Ernst Bloch, Georg Lukács, Bertolt Brecht, Walter Benjamin and Theodor Adorno*. London: NLB, 1977.

Bourdieu, Pierre, *Distinction: A Social Critique of the Judgement of Taste*. London: Routledge & Kegan Paul, 1984.

Brady, Anita, 'Taking Time between G-string Changes to Educate Ourselves: Sinéad O'Connor, Miley Cyrus, and Celebrity Feminism', *Feminist Media Studies*, 16.3 (2016), 429–44.

Braidotti, Rosi, 'Cyberfeminism with a Difference', *New Formations* 29 (1996), 9–25.

Braun, Rebecca, 'Embodying Achievement: Thomas Bernhard, Elfriede Jelinek, and Authorship as a Competitive Sport', special issue of *Austrian Studies, Elfriede Jelinek in the Arena: Sport, Cultural Understanding and Translation to Page and Stage*, ed. by Allyson Fiddler and Karen Jürs-Munby, 22 (2014), 121–38.

Braun, Rebecca, 'Prize Germans? Changing Notions of Germanness and the Role of the Award-Winning Author in the Twenty-First Century', special issue of *Oxford German Studies, Post-War Literature and Institutions*, ed. by Sean Williams and Daniel Wilson, 43.1 (2014), 37–54.

Brennan, Karen, 'The Geography of Enunciation: Hysterical Pastiche in Kathy Acker's Fiction', *boundary 2*, 21.2 (1994), 243–68.

Brooks, Ann, *Postfeminisms: Feminism, Cultural Theory, and Cultural Forms*. New York: Routledge, 1997.

Brown, Wendy, 'Wounded Attachments', *Political Theory*, 21.3 (1993), 390–410.

Brunst, Klaudia, 'Frau gegen Frau', *Die Zeit*, 16 June 2005.

Brunst, Klaudia, *Je später der Abend… Über Talkshows, Stars und uns*. Freiburg: Herder, 2005.

Burke, Kenneth, *A Rhetoric of Motives*. Berkeley: University of California Press, 1969.

Butler, Judith, *Bodies that Matter: On the Discursive Limits of 'Sex'*. New York; London: Routledge, 1993.

Butler, Judith, 'Bodies that Matter', in *Engaging with Irigaray*, ed. by Carolyn Burke, Naomi Shor, and Margaret Whitford. New York: Columbia University Press, 1994.

Butler, Judith, *The Psychic Life of Power: Theories in Subjection*. Stanford, CA: Stanford University Press, 1997.

Butler, Judith, *Giving an Account of Oneself*. New York: Fordham University Press, 2005.

Butler, Judith, *Gender Trouble: Feminism and the Subversion of Identity*. 3rd edition. New York; London: Routledge, 2006.

Caputo, John D. and Mark Yount, *Foucault and the Critique of Institutions. Studies of the Greater Philadelphia Philosophy Consortium*. University Park: Pennsylvania State University Press, 1993.

Carr, Cynthia., 'The Legacy of Kathy Acker, Theoretical Grrrl', *Village Voice*, 5 November 2002.

Carter Olson, Carti, '#BringBackOurGirls: Digital Communities Supporting Real-world Change and Influencing Mainstream Media Agendas', *Feminist Media Studies*, 16.5 (2016), 772–87.

Cavarero, Adriana, *Relating Narratives: Storytelling and Selfhood*, trans. by Paul A. Kottman. London: Routledge, 2000.

Colebrook, Claire, 'From Radical Representations to Corporeal Becomings: The Feminist Philosophy of Lloyd, Grosz and Gatens', *Hypatia*, 15.2 (2002), 76–93.

Colebrook, Claire, *Gilles Deleuze*. London: Routledge, 2002.

Connell, Raewyn, 'Understanding Neoliberalism', in *Neoliberalism and Everyday Life*, ed. by Susan Braedley and Meg Luxton. Montreal: McGill-Queen's University Press, 2010.

Daley, Chris, 'Of the Flesh Fancy: Spanking and the Single Girl', in *Jane Sexes It Up: True Confessions of Feminist Desire*, ed. by Merri Lisa Johnson. New York: Four Walls Eight Windows, 2002.

Day, Elizabeth, ' "The Buck Stops Here…I've got Bad Blood". Novelist Gwendoline Riley Talks about her Obsessive Need to Write, and Why she'll Never have Children', *The Observer*, 18 May 2012.

De Jour, Belle, *The Intimate Adventures of a London Call Girl*. London: Weidenfeld & Nicolson, 2005.

De Jour, Belle, *The Further Adventures of a London Call Girl*. London: Phoenix, 2007.

Delany, Paul, *Literature, Money, and the Market: From Trollope to Amis*. Basingstoke: Palgrave, 2002.

Deleuze, Gilles, *Différence et répétition*. 4th edition. Paris: Presses universitaires de France, 1981.

Deleuze, Gilles and Félix Guattari, *Anti-Oedipus: Capitalism and Schizophrenia*, trans. By Robert Hurley, Mark Seem, and Helen R. Lane. London: Continuum, 2004.

Deleuze, Gilles and Félix Guattari, *A Thousand Plateaus: Capitalism and Schizophrenia*, trans. Brian Massumi. London: Continuum, 2004.

Delius, Mara, 'Mir zerfallen die Worte im Mund wie schlechte Pillen', *Frankfurter Allgemeine Zeitung*, 22 January 2010.

Delorme, Wendy, *Quatrième Génération*. Paris: Bernard Grasset, 2007.

Devitt, Amy J., *Writing Genres*. Carbondale: Southern Illinois University Press, 2008.

Dick, Leslie, 'Feminism, Writing, Postmodernism', in *From My Guy to Sci-Fi: Genre and Women's Writing in the Postmodern World*, ed. by Helen Carr. London: Pandora, 1989.

Dirke, Sabine von, 'Pop Literature in the Berlin Republic', in *Contemporary German Fiction: Writing in the Berlin Republic*, ed. by Stuart Taberner. Cambridge: Cambridge University Press, 2007.

Downes, Julia, 'Riot Grrrl: The Legacy and Contemporary Landscape of Feminist Cultural Activism', in *Riot Grrrl Revolution Girl Style Now!*, ed. by Nadine Monem. London: Black Dog Publishing, 2007.

Driscoll, Catherine, *Girls: Feminine Adolescence in Popular Culture and Cultural Theory*. New York: Columbia University Press, 2002.

Drügh, Heinz, 'Konsumknechte oder Pop-Artisten? Zur Warenästhetik der jüngeren deutschen Literatur', in *Konkurrenzen, Konflikte, Kontinuitäten: Generationenfragen in der Literatur seit 1990*, ed. by Andrea Geier and Jan Süselbeck. Göttingen: Wallstein, 2009.

Duggan, Lisa, 'The New Homonormativity: The Sexual Politics of Neoliberalism', in *Materializing Democracy: Toward a Revitalized Cultural Politics*, ed. by Dana D. Nelson and Russ Castronovo. Durham, NC; London: Duke University Press, 2002.

Dworkin, Andrea, *Pornography: Men Possessing Women*. London: Women's Press, 1981.

Dworkin, Andrea, *Intercourse*. London: Secker & Warburg, 1987.

Edelman, Lee, *No Future: Queer Theory and the Death Drive*. Durham, NC: Duke UP, 2004.

Eisenstein, Hester, *Feminism Seduced: How Global Elites Use Women's Labor and Ideas to Exploit the World*. Boulder, CO: Paradigm Publishers, 2009.

Ernst, Thomas, *Popliteratur*. Hamburg: Europäische Verlagsanstalt/Rotbuch, 2001.

Ernst, Thomas, '"The Author is a DJ!" Plagiarism vs. Intertextuality in the Discourse of Pop Literature. A Look at Helene Hegemann's *Axolotl Roadkill*', in *German Pop Literature: A Companion*, ed. by Margaret McCarthy. Berlin: De Gruyter, 2015.

Evans, Mary, 'Feminism and the Implications of Austerity', *Feminist Review*, 109 (2015), 146–55.

Faludi, Susan, *Backlash: The Undeclared War against Women*. London: Vintage, 1992.

Feigenbaum, Anna, 'Remapping the Resonances of Riot Grrrl: Feminisms, Postfeminisms, and "Processes" of Punk', in *Interrogating Postfeminism: Gender and the Politics of Popular Culture*, ed. by Yvonne Tasker and Diane Negra. Durham; London: Duke University Press, 2007.

Feldman, Gayle, 'Going Global', in *Publishers Weekly*, 19 December 1986.

Felski, Rita, *Beyond Feminist Aesthetics: Feminist Literature and Social Change*. London: Hutchinson Radius, 1989.

Ferree, Myra Marx, *Varieties of Feminism: German Gender Politics in Global Perspective*. Palo Alto: Stanford University Press, 2012.

Ferriss, Suzanne and Mallory Young, eds., *Chick Lit: The New Women's Fiction*. New York: Routledge, 2006.

Finlay, Frank, 'Literary Debates and the Literary Market since Reunification', in *Contemporary German Fiction: Writing in the Berlin Republic*, ed. by Stuart Taberner. Cambridge: Cambridge University Press, 2007.

Flood, Alison, 'Novelist Ditches Publisher at Book Launch for "Condescending" Treatment', *The Guardian*, 15 September 2011.

Foucault, Michel, 'The Subject and Power', in *Michel Foucault: Beyond Structuralism and Hermeneutics*, ed. by Hubert L. Dreyfus and Paul Rabinow. Brighton: Harvester, 1982.

Foucault, Michel, 'Technologies of the Self', in *Technologies of the Self: A Seminar with Michel Foucault*, ed. by Luther H. Martin, Michel Foucault, Huck Gutman, and Patrick H. Hutton. London, Amherst: University of Massachusetts Press, 1988.

Foucault, Michel, 'The End of the Monarchy of Sex', in *Foucault Live: Interviews, 1966–1984*, ed. by Sylvere Lotringer, trans. John Johnston. New York: Semiotext(e), 1989.

Foucault, Michel, *The History of Sexuality*, 3 vols., trans. Robert Hurley. Harmondsworth: Penguin, 1990.

Foucault, Michel and Colin Gordon, *Power/Knowledge: Selected Interviews and Other Writings, 1972–1977*. Hemel Hempstead: Harvester Wheatsheaf, 1980.

Fraser, Nancy, 'Feminism, Capitalism and the Cunning of History', *New Left Review*, 56 (2009), 97–117.

Friedman, Ellen G., 'A Conversation with Kathy Acker', *The Review of Contemporary Fiction*, 9.3 (1989), 12–22.

Friedman, Ellen G., '"Now Eat Your Mind": An Introduction to the Works of Kathy Acker', *The Review of Contemporary Fiction*, 9.3 (1989), 37–49.

Frow, John, *Genre*. London: Routledge, 2006.

Frye, Northrop, *Anatomy of Criticism: Four Essays*, ed. by Robert D. Denham, *Collected works of Northrop Frye*. Toronto, ON; London: University of Toronto Press, 2006.

Fuss, Diana, *Essentially Speaking: Feminism, Nature and Difference*. London: Routledge, 1990.

Genette, Gerard, *Palimpsestes*. Paris: Seuil, 1982.

Genz, Stéphanie, 'Third Way/ve: The Politics of Postfeminism', *Feminist Theory*, 7.3 (2006), 333–53.

Genz, Stéphanie and Benjamin A. Brabon, *Postfeminism: Cultural Texts and Theories*. Edinburgh: Edinburgh University Press, 2009.

Giddens, Anthony, *Modernity and Self-identity: Self and Society in the Late Modern Age*. Cambridge: Polity, 1991.

Gill, Rosalind, 'Postfeminist Media Culture: Elements of a Sensibility', *European Journal of Cultural Studies*, 10.2 (2007), 147–66.

Gill, Rosalind, 'Post-postfeminism? New Feminist Visibilities in Postfeminist Times', *Feminist Media Studies* 16.4 (2016), 610–30.

Gill, Rosalind and Christina Scharff, eds., *New Femininities: Postfeminism, Neoliberalism and Subjectivity*. Basingstoke: Palgrave Macmillan, 2011.

Gilmore, Leigh, 'Autobiographics', in *Women, Autobiography, Theory: A Reader*, ed. by Sidonie Smith and Julia Watson. Madison, WI: University of Wisconsin Press, 1998.

Gleba, Kerstin and Eckhard Schumacher, 'Vorwort', in *Pop seit 1964*, ed. by Kerstin Gleba and Eckhard Schumacher. Cologne: Kiepenheuer & Witsch, 2007.

Gleba, Kerstin and Eckhard Schumacher, eds., *Pop seit 1964*. Cologne: Kiepenheuer & Witsch, 2007.

Greer, Germaine, *The Female Eunuch*. London: Harper Perennial, 2006.

Guest, Katy, 'Young Gifted and Bold as Brass', *The Independent*, 7 March 2008.

Gwynne, Joel, *Erotic Memoirs and Postfeminism: The Politics of Pleasure*. Basingstoke: Palgrave Macmillan, 2013.

Hagberg, Garry L., 'Self-Defining Reading: Literature and the Constitution of Personhood', in *A Companion to the Philosophy of Literature*, ed. by Garry L. Hagberg and Walter Jost. Oxford: Wiley-Blackwell, 2010.

Hage, Volker, 'Ganz schön abgedreht', *Der Spiegel*, 12 (1999), pp. 244–6.

Halberstam, Judith, *In a Queer Time and Place: Transgender Bodies, Subcultural Lives*. New York: New York UP, 2005.

Harvey, David, *A Brief History of Neoliberalism*. Oxford: Oxford University Press, 2005.

Harvey, Laura and Rosalind Gill, 'Spicing it Up: Sexual Entrepreneurs and *The Sex Inspectors*', in *New Femininities: Postfeminism, Neoliberalism and Subjectivity*, ed. by Rosalind Gill and Christina Scharff. Basingstoke: Palgrave Macmillan, 2011.

Heath, Stephen, 'The Politics of Genre', in *Debating World Literature*, ed. by Christopher Prendergast and Benedict Anderson. London: Verso, 2004.

Hemmings, Clare, *Why Stories Matter: The Political Grammar of Feminist Theory*. Durham, NC: Duke University Press, 2011.

Hermand, Jost, *Pop international: Eine kritische Analyse*. Frankfurt am Main: Athenäum, 1971.

Hogeland, Lisa Maria, *Feminism and its Fictions: The Consciousness-Raising Novel and the Women's Liberation Movement*. Philadelphia: University of Pennsylvania Press, 1998.

Huddle, David, 'Report from the Darkest Interior (of Us): The Fiction of Mary Gaitskill', *The Hollins Critic*, XXXVII.3 (2000), 1–16.

Hughes-Warrington, Marnie, ed., *The History on Film Reader. Routledge Readers in History*. London: Routledge, 2009.

Hughes, Sarah, 'Farewell Bridget Jones – Hello Literary Bad Girls', *The Guardian*, 18 February 2014.

Hutcheon, Linda, 'Irony, Nostalgia and the Postmodern' in *The History on Film Reader*, ed. by Marnie Hughes-Warrington. London: Routledge, 2009.

Hutcheon, Linda, *A Poetics of Postmodernism: History, Theory, Fiction*. New York; London: Routledge, 1988.

Iqbal, Nosheen, 'Femvertising: How Brands are Selling #Empowerment to Women', *The Guardian*, 12 October 2015 https://www.theguardian.com/lifeandstyle/2015/oct/12/femvertising-branded-feminism [accessed 16.02.2017].

James, Robin, *Resilience and Melancholy: Pop Music, Feminism, Neoliberalism*. Alresford: Zero Books, 2015.

Jameson, Fredric, *The Political Unconscious: Narrative as a Socially Symbolic Act*. London: Routledge, 2002.

July, Miranda, *The First Bad Man*. Edinburgh: Canongate, 2015.

Kantola Johanna and Judith Squires, 'From State Feminism to Market Feminism', *International Political Science Review*, 33.4 (2012), 382–400.

Kauer, Katja, *Popfeminismus! Fragezeichen! Eine Einführung*. Berlin: Frank & Timme, 2009.

Kaulen, Heinrich, 'Popliteratur als Generationsphänomen: Jugendliche Lebenswelten im Spiegel der Popliteratur der 1990er Jahre', in *Konkurrenzen, Konflikte, Kontinuitäten: Generationenfragen in der Literatur seit 1990*, ed. by Andrea Geier and Jan Süselbeck. Göttingen: Wallstein, 2009.

Kelly, Stuart, 'Is This the End of Fiction's Genre Wars?', *The Guardian*, 17 May 2013.

Kendall, Mikki, '#SolidarityIsForWhiteWomen: Women of Colour's Issue with Digital Feminism', *The Guardian*, 14 August 2013.

Kennedy, Colleen, 'Simulating Sex and Imagining Mothers', *American Literary History*, 4.1 (1992), 165–85.

Kiraly, Miranda and Meagan Tyler, eds., *Freedom Fallacy: The Limits of Liberal Feminism*. Brisbane: Connor Court, 2015.

Kraus, Chris, *I Love Dick*. London: Tuskar Rock Press, 2015 [1997].

Kristeva, Julia, *La révolution du langage poétique*. Paris: Éditions du Seuil, 1974.

Kullmann, Katja, *Generation Ally: Warum es heute so kompliziert ist, eine Frau zu sein*. Cologne: Eichborn, 2002.

Lacan, Jacques, *Écrits: The First Complete Edition in English*, trans. Bruce Fink. New York; London: W.W. Norton, 2006.

Lahann, Brigitte, 'Elfriede Jelinek im Gespräch mit Brigitte Lahann: "Männer sehen in mir die große Domina"', *Der Stern*, 8 September 1988, p. 78.

Laing, Olivia, 'Grrrls Who Wanted More than Just Fun...', *The Observer*, 30 June 2013, pp. 26–7.

Layton, Lynne, 'Trauma, Gender Identity and Sexuality: Discourses of Fragmentation', *American Imago*, 52.1 (1995), 107–25.

Lecarme, Jacques, 'Autofiction: un mauvais genre?', *Autofictions & Cie.*, RITM, 6.1 (1993), 227–49.

Linklater, Beth, 'Germany as Background: Global Concerns in Recent Women's Writing in German', in *German Literature in the Age of Globalisation*, ed. by Stuart Taberner. Birmingham: University of Birmingham Press, 2004.

Lury, Celia, 'Reading the Self: Autobiography, Gender and the Institution of the Literary', in *Off-Centre: Feminism and Cultural Studies*, ed. by Sarah Franklin, Celia Lury, and Jackie Stacey. London: HarperCollins Academic, 1991.

MacKinnon, Catharine A. and Andrea Dworkin, *In Harm's Way: The Pornography Civil Rights Hearings*. Cambridge, MA; London: Harvard University Press, 1997.

Maitland, Sarah, 'Futures in Feminist Fiction', in *From My Guy to Sci-Fi: Genre and Women's Writing in the Postmodern World*, ed. by Helen Carr. London: Pandora, 1989.

Manners, Marilyn, 'The Dissolute Feminisms of Kathy Acker', in *Future Crossings: Literature Between Philosophy and Cultural Studies*, ed. by Krzysztof Ziarek and Seamus Deane. Evanston, IL: Northwestern University Press, 2000.

Marcus, Laura, 'Feminist Aesthetics and the New Realism', in *New Feminist Discourses: Critical Essays on Theories and Texts*, ed. by Isabel Armstrong. London; New York: Routledge, 1992, 11–25.

Martin, Courtney E. and Vanessa Valenti, '#FemFuture: Online Feminism', *New Feminist Solutions*, 8.1 (2012), 1–34.

Marven, Lyn and Stuart Taberner, eds., *Emerging German-Language Novelists of the Twenty-First Century*. Rochester, NY: Camden House, 2011.

Marx-Ferree, Myra, *Varieties of Feminism: German Gender Politics in Global Perspective*. Stanford: Stanford University Press, 2012.

Mazza, Cris, 'Editing Postfeminist Fiction: Finding the Chic in Lit', *symplokě*, 8.1/2 (2000), 101–12.

Mazza, Cris, 'Chick-Lit and the Perversion of a Genre', *Poets & Writers*, 33.1 (2005), 31–7.

McCaffery, Larry, 'The Path of Abjection. An Interview with Kathy Acker', in *Some Other Frequency: Interviews with Innovative American Authors*, ed. by Larry McCaffery. Philadelphia: University of Pennsylvania Press, 1996.

McCarthy, Margaret, 'Feminism and Generational Conflicts in Alexa Hennig von Lange's *Relax*, Elke Naters' *Lügen*, and Charlotte Roche's *Feuchtgebiete*', *Studies in 20th and 21st Century Literature*, 35.1 (2011), 56–73.

McCarthy, Margaret, ed., *German Pop Literature: A Companion*. Berlin: De Gruyter, 2015.

McNay, Lois, *Gender and Agency: Reconfiguring the Subject in Feminist and Social Theory*. Cambridge; Malden, MA: Polity Press, 2000.

McRobbie, Angela, 'Post-feminism and Popular Culture', *Feminist Media Studies*, 4.3 (2004), 255–64.

McRobbie, Angela, *The Aftermath of Feminism: Gender, Culture and Social Change*. Los Angeles; London: SAGE, 2009.

Mendible, Myra, ed., *American Shame: Stigma and the Body Politic*. Bloomington: Indiana University Press, 2016.

Mennel, Barbara, 'Alina Bronsky, *Scherbenpark* (2008): Global Ghetto Girl', in *Emerging German-Language Novelists of the Twenty-First Century*, ed. by Lyn Marven and Stuart Taberner. Rochester, NY: Camden House, 2011.

Miller, D. A., *Narrative and its Discontents: Problems of Closure in the Traditional Novel*. Princeton: Princeton University Press, 1981.

Minda, Gary, 'Lessons from the Financial Meltdown: Global Feminism, Critical Race Theory, and the Struggle for Substantive Justice', *American University Journal of Gender Social Policy and Law*, 18.3 (2010), 649–83.

Mißler, Heike, *The Cultural Politics of Chick Lit: Popular Fiction, Postfeminism and Representation* (New York; Abingdon: Routledge, 2016).

Mohanty, Chandra Talpade, *Feminism Without Borders: Decolonizing Theory, Practicing Solidarity*. Durham, NC; London: Duke University Press, 2003.

Moi, Toril, *Sexual/Textual Politics: Feminist Literary Theory*. London: Methuen, 1985.

Mueller, Agnes C., 'Introduction', in *German Pop Culture: How 'American' is it?*, ed. by Agnes C. Mueller. Ann Arbor: University of Michigan Press, 2004.

Mulvey, Laura, *Visual and Other Pleasures*. Basingstoke: Palgrave Macmillan, 1989.

Myles, Eileen, *Chelsea Girls*. New York: HarperCollins, 2015 [1994].

Negra, Diane, 'Claiming Feminism: Commentary, Autobiography and Advice Literature for Women in the Recession', special issue of *Journal of Gender Studies*, 'Feminism, Academia, Austerity', ed. by Helen Davies and Claire O'Callaghan, 23.3 (2014), 275–86.

Negra, Diane, and Yvonne Tasker, eds., *Gendering the Recession: Media and Culture in an Age of Austerity*. Durham, NC: Duke University Press, 2014.

Nguyen, Mimi Thi, 'Riot Grrrl, Race, and Revival', *Women and Performance*, 22.2–3 (2012), 173–96.

O'Hagan, Andrew, 'Travelling Southwards', *London Review of Books*, 34.14 (2012), 29.

P., Melissa, *One Hundred Strokes of the Brush Before Bed*, trans. by Lawrence Venuti. London: Serpent's Tail, 2004.

Paul, Georgina, *Perspectives on Gender in Post–1945 German Literature. Studies in German Literature, Linguistics, and Culture*. Rochester, NY; Woodbridge: Camden House, 2009.

Paul, Pamela, *Pornified: How Pornography is Transforming our Lives, our Relationships, and our Families*. New York: Times Books/Henry Holt & Company, 2005.

Peglow, Katja and Jonas Engelmann, eds., *Riot Grrrl Revisited: Geschichte und Gegewart einer feministischen Bewegung*. Mainz: Ventil, 2011.

Perreault, Jeanne, 'Autograph/Transformation/Asymmetry', in *Women, Autobiography, Theory: A Reader*, ed. by Sidonie Smith and Julia Watson. Madison, WI: University of Wisconsin Press, 1998.

Persis Murray, Dara, 'Branding "Real" Social Change in Dove's Campaign for Real Beauty', *Feminist Media Studies*, 13.1 (2013), 83–101.

Plant, Sadie, *Zeros and Ones: Digital Women and the New* Technoculture. London: Fourth Estate, 1998.

Plummer, Kenneth, *Telling Sexual Stories: Power, Change, and Social Worlds*. London: Routledge, 1995.

Politycki, Matthias, 'Literatur muss sein wie Rockmusik', *Frankfurter Rundschau*, 7 October 1995.

Politycki, Matthias, 'The American Dead End of German Literature', in *German Pop Culture: How 'American' is it?*, ed. by Agnes C. Mueller. Ann Arbor: University of Michigan Press, 2004.

Pompeo, Joe, 'Original "riot grrrl" Kathleen Hanna meets the press, and this time it's happy', *Capital New York*, 31 May 2013.

Projansky, Sarah, 'Mass Magazine Cover Girls: Some Reflections on Postfeminist Girls and Postfeminism's Daughters', in *Interrogating Postfeminism: Gender and the Politics of Popular Culture*, ed. by Yvonne Tasker and Diane Negra. Durham; London: Duke University Press, 2007.

Prügl, Elisabeth, 'Neoliberalising Feminism', *New Political Economy*, 20.4 (2015), 614–31.

Pusch, Luise F., *Das Deutsche als Männersprache: Aufsätze und Glossen zur feministischen Linguistik*. 1st edition. Frankfurt am Main: Suhrkamp, 1984.

Quan, Tracy, *Diary of a Manhattan Call Girl*. New York: HarperCollins, 2001.

Radisch, Iris, 'Die alten Männer und das junge Mädchen: Warum das männliche Kulturestablishment auf Helene Hegemann einschlägt', *Die Zeit*, 18 February 2010.

Reichwein, Marc, 'Helene Hegemann, das Fräuleinwunder im Medienzoo', *Die Welt*, 20 August 2013.

Rossi, Sonia, *Fucking Berlin*. Berlin: Ullstein, 2008.

Sanders, Hannah E., 'Living a *Charmed* Life: The Magic of Postfeminist Sisterhood', in *Interrogating Postfeminism: Gender and the Politics of Postfeminist Culture*, ed. by Yvonne Tasker and Diane Negra. Durham; London: Duke University Press, 2007.

Scharff, Christina, *Repudiating Feminism: Young Women in a Neoliberal World. The Feminist Imagination: Europe and Beyond*. Farnham; Burlington, VT: Ashgate, 2012.

Schirrmacher, Frank, 'Idyllen in der Wüste', *Frankfurter Allgemeine Zeitung*, 10 October 1989.

Scholder, Amy and Dennis Cooper, eds., *Essential Acker: The Selected Writings of Kathy Acker*. New York: Grove Press, 2002.

Schui, Herbert and Stephanie Blankenburg, *Neoliberalismus: Theorie, Gegner, Praxis*. Hamburg: VSA, 2002.

Schwarzer, Alice, *Der kleine Unterschied und seine großen Folgen: Frauen über sich, Beginn einer Befreiung*. Revised edition. Frankfurt am Main: Fischer Taschenbuch, 2007.

Schwarzer, Alice, *Die Antwort*. Munich: Wilhelm Heyne, 2008.

Sciolino, Martina, 'Kathy Acker and the Postmodern Subject of Feminism', *College English*, 52.4 (1990), 437–45.

Siegel, Deborah, *Sisterhood, Interrupted: From Radical Women to Grrls [sic] Gone Wild*. New York; Basingstoke: Palgrave Macmillan, 2007.

Sincero, Jen, *You Are a Badass: How to Stop Doubting Your Greatness and Start Living an Awesome Life*. Running Press: 2013.

Smelik, Anneke, 'Die virtuele matrix. Het lichaam in cyberpunkfilms', *Tijdschrift voor Genderstudies*, 3.4 (2000), 4–13.

Smith, Clarissa, 'Pleasing Intensities: Masochism and Affective Pleasure in Porn Short Fictions', in *Mainstreaming Sex: The Sexualisation of Western Culture*, ed. by Feona Attwood. London: I.B. Tauris, 2009.

Smith-Prei, Carrie, ' "Knaller-Sex für alle": Popfeminist Body Politics in Lady Bitch Ray, Charlotte Roche, and Sarah Kuttner', *Studies in 20th and 21st Century Literature*, 35.1 (2011), 18–39.

Soiofi, Mona Hanafi El, Jennifer Moos, and Liane Muth, 'Feminisms Revisited: Einleitung', in *Feminisms Revisited*, ed. by Meike Penkwitt. Leverkusen-Opladen: Budrich UniPress, 2010.

Sonnabend, Lisa, 'Blogger entlarvt Fräuleinwunder', *Süddeutsche Zeitung*, 17 May 2010.

Spender, Dale, *Nattering on the Net: Women, Power and Cyberspace*. North Melbourne: Spinifex Press, 1995.

Spiers, Emily, '"Mädchen haben keine Lobby im Pop": Writing the Performative Popfeminist Subject,' in *German Pop Literature: A Companion*, ed. by Margaret McCarthy. De Gruyter, 2015, 143–65.

Spiers, Emily, 'The Long March through the Institutions: From Alice Schwarzer to Pop Feminism and the New German Girls,' *Post-War Literature and Institutions*, special issue of *Oxford German Studies*, ed. by Sean Williams and Daniel Wilson, 43.1 (2014), 69–88.

Spiers, Emily, 'Performing the "quing of berlin": Transnational Digital Interfaces in Queer Feminist Protest Culture', special issue of *Feminist Media Studies* 'Digital Feminisms: Transnational Activism in German Protest Cultures', ed. by Maria Stehle, Carrie Smith-Prei, and Christina Scharff, 16.1 (2016), 128–49.

Stehle, Maria and Carrie Smith-Prei, *Awkward Politics: Technologies of Popfeminist Activism*. Montreal: McGill-Queen's University Press, 2016.

Stehle, Maria, Carrie Smith-Prei, and Christina Scharff (eds.), 'Digital Feminisms: Transnational Activism in German Protest Cultures', special issue of *Feminist Media Studies*, 16.1 (2016).

Stehle, Maria, 'Pop, Porn, and Rebellious Speech: Feminist Politics and the Multi-Media Performances of Elfriede Jelinek, Charlotte Roche, and Lady Bitch Ray', *Feminist Media Studies*, 12.2 (2012), 229–47.

Sundén, Jenny, 'What Happened to Difference in Cyberspace? The (Re)turn of the She-cyborg', *Feminist Media Studies*, 1.2 (2001), 215–32.

Taberner, Stuart, ed., *German Literature of the 1990s and Beyond: Normalization and the Berlin Republic*. Rochester, NY; Woodbridge: Camden House, 2005.

Taberner, Stuart, 'Literary Debates since Unification: "European" Modernism or "American" Pop?', in *German Literature of the 1990s and Beyond: Normalization and the Berlin Republic*. Rochester, NY: Camden House, 2005.

Taberner, Stuart, *Contemporary German Fiction: Writing in the Berlin Republic*. Cambridge: Cambridge University Press, 2007.

Taormino, Tristan, Celine Parrenas Shimizu, Constance Penley, and Mireille Miller-Young, eds., *The Feminist Porn Book: The Politics of Producing Pleasure*. New York: Feminist Press at the City University of New York, 2013.

Tasker, Yvonne and Diane Negra, 'Introduction: Feminist Politics and Postfeminist Culture', in *Interrogating Postfeminism: Gender and the Politics of Popular Culture*, ed. by Yvonne Tasker and Diane Negra. Durham; London: Duke University Press, 2007.

Taylor, Anthea, *Celebrity and the Feminist Blockbuster*. London: Palgrave Macmillan, 2017.

Tuzcu, Pinar, '"Allow Access to Location?" Digital Feminist Geographies', *Feminist Media Studies*, 16.1 (2016), 150–63.

Vernon, Polly, *Hot Feminist*. London: Hodder & Stoughton, 2016.

Venuti, Lawrence, ed., *Rethinking Translation: Discourse, Subjectivity, Ideology*. London; New York: Routledge, 1992.

Whelehan, Imelda, *Overloaded: Popular Culture and the Future of Feminism*. London: Women's Press, 2000.

Whelehan, Imelda, *The Feminist Bestseller: From Sex and the Single Girl to Sex and the City*. Basingstoke: Palgrave Macmillan, 2005.

Whiteside, Thomas, *The Blockbuster Complex: Conglomerates, Show Business, and Book Publishing*. Middletown, CT: Wesleyan University press, 1981.

Williams, Sherri, '#SayHerName: Using Digital Activism to Document Violence against Black Women', *Feminist Media Studies*, 16.5 (2016), 922–5.

Williams, Zoe, 'Survival of the Fittest', *The Guardian*, 20 March 2004.

Winkels, Hubert, 'Grenzgänger. Neue deutsche Pop-Literatur', *Sinn und Form*, 51.4 (1999), 581–610.

Wittstock, Uwe, *Leselust: Wie unterhaltsam ist die neue deutsche Literatur? Ein Essay*. Munich: Luchterhand, 1995.

Wolf, Naomi, *Promiscuities: A Secret History of Female Desire*. London: Vintage, 1998.

Wydeven, Joseph, 'Mary Gaitskill', in *Dictionary of Literary Biography: American Short-Story Writers Since World War II*, ed. by Patrick Meanor. 4th edition. Detroit: Thomson Gale, 2001.

Zambreno, Kate, *Heroines*. Los Angeles: Semiotexte/Active Agents, 2012.

Zeisler, Andi, *We Were Feminists Once: From Riot Grrrl to CoverGirl®, the Buying and Selling of a Political Movement*. New York: PublicAffairs, 2016.

Films

The Punk Singer, directed by Sini Anderson (opening band films, 2013).

Secretary, directed by Steven Shainberg (Lionsgate, 2002).

Lectures, Audio, and Interviews

Clare, Stephanie, 'New Material Feminisms', *Gender Studies Lecture*, Oxford University, 16 February 2012.

Colvin, Sarah, 'You have to Change Your Life?', *Schröder Lecture* (unpublished), Cambridge, 25 October 2013.

Frostrup, Mariella, *A History of Women's Writing (Part 4)*, BBC Radio 4, 31 July 2011.

Morgan, Clare, *Gender, Literature and Culture Seminar*, 'What is Women's Writing?' Interdisciplinary Research Group, University of Oxford, 25 October 2013.

Thomas, Scarlett, Interview by Emily Spiers (unpublished), 13 June 2012.

Digital Sources

'About Us', Bitch Media (2013) <https://www.bitchmedia.org/about-us> [accessed 03.10.2017].

'About Bust', Bust (2013) <http://www.bust.com/info/about-bust.html> [accessed 02.10.2013].

'Advertise with Bust', Bust (2013) <http://www.bust.com/advertise-in-bust.html> [accessed 02.10.2013].

Allen, Katie, 'Mantel, Kingsolver Make Orange Shortlist, as Indies Dominate', *The Bookseller*, 20 April 2010 <http://www.thebookseller.com/news/mantel-kingsolver-make-orange-shortlist-indies-dominate.html> [accessed 21.10.2013].

Baum, Antonia, 'Wie ich einmal vorlas', *Frankfurter Allgemeine Feuilleton*, 10 July 2011, available at http://www.faz.net/aktuell/feuilleton/buecher/autoren/bachmannpreis-in-klagenfurt-wie-ich-einmal-vorlas-13739.html [accessed 16.02.2017].

Blase, Cazz, 'But What of Us? UK Riot Grrrl (Part 1)', The F-Word (2005) PM normal code? <http://www.pressgazette.co.uk/loaded-owner-paul-baxendale-walker-reveals-all-dont-worry-ill-keep-my-clothes/> [accessed 3.10.2017].

Blasé Cazz, 'But What of Us? UK Riot Grrrl (Part 3)', The F-Word (2005) <https://www.thefword.org.uk/2005/01/but_what_of_us_uk_riot_grrrl_part_3/> [accessed 3.10.2017].

——, 'But What of Us? UK Riot Grrrl (Part 4), The F-Word (2005) <https://www.thefword.org.uk/2005/04/but_what_of_us_uk_riot_grrrl_part_4/> [accessed 3.10.2017].

'Box Office Mojo', International Movie Database (2013) <http://www.boxofficemojo.com/movies/?id=secretary.htm> [accessed 18.04.2013].

Bradley, Jane, 'What's On the Inside', *The Bookseller*, 20 September 2011. <http://www.thebookseller.com/blogs/whats-inside.html> [accessed 21.10.2013].

Buhr, Elke, 'Weil ich ein Mädchen bin: Kerstin Grether ist Zuckerbaby', in *Frankfurter Rundschau*, 23 April 2004 <http://www.fr.de/kultur/literatur/weil-ich-ein-maedchen-bin-a-1201298> [accessed 3.10.2017].

'Bust Boobtique', Bust (2013) <http://www.bustboobtique.com/> [accessed 03.10.2013].

Caesar, Ed, 'Charlotte Roche is an Unlikely Shock Artist', *Timesonline*, 1 February 2009. [no longer available online].

Crane, Antonia, 'Growing Up: The Rumpus Interview with Michelle Tea', 30 April 2015, available at http://therumpus.net/2015/04/growing-up-the-rumpus-interview-with-michelle-tea/ [accessed 16.02.2015].

Deresiewicz, William, 'When the Whip Comes Down: On Mary Gaitskill', *The Nation*, 11 May 2009 <http://www.thenation.com/article/when-whip-comes-down-mary-gaitskill?page=0,1> [accessed 11.07.2013].

Dzodan, Flavia, 'US Centrism and Inhabiting a Non-Space in #femfuture', *Red Light Politics*, 10 April 2013 <http://www.redlightpolitics.info/post/47611939840/us-centrism-and-inhabiting-a-non-space-in-femfuture> [accessed 05.10.2013].

'Fiction in German makes it to pole position', *The Economist*, April (2008) <http://www.economist.com/node/10952281> [accessed 21.08.2014].

FrauenMediaTurm, Das Archiv und Dokumentationszentrum (2013) <http://www.frauenmediaturm.de/home/> [accessed 05.08.2013].

Friedman, Ann, 'Pop Feminism Doesn't Mean the End of the Movement', nymag.com, 1 June 2016, available at https://www.thecut.com/2016/05/andi-zeisler-pop-feminism-movement.html [accessed 3.10.2017].

Gormley, Sarah, 'Introduction: Chick Lit', Working Papers on the Web (2009) <http://extra.shu.ac.uk/wpw/chicklit/gormley.html> [accessed 19.12.2013].

Grossman, Lev, 'Man, oh manifesto! Brash Band of Young Writers Calls for Return to Storytelling', *Salon Magazine*, 22 November 2000. <http://archives.cnn.com/2000/books/news/11/22/salon.manifesto/> [accessed 14.05.2012].

Harrington, Joshua, 'All Indie Shortlist for Dylan Thomas Prize', *The Bookseller*, 7 November 2013 [no longer available online].

Keller, Jessalynn and Maureen Ryan, 'Call for Papers: Emergent Feminisms and the Challenge to Postfeminist Media Culture', 2015 http://arcyp.ca/archives/4244. [accessed 16.02.2017].

Kraus, Chris, 'The New Universal', *Sydney Review of Books*, 17 October 2014, available at http://sydneyreviewofbooks.com/new-universal/ [accessed 23.01.2017].

Kraus, Chris, 'I Love Dick happened in real life, but it's not a memoir', *The Guardian*, 17 May 2016, available at https://www.theguardian.com/books/2016/may/17/chris-kraus-i-love-dick-happened-in-real-life-but-its-not-a-memoir [accessed 16.02.2017].

Laity, Paul, 'Maggie Nelson interview: 'People write to me to let me know that, in case I missed it, there are only two genders', *The Guardian*, 2 April 2016, available at https://www.theguardian.com/books/2016/apr/02/books-interview-maggie-nelson-genders [accessed 10.02.2017].

'Loaded Mag Sold to Adult Film Company', *Press Gazette*, 30 April 2012 <http://www.pressgazette.co.uk/loaded-owner-paul-baxendale-walker-reveals-all-dont-worry-ill-keep-my-clothes/> [accessed 3.10.2017].

Lutz, Cosima, 'Helene Hegemann beraubt ihre Freunde schonungslos', *Welt Online*, 10 February 2010 <http://www.welt.de/News/article6329626/Helene-Hegemann-beraubt-ihre-Freunde-schonungslos.html> [accessed 10.12.2012].

Maedchenmannschaft.net <http://maedchenmannschaft.net/>.

Marshall, Richard, 'All Hail Matt Thorne: Matt Thorne interviewed by Richard Marshall', *3am Interview*, 3ammagazine.com (2003). <http://www.3ammagazine.com/litarchives/2003/nov/interview_matt_thorne.html> [accessed 11.05.2005].

Moritz, Rainer, 'Und alles riecht nach Zimt', *Die Welt*, 28 August 2008 <http://www.welt.de/welt_print/article2342417/Und-alles-riecht-nach-Zimt.html> [accessed 27.09.2012].

'Le Tigre Talks Song-Writing, Politics and *Spin* Magazine', *The Huntington News*, 24 October 2004 <http://huntnewsnu.com/2004/10/le-tigre-talks-song-writing-politics-and-spin-magazine/> [accessed 19.04.2013].

Nussbaum, Emily, 'Mary, Mary, Less Contrary', *New York Magazine*, 6 November 2005 <http://nymag.com/nymetro/arts/books/14988/> [accessed 13.03.2013].

Page, Benedicte, Felicity Wood, and Philip Stone, 'Women's Brands Hard Hit by Downturn', *The Bookseller*, 23 September 2011 <http://www.thebookseller.com/news/womens-brands-hard-hit-downturn.html> [accessed 30.05.2014].

Power, Nina, 'The Dirty Girl. Nina Power Interviews Charlotte Roche', *Salon*, 4 April 2009 <http://www.salon.com/2009/04/04/charlotte_roche/> [accessed 16.07.2013].

Schrader, Carsten, 'Literatur statt Russendisko', *umagazine.de*, 10 October 2008 <http://www.umagazine.de/artikel.php?ID=107601> [accessed 27.09.2012].

Schwarzer, Alice, Website (2014) <http://www.aliceschwarzer.de/start/> [accessed 28.08.2014].

Sharpe, Matthew, 'Interview with Mary Gaitskill', *Bombsite*, 107, Bombsite (2009) <http://bombsite.com/issues/107/articles/3265> [accessed 14.03.2013].

Secretary, on IMDb.com (2013) <http://www.imdb.com/title/tt0274812/> [accessed 18.04.2013].

Smith, Rachel, 'Revolution Grrrl Style, 20 years later', *NPR music*, 22 September 2011 <http://www.npr.org/blogs/therecord/2011/09/20/140640502/revolution-girl-style-20-years-later?sc=tw&cc=share> [accessed 04.10.2013].

Stone, Philip, 'Boys to Men', *The Bookseller*, 24 June 2013 <http://www.thebookseller.com/blogs/boys-men.html-0> [accessed 19.03.2014].

Sturgeon, Jonathan, '2014: The Death of the Postmodern Novel and the Rise of Autofiction', *Flavorwire*, 31 December 2014, available at http://flavorwire.com/496570/2014-the-death-of-the-postmodern-novel-and-the-rise-of-autofiction [accessed 23.01.2017].

Tivnan, Tom, 'Is the Future Female?', *The Bookseller*, 17 June 2011 <http://www.thebookseller.com/blogs/future-female.html> [accessed 25.04.2014].

Westfall, Stephen, 'Interview with Mary Gaitskill, *Bombsite*, 30, Bombsite (1990) <http://bombsite.com/issues/30/articles/1290> [accessed 15.03.2013].

Witt, Emily, 'The Poet Idolized by a New Generation of Feminists', Interview with Eileen Myles, *New York Times Style Magazine*, 15 April 2016, available at http://www.nytimes.com/2016/04/15/t-magazine/poet-eileen-myles-chelsea-girls.html?_r=0 [accessed 16.02.2017].

Wood, James, 'Celluloid Junkies', *The Guardian*, 16 September 2000. <http://www.guardian.co.uk/books/2000/sep/16/fiction.reviews1> [accessed 15.05.2012].

Young, Holly, 'The Digital Language Divide: How Does the Language you Speak Shape your Experience of the Internet?', *The Guardian*, available at http://labs.theguardian.com/digital-language-divide/ [accessed 16.02.2017].

Zeilinger, Julie, *The f bomb* (2009) <http://thefbomb.org/about/> [accessed 04.10.2013].

Zylka, Jenni, 'Schleimporno gegen Hygienezwang', *Die Tageszeitung*, 28 February 2008 <http://www.taz.de/!13560/> [accessed 23.06.2012].

Index